BORDER VISIONS

Border

Visions

» » » » »

Mexican Cultures of the

Southwest United States

» » » » »

CARLOS G. VÉLEZ-IBÁÑEZ

The University of Arizona Press » Tucson

01   00   99   98   97   96   6   5   4   3   2   1

Library of Congress Cataloging-in-Publication Data

Vélez-Ibáñez, Carlos G., 1936–
    Border visions : Mexican cultures of the Southwest United States /
Carlos G. Vélez-Ibáñez.
       p.   cm.
    Includes bibliographical references and index.
    1. Mexican Americans—Southwest, New.   2. Mexican-American Border
Region.   3. Mexican Americans—Southwest, New—Social conditions.
4. Mexican Americans—Southwest, New—Ethnic identity.   5. Mexico—
Emigration and immigration.   6. Southwest, New—Emigration and
immigration.   I. Title.
    F790.M5V45   1996
    305.868'72073—dc20   96-10100
                                                                              CIP

British Library Cataloguing-in-Publication Data
A catalogue record for this book is available from the British Library.

Publication of this book is made possible in part by the proceeds of a permanent endowment created with the assistance of a Challenge Grant from the
National Endowment for the Humanities, a federal agency.

Para mi Padre, quien en su último suspiro

al ser preguntado por el sacerdote si le permitía

darle la última bendición, él con una media mirada,

le contestó: "No me quiero comprometer."

    y

Para Nayely Luz,

que tenga este recuerdo

de su padre.

Contents

Illustrations

MAPS

TABLES

Acknowledgments

THIS WORK could not have been written without the generosity of the University of Arizona, which provided an important portion of the financial support that allowed me to fulfill a fellowship at the Center for Advanced Study in the Behavioral Sciences at Stanford. Especially important in gaining this support were President Manuel Pacheco, Provost Paul Sypherd, and Dean Holly Smith. In addition, the work could not have been concluded without the financial, material, and human support afforded me during the fellowship year, 1993–1994, by the Center for Advanced Study in the Behavioral Sciences. I would like to thank Robert Scott, associate director, who in good fellowship provided time and energy to hear out some ideas and to many of the staff of the center without whom I could not have completed this study: Ann Fidrich, Diana Knickerbocker, Jessie Louis, Virginia MacDonald, Joy Scott, and Felicia Whitside, and the crew of the cafeteria Shanon Green and the capable Marco Dueñas and Estela Pérez.

Beyond the material, human, and financial support, the Center for Advanced Study in the Behavioral Sciences as a place for serious and sustained scholarship has no peer, and I appreciate the opportunity to have spent time there. I wish to recognize the invaluable support and assistance of my colleagues Arthur Kleinman and David Montejano. I am very grateful to Luis Fraga and Charlene Aguilar, of the Chicano Studies Research Center, and Jane and George Collier and Renato Rosaldo, of the Department of Anthropology at Stanford, who provided me opportunities to test out ideas in this book at various colloquia at Stanford University. At the University of California, Riverside, I am very grateful to Professor Emory Elliot who afforded me much appreciated guidance in the literature chapter and without whom I would have committed serious errors.

Intellectually, I owe much to the many rich, theoretical and substantive conversations with James B. Greenberg, colleague and collaborator on so many projects for ten years at the Bureau of Applied Research in Anthropology. Also to my colleague Norma González, of the same organization, who was instrumental in my focusing on the place of emotive patterns and feelings within ethnography; and to my colleague Tim Finan for providing me insights into the economic life of people outside of anthropology. The most substantive influence in this work has come from Eric R. Wolf, who demonstrates a rare combination of high intellectualism and human warmth toward the topics of his research and the populations with whom and about whom he has written.

To Christine Szuter, editor of the University of Arizona Press, who often pressed me to maintain the honesty of the word, especially in those areas that were closest to me and even those more removed, I offer my gratitude and appreciation for her constant encouragement and good fellowship. To the unnamed book manuscript reviewers my profound gratitude for their comments and direction for improvements and for their ability to steer me from serious factual and theoretical mishaps.

Last, but not least, whatever errors of omission and commission there may be, the responsibility is mine alone.

BORDER VISIONS

INTRODUCTION

» » » » »

"Cultural Bumping"

and the Movement of

Populations North

I HAVE WANTED to conduct this research and write about its results for much of my adult life. After almost a half century of breathing and smelling the dust of desert evenings in Arizona and watching the brilliance of the orange sun slowly dip down behind my ocotillo fence, I think I may know enough to say something of value about the Mexican populations that inhabit this "Greater Mexican Southwest" area, or the U.S. Southwest as it is most commonly known.

One reason for writing about this population is purely personal and experiential. I was born *con un pie en cada lado;* that is, born with one foot on each side of the political border between Mexico and the United States. It is only by chance that I was not born in Sonora rather than Arizona, and that happenstance is repeated literally today by thousands of others like me.

For my generation, being born either in Sonora or Arizona did not really matter too much because becoming a citizen was a simple matter of where parents chose for children to be born or for themselves to become "naturalized." For my father and mother's generation there was little difference between the two areas; only forty-three years before their birth it had all been Sonora, and the stories of wagon trains, incessant combat with Apaches, and land grants were part of their daily tradition. For my generation, Sonora was a place where family contacts and visits were numerous, while in Arizona these seemed to have thinned out and did not seem to matter quite as much. Sonora was a place where my parents frequently went to be culturally recharged; so it was not surprising that during one of their many return trips to Tucson from Magdalena, Sonora, I was born in Nogales, Arizona, exactly midpoint between the two towns. Even St. Joseph's Hospital where I was born was built only a few feet north of the Cyclone fence that separated the countries south from north.

As I was growing up these visits taught me much about history, ways of thinking, and the courage of people fighting to survive. From one such visit, I can recall Don Melitón, a man who had been tortured during the Yaqui wars forty years before by having the tendons of his calves severed. After these had healed they permanently pulled up the heels of his feet so that he appeared to walk like a slightly inebriated ballet dancer trying to gain his balance. He nevertheless always maintained his dignity by wearing a carefully placed fedora, long coat and tie, and knife-creased trousers.

These and many other experiences I cherish today, fifty years later, but from these experiences I came away also curious and inquisitive about why it always seemed that people from the south were kept separate from the north. On many return visits, I looked at the Cyclone fence next to which I was born, and it appeared to have only one side although identical when viewed from either the south or the north. It seemed that while it separated people, the separation was one-sided: the north trying to keep out the south, whereas from the south there was little or no perception of excluding those from the north. Eventually these puzzling perceptions led me to wonder and to question the underlying reasons for and assumptions behind my curiosity about this region. Finally, they led me to seek answers, some of which I provide here.

There are different labels for this area—the Spanish Borderlands, the Greater Southwest, the Greater Mexican Northwest, and even Northern Mesoamerica. Whatever label is used, for me the area encompasses the southwestern United States and northern Mexico. However, this is not a book of "place" as such, but rather an attempt to piece together the history and understand the processes by which human beings with their own ideology moved into the U.S. Southwest and created a sense of cultural place and try to understand the attempts by others to define or deny that cultural place by building fences of various sorts. The first fence creates a misunderstanding of the Mexican population of the region by using political instead of cultural definitions. Nations provide rights of citizenship but do not necessarily define the "cultural" systems that people use to survive when facing problems of daily subsistence. The differences between nations are more a matter of how supralocal institutions like the state decide who may be "naturalized" and then create the prisms of acceptable cultural characteristics usually based on myth, language, and ideology. These characteristic "norms" may have little to do with the way in which local culture develops and later flourishes. Especially when conquest, war, and expansion have decided them, national or "imperial" prisms will become imposed on others previously present and those close by. In order to understand the Mexican population of this region and the cultural systems they have developed, it will be necessary to examine the way in which this population organizes itself on social and work-related levels, what they have to do to earn sufficient income to subsist, the reason for labor being defined as a commodity, and why basic ideas and values are more important than citizenship. It is not that the nation-state has no influence on the U.S. Mexican population, but rather that local versions of culture emerge sometimes in resistance to and sometimes in accommodation of the national prism.

The second fence is the mistaken idea that human populations somehow are culturally "pristine." There is no reason to believe that any human population was so isolated that it did not "bump" into another at one time. All human populations move from one area to another for the same basic reasons, both in the past and at present: to subsist. In so doing, they bump into each other and the way in which these processes unfold becomes crucial to understanding the formation of a regional and subregional cultural identity. Sometimes the bumping process is so onerous that it eliminates much of the "bumped" population by a combination of disease, famine, and war. In other instances, combinations of repression, accommodation, and integration within specific class groups unfold and reshape the structure of relations within the impacted population. At other times even the conqueror changes, and the local versions of culture become refreshed and enhanced by the conquering population. Whether divided by geography, language, or culture, human populations often may become more distinct but some-times more similar after bumping into one another.

The "bumping" process in the Southwest has a long history, begin-ning before the arrival of Europeans in the sixteenth century. In pre-Hispanic times south to north bumping included periods of conquest, trading, and even movement of labor (Reff 1991, 80). The bumping process of peoples and institutions continues to this day and in the same south to north direction.

Because the scope of the text is so broad, it requires a treatment that for the most part is multidimensional as to materials covered, explana-tion, and approach. The book is organized along three main axes con-sisting of "mini-ethnobiographies," which provide a type of cultural glue to the chapters themselves. Each part provides a personal view, history, or insight that initiates the discussion of the chapters that fol-low so that each major part is also an important lived experience, thus the name ethnobiography. The glue is the experiential dimension that as anthropologists we often have access to and which we claim to be es-sential to understanding our work. It is of the same quality as the idea of "thick description," which provides not only the temporal and spa-tial dimensions of the experience, but a highly contextualized sense of the experience itself.

For this work I use archaeological, historical, demographic, ethno-graphic, and ethnobiographical information to explain and describe the manner in which populations and ideas have persistently moved from the peripheries of Mesoamerica to what is now called the U.S. Southwest. This direct or indirect south to north movement of human populations and their cultural inventions, since at least pre-European periods to the present, has been a dynamic process in which various groups have "bumped" into one another, and at times they either com-bined, resisted, or were decimated. This south to north search for "cul-tural space and place," the major theme of this work, brought various groups into the same geographical arena in which new cultural, class, and group formations were developed in the intense "bumping" processes between various opposing and accommodating populations: Native American, Spanish, and Mexican.

In the ensuing chapters I discuss the manner in which the Anglo American *entrada* into the Southwest initiated, through practices on both sides of the border, the formation of an undervalued commodity:

the Mexican population and its labor, even though this group of people provided the knowledge and training crucial to the economic development of the entire region. Identity encompasses the general cultural outlines by which people refer to themselves and to others and by which they define the social, economic, and political relationships that emerge between people. As mentioned above, one significant identity imposed on Mexicans is that of being a "commodity." In a capitalistic economic system, things such as labor, materials, and processes can be bought and sold for a price, and conditions are created in which some populations may be regarded primarily as a type of price-associated group to be used and discarded not unlike disposable materials or any used manufactured goods.

After the development of American capitalism and its penetration into the U.S. Southwest and Northwest Mexican region, Mexicans as a group were generally regarded as "cheap labor" and are even today. Individual variation aside, the history of Anglo-Mexican relations has often been defined by this imposed "commodity identity," a determining but not absolute condition that has strongly influenced how Mexicans are perceived by others and how Mexicans perceive themselves.

Despite such identification, Mexicans have developed vibrant communities with continuous cross-border exchanges and relationships in spite of an intense "barrioization" process in which Mexicans were compressed into largely Mexican communities within larger Anglo domains. A major part of the work that follows takes up the manner in which Mexicans have created political and cultural organizations including voluntary associations, labor unions, cultural movements, and household mechanisms to accommodate and resist the larger economic and political processes of commoditization in the population's search for cultural place and space. It is within this framework that such processes are also shown to have an impact on what I have termed "the distribution of sadness," that is, the overrepresentation of Mexicans in statistics on poverty, crime, illness, and war.

Regardless of such overrepresentation, Mexicans continue the search for place and space; this search and the "sadness" are themes expressed creatively in literature and art. I show the manner in which selected novels and expository narratives explicitly treat these themes but in a highly "holographic" manner. Similarly, mural art is discussed as the culminating form by which the search for place and space is not only represented but new issues and forms are also incorporated within their expression. Even though new generations of Mexicans replace those from before, the search for cultural place and space nevertheless continues to this moment.

In toto the work seeks to provide a basic template for understanding why Mexicans have seldom permitted themselves as a group to live out their lives based on the "commodity identity." They have created enormously adaptive and imaginative human cultural systems not as a response to such commoditization but rather as a series of human inventions accumulated through time and that through trial and error contributed to the Mexican "cultural identity" and provided social platforms from which following generations could emerge in relatively sound health. These systems include transborder ideas of identity, cross-border households, clustered households, particular variations of "patriarchy," ways of raising children, reciprocity and *confianza*, and particular political, economic, and social community organizations built around the central principle of exchange, multiplicity, and density of relationships and mutuality. Similarly, such identity includes means of expression that are not bimodal but multidimensional and holographic.

This book is organized around the major idea that Mexicans like other human populations have long moved from their points of origin in the south to the north and that such movement is an ancient one in which the present and the past are continuously engaged by the accompanying movement of ideas, practices, inventions, as well as conflicts between populations. The discussion here questions a cultural "interruption" between the peripheries of Mesoamerica and the Greater Southwest from the pre-Hispanic through the Spanish colonial and Mexican periods. In fact, much is owed to the peripheries of the central Mexican core institutionally, culturally, economically, and politically, and the Greater Southwest region cannot be understood as a separate or isolated region during any one of these periods. Imaginary political borders do not define the historical and cultural mosaic of this region nor of its Mexican population in the present. Rather than assuming that the population is only another immigrant group defined as such by a political border, the vision here is that the population is engaged in the processes of cultural creation, accommodation, rejection, and acceptance—all occurring simultaneously over a very long period of time. The vision emerging from this approach will differ markedly from a more politically bound analysis of the population.

The text experiments with various ways of presenting material, using personal and highly interpretive methods to contextualize ideas so that an emotive vision is more likely to emerge in comparison to a nomothetic vision of statistical information, numeral protocols, or inferential enumerations. The latter almost obscure the imagination and cognition and flatten emotion. On another level, the discursive and expository text attempts various settings so that the style is more akin to a diary than to an objectification of information, and the narrative may be shaped differently than a strictly essentialist rendition. I have used these sorts of textual presentations because the reality of the border demands different types of lenses and foci. The region is a polyphonic and polycultural mosaic, and in this text I try to map its multidimensionality of events, ideas, and behaviors by experimenting with textual form and function.

On Method
» » »

This book is based on a "mixed methods" approach rather than a strictly organized experimental approach, which insists on tight, almost laboratory models of presentation in which hypotheses are provided, a series of testing approaches are presented, then data are generated to show how the original hypotheses were validated or not. I have not relied completely on its opposite "interpretive" approach in which only a personal view or interpretation is provided and in which the author is as much the text as the text itself. I have taken a middle ground that recognizes that too many processes that we are not cognizant of or are oblivious to truly guide our hands and our minds so that what we present as "scientific" or as an objective rendition in fact is not. After all, those of us in anthropology who rely on human experience rather than its representation in abstract form depend on that experience to guide our understanding and provide insights. (An anthropologist who does not use fieldwork and human experience as the basis for research can speak only in abstractions.)

This work is "an anthropology" not "the anthropology" of a population in the Southwestern United States. Anthropologists for too long have constructed versions of other people's cultures as a reflection of their own. They consider themselves the final authorities and legitimate references for gaining an understanding of "us" and the multiplicity that we are. At one time populations studied by anthropologists were described as unchanging in the "anthropological present." Although these frozen-in-time descriptions provided valuable insights, they still made too much of the temporal and spatial boundaries that constituted human experience. For the most part, such ethnographies laid out the bare skeletal remains of human experience without reference to joy, hate, love, cowardice, loyalty, bravery, and the literally hundreds of human emotions and sentiments that drive much of what we are, and simultaneously they omitted a discussion of the cultural heterogeneity of the population. The latter point especially reduced the population to brush strokes of a much more detailed canvas.

Similarly to pretend that the anthropologists' own culture does not consistently and continuously guide, shield, and mask that which we select as topics, ideas, and populations for analysis is naive at best and foolish at worst. Even the experimentalist who reduces experience to a factor, a variable, or some other representation is doing so at the behest of often hidden dimensions too complex to recognize at first hand. For the most part many of us are neither aware of these dimensions nor are we likely to defend their invisibility.

Taking all these factors into account, I chose to treat this many-faceted topic by describing that which impressed me most about this border vision of the population called Mexican in this region called the Southwestern United States. I have been influenced and moved by the joys, but also the sufferings, of the man who more than anyone else gave me insights into this vision of the region—my father—a man of the border region of two nations and the cultures that make it up. In part this work is his view that the political border divided a cultural population and that the two nations demanded political allegiance without reference to cultural reality. His vision recognized the inalienable right of people to earn a living regardless of location, and therefore his vision included a broad appreciation for all people who were adaptive, skilled, and ready at a moment's notice to seek more agreeable conditions for self and household. This is what the border region in fact requires in light of both the speed and scale of constant economic and physical changes in the region. However, this regional demand for adaptation also involves a certain amount of willingness to put up with uncertainty, and those unable to do so are at a distinct disadvantage. In this border vision of one cultural group, those people who are at an advantage have a built-in aptitude for change and invention and for discarding what is generally not functional. In this border region the population under consideration here does come in contact with many other non-Mexicans. Simultaneously, Mexicans do seek solace from finding a place and creating a space that is their own, even though they may change quickly to advantage themselves and their families. Mexicans are easily able to incorporate others—Mexicans and non-Mexicans—and the boundaries of culture are more like a permeable membrane not unlike the imaginary political border constructed through war and treaty. This was my father's vision and it is mine, too.

» » » » »

PART 1

The Continuing Process:

An Ethnobiography

ADALBERTO VÉLEZ GARCÍA was born in Altar, Sonora, in 1901. His mother, Francisca García Terán, had been born in Tubutama, Sonora, in 1875 although she frequently visited and lived with relatives in Tubac, Arizona, 120 miles north of her birthplace.[1] His father, Manuel Vélez Escalante, was born in Arizpe, Sonora, twenty years before the birth of Adalberto's mother—that is, a few years before the Gadsden Purchase; and at that time Arizpe and Tubac were both in Sonora.

Manuel and Francisca would travel with the family of seven in the early 1900s from Magdalena, Sonora, where they lived, to Tubac and then on to Tucson to visit relatives, especially during the Fiesta de San Agustín. Travel was straightforward although

physically taxing in the early 1900s. The border crossing was only a formality, and visas for Mexicans were not a necessary condition. Another
reason that travel was not too onerous was that the family would stop
along the way with relatives who lived on small *ranchos* along the Santa
Cruz basin, which extended 60 miles from slightly south of present-
day Nogales, Arizona, to Tucson. They were able to visit in this manner
until most of their relatives lost their ranches to taxes and promises by
the American way of doing things. This same travel scheme was followed by many including Adalberto's maternal uncle, Tío Tomás, who
often took Adalberto as a five-year-old from Magdalena to Tucson in a
Conestoga wagon, carrying merchandise for sale piled up to its canvas
roof, under which Adalberto lay peeking out at the pulling mules while
his uncle snapped his long guide whip over the recalcitrant animals.

Only fifteen years before, and prior to Adalberto's birth, his father
Manuel had made similar visits to Francisca in Tubac during their
courtship, but then heavily armed with a Winchester repeater, a Colt
six-gun, and lots of ammunition and food carried on two pack horses.
At least three other friends also heavily armed would accompany him;
some of them were tough trail-wise *fayuqueros* (traders) like Tío Tomás,
who had driven wagon trains before the advent of the railroad in 1880.
Although the probability for Apache attack in 1890 was remote, only
ten years before Mexican rancheros along the Santa Cruz had carried
their weapons on trips to their grazing cattle and to irrigate fields and
had lookouts posted on high ground around their *ranchitos*. Manuel
did not take chances in those days.

After this long-distance courtship, Francisca and Manuel were married and raised seven children in Magdalena, Sonora, where the family
established a blacksmith foundry in which hand-crafted surreys, carriages, stage coaches, and mining and Conestoga wagons were manufactured until 1913. The family concern employed fifty men to make
mesquite wagon hubs, spokes, wheels, wagon bodies, finely made iron
fastenings to hold the wood together, as well as tools and implements
forged from Norwegian iron.

Manuel sold his finished carriages and wagons in Sonora and also in
Arizona to Federico Ronstadt's hardware and livery store in Tucson.
Ronstadt (Linda Ronstadt's grandfather), who also constructed similar
vehicles, then evidently sold the Sonoran versions with his nameplate,
which in this period was probably one of the first examples of a cross-

border *maquiladora* arrangement. Manuel and Francisca had done so well that they kept a chest half filled with gold coin.

After 1912, however, three events interrupted this long-term arrangement: the Mexican Revolution, World War I, and the further penetration of American capital in the form of the automobile. The revolution pushed the Vélez family north to Tucson where Adalberto had been living with his mother's cousins since he was six years old. He had been sent there earlier to learn to speak English fluently because his father Manuel had considered opening a comparable business in Tucson to take advantage of the mining market in nearby Ajo to the west and in southeastern Arizona and in the northeastern silver mines. Adalberto had stayed in Tucson and attended elementary and later secondary schools with his cousins, played football on bare fields covered with rocks, watched Barney Oldfield race on Speedway Avenue, and worked as a delivery boy for Western Union and the Bonanza department store, owned by his father's *compadre*, Carlos Jacome.

However, during the earlier revolutionary period, Adalberto's eldest brother Lauro had been scheduled for execution by one of the many revolutionary colonels who had settled a personal score by executing one of Lauro's compadres who had been the mayor of Magdalena, Sonora. Lauro had taken over his compadre's post and had taken it upon himself to support the man's widow. Evidently the colonel became upset at this turn of events and ordered his soldiers to execute all the male members of Manuel and Francisca's household in retaliation.

As the story goes, Manuel, with three of his sons, escaped death by a whisker by fleeing in a 1915 Hupmobile to Tucson but only after a series of punctured tires, broken axles, lack of gasoline, and overheated radiators along the way. Evidently, the revolutionaries who were on horseback almost caught up with them at the border but had to rein in their steeds at the yellow boundary marker, the only physical separation between Sonora, Mexico, and Arizona, United States, in that period.

Two years later, Adalberto returned to Magdalena with his brothers and father so that Lauro would not be drafted into the U.S. Army when the United States entered World War I, and upon their return they finished turning the livery, carriage, and blacksmith shop into an automobile garage where Adalberto and the rest of his brothers learned the mysteries of combustion engine–driven buggies called Model T Fords. Tens of hundreds of automobiles were developed in that early period

Plate 1.1
Adalberto G. Vélez, right, and unidentified coworker in Lester Lawrence
Garage, ca. 1927, Walnut Creek, California

of automobile manufacturing. The garage stood next to Manuel's home
for the next seventy years, with the eldest son taking over from father
and, except for Adalberto, younger brothers taking over from elder
brothers.

A few years after their return to Magdalena, however, Adalberto
went back to Tucson where he got a job as a mechanic in one of the
many newly founded automobile shops and until 1927 lived with his
aunts and uncles in the same house he had stayed in as a youngster. He
was then offered a job by one of the customers who had taken his car to
the garage where Adalberto worked. The customer, Lester Lawrence of
Walnut Creek, California, was so impressed with this twenty-seven-
year-old mechanic that he doubled his salary, paid for his travel to
Northern California, and for the next eight years Adalberto remained
in his employ in "Lester Lawrence Garage and Service" as his stellar
letter of recommendation shows.[2]

In 1929 Adalberto married Luz Ibáñez Maxemín from Tepic, Nayarit,
after they had met at a dance in Magdalena, Sonora, during one of
Adalberto's frequent visits. She was the daughter of a Mexican colonel
in the federal cavalry, Julio Ibáñez Camarillo, who had been killed in

Plate 1.2
Wedding picture of
Luz Ibáñez Maxemín
and Adalberto G.
Vélez, April 28, 1929,
Magdalena, Sonora

the Battle of Saltillo in 1913, and of Josefa Maxemín Estévez from Mazatlán, Sinaloa, who had died in 1920. After the death of her mother, Luz, her nephew, sister, and her sister's husband, a doctor, moved to Magdalena, Sonora, when massive floods in Santiago, Nayarit, had wiped out the Ibáñez household goods.

In 1929, both Adalberto and Luz returned to foggy Walnut Creek, California, where two children were born. However, in 1935 the family returned to Tucson so that Luz could escape the chilblains caused by the damp Bay area climate and in order for Luz to be closer to her sister who lived in Magdalena and to Adalberto's relatives in Tucson and Magdalena.

For the next fifty years, in the midst of which I was born, Luz and Adalberto made their home in Tucson, and every day Adalberto returned home after working eight to ten hours, washed his grease-

Plate 1.3
Adalberto G. Vélez,
1936, downtown
Tucson, Arizona

stained hands, and helped take care of his family with love, affection, and patience. He enjoyed dressing well and taking the family on Sunday drives, especially past the then not-quite-so-huge University of Arizona, where he told us, "que allí se hallaba toda la sabiduría del mundo" (There, all of the world's knowledge was found).

He was respected by most of his fellow workers at his place of employment, although earning no more than $75 a week, and he was an expert at repairing huge truck transmissions, differentials, and gasoline engines for which he was responsible for factory manual changes in gear ratios that engineers had misjudged in International Harvester and General Motors trucks. He would come home and proudly tell the family of his day's accomplishments, even though we could not tell a gear bushing from a piston sleeve, the parts which he had so expertly fitted and repaired that day. He was proud of his work even though he was hurt many times and twice seriously by falling engine blocks and slipping transmissions that broke his arms, cracked his skull, and damaged his vertebrae so that he could not turn his neck to look to either side of him much less behind him.

In spite of this, he still came home every day to tell of his achievements until one day when I, still a teenager, saw him come home with saddened eyes and his head hung low. He had been told by a foreman to go back to where he had come from when he complained about his low wages and long hours. He was after all only a "Mexican," and there were plenty where he had come from according to his foreman. After that my father seldom mentioned his work again, even though my mother tried to stroke his hurt away by smoothing his brow. Instead, for years this gentle, loving man had to return to work to be seen as a thing called "Mexican."

However, before him there had been Mexicans and non-Mexicans as well who had crossed back and forth over that imaginary political division called the U.S.-Mexican border. That migration began in pre-European times and has lasted to this moment. This circuitous route to an explanation was taken because explaining the beginnings helps explain the present circumstances in which people like my father continue to be subjected to the indignities created by ignorance and misinformation as well as by an artificial border vision created long ago through war.

CHAPTER 1

» » » » »

Without Borders,

the Original Vision

I T I S H I G H L Y L I K E L Y that major parts of the Northern Greater Southwest were well populated at the time of Spanish expansion in the sixteenth century. It is also probable that Indian populations were concentrated in urban agricultural pueblos and/or in small dispersed agricultural settlements (*rancherías*) along riverine systems. Uto-Aztecan speakers came out of the south from the Mesoamerican region carrying maize and squash and "bumped" into recipient populations from as early as 300 B.C. From A.D. 1 on, peripheral Mesoamerican groups may have introduced pottery to the region and inspired the adoption of certain practices, such as the construction and use of ball courts (ideas which may have emerged from the south as early as A.D. 500–700), exemplified in Arizona alone by the 189 courts documented at 149 sites.[1]

Although there is some controversy as to whether early peoples such as the Hohokam, Mogollon, or Anasazi were direct ancestors of the concentrated populations the Spanish bumped into in the sixteenth century, there is no doubt that these groups had developed complex social and economic systems. The Opata of northern Sonora alone numbered 60,000 persons and inhabited hierarchically stratified systems of rancherías, villages, and towns containing public monuments at the time they were encountered by Spanish explorers and missionaries. The notion that this region was only sparsely settled prior to the arrival of the Spanish is not borne out by recent work demonstrating that the region of the northwestern borderlands was inhabited by Pueblos, Opata, and Pimas Altos who numbered 220,000 prior to the Spanish expansion, but who were decimated by pathogens perhaps even before the actual physical encounter so that by 1764 only 32,000 of that number remained.[2] Between the early contacts of explorers in the sixteenth century who described "kingdoms" with well-populated complex urbanized settlements and later descriptions by Jesuits who described only remnants of decayed centers and dispersed rancherías, an ahistorical "gap" was created that later supported the stereotype of the region as an empty physical and cultural space. Only recently has significant attention been paid to the impact of disease on settlements in this region during the fifteenth and sixteenth centuries.[3]

It is probable that prior to the Spanish influx the region was composed of permanent villages and urbanized towns with platform mounds, ball courts, irrigation systems, altars, and earth pyramids.[4] The agricultural techniques common to the area included floodwater farming, canal irrigation, and wetland agriculture. A surplus, sufficient to support craft production and long-distance trade between adjoining populations and those stretching from and into central Mexico, was created, thus establishing precapitalist commodity relations between populations. One example of this type of political and economic creation in Mesoamerica is that of the Southern Mogollon of Casas Grandes in Northern Chihuahua, whose activity, however, had declined by the 1500s.[5]

Even though many of the highly complex social and economic systems, such as that of the Hohokam, had all but disappeared by the mid-1400s, intensive and extensive trading and slaving had already been established. By the 1500s, Apaches, for example, marketed not only hides and meat to the Pueblos of Northern New Mexico but human beings as well. Thus, at the time of conquest, the region was not an empty physical space bereft of human populations but an area with more than likely a lively interactive system of "chiefdom"-like centers or rancherías, each with its own *cazadores* (hunters), material inventions, and exchange systems.

It was only in the aftermath of the introduction of European pathogens, which virtually decimated indigenous populations, that the region actually came to be defined in European terms as an empty vessel to be filled with colonizers. The survivors among the local populations became sources of cheap labor; and in their weakened condition, entire communities of the physically exploited were also made spiritually captive by an enforced religious ideology. The actual physical demise, with its attendant created "space," was reinforced by coterminous ideological commitments to the notion of political and cultural superiority.

Los Primeros Pobladores: The Development of Early Southwestern Cultural Centers

» » »

Anthropologist Henry Dobyns posed an interesting question on the 501st anniversary of the incipient European inundation[6] of the indigenous worlds of the American continents, "What was here . . . in 1492?"[7] Dobyns answered his own question by stating that unlike the way most North American newcomers arrived in this region in the nineteenth century from the East, most major human trails of the region ran from south to north. He stated that such trails were a result of the economic links within the urban population of almost 2 million in the various cities of the Valley of Mexico. Although there is a great deal of controversy among different archaeological authorities concerning this theory, compelling evidence does exist to support Dobyns's point of view.[8] We can divide the issue into two basic questions: what were the processes that enabled these 2,000-mile links to develop, and how were these links to which Dobyns refers established?

The answer to the first proposition begins with the idea that the south to north movement is an old one. Haury (1986b, 443), although he had revised his earlier estimates of the arrival time of Mesoamerican populations to the region, placed the movement of populations carrying maize from the northwestern frontier of Mesoamerican "high cultures" to central Arizona at about 300 B.C.[9] Especially pertinent to this view is the triad of complex agriculturally based societies that includes the Hohokam of Southern Arizona and Sonora, perhaps the Mogollon of Casas Grandes, Chihuahua, Mexico, and the mountain Mogollon of Southwestern New Mexico, and to a lesser extent the Anasazi of Chaco Canyon and Mesa Verde who inhabited the Four Corners area of New Mexico, Arizona, Utah, and Colorado.

Over a period of sixty years as a preeminent authority on Southwestern peoples, Haury concluded that "the richness of the oldest Hohokam ceramic tradition, their lithic technology, irrigation capability from the start, and echoes of Mesoamerican beginnings persuade me to hold fast" to the idea that an immigrant group from Mexico carried with them the technological hardware and cultural "funds of knowledge" to establish themselves in the aridity of the Sonoran desert region.[10] For Haury, the Hohokam complex began with the migration of agriculturally sophisticated peoples into the Gila River Valley somewhat south of present-day Florence, Arizona.[11] There they not only pursued complex irrigation agriculture, the knowledge of which they had brought with them, but they also developed hybrids of maize adapted to an arid environment.

These populations of the Greater Southwest,[12] as Haury suggested, eventually inhabited and developed a technologically complex agricultural geographic area of 45,000 square miles (excluding probable Sonoran equivalents) over a period of almost 2,500 years. The Hohokam, it was proposed, were more than likely direct migrants from Mesoamerica who bumped into the hunting and gathering peoples who were already present at their arrival.[13] By the twelfth century, they had developed a "core" area of the Phoenix basin and eight peripheral areas.[14]

From their very origin in 300 B.C. the Hohokam were a "frontier, spacially displaced Mesoamerican society" (Haury 1976, 351). This interpretation hypothesizes that the Hohokam came from Mexico and after settling to the north maintained contact and were stimulated to develop culturally by periodic "infusions" from Mesoamerica. For a thousand years the Hohokam developed complex cultural forms and peaked both politically and economically about A.D. 700–900 with a final decline in A.D. 1450 only shortly before the intrusion by the Spanish (Haury 1976, 352).

There is, however, an opposite point of view that does not automatically deny influence from the south but denies that the Hohokam complex originated in Mesoamerica or its peripheries. Most recently, scholars have suggested that the complex Hohokam development occurred incrementally and that by the time of Christ, numerous groups in the region had already developed incipient agricultural "archaic" production patterns.[15] Thus local groups after A.D. 700 had already developed a number of distinctive regional traditions and created interactive trade networks, major agricultural systems of production, social stratification, and other complex political and organizational forms. However, even those scholars that emphasize this point of view do not deny that by A.D. 1100 imported Mesoamerican ideas, practices, objects, and more than likely peoples were present among the Hohokam.[16] Fish (1989, 21), who is less predisposed to the Mesoamerican origination thesis, states unequivocally that what especially differentiates Hohokam public architecture such as platform mounds and ball courts from Pueblan complexes is their "Mesoamerican antecedents."[17]

The resolution to the debate between origination and the influence of Mesoamerican traditions in the Southwest, I would suggest, is not an either/or matter. Rather it should be understood that the origination of complex production forms by early peoples in the region occurred differentially, and different complexes like the Hohokam, Mogollon, and Anasazi developed local systems and to different degrees were influenced by Mesoamerican traditions, ideas, and peoples.

For the Hohokam, influences probably originated out of northern Michoacán, Guanajuato, Aguascalientes, southern Zacatecas, and western Mexico and probably followed a coastal route, given the fact that the maize of the early Hohokam type more than likely was diffused from western Mexico. Once established, the Hohokam/Mesoamerican connection is best exemplified by (1) direct imports and (2) ideas and practices that led to their replication and adoption.[18]

Figure 1.1 represents the various cultural items and influences transmitted from Mesoamerica before A.D. 1 (according to the Haury thesis), although the chronology may be questionable given the most recent estimates.[19] These influences range from complex irrigation agriculture to pottery making itself, although there is evidence the Hohokam themselves developed an incipient form of agriculture after A.D. 1 and developed pottery as well.[20] In fact, the latest work on the Hohokam indicates that the development of an advanced agricultural way of life occurred more probably after A.D. 200,[21] so that the Hohokam complex is much later than Haury originally estimated. Therefore, agriculture among the Hohokam was probably locally developed but also influenced by practices introduced by another source from the south. This "bumping" must have been a dramatic and intrusive process in the lives of the hunters and gatherers and original small-scale agricultural villages.[22] Some types of pottery, stone sculptures, turquoise mosaics, censors, anthropomorphic figures, as well as the triad of Mesoamerican

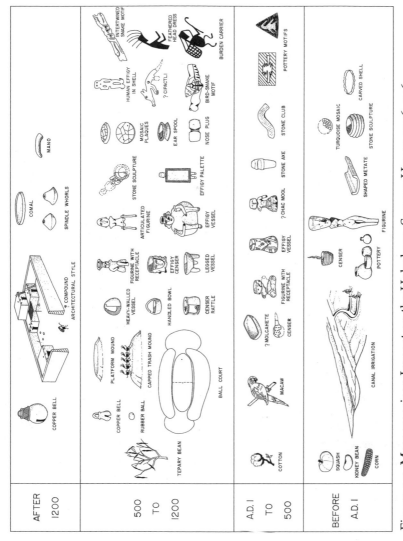

Figure 1.1 Mesoamerican Impact on the Hohokam. Source: Haury 1976, 346.

foods, kidney beans, squash, and new varieties of corn, were to different degrees influences from the south.[23]

Chronological veracity aside, Haury supports the thesis that the major influences from the south included representative ceramics such as a Chac Mool–like figure, crematory and funerary practices, and artifacts, such as handled incense burners. In addition, the appearance of the macaw seems to indicate a greater and greater expansion of ceremonialism, and simultaneously of art styles and pottery painting with motifs similar to that of the "Quetzalcoatl cross" (as shown in figure 1.1 in the left pottery motif of the A.D. 1 to 500 period). The introduction in this period or perhaps earlier of human and bird effigy jars and of cotton shows an increasing complexity of ritual and ceremony, in which the former were used, and of important productive and economic infusions, in the case of the latter.[24]

The importance of the imported ideas and practices should not be underestimated, for they may have influenced social complexity, environmental change, and cultural experimentation in the region. The use of irrigation systems alone required labor organization, knowledge of planting, crop tilling, harvesting, and plant rotation (all undertaken at appropriate times of the year). Undoubtedly, this information was integrated into a wider "fund of knowledge" concerning summer and winter solstices, ceremonial preparations, and sacrifice expressed in cosmological terms by priest specialists. Thus, it can be seen that influences from the south combined with technologies already present in the region, if the origination thesis is tempered to focus upon southern influences from A.D. 300 on. In the period A.D. 300–700 ceramic figures are similar to those from Mexico and tend to portray especially the idea of fertility and procreation. It is at the beginning of this period that a shift to agriculture from a reliance on hunting takes place, and the link between fertility and crop production rather than hunting also evolves.[25] The belief in death and rebirth, perhaps associated with cremation practices and new crops, probably became part of the ancient world views that bind the present-day Pima and Tohono O'odham to their past.[26] In fact, it may be that before the European inundation ceremonial ball games were conducted by their Hohokam ancestors to celebrate ancient versions of what are today known as Green Corn maturation ceremonies.[27]

The period of greatest Mesoamerican influence in the region occurred between A.D. 800 and 1200, even though Haury's estimate is some two hundred years earlier.[28] Platform mounds and ball courts are two examples of that influence. The artificial elevated platforms, which were widely diffused to the southeastern United States from Mesoamerica in an earlier as well as contemporary period to that of the Hohokam, serve as symbols of an important architectural and ritual shift within this group.[29] Although introduced much earlier than were ball courts, platform mounds of the Hohokam became central locations for ritual. Constructed in a layered manner, with the use of steps not unlike Mesoamerican models, the Hohokam platform mound imitated its southern model by shifting its geographical center as changes in the calendric cycle occurred. In the last period of their existence in the Classic period (1450), massive mounds were built with houses on top at various sites in the Salt River Valley of Arizona.[30]

The eventual construction of some 200 ball courts (see figure 1.1),[31] the game itself, in which a rubber ball was used,[32] and the attendant cultural practices are among the most obvious expressions of the influence of the Mesoamerican belief system and public ceremonial architecture, despite the views of some who would depict the structures as dance plazas rather than ball courts.[33] As Olson so eloquently stated, "There is no reason why we should deny all but material traits to the people migrating to the New World."[34] Other ideas related to macro-Indian cosmology that were imported and developed in the region and are associated with the ritual ball game would include "shamanism, vision quests, cosmologies of Earth Mother and Sky Father, moiety divisions and the conception of a cosmic whole formed from the relations of an underworld and an upperworld" (Wilcox 1991, 101–2). In this vein, the game was traditionally an important part of the Mesoamerican cult of Quetzalcoatl/Tezcatlipoca and in its play articulated symbolically the struggle between good and evil represented respectively by the mythic brothers Quetzalcoatl and Tezcatlipoca—God of Life and Light and God of Death and Darkness.[35] There is as well an indication that fertility-associated bone implements excavated at Snaketown, Arizona, may have been used as part of bloodletting ceremonies congruent with Mesoamerican and Maya practices.[36]

Entire sets of ideas concerning the manner in which the world works were diffused at the same time as other sorts of ideas; and the ball court "way" was not merely a sport played as a competitive game between individuals and their teams, but was, as has been stated, a reflection of fundamental beliefs about the world. Much like the martial arts of premodern Asia in which there was a great difference in the combat between groups representing the corporate interests of communities and combat between lineages and their ancestors, ball court "ways" might have functioned and expressed the corporate interests of communities, their lineages and moieties, and their spiritual corporate ancestors. The ball game as a possible predictive device may have been played to reduce the uncertainty of life in a desert environment in which a combination of scarce rainfall, constructed irrigation works, and fragile water wells made a lack of resources an overriding probability. The ball game may have functioned psychologically to reduce the anxiety of the likelihood of failure by testing possible outcomes with one team representing success in predicting rainfall, crop success, favorable trading exchange, and the outcome of conflicts with neighbors. In addition, the ball game might have tested man's relations with the supernatural because the outcome of the game was in the province of the gods alone, and their beneficence would be expressed if the winning side represented a successful agricultural year.[37]

Mesoamerican influence extended beyond the areas of architecture, agricultural technology, ceremonial practices, and beliefs already discussed. Artifacts from the period of contact provide evidence of some unspecific exchange between the cultures. About two hundred copper bells (spectrographic analyses have identified them as originating in the Mexican states of Jalisco and Nayarit),[38] approximately one hundred highly reflective mosaic mirrors, pottery shapes like three-legged vessels, and stone sculptures are all indicative of the types of trade goods imported from distances to the south. In only probing these materials of the mirrors and the bells, it is clear that both are Mexican. Identical mosaic mirrors have been recovered from archaeological sites in Jalisco, Mexico, and as far as Guatemala among Mayan ruins. The mirrors found among the Hohokam are of Mexican derivation in both style and technique, and they are associated with death and cremation and anthropomorphized just as those in Guatemala are.[39] However, more important is the strong association with the Quetzalcoatl-Tezcatlipoca cult: the mirrors were found primarily at Hohokam cremation sites, and among Mesoamericans such identical mirrors were sacrificed yearly to their warriors.[40] Even today the Quetzalcoatl plumed snake seems to continue as "Corua," or water snake, in the myths and folk beliefs of U.S. Mexicans in the Southwest.[41]

At the representational level, figure 1.1 shows some of the important Mesoamerican influences, one of which is the bird-snake combination. This is of particular interest because the bird-snake motif often served as a covert form of Quetzalcoatl, the plumed serpent, the mythic god-man who was related to the sea and wind, and had journeyed and reached the central plateau of Mexico and established himself at Teoti-huacán. After his destruction in A.D. 650,[42] the mythic personality reappeared at Tula where he rose again and with him the great Toltec center of Tula. The god-man was then exiled from Tula in A.D. 987, later to appear in a number of Mesoamerican and Northwestern Mexican cultural areas such as Tenayuca, Chulhuacan, Cholula, Cempoala, and finally to the desert.[43] Reminiscent of the death and rebirth myth common to the Amerindian world of the Southwest, Quetzalcoatl as myth, together with his mythic journey, is of ancient origin and much older than his Nahuatl name.[44]

The Hohokam were not merely passive recipients of Mesoamerican influences; they created extensive commercial exchange systems, especially between A.D. 800 and 1100, maintaining "core" or middleman exchange relations with a number of other groups in other directions. For example, the Hohokam acquired shell on the California coast (both on the Baja Peninsula and northward) from which they produced bracelets that were exchanged for Cerillos turquoise in the Chaco Mogollon area. Other Hohokam derived, produced, or transferred goods, sent through their trade networks, included cotton, salt, lac, ground-stone tools such as metates, and finished pottery.[45] After 1200, Mesoamerican influence in the region seemed to wane, possibly as an aftereffect of other than local environmental processes or ecological imbalances. Haury (1976, 347) speculated that Mesoamerican influence lessened because of the crumbling of Toltec cities and empires in that period.

The Hohokam as a regional system did shrink in this period; settlements became more concentrated in the Gila and Salt basins, architecturally adobe rooms above ground replaced pithouses, and even administrative centers like Casa Grande outside of Coolidge, Arizona, arose and traded with Casas Grandes of Chihuahua. By 1450 or so, most of the population centers had been abandoned; environmental causes such as water logging and salt concentration in the irrigation fields were partially to blame, but more than likely this collapse was also associated with the interruption of regional trading patterns with other cultural complexes such as the Mogollon, Anasazi, and Patayan. By the time of the Spanish inundation, the Hohokam population had been reduced to a tenth of its preconquest level; but at the same time a number of highly mobile, culturally diverse groups created less concentrated population centers with little reliance on large-scale irrigation-based agriculture.[46] Despite the decline of the Hohokam, new forms of macroeconomic relations emerged that permitted contact and extensive trade between groups in the same region.

With regard to the Mogollon complex, the second of the triad of complex Southwestern and Northern Mexican societies, Haury (1986, 455) suggested that the Mogollon north of the present Mexican border were in reality no more than technologically well developed populations from a "heartland centered in the Sierra Madre Occidental of Mexico." Casas Grandes in Chihuahua was thought to have served as a major trading and manufacturing center on the northern frontier within Mesoamerica, and northwestern peoples were agents of cultural exchange and trade between Mesoamerica and complexes further north.[47] Although Haury is partially correct, it is clear that Casas Grandes was not developmentally contemporaneous with the Anasazi but instead with their later survivors in the fourteenth century and with the Hohokam in the early 1300s.[48]

The Chaco Anasazi and the Eastern Anasazi provide the strongest case for a slowly developing complex that was not directly derived from Mesoamerica but which, nevertheless, may have been strongly influenced by long-distance trade relations with Mesoamerica especially through groups that influenced local Anasazi culture.[49] Even though this position is in direct opposition to that held by some,[50] a convincing argument is made by others who state that Mesoamerican goods like macaws, copper bells, and Mesoamerican cloisonné items were more than likely high-value commodities used as the basis of economic exchange between elites of Chaco and other elites of the Southwest and West Mexico.[51] In addition, the compelling "astroarchaeological" analysis by Reyman (1971, 283), who focused on the impact of Mexican influences on Anasazi ceremonialism, concludes that "Chaco Canyon appears to have been a central receiving and distribution area for Mexican trade in the 11th and 12th centuries."[52] How that occurred prior to the emergence of Casas Grandes is difficult to discern considering that Casas Grandes would have been the most likely trade transfer point; however, the Chaco core dissolved almost at the advent of Casas Grandes in 1150.[53] In terms of Mesoamerican connections there is overriding evidence that appears to be solely an importation from tropical Mexico (Oaxaca and southern Tamaulipas): the Scarlet Macaw (*Ara macao*), which was found in the ruins of Pueblo Bonito, the largest Chaco site of the tenth century.[54] One doubts a "flying saucer connection."

Without speculating as to the efficacy of the cultural influence of Mesoamerican traders on Chaco, suffice it to say that Mesoamerican trade items were highly valued and served as symbols of elite status.[55] However, it is probable that Southwestern ceremonialism at Chaco was significantly influenced by Mexican sources.[56] What has to be sorted out is whether all three cultural complexes either originated in Mesoamerica, were recipients of Mesoamerican cultural influence but did not play an important role in economic or political relations, or played a crucial role in the Southwestern-Mesoamerican connection.

First, it should be understood that the Hohokam, Mogollon, and Anasazi rose and fell in different periods and were more than likely connected one to the other by trade and exchange relations at different times. During the historical existence of these cultural centers, each served as a core area of an "interaction sphere" expanding its trade and communication networks and routes throughout the Greater Southwest and beyond.[57] In some cases (Hohokam and Chaco), they interacted one with the other and were to varying degrees trading partners and cultural bearers and borrowers.[58] What seems clear is that they were never isolated from either each other or other groups and certainly not from Mesoamerica. Second, it is probable that their connections to Mesoamerica were generally not direct (except perhaps for the Hohokam) and that complexes in Northern and Western Mexico served as transit and transfer points for goods and populations.

María Teresa Cabrero (1989, 49–50) states that the Chalchihuites cultural center of Zacatecas was a transfer point because it had the closest connections with the Greater Southwest. Even though it was an extension of Mesoamerican centers, it also developed its own original complex cultural system. Its province eventually extended north to Durango and to the south strongly influenced the Malpaso and Bolanos-

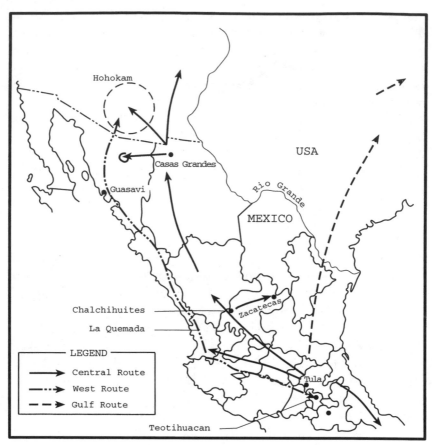

Map 1.1 Commercial Routes of Mesoamerica (A.D. 350–1350). Source: Cabrero Garcia 1989, 48.

Julchilpa cultures. During the Pre-Classic period of Teotihuacán ca. A.D. 200, Chalchihuites served primarily as an autonomous transfer point, but by A.D. 350 (during the Classic period) it had become a core periphery. The interest in the center was probably increased because of the availability of turquoise in the Greater Southwest (particularly in New Mexico); in addition, Chalchihuites served as a major mining center for the mineral chalchihuite so that after A.D. 350 exploitation of the area increased, as map 1.1 illustrates.⁵⁹

It has been suggested that with the fall of Teotihuacán, Tula became the main trade center for minerals in Mesoamerica, and Casas Grandes, situated in the middle of Chihuahua and La Quemada in central Zacatecas, was thought to have been the principal commercial center on the trade route to Tula. However, this analysis has been completely revised by recent findings that date the advent of Casas Grandes much too late for it to have served as a commercial center on the route from Tula to La Quemada and then on to Durango with commercial exchange taking place in Zape until it was transferred to Casas Grandes from where it continued on to the Hohokam and Mogollon. However, it is certain that Chalchihuites served as a transfer site for New Mexican turquoise, which was more than likely carried there beginning in 350 A.D. and continuing perhaps until the twelfth century. At El Vesuvio and Cerro de Moctezuma, two Chalchihuites culture areas located near each other, X-ray diffraction techniques have identified eighty turquoise artifacts as having come from turquoise mines in New Mexico, probably from the Cerrillos mines near Santa Fe, New Mexico,⁶⁰ during that area's formative development (Basketmaker Period). It is also possible that expeditions formed in Chalchihuites were organized to exploit this resource in the early phases of New Mexican turquoise export.⁶¹

There was a probable connection between Casas Grandes and the Durango area, but at a later period in time and through the trade center of Cañon de Molino in the early fourteenth to late fifteenth century. In addition, it is more than likely that Casas Grandes would have established exchange relations with coastal Sinaloa and Guasave and would have interacted with Sonora statelets and the Hohokam.⁶²

To return, however, to the period 350–1100, turquoise did become the mineral of choice for the various elites of the Greater Southwestern centers, their Northwestern Mexican counterparts, and for the Toltec lords of Tula. As late as 1492 turquoise was the most important item to be traded to the south, and the trade routes followed what Dobyns (1993, 5) has termed "Mesoamerica's Western Turquoise Trail," by means of which Mesoamericans imported turquoise from Los Cerrillos in New Mexico, the Gleason deposit in Southwestern Arizona, and from the Cerbat Mountains in the Mojave, California, area. They also imported green hyaline opals from the upper Rio Grande in the same period.[63]

Some scholars have suggested that the Greater Southwest maintained peripheral trade relations with Mesoamerica from at least A.D. 1050 to 1350.[64] However, this position is difficult to maintain since there would be little if any political authority, physical force, or conviction to coerce such distant peripheral centers. Rather, they were probably relatively equal "core" trading partners one with the other; in the case of Casas Grandes, it probably was part of a peripheral trade system into the late fifteenth century.

Thus, at the time of conquest, the Northern Greater Southwest region was not an empty physical space bereft of human populations even after the demise of great urban centers, but more than likely was a lively interactive system of "chiefdom"-like centers, *rancherías*, and *cazadores* (hunters) with their material inventions and exchange systems. Elaborate trade systems in the protohistorical period may have been in operation and goods, traders, ideas, and innovations continued to flow up to the time of the Spanish inundation and perhaps afterwards to a much more limited degree.[65]

Certainly, by A.D. 300 people and ideas may have moved from the south, as was the case with the Hohokam, and influenced the technological and productive ways of organizing natural resources, labor, and agricultural activity. The impact of ideology ebbed and flowed as some compact cultural centers like the Mogollon rose and fell because of environmental reasons, as was the case for Casas Grandes, razed by invasion and fire. Even when such a grand center as the Chaco Canyon complex deteriorated to the degree that the human inventors abandoned it, others slipped in behind or traveled further north and south to form even more complex systems, or much more compact systems in the south known as Pueblos in the various provinces described.

Yet what has to be understood is that all of these populations of the Greater Southwest did in fact interact directly in some cases or indirectly in others with complex systems further into what is known as Mesoamerica. There is little evidence to lead one to think that by some means Teotihuacán, Tula, Tarasca, or Tenochtitlán, considering the great distances involved, maintained coercive relationships with other populations, inducing them into a politically subservient position to be controlled economically without the use of force. However, there is sufficient evidence to conclude that for at least 1,696 years the pre-Hispanic Greater Southwest was part of a series of exchange systems made up of centers of production, trade, and redistribution that functioned according to the availability of food and its acquisition. When this process was made impossible because of drought, flooding, wars, and/or pestilence, the centers died out and others eventually took their place. What can be concluded is that the environmental, social, and economic dynamics of the Greater Southwest demanded that its populations be amazingly adaptable, which at times meant learning from or becoming amalgamated with other groups. Simultaneously, they created rituals—ceremonial, artistic, and physical expressions—that reflected ancient ideas from the south but included as well their own versions that tended to better fit the existing conditions in which they found themselves.

The Second Settlers: North from New Spain[66]

» » »

The second great south to north movement of ideas and populations from the Mexican south into the North American Greater Southwest region occurred in the midst of the protohistoric trade and exchange dynamics during the sixteenth and seventeenth centuries, not discussed here. Map 1.2 illustrates the major trade routes northward from Mexico, which are remarkably similar to those of map 1.1 for the simple reason that these routes were basically the same as those taken by the ancient explorers, traders, migrants, and entrepreneurs since A.D. 300.

The second movement, in contrast to the first, is more direct and to varying degrees intrusive and destructive to the populations present. The penetration by Hispanos/Mexicanos from the south into the Northern Greater Southwest was dramatically different depending on the region in which it occurred. Compared to the suddenness and vio-

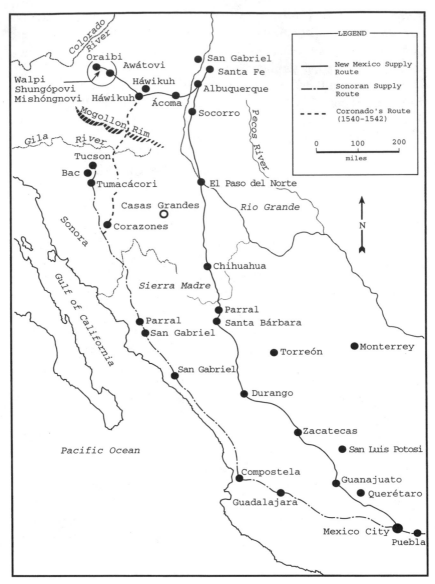

Map 1.2 Nueva España in the Seventeenth and Eighteenth Centuries. Source: Officer 1989.

lence of Coronado's expedition to the New Mexico region,[67] the 100-year occupation—after the capture in 1580 by Juan de Oñate and his soldier colonists of parts of northern New Mexico and before their reconquest by the Spanish in 1693 after the various Pueblo Revolts of 1680–1696—the establishment of colonial hegemony over Sonora/Arizona, California, and Texas were slow accretions. In this region, just as in New Spain, the mestizo Hispano/Mexicano culture continued to develop; and during the Spanish Colonial period to 1821 their cultural communities came to be known as Las Provincias Internas—the internal provinces.

The Second Settlers: Nuevo México

The initial bloody confrontations between the Franciscan missionaries, Hispano/Mexicano soldiers with Tlascalan allies and Native Americans in New Mexico created great enmity and cultural conflict. Following the reconquest by De Vargas in 1693, the returning colonists (who had left the area during the Pueblo Revolts) were not of the *adelantado*[68] type, demanding tribute from Native Americans, holding slaves, and encroaching upon native lands. Fewer than forty families returned from the original group of exiles. Sixty-seven new families returned with De Vargas from central Mexico in 1693 and 1694, and twenty-seven more from Zacatecas moved north to Santa Fe in 1695. It is interesting that in fact these families were described as "Españoles Mexicanos" by De Vargas, which indicated southern origin and a classification outside of the caste system of the period.[69] These are the "Segundos Pobladores" for this and for the rest of the region.

Although the subjugation of the Pueblos was conducted through a war of attrition by soldiers, many of the new colonists, besides the military, were weavers, blacksmiths, hatmakers, leather workers, and farmers. These were not the displaced soldier-sons seeking booty, tribute, riches, and gold, but rather rural and urban peoples looking for a place to create and develop through their own efforts and to escape the restrictions of a caste-ridden colonial regime. In addition, some coming from Zacatecas were more than likely skilled miners and like many Mexicans even to this day possessed knowledge of and a variety of skills in such areas as animal husbandry, irrigation farming, and construction.[70] These colonists, in fact, could not depend on Indian tribute, forced labor, slavery, or usurped lands as had the colonists and soldiers before them; and the Franciscan friars were less likely than their predecessors to engage in religious pogroms. The hated *encomienda* system, which made Spaniards lords of not only the land but the bodies and souls of the native peoples, died with the Pueblo Revolt. In addition, the use of household slaves, non-Indian and Indian, decreased by two-thirds between 1680 and 1790, which illustrates the impact the Pueblo rebellion had on Spanish colonial policy and, just as important, on the relations between Hispanos/Mexicanos and Pueblo peoples.[71] What developed between the segundos pobladores and native peoples was a series of cultural accommodations each of which tied one to the other in a common purpose: their defense against Utes, Apaches, and Navajos. It was especially the highly marginalized "Genizaros" (outcasts) from the Pueblos, many of them former slaves or servants, that formed the most fearsome allies of the Hispanos/Mexicanos.[72]

These relationships should be distinguished from the exploitive relations created by long-practiced institutions such as the *repartimiento*, which in spite of rigid safeguards compelled Indians to carry out "public" labor. Mostly an abusive and exploitive form of forced labor demanded by Spanish officials, soldiers, and upper-caste settlers, the repartimiento lasted long after it was abandoned in colonial Mexico and Peru.[73] This institution, however, was primarily the tool of the landed aristocracy, pernicious officials, and unproductive soldiers who still depended on Indian labor as the means of their own livelihood, but had little to do with most of the Hispano/Mexicano agropastoralists from the south who were in many ways more like the Pueblos' agrarian subsistence farmers than their upper-class, upper-caste "Spanish" brethren.

Intermarriage between colonists and the indigenous populations accentuated mestizo culture by increasing the Hispano/Mexicano population, which grew at a rate almost seven times that of the Pueblos between 1700 and 1840. This increase was due to a combination of natural population growth, creation of *hijos de la iglesia* (illegitimate offspring) who composed about 10 percent of the population legally married between 1700 and 1846, and the flight of Genizaros (Pueblo outcasts) to the towns, assuming only a marginal Hispano/Mexicano identity.[74]

As important as intermarriage was to population growth and the development of the regional cultural system, the continued migration, especially after 1700 from north-central Mexico, of craftsmen and of people seeking land to farm also had an impact. Great pressures were placed on available arable land, and in fact both migrants and *vecinos*[75] rented land from the Pueblos or purchased agricultural goods from them. The migrants from the south changed the relation between Hispano/Mexican and Pueblo farmers, with an emphasis more on cordiality, economic self-interest and *confianza* (mutual trust); and with the reduction of the Franciscan fervor to stamp out Pueblo religion, mutual self-interest between small-scale farmers and Pueblos was made possible, continuing to Mexican Independence (1821) and beyond.[76] In addition, the huge volume of trade between Santa Fe and Chihuahua culminated yearly in fairs, during which many Chihuahuan women married traders from the north; and present-day descendants continue to trace their descent matrilineally.[77]

In fact, the key to understanding Hispano/Mexicano communities in Colonial and post-Colonial periods lies not simply on the often cited caste categories, religious "folk" ideas, linguistic forms, or ideological "Hispanic" belief systems that differentiate this population from Pueblos or other regions of the Northern Greater Southwest, but in addition on the fact that for the most part this population consisted of farmers, artisans, and wage workers in small-scale, intensive agrarian systems of subsistence and exchange, and traders, mule drivers, and packers in commerce in a harsh and unforgiving land.[78]

Certainly much of daily living for most of the Hispano/Mexicano population was focused on agriculture and livestock raising; they were essentially "agropastoralists" in the post–Pueblo Revolt period.[79] Sharing available water drawn from existing floodplains along the Rio Grande for crops in cooperative irrigation systems called *acequias* and running cattle and sheep on the uplands, these farmers/ranchers basically grew and raised only what they needed, relied on relatives and kin for communal labor to clean the irrigation ditches, and generally formed small closely knit agrarian communities bound by reciprocity and mutual trust within extended domestic units. Except for the dangers and inconveniences of rattlesnakes, drought, pestilence, storms, floods, and Apache, Comanche, Navajo, and Ute raids, the northern Hispano/Mexicano farmers like many of the Pueblos became relatively successful in an arid ecological environment of great climatic extremes.[80] The originality and creativity of this region was apparent at the local level; the *paisanos*[81] created and formed the basis of Nuevo

Mexicano regional culture of that period and somewhat into the present. The cultural referent in this case is certainly not a pseudo–peninsular Spanish colonial tradition of false caste pretensions, imperial dictums, and a European theology largely ignored.

There is little doubt that the so-called Spanish population was in reality mostly Hispano/Mexicano agropastoralists, artisans, and workers (many from the south), and acculturated Genízaros, with only a tiny portion made up of either Spanish born or Spanish descendants, who maintained rigid genealogies to denote their "purity" of descent. Therefore, the use of the term "Spanish" to denote social stratification obliterates the obvious class lines present within these populations, as well as the important role of the south to north migration of Hispanos/Mexicanos to the area. Using colonial census categories according to "caste" becomes very problematic analytically as a means of determining processes like intermarriage, designations of occupations, and demographic characteristics. This conflating of a cultural category with an analytical one contributes to the myth of "Spanish" culture in this region and the denial of a process that created a northern Hispano/ Mexicano subregional culture of New Mexico that took root after the Pueblo Revolt and was periodically reinforced by south to north migration, which extended into the twentieth century.[82]

The Second Settlers: Pimería Alta

Other than perhaps the southeastern valley portion of Texas, which identifies strongly with Nuevo Santander, there is no other region of the Northern Greater Southwest that has been so stubbornly and persistently Sonoran in its regional identity than what is now known as Arizona or Pimería Alta, as it was known by some even into the twentieth century.[83] Most recently the description of the underlying pattern of movement that distinguishes this area from others was so well told that it bears being repeated here.

Juan Bojórquez was a corporal in the military garrison of Tucson when Mexican soldiers finally left that post in March 1856, nearly two years after ratification of the Gadsden Purchase Treaty. Like many of the soldiers and most of the civilians who returned to Mexico at that time, Bojórquez lingered only briefly in his native country, then returned to Tucson where he established a business, reared a family, and spent the remainder of what turned out to be a very long life. On December 11, 1920, they buried him in Tucson, Holy Hope Cemetery.[84]

The previous passage contains the keys to understanding the regional cultural identity of the Sonoran of Arizona. Of all the regions of the Northern Greater Southwest, Sonora/Arizona's culture was shaped by its reliance on force of arms for basic survival, its continuous relations with the south, its very late disengagement from the Republic of Mexico, and the ease with which populations moved north to south and back again. Another aspect of the culture of the region was its dependence upon the riverine systems that provided precious water for its acequia systems and for the cattle and horses the migrants brought with them. Like their New Mexican *paisanos*, Sonorans were primarily agropastoralists. For survival they depended not on the largess of a central government 1500 miles away in Mexico City but, like their counterpart Hispanos/Mexicanos of New Mexico, on Indian allies and on their own skills of adapting the farming and livestock-raising techniques inherited from their Spanish ancestors and learned from the native peoples of the area to meet the requirements of an arid environment. The Sonorans relied on the Pima-speaking Tohono O'odham, instead of on the Tewas, to protect them from the recently migrated western Apaches;[85] and instead of the Genizaros, presidial companies of Pimas protected the missions and *vecinos* from the raiding of the formidable Athabascans. (Map 1.3 shows the Indian raiding patterns during this period.)[86]

Most agrarian settlements were established late into the eighteenth century although some were established as early as the late seventeenth century. However, much of the initial impetus for such settlements was established by the missionizing efforts of the Jesuit order and especially of Eusebio Francisco Kino, who began his work in 1691 and traveled as far north as Tumacácori.[87] This effort, however, was preceded by the Jesuit missionary *entrada* into Sinaloa in 1591, and as early as 1617 the Jesuits had established regular contact with the Yaquis. On their continued south to north movement, the missionaries carried with them not only the Jesuit version of ideological Catholicism but new skills in agricultural management and production as well, many of which were adopted by indigenous groups like the Yaqui and Lower Pima.

As map 1.4 shows, Kino and those who followed him founded missions along the same riverine systems that previous groups had used as the basis of their settlement efforts in the protohistoric and prehistoric

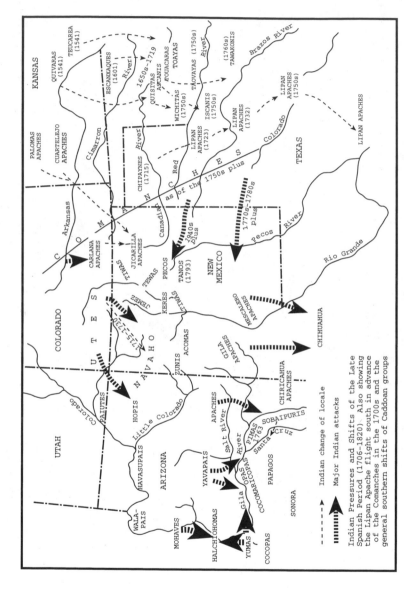

Map 1.3 Indian Pressures and Shifts of the Late Spanish Period (1706–1820). Source: Schroeder 1979, opposite 247.

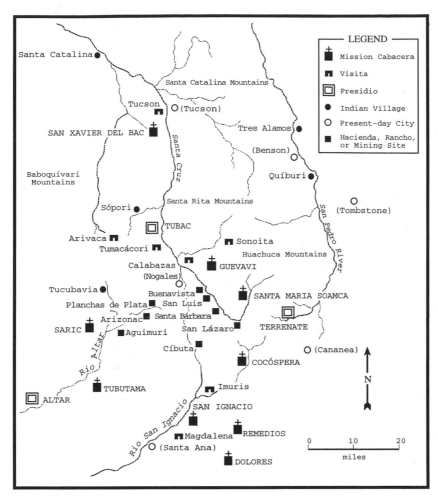

Map 1.4 The Northern Primería Alta (1691–1767): Sonora's Military Frontier in Spanish Times. Source: Officer 1987, 29.

periods. Although there were in fact few Hispano/Mexicano settlers in the region, there is sufficient evidence to show that some agropastoralists did settle at the south end of the Huachuca mountains and the San Luis Valley just south of the presidio of Santa Cruz de Terrenate and north of Las Nutrias as early as 1680.[88]

It was undoubtedly the 1736 discovery of silver slabs and chunks on the ground at a site a few miles southwest of Nogales at "Arizonac" that piqued the particular interests of Colonial authorities and stimulated the northward migration of Sonora-born Hispanos/Mexicanos, most of whom were not members of any "Spanish" elite category but rather were the mestizo offspring of Spaniard and Indian. Although the population of the Pimería Alta, as southern Arizona was known to Sonorans, exceeded one thousand by 1820, the initial nonmilitary, nonreligious population was made up mostly of prospectors who directed their attention to the Arizonac silver find. From that location they migrated northward and became agropastoralists. For the remaining Colonial and Mexican periods and into the American period, these transplanted Sonorans faced a harsher environmental and social reality than their Nuevo Mexicano *paisanos*.[89]

Facing a similar type of Pueblo Revolt, that of the Pima Indians in 1751, incessant Apache attacks that decimated herds and fields, and extreme difficulties in growing sufficient subsistence crops for survival, the population of Northern Sonorenses fluctuated, but declined particularly during the 1750s due to death at the hands of Apaches, and populations moving to escape from the religious strictures of the Jesuits and to find relief from the Apaches.[90] Barely hanging on at Santa Cruz, Tumacácori, Tubac, and Tucson and in fact abandoning them one for the other at different periods, the Hispanos/Mexicanos nevertheless managed to develop a social and economic presence.

Like the area in the northeast of New Mexico, the Sonoran regions of both Pimería Alta and Baja were populated primarily by Hispano/ Mexicano mestizos, or Coyotes, as they were known in Sonora. Very few criollos, in fact, inhabited Sonora; and according to Officer (1989, 41), one of the German Jesuit missionaries, Father Ignacio Pfefferkorn, stated that "besides the governor of Sonora, the officers of the Spanish garrisons, and a few merchants . . . there is hardly a true Spaniard in Sonora." Like Nuevo Mexicanos, the Creoles created a military-merchant-bureaucracy class, which was reinforced through intermarriage. Their children in turn fed back into the social sector by continuing these alliances through further marriage and by maintaining a "Spanish" genealogy from which the majority of the agropastoralists, wage workers, and artisans were excluded. Even though Tucson seemed to have formed a stratified system according to ethnicity, caste designations were quite fluid, and a propensity for "whitening" seemed to be the rule by which persons claimed Creole descent. Even gender divisions do not seem to have been of primary concern, especially in the less affluent sectors of society. Both men and women had to defend themselves, and women were more than likely to be just as adept at handling weapons as men, especially when the latter were on counter raids against Apaches. While the domestic unit of the household was most certainly divided by gender, there is no doubt that frequent spousal changes occurred as a result of early widowhood and because of male absences. In addition, self-assuredness acquired through sheer survival in the midst of onerous conditions did not induce women to readily accept a passive role.[91]

By 1767 the Pimería Alta's 500 or so settlers and presidial soldiers not only had to withstand more Apache attacks, outbreaks of measles, drought, and floods but by 1772 were unable to carry out retaliatory raids because many of the horse herds at the presidios of Tubac and Terrenate had been stolen. In fact, the dangers of Apache attacks were such that most farming activities had to be conducted under the guard of presidial soldiers;[92] and indeed few farmers were safe outside of earthenworks or presidial walls.

Despite the difficulties, many Hispano/Mexicano families had been established in the area before the founding of the Presidio of San Agustín de Tucsón in 1776 and of Tubac twenty-five years earlier; and in spite of Apache raids, which pushed Hispanos/Mexicanos from their lands, they kept returning to their small ranches and to the small settlements of Sopori, Calabazas, and Arivaca to carry out their farming and ranching activities.[93] It is these ranches that, in fact, extended the Sonoran rancher tradition north and established the basis for the creation of the cultural stereotype of the independent and no-nonsense Sonoran *vaquero* ranching families of Pimería Alta. In fact, the *vaquero* tradition is responsible, as well, for whatever later Anglos learned about the region and about how the families and cattle managed to survive in these arid lands beset by drought, heat, floods, epidemics, and Apache raids.

However, even presidial walls were insufficient to prevent Apache attacks; and in a direct attack on the Royal Presidio of San Agustín de Tucsón in 1782 by some 500 warriors, only the courageous defense by eighteen soldiers and two *vecinos* prevented the storming of the presidio, mission, and the pueblo of Tucson.[94] Such bravery was, of course, not surprising because such Sonoran men and women, led by Juan Bautista de Anza, traveled the overland route to California, and as expeditionary parties, founded the present-day city of San Francisco.[95]

These settlers, however, could only have persisted with the cooperation of the Pimas, Tohono O'odham, and Sobiapuris who served as presidial soldiers, "flying" companies, and raiders. It was only with such cooperation that the eighteenth century became such an improved period for the Pimería Alta Sonorans and enabled the construction of the mission "Dove of the Desert" of San Xavier del Bac to be dedicated in 1797.

After Mexican Independence (1821) a second migration from south to north began with the prospect of land grants being issued by the new Mexican government. However, this movement had barely begun when it was interrupted by large-scale Apache raids during which many of the grantees temporarily abandoned their ranches in favor of the protection of the presidios of Tucson and Tubac until the raids subsided. This level of Apache attack occurred as an aftermath of an American/Apache arms market in which Apaches traded stolen Mexican cattle, horses, and goods for American-made guns and ammunition. Because of this lucrative market, for the next twenty-five years vicious no-quarter-given combat raged between former presidial soldiers, who became members of the Mexican militia, Indian allies, Sonoran agro-pastoralists, and their Apache foes.

By 1840, Tucsonans of Pimería Alta were so inadequately supplied with arms that after one ambush in which fifteen presidial soldiers were killed in the Whetstone Mountains by weapons provided through the American arms market, their surviving companions could not recover their bodies. In a small-scale, Catholic agrarian community of mostly kinsfolk that by 1840 numbered only 500 and a presidial force of 52, this loss of fifteen soldiers represented almost 30 percent of its armed force and almost 3 percent of its total population in one battle alone.[96]

This process of constant attack, withdrawal, resurgence, and aggregation was the pattern that Los Sonorenses of Pimería Alta suffered up to the American period. Such a process did not select for stable villages, as was the case for New Mexico, except for Tucson and Tubac. Largely, Sonorenses tried valiantly to maintain their livestock and food production, and to eke out a subsistence living on family *rancherías* and near the presidio walls, in the face of overwhelming odds at the hands of Apaches, while still trying to maintain social relations through ritual, marriage, *compadrazgo* (co-godparenthood), economic exchange, and celebrations. Tied basically to rivers like the Santa Cruz, the vecinos co-operated in the acequia system that was managed by an elected *zanjero* (water judge), who organized the construction and repair of irrigation canals for diverted water. Growing wheat, barley, and corn for fodder, these second settlers had to be self-sufficient and cooperative at the same time.[97] This required intense cooperation with Indian peoples in the sharing of resources so that water, which originated from springs on Indian land, was diverted in a one-third to two-thirds sharing formula, with the former the amount provided to the fields around the presidio of Tucson and the latter to Indian fields. Simultaneously, their exchange alliances with Apache "Mansos,"[98] Gila River peoples, and Tohono O'odham provided them part of the combat forces needed to defend themselves. It was in this manner that the *vecinos* managed their survival in the midst of great scarcity and deadly attacks. That they succeeded at all is a testament to their ability to cooperate, develop exchange relations, and create a functional, though precarious, social and political fabric among themselves and others in Sonoran Pimería Alta.

The Second Settlers: Los Tejanos

"Tejas"[99] (Texas), like California, was initially penetrated and settled in response to the threatened incursions by European rivals to the Spanish crown—French expansion in the Arkansas/Texas area and Russian expansion in California and the Northwest. As in other regions, the Spanish colonial authorities chose missionaries to begin this process of defense because it was the least expensive and certainly the least threatening, thus to avoid warlike responses from the French who controlled the territory adjacent to Texas.

Similar to the initial missionizing and colonizing attempts in New Mexico, the Texas process was eventually composed of the same institutional trinity of mission-presidio-settlement; and as in the New Mexican process, Tlascalan Indians played an important role. Although serving initially as scouts and auxiliary soldiers on various expeditions beginning in 1688, the Tlascalans' actual settlement at the presidio of San Juan Bautista near Eagle Pass in 1700 was reminiscent of their establishment in Santa Fe in the barrio of Analco after the founding of that *villa* (town) in 1606.[100]

In a second similarity to that of New Mexico (in which Spaniards bumped into sedentary Pueblos), the initial penetration forces bumped into the sedentary Caddos Indians who lived in the woodlands between the Trinity and Red rivers in present-day Eastern Texas and Western Louisiana. Like the Pueblos, the Caddos lived in houses and in twenty-five compact villages, combined agriculture, hunting, and trade as productive systems, and evidently were organized in a political structure made up of three cooperating confederacies: the Hasinai, the Kadohadacho, and the Natchitoches.[101] In addition, two elements favored the relative independence of the Hasinai from any mission or presidial attempts at ideological or physical coercion and that is that they had a choice to ally themselves to the nearby French and acquire guns and horses through trade, and the Spanish supply line to accomplish the same thing was impossible to maintain because of the long overland route by way of New Spain.[102]

Although initially receiving the Spanish missionaries with courtesy and a warm welcome, the Caddos soon learned the Spaniards also carried smallpox, which killed many of their numbers. Unimpressed with priestly explanations of celestial will for their illnesses, the Caddos promptly warned the priests and gave them a choice to leave or die. In this case, the missionaries did not choose martyrdom and quickly buried the church bells, gathered their belongings, and burned their mission down before leaving in 1693. Ironically, some of the same priests died during other Pueblo revolts five years later and became martyrs to the faith.[103] Eventually, however, the institutional trinity took hold with the founding of various missions, presidios, and towns.

In 1718 the presidio of San Antonio de Béjar was dedicated, the mission of San Antonio de Valero with its later well known chapel of the Alamo was founded, and the Villa of San Fernando de Béxar, the civil settlement, was laid out. Map 1.5 shows the range of colonial settlements between 1685 and 1721.

The settlers themselves were an interesting combination of Hispano / Mexicano colonists, who had gone to Texas with the early expeditions of Domingo Ramón, Martín de Alarcón, and the Marquis de Aguayo, and Canary Islanders, who arrived in San Antonio in 1731 and created

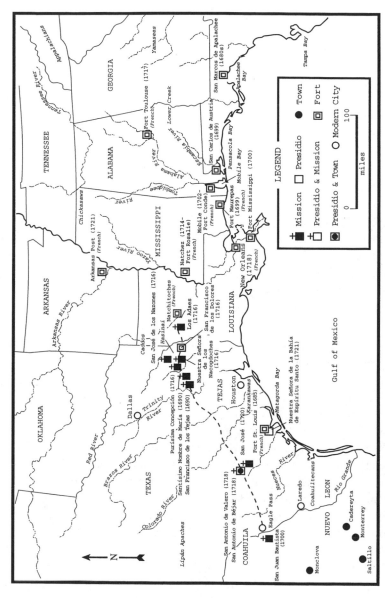

Map 1.5 Colonial Settlements, Texas and Gulf Coast. Source: Weber 1992, opposite 151.

their own sense of exclusivity in contrast to the Hispanos/Mexicanos from the north of Mexico. Combined, the population of the entire province of Tejas numbered only 500, yet both groups managed to come to terms with the reality of a hostile environment and formed agro-pastoral adaptations around the their settlements similar to those of Pimería Alta and New Mexico. Simultaneous to this formation of agro-pastoralism, the subsidized Franciscan missions developed large-scale irrigation agriculture and well-managed herds, both of which were totally dependent on Indian labor. The *vecinos* simply could not compete with such subsidized production in the sale of agricultural goods and livestock to the presidio, which throughout the Northern Greater Southwest was an important source of revenue for agropastoralists.[104]

To the south of Tejas, the province of Nuevo Santander, which had been founded by nonmilitary, nonreligious colonists, developed far more quickly than did Tejas; and by 1755 it boasted 6,000 inhabitants, twenty-three towns, and fifteen missions. By 1790 Tejas had a population of only 2,510 in the entire province, while at the same time the proximal province to the south had ten times that many.

We must ask, however, who were these Tejas *vecinos?* Like their *paisanos* of Nuevo México and Sonoran Pimería Alta, they were primarily northern Hispanos/Mexicanos. Most came from Coahuila, the adjacent province to the south of Texas; and except for the Tlascalans and Canary Islanders, this population was mostly Hispanos/Mexicanos who also mixed with native Indians especially through the institution of *barraganía*.[105] These settlers together with families of soldiers set up extralegal settlements close to the missions and presidios around Goliad, Nacogdoches, and San Antonio.

Eventually, by the 1750s, after a peace treaty had been negotiated with Lipán and Natage Apaches, both large- and small-scale ranching was made possible, and the development of the South Texas ranchero cultural system of independent producers of "protein on the hoof" was established.[106] Unlike Pimería Alta, which developed a much later ranchero tradition, the 1749 treaty permitted the development of the basis of the Norteño Tejano stereotype that came to be associated with tough, independent and no-nonsense types of individuals. However, before this stereotype could unfold completely, new hostilities arose with the "Northern Nations" like the Caddos, Wichitas, Tonkawas, and their allies—the Comanches.[107] As these hated foes of the Apaches began raiding the newly established ranches, Apache-populated missions, and farms surrounding the presidios, missions, and towns, the exact same process of ranch, farm, and settlement abandonment that had occurred in Pimería Alta took place here. For example, San Antonio's entire presidial horse herd was taken by Comanches in 1774, making defense impossible, and by 1778 the entire province of Tejas numbered only 3,103 inhabitants, and the only remaining settlements of note were the *villa* of San Antonio, two presidios at Béxar and La Bahía, and seven missions with few converts.[108] It was only after 1810 that the abandoned ranches between Béxar and Goliad experienced a resurgence, and new ranches were established along both sides of the San Antonio River and its tributaries.[109] All this activity was made possible through peaceful alliances between Spanish colonial authorities and most Native Americans before 1800; one specific example is the Comanche alliance of 1788 successfully negotiated by the Sonoran, and then governor of New Mexico, Juan Bautista de Anza the Younger.[110] With only relatively small breaches of the peace around San Antonio committed by Comanches and Northern peoples while chasing Apaches southward, the 1800s were generally favorable for the development of the Norteño Tejano throughout the region.[111] A demographic snapshot of San Antonio de Béxar between 1720–1790 provides some similarities and marked differences to the demographics of Pimería Alta and of Tucson and Tubac. As in Pimería Alta towns, hostile Apache and Comanche raids in Texas created great suffering and induced high early death rates throughout the eighteenth century. The high mortality rates due to permanent warfare plus the extremely high infant mortality rates due to smallpox and *matlazahuatl* fever caused relatively slow demographic expansion in San Antonio, similar to that in the rest of Texas.[112]

Expansion was primarily the result of migration from the northern and central provinces of Mexico, with adults making up two-thirds of the population in Texas and 68 percent of the population of San Antonio over a 16-year period.[113] Most were Hispano/Mexicano migrants from Saltillo, Camargo, Monterrey, Monclova, and Río Grande, although some were from central Mexican towns like Querétaro, Mexico City, and Guadalajara.[114] Given the circumstances of migration from Northern Mexico, ethnic stratification was based only on the language of claims—that is, the attempt to "whiten" a person's social category in order to gain access to legal, economic, and/or political privilege. The fact of the matter is that caste mobility demanded the creation of the language of caste claims when these categories fell apart in the face of social reality. For the most part, the majority of the non-officer ranks of all presidios throughout the Greater Southwest were non-Peninsular or non-Creole, yet they were not classified as mestizos in proportion to their actual number. In this sense people claimed caste membership in spite of the fact that they were not members legally.

Similarly, in examining the number of native born versus migrants, 43 percent of household heads were non-native born of which 17 percent were *labradores*—a census category designating individuals with direct access to land or tenancy. This category included the most affluent *hacendados* to the owners or renters of small gardens and farms. Three percent were merchants, 16 percent were artisans, 18 percent were widows, and 46 percent were laborers. Even using the claim language of caste, it is obvious that many of the migrants were non-"Spanish" but rather Hispanos/Mexicanos from the northern provinces of Mexico, seeking land, wages, and cultural and physical location.[115]

The town of San Fernando (Antonio) de Béxar, which was the third leg of the original trinity of colonial settlement, was not unlike Santa Fe and Tucson in its class stratification. It was composed of four barrios: (1) the South, in which descendants of the original Canary Islanders lived; (2) the North, where the wealthiest resided; (3) Valero, in which active and retired presidial soldiers dwelled; and (4) Laredo, for which there is no historical record,[116] but given the general characteristics of the population and the structure of eighteenth-century settlements, the residents were more than likely Hispanos/Mexicanos who may have been artisans, wage earners, or small landholders.

Like their counterparts in New Mexico and Pimería Alta, Tejano stratification along class, caste, and ethnic cultural lines became blurred by isolation from central authority, population admixture due to marriage and concubinage, and close physical proximity of all groups. However, gender divisions do not seem to have been as equally blurred, for women suffered higher mortality rates then men; and of those remaining women, as many as 30 percent were widowed, leaving many of them to eke out a living in a largely patriarchal system. Also the practice of concubinage did not provide women in such circumstances with any legal protection in domestic disputes nor were they even counted as part of the census taken at the time.

Nevertheless, class, ethnic, and caste lines seemed to have blended with the use of fictive kinship tools like *compadrazgo,* which crosscut segmentation because of the necessity for alliances with Indians and the creation of relatively independent farming and ranching communities that led in large part to the creation of a relatively unified Tejano identity, which persists to this day. However, the basic cultural and institutional debt owed is one credited to the south and the Tejanos' own cultural adaptations dictated by context and the "bumping process."

The Second Settlers: Alta California

While Spanish colonial policy with regard to Alta California sought to avoid Russian intrusion by missionizing and creating presidios in the Californias,[117] it was also directly influenced (particularly in the formation of settlements) by the rebellions of indigenous peoples and the moral concern of missionaries about sexual violations of native women by Spanish presidial troops. Although rape in New Mexico was not unknown, and certainly Zunis and other Pueblos rose up in response to the violation of indigenous women, the widespread sexual abuse of native women in Alta California seems unprecedented in scope due either to poor documentation in other regions and/or better documentation in the California case.[118] While in the New Mexico region the rape of women who were servants seemed to be prevalent, there was no attempt to affect colonial behavior by preventing repeated occurrences, even though such attacks were considered an abomination by the mission priests and church doctrine.[119]

Therefore, most of the second settlers were sent from the south as domestic units[120] as they had been in the other regions as well in order to ensure the crown's overseas possessions and produce needed subsistence items but also to fill the cultural space of others with their own. It does seem that the transmission of the Hispano/Mexicano domestic unit was specifically meant to limit the onerous damage done by violation of the Spanish version of the indigenous domestic unit by the rapes carried out by Spanish soldiers. It is not the case that Spanish missionaries sought to protect the indigenous domestic unit, but rather they sought to ensure the cultural transformation of that unit into the colonial patriarchal form.[121] This could only be accomplished if native peoples who were not in sedentary settlements were induced to settle in *reducciones* (the practice of settling Indians around missions).

The third element, besides rape and the colonial domestic unit response, that distinguished Alta California from other regions is the clear absence of continuous warfare with native groups, especially equivalents to Apache and Comanche warriors. In fact, such intensive conflict, due to the breakdown of political control by Mexican authorities and the gun running of American entrepreneurs, does not emerge until sixty years after the founding of San Diego (1769).[122] However, there is no doubt that many native peoples of the region both protested and occasionally rebelled against not just the ideology that was imposed on them, but against the harsh measures that were dealt them at any sign of resistance to labor and *reducciones*. The rebellions were quickly squashed by lashing, burning, and executions. Although the Ipais burned down the mission of San Diego in 1775 and a number of other rebellions along the coast ensued, they were quickly extinguished by superior firepower and technology.[123]

All-male attempts then at colonization in California proved to be disastrous for missions, presidios, and most of all for the native peoples because of the harsh treatment meted out for resistance to the sexual violations of native women by Spaniards, and the attempts to "reduce" them to centralized settlements (*reducciones*). It was only after the arrival of the colonists who founded San Francisco and Santa Bárbara and populated some of the areas around San Gabriel by 1781 or so that Hispano/Mexicano communities could emerge, as map 1.6 illustrates.

There is a myth concerning Hispanos/Mexicanos of this region: the idea that the "Californios" were originally "Spanish" Dons, a stereotypic landed gentry owning thousands of acres filled with cattle, and were the creators of the social structure of California. That large land grants existed was the case, but in general these did not develop until the post-1821 Mexican period and particularly after 1834 with the secularization of mission lands. Before 1821 less than 20 ranches of varying sizes were given as grants, but after 1834 about 700 ranches were granted by the then governors of California.[124] For example, in the post-1821 period José de la Guerra y Noriega was granted a ranch of over 250,000 acres with more than 50,000 head of cattle, while others of lesser size were granted in the same period.[125] Therefore, like the mythic "Spanish" heritage of the New Mexican who owes much in the way of substantive cultural tradition to northern Mexicans, the actual-

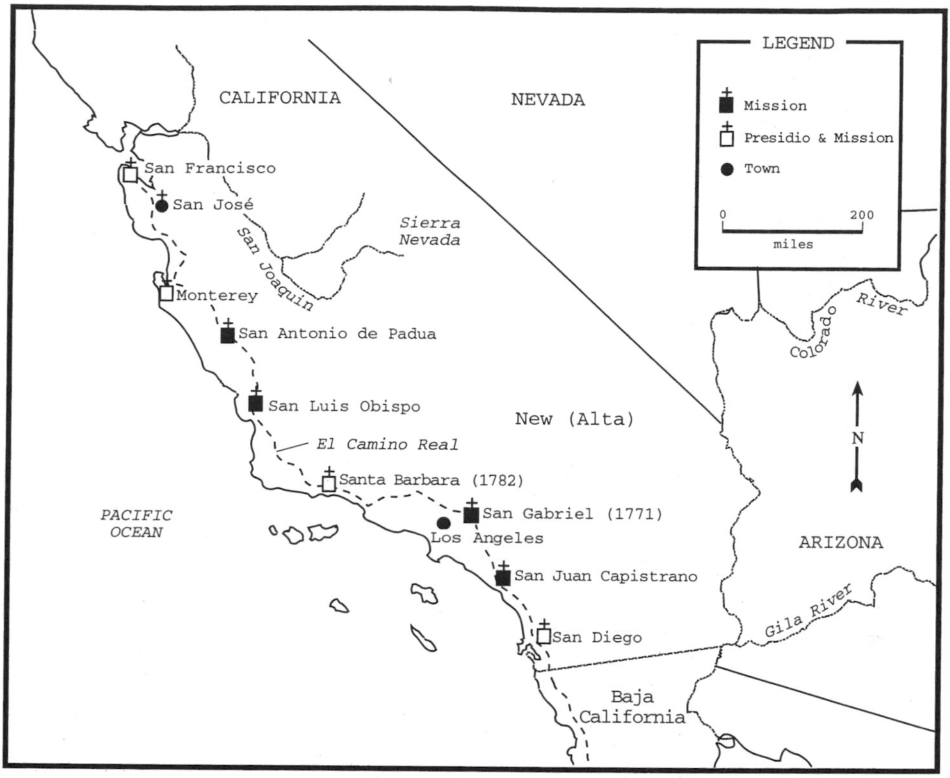
CALIFORNIA
NEVADA
LEGEND
Mission
Presidio & Mission
Town
0
200
miles
San Francisco
San José
Sierra Nevada
San Joaquin
Monterey
San Antonio de Padua
Colorado River
San Luis Obispo
New (Alta)
N
El Camino Real
Santa Barbara (1782)
San Gabriel (1771)
PACIFIC OCEAN
Los Angeles
ARIZONA
San Juan Capistrano
Gila River
San Diego
Baja California

Map 1.6 Spanish Settlements in New California (1784). Source: Weber 1992, 262.

ity of the Spanish Don tradition owed much to the 1834 Mexican Secularization Proclamation, which dismantled mission structures, distributed lands to a few politically connected individuals, and supported the aggrandizement of the Don complex.

For the most part, the California colonial and postcolonial class structure in varying degrees resembled that of New Mexico, Pimería Alta (Arizona), and Texas with a small class segment of wealthy cattle and land owners (who formed the backbone of the tallow and hide export business) and political officials and merchants who supported them. In addition, there was a sizable sector of agropastoralists who simultaneously farmed, ran cattle, irrigated lands, and provided most of the agricultural and subsistence products for the region. The last and largest of the Hispano/Mexicano sectors was made up of artisans, vaqueros, seasonal workers, landless laborers, and construction workers who lived in Los Angeles, San José, or Branciforte or around the presidios of San Diego, Santa Bárbara, Monterey, San Francisco, and in small rancho sites. By 1821, 3,200 Californios of varying social sectors were spread out within a 500 mile corridor among an indigenous population of declining numbers.[126]

As can be surmised from the discussion above, the Southwest region was partially populated by a small but adaptive population that owed its primary cultural existence to northern migrations of Hispanos/Mexicanos. Nevertheless, with much larger indigenous populations in various cooperative and antagonistic relationships with the Hispanos/Mexicanos, the region was an arena of constant turmoil and dynamic change.

CHAPTER 2

» » » » »

The American *Entrada:* "Barrioization"

and the Development of Mexican

Commodity Identity

IN THE 1967 PREFACE to the reprint of his book, *Forgotten People: A Study of New Mexicans,* George I. Sánchez asked the rhetorical question: "Where are our land grants, for example." This question, asked more than 100 years after the American war against Mexico and after the Gadsden Purchase, has not only plagued New Mexicans but segments of the population in California, Arizona, and Texas who either lost their land grants through chicanery or sold them legally. Whether large or small, Spanish and/or Mexican land grants for most Hispanos/Mexicanos of Sánchez's generation and before, and for the political activists of the 1970s, were symbolic not just of land juridically usurped, purchased, annexed, or placed in limbo because of legal delay, but of a historical and cultural place and past. Land grants were geographically specific indicators of Hispano/Mexicano past and potential presence in the area. Regardless of a cultural redefinition due to economic conditions, for the Hispano/Mexicano population land grants were tied to values of control, space, production, and relations with a vague and perhaps romanticized past.

Even though the Mexican war is often considered to be the most important episode of the American *entrada* into the Northern Greater Southwest, it should be considered as the end of a long process by which the United States took advantage of the unstable Mexican political structure of the Southwest. This instability, created after Mexican independence in 1821, was a result of the American penetration of the region through long-distance trade and the social and cultural penetration effected by American trappers and entrepreneurs. Probably more important than either of these factors is the consistent destruction of Mexican communities and their political structure by those Americans who were involved in illegal trade with and in fact sponsored and supported raids carried out by Apaches, Comanches, Ute, and other native peoples.[1]

To reiterate, the eventual cultural subordination of the Mexican population is the aftermath of a series of processes. The first involves the rise of Anglo trapping and commercial activities in the region, and the second, the joining of Anglo trappers and merchants and elite Hispano/Mexicano families through marriage, partnerships, and alliances. This latter process, in particular, was upheld by liberal Mexican laws, which granted citizenship to Americans and other foreigners of a social status equal to that of Mexican citizens. Parallel to both processes, but more important, is the destructive effect on Hispano/Mexicano ranching, farming, and community stability caused by an illegal arms trade, which supplied Apache, Comanche, Ute, and other regional native peoples with guns and ammunition for stolen cattle, goods, and even Mexican captives. As will be shown, this last process decimated populations, their economic and social structure, and together with the other two processes created a willingness within local populations to seek political and military solutions with the United States. The 1836 Texas war of independence, the Mexican war of 1846, and the subsequent penetration of the region by intensive capitalist enterprises were in reality the culmination of a series of events, which led to the eventual political and cultural subordination of Hispanos/Mexicanos in stratified-class communities.

During the Mexican period Hispano/Mexicano communities were faced with the expansion of American colonialism and the diminution of the Spanish colonial version. Mexican trading policy, which opened the Santa Fe trail and allowed American fur trappers and traders into the New Mexico and California regions, assured the inclusion of this important area in the American economic market and political sphere of influence. Simultaneous with the American penetration of the region was the granting to Americans, by the newly established Delegation of New Mexico (the regional legislative body), a political status equal to that of Mexican citizens of New Mexico, as long as they paid taxes and other surcharges.[2] Even more liberal were the laws created for the colonization of Texas and California, which stated that the only requirements for citizenship were that Anglos and other foreigners had to become Catholics and pay residency and land ownership taxes.

With access to and citizenship in the regions of New Mexico, Texas, California, and Sonora made so easy, American traders, merchants, craftsmen, vagabonds, land seekers, political agents, and eventually southern immigrant families from slave-holding states began to exert great influence in the Northern Greater Southwest. However, there was a second order of influence that made the nexus of commercial and economic relations much denser, and that was the extensive kinship alliances between elite Hispano/Mexicano landowners and American traders, trappers, and merchants. Prior to the Mexican war, for example, the landed elite of Los Angeles included Mexicanized Anglos who through marriage and land ownership became cultural copies of the small Hispano/Mexicano landed gentry. Thus Abel Stearns, "Juan José" Warner, "Don Benito" Wilson, John Temple, William Wolfskill, and Louis Vignes married Hispanas/Mexicanas and assumed a bicultural identity and important political and class relationships with local Dons.[3] Certainly prior to the Texas revolution of 1836, marriage between single American males and Mexican females was quite the norm, as the marriages of Stephen Austin, Jim Bowie, Davey Crockett and sundry other famous Texans attest. However, in many semicolonial arenas these were usually between daughters of landed elites and the new "Mexican Texans" who only a few years previously had been uprooted Mississippians, Alabamans, Kentuckians, or Carolinians. Likewise, in New Mexico marriages between the daughters of Nuevo Mexicano elites and Anglo or French merchants and trappers were not unusual after Mexican independence.

These marriage ties encouraged economic and commercial relations between Mexicanized Anglos and Hispano/Mexicano elites, who together formed networks of cultural, property, and class interests. On a broader scale, the networks spun off regional political allegiances in opposition to a Mexican political system nominally controlled from Mexico City, some 1,500 miles away. In fact, one commentator of the period in California stated that "the much stronger ties of marriage and property . . . [created a regard by Californios for Americans] . . . as brothers" and was more important than the commercial relationship.[4] However, the alliances between and mutual interests of Anglos and Hispanos/Mexicanos in California, New Mexico, and Texas simply could not prevent wholesale land redistribution from Hispano/Mexicano elites to Anglos after both the Texas rebellion and the Mexican war, as a later discussion will illustrate.

On a different scale of social activity throughout the Northern Greater Southwest, the Hispano/Mexicano villager, ranchero, agro-pastoralist, and wage worker held few pretensions of alliances with Anglos and a resulting economic advantage. Rather, they were accustomed to confronting the hardships of subsistence survival and having to face an onslaught of Apache, Comanche, Ute, and other Native American attacks.

In 1803 the illegal trade mentioned above originated and continued unchecked for many years. By the time of Mexican independence, Anglo traders from Louisiana were receiving horses and mules stolen from San Antonio by Comanches, Apaches, and Taovayas in exchange for guns and ammunition. In Stephen Austin's colony in Texas, Texas Anglos served as middlemen for Comanches by buying their stolen Mexican furs and other goods and then selling them in Louisiana. The illegal economy of stolen goods, horses, furs, and even human beings brought about the establishment of a series of trading posts along the Red River in the area where it formed the pre-Mexican war boundary.[5]

Further north, the Missouri-Santa Fe trail became an avenue for the importation of arms and ammunition to Taos, Santa Fe, and El Paso by American traders who then traded the munitions to Apaches, Comanches, and Caddos in West Texas, Chihuahua, and Sonora. The arms were used extensively against the residents of the Northern Greater Southwest, with very little of the area being spared; in fact, Comanches raided as far south as 135 miles north of Mexico City.[6] It was by this means that the balance of power between Navajos and New Mexicans was completely overturned. Although most goods from Missouri were brought to the Southwest by Anglo traders, some New Mexicans participated in the same trade and exchanged guns and ammunition for goods and horses taken perhaps from their own communities.[7] In addition to the those along the Red River, Americans also constructed trading posts outside the Mexican political sphere in Southern Colorado. There Bents Fort and Forts Vásquez, Jackson, and Lupton all served as trading centers for guns and ammunition. These forts could not have been used as centers for illegal trade without the acquiescence of American authorities. It is possible that these forts were instruments of American policy, which aimed at forcing Hispanos/Mexicanos from their settlements, missions, forts, farms, and ranchos so that they might seek protection.[8]

American traders and trappers also expanded their illegal trade into California. Horses and goods were stolen from northern California ranches by New Mexicans, Anglos, California Indians, Navajos, Nez Percés, Yakimas, and Cayuses (all driven from their own territory by encroaching U.S. settlements). Cattle, stolen by Utes on the West Coast, were driven east and sold, in some cases to Mormons in Salt Lake City. From as far away as Wisconsin, Delaware, Alabama, and Pennsylvania, Delawares, Shawnees, and other groups, displaced by continued American expansion, also traveled west to California and preyed upon the ranchos.[9]

Raids, such as those described above, by Apaches, Utes, as well as by Comanches and literally dozens of other native peoples cannot be understood as the idiosyncratic activities of "hunters and gatherers." Rather, this facet of the illegal economy should be considered an important, and perhaps the major, covert instrument of American expansionist policy and an encroaching capitalist economy. Nevertheless, from whatever point of view, the result was the same throughout the region: devastated ranches, burned-out villages, and abandoned farms. More importantly it set the stage for Hispanos/Mexicanos to seek alternative means of survival, which they saw in the promises offered by U.S. arms and wealth. The Mexican war was perceived by most Hispanos/Mexicanos of the Northern Greater Southwest not as the end of a cultural system but rather as a means of surviving physically. Culturally, the Hispano/Mexicano had seen the ease with which the first Anglos married Mexican women, acculturated to Mexican religion and customs, and generally seemed to have taken on the behaviors appreciated by Mexicans, who came to regard them as "Americanos simpáticos." Throughout the region many Hispanos/Mexicanos initially welcomed the large-scale presence of Americans and their entrepreneurial skills.

The Mexican war, American land policies, the rapid expansion of a capitalist market, and ethnocentric and racist attitudes compressed Hispanos/Mexicanos into a culturally and politically subordinated population, and with reason their attitude toward the Anglo interlopers changed. After the Texas revolution, the Mexican war, and the Gadsden Purchase of 1856, the basic U.S. strategy for acquiring property around former missions, presidios, and large and small towns was to use taxation, boundary manipulation, theft, and juridical means such as delaying land grant claims in order to possess Mexican productive resources. The result was that an already hard-pressed population lost its land-holding power and control. In a very particular sense most people in Tucson, San Antonio, San Diego, Los Angeles, Santa Fe, and rural areas became subordinated not because of some cultural trait or practice but because of American economic policy. A few Hispano/ Mexicano families, who were either joined in marriage to Anglos or had learned to manipulate the Anglo legal and commercial systems, retained their possessions; however, most of the wealth, land, and even knowledge of survival for Anglos in the region arose from the labor and ashes of Mexican communities. From this point on Hispanos/ Mexicanos came to be thought of as a commodity to be bought, sold, and periodically expelled, becoming what Weber has so masterfully termed, "Strangers in their own land."[10]

"Barrioization," Cultural Creation, and Resistance

» » »

Hispanos/Mexicanos managed to retain and embellish cultural systems, which continue to this day, in spite of massive acculturation and institutional mechanisms that sought to culturally eradicate them. From the time of the American occupation to the Mexican Revolution of 1910, each region developed a similar process: the encapsulation of segments of the population into class-stratified communities and heterogeneous barrios within urban centers. The creation of this type of community and the cultural and geographical space in which to locate became the developmental platform for generations of Mexicans in the region and was enhanced by enduring social ties and familial relationships south of the political border.

To varying degrees, Tucson, Arizona, may serve as a case study of the creation of a stratified community and of a working-class sector. Tucson is representative of a process that also came about in Los Angeles, El Paso, Santa Barbara, San Antonio, and Albuquerque.[11] At the root of such a process, however, are major economic changes in the region, which include the introduction of mining, construction, cattle ranching, and other land use. A key shift occurred after the introduction of the Southern Pacific Railroad in 1870 connected Tucson to markets in the East and brought about the inevitable process of making Mexican land, resources, and labor part of market forces much beyond their local control. In the other regions, simple variants of this deep capitalist penetration occurred.

El Barrio y Comunidad Mexicana: The Case of Tucson to 1910[12]

In his ninety-fourth year, Elízar Herrera recalled: "We used to leave our doors open and nobody would bother us and anytime anyone wanted to come over or to visit from Sonora, they just dropped in. Sometimes they stayed for months but it did not matter for they were either relatives or *conocidos* (known persons), and if they needed help like almost everyone did, you know, *con confianza*." That is how Elízar Herrera recalled his earliest memories of the late 1890s in Tucson's Mexican neighborhoods or *barrios* and the system based on reciprocity, exchange, and need.[13]

For Elízar Herrera, whose father was a blacksmith, growing up in Tucson consisted of taking dips in the then-running Santa Cruz River, being chased by newly hired truant officers, and avoiding the sun in an "air-conditioner-less" Tucson. Mexican neighborhoods had no boundaries south past the border. Relatives not only visited, but stayed and worked and married other Sonorenses whose relatives had done the same thing. For Elízar the movement of populations from the south into Mexican neighborhoods of Tucson was not a cause for alarm, but rather for acceptance of a process as normal as rising in the morning.

This process was not only, however, a norm for the working class but also extended to the elite of Tucson who lived in the same or adjoining neighborhoods. Among the wealthiest Mexicanos in Tucson in 1870, twenty-seven were from Sonora, three from Chihuahua, one from Sinaloa, two from Spain, and one from Chile. Most of their wealth was earned from commercial occupations such as retail merchandising and trading; and for the most part, these families had not combated Apaches as a few of the remaining pre-Gadsden Purchase families had done. The old presidial and village families in the area were respected for their leadership and knowledge of the ways of desert, Apaches, and ranching and farming; but they had not become wealthy like the Mexicano residents of Tucson who had more recently come from the south.[14]

The rest of the Mexicano community in the same period, 1860–1880, shows the same demographic characteristics in terms of origin. In 1860, 62.6 percent of the Mexican population had been born north of the newly established Gadsden Purchase line. By 1880, 70.2 percent had been born south of that line in Sonora. Twenty years later this evened out with almost an equal proportion born north and south of the line (58.2 and 41.5 percent, respectively). In terms of wealth as indicated by occupation, in 1860 over 80 percent of Mexicanos were in blue-collar occupations while twenty years later not quite 80 percent were so represented. By 1900 only slightly over 70 percent were in blue-collar occupations and the rest in white collar. However, what is even more important during this period for the Mexicano is that in 1860 almost 12 percent of the population were agropastoralists, but thirty years later this occupational category accounted for only 2.4 percent.[15]

This pattern of a declining Mexicano participation in farming and ranching was not just a local phenomenon; in fact, it was a process that occurred over much of the Chihuahua and Sonora region in the aftermath of Porfirian land policy implementation. On the American side of the border the decline of Mexican ranchos began after the introduction of American capitalist enterprises in the form of cattle companies and industrialized agricultural production and was coupled to large-scale land fraud and lack of legal land grant and Homestead Act recognition. José Moreno, an old Mexican cowboy, recounted the bitter experience of most Mexican ranchos in the Tanque Verde area then east of Tucson:

> Before the big ranchers came to Tanque Verde, men had small spreads and made a living not so much by raising beef as by simple dairy farming. All of that ended when the Americans came into the area. Before, all of the places were pure Mexican ranches. No sooner did the Americans come than the small Mexican ranches were finished.[16]

Together with large-scale cattle ranching and industrialized agricultural production, the introduction of the railroad to Tucson (which opened the entire southern Arizona region to intensive capitalist penetration) created the need for labor from the south, thus stimulating migratory pressures. Populations were forced to migrate just as their ancestors had done, with occupationally adaptive Mexicanos moving to cities like Tucson, El Paso, Albuquerque, San Diego, San Antonio, and Los Angeles, thus accounting for much of the increase in the Mexican population in those cities and the decline of the agropastoralist occupational status in Tucson.[17]

Mexicanos, as urban populations, concentrated in specific areas of cities like Tucson, in barrios made up of a heterogeneous middle- and working-class population like that described by Elízar Herrera. Within these neighborhoods, just as today, one could find *boticas* where, among other things, Lady Lipton's Elixir for constipation and *yerba buena* (mint) for hangovers and stomach pains were sold. The butcher, barber, and blacksmith shops together with the local Catholic Church, saloons, newspaper and assay offices, restaurants, laundries, and Mexican variety theaters filled much of the daily economic ritual and recreational activity of working- and middle-class and nearby elite residents. It is within the barrio shops of the service providers, merchants, and skilled artisans that between 1860 and 1900 the Mexican middle class expanded through internal growth and Sonora to Tucson migration; so that of all occupations in Tucson in 1900, 40 percent of employed Mexicans occupied white- and skilled blue-collar jobs, an increase of 10 percent from twenty years before.[18]

An integral aspect of these barrios, however, was the poverty bred by a dual labor system that paid Anglos more than Mexicans for the same job. The backbreaking job of laying tracks for the Southern Pacific Railroad, where most Mexicans who worked on the railroads were concentrated, was an especially onerous task in 115-degree heat and selected for early retirement due to death or injury, as was the case in most jobs held by Mexican men. By 1900 more than 25 percent of all Mexican households were headed by widows.[19] Four out of every ten Mexicanos worked at dollar-a-day unskilled jobs, which, however, does not mean that they were unskilled themselves.[20] Rather, the structure of the economy rested on the need for a large reserve of labor for mines, railroad, construction, and cattle ranching. This reserve, as in the present, although highly skilled in a variety of occupations such as carpentry, mining, agriculture, and construction, was not employed according to ability. In other words, regardless of skill and knowledge, Mexicanos were no more nor less than a commodity to be used when the need arose and were paid less than Anglos for comparable work.

Added to the labor picture was the increasing cultural subordination of the population made possible especially through the educational system, which taught Mexican children from the 1870s on that the only way to be a good American was to reject Mexican culture. Even though the public school system of Tucson was originally developed in 1871 by Estevan Ochoa, former Tucson mayor and prominent merchant, the Chihuahua-born Mexican could not have predicted that what he helped create would be a major mechanism for cultural subordination.[21] Perceived only as other immigrants, Mexican children not only became foreigners in their own land but were given the distinct message that their considerable poverty stemmed from their backward Mexican culture and language. Therefore, the general educational strategy was to "Americanize" children by eliminating obviously "foreign" accents in Spanish, prohibiting the language from being spoken, and advising "that Anglo Saxon models of work, morality, and government" were to be imitated, inferring that Mexican models were somehow inferior.[22] Taught by largely well-meaning but ethnocentric Anglo teachers, the school curriculum was designed to erase language, culture, social relations, food preference, and a sense of cultural lineage.

However, beyond such an educational process was an even more pernicious belief: that being a Mexican was equated with ignorance, laziness, and a notion of illegitimacy because of Indian-Spanish admixture. Underlying this notion was a larger pattern in which Mexican children were perceived, like their parents, as a commodity for the job market but of less value than their Anglo counterparts. For Mexican elites, however, this was not the case because they developed their own private Catholic schools for girls and boys in 1870 and 1874 respectively.[23] This separate but unequal schooling of Mexican elites and aspiring middle-class individuals created a real and lasting distinction within the Mexican community that can be perceived to this day.

Thus, class stratification and class alliances and interests between the Mexican and Anglo elites only accentuated class distinctions. Mexican elites and the struggling middle-class sectors of Tucson perceived the working-class Mexican population (some 70 percent of the total) as *pelados,* or skinned ones, who lived in the Barrio Libre or "Free Neighborhood," whose boundaries changed as more persons sought cheap housing, thus expanding its domain. Amalgamated to this distinction in classes was the designation of just about any Mexican, regardless of class origin in Sonora, as a *pelado*.

For the aspiring Sonorense individual and family from the south, "proving" and gaining class legitimacy was a major effort. Thus, among the most serious class statements that could be made from the nineteenth century to the present was not only which designated Catholic Church was attended, because these too had class associations, but as well how soon one's Mexican children were placed in Catholic schools. The irony of the situation was that within Mexican Catholic schools great attention was paid to Latin America, culture, language, and manners, and distinctions were made between themselves and Anglos who were perceived as ill mannered.[24]

This stratification of the population was crosscut by a variety of community and regional mechanisms that gave the Mexican community its dynamic character. The maintenance of kinship systems across the newly defined U.S.-Mexico border provided avenues for continued migration from the south, with the ebb and flow depending on regional economic circumstances. The main transport and communication lanes used by Mexicanos then and now provided easy access to the north for refugees from many of the Sonoran political conflicts in the nineteenth century. Thus it was that intellectuals, writers, and revolutionaries joined their relatives in Tucson, and many became residents and citizens. They provided much of the leadership and commercial vitality to the Mexican community within Tucson in the 1870–1910 period. Writer, judge, politician, and scholar, Carlos Velasco left Sonora for Tucson in 1865 in the aftermath of the French intervention; in 1878 he founded the newspaper *El Fronterizo* and led the fight to eradicate discrimination against Mexicans.[25]

Although diminishing after 1880 with the influx of Anglo immigrants to Tucson, intermarriage between Mexicans and Anglos was an important tie, especially in later Anglo nativist and racist periods during the depression of 1890 and into the Mexican Revolutionary era. Intermarriage accounted for twenty-three percent of all marital unions between 1870 and 1880. As in most demographically unbalanced situations in which immigrating single men lack marriageable partners of the same cultural group, 96 percent of all marriages were between

Mexican women and Anglo men, with the former usually the well-heeled daughter of a prominent Mexican family. It is interesting that by 1860, Anglos, most of whom were male and constituted only 20 percent of the population, controlled 87 percent of real and personal property. In contrast, the Mexican population, which constituted 71 percent of the total, controlled only 13 percent of real and personal property.[26]

Intermarriages, however, waned, reflecting the pattern that was to emerge, as the economic structure of Tucson drew more Anglos into the area. The percentage of intermarriages reduced from 23 percent in the twenty year period 1870–1890 to 9.1 percent in the decade 1900–1910.[27] It would seem as well that as Anglos assumed more and more control of land, resources, and labor an inverse relationship between Mexican and Anglo marriage emerged. Thus by 1900, over 44 percent of Anglos held white-collar occupations while Mexicans held half that number, even though Mexicans and Anglos were almost equal in total numbers in occupations: 1,115 Mexicans to 1,328 Anglos.[28]

Nevertheless, early families of mixed parentage like the Tullys, Brictas, Wards, and Browns were important cultural bearers. In the midst of Anglo racist hysteria during the depression of the 1890s and the post-1910 migration from Mexico, these families served as cultural brokers and managed to calm and provide cooler voices to potential ethnic conflicts.[29]

In addition, the religious activities of sodalities such as the Sociedad Guadalupana, St. Vincent de Paul Society, Knights of Columbus, Club San Vicente, and Club Santa Teresita helped the indigent and provided support in raising funds for church and community improvement, regardless of class association. The important religious and lay *fiestas* were celebrated by the entire community; one example was the celebration honoring the patron saint of Tucson, San Agustín, which began on August 28 and lasted for two or more weeks until September 16, Mexican Independence Day.[30] Other feast days, such as those of St. John the Baptist (Día de San Juan) and San Isidro, were coupled with the many saint's days that individuals and families celebrated. When combined with the traditional Christmas, New Year, and Easter holidays as well as the life cycle rituals, such as baptisms, confirmation, birthdays, weddings, and funerals, the community was provided with opportunities for elite, middle-, and working-class populations to meet if not touch across class lines. As later chapters will discuss, these celebrations formed the early versions of still-operating "Ritual Cycles of Exchange" in which rituals are used as means of articulating social relations and provisioning households beyond economic limitations.

As in San Diego, Los Angeles, El Paso, Albuquerque, Laredo, San Antonio, and almost anywhere Mexicans lived, in Tucson most middle- and working-class people came to rely more and more on the process of visitation, which Elízar Herrera recalled as "where they just dropped in." That is, institutional subordination in employment, education, politics, economy, and even recreation, as later chapters will illustrate, were resisted by developing household strategies that modified and soothed the terrible impact of social, educational, and cultural discrimination and economic commoditization. In addition, from these sectors arose political leadership that constantly tried to support community sodalities, voluntary associations, and self-help groups like the Alianza Hispano Americana (1894) and the Sociedad Zaragoza (1901), which were the precursors of many similar organizations to follow.[31]

For the elites, theirs was a double responsibility that was sometimes distributed positively and sometimes negatively. While Anglos, who came to completely control the political and economic life of the southern Arizona region including Tucson, often sought their advice on such matters as resisting employees who demanded better wages or working conditions, more than likely Mexican elites sided with Anglos over such matters. In fact, it would not have been in their own self-interest to support workers because they themselves were frequently partners in or owners of the commercial concerns that benefited when mining, construction, or railway strikes were quickly stopped.

Some elites assumed the mythic trappings of the *hacendado,* not unlike their New Mexico, California, and Texas counterparts. This group not only assumed a false identity but made others who were economically less fortunate than themselves feel unworthy of attention by using that false identity to distance themselves culturally and socially. A hundred years later their alleged descendants rode about in parades on community feast days wearing Spanish Don helmets in 110-degree weather, unlike their more sensible pseudoancestors. Others, however, provided real and lasting leadership while serving as state legislators, creating opportunities for the less fortunate, and, like their middle- and working-class counterparts, supporting sodalities and self-help societies. A hundred years later some of their descendants would oppose Jim Crow laws in Tucson and in the rest of the region, oppose segregation in schools and in public facilities, and provide an opportunity base for other Mexicanos less fortunate than themselves.

Tucson's Mexican community had begun to decline from 1890 on because of the depression and declining migration from the south. Nevertheless, by 1909 the community had already established the social structure, associations, neighborhoods, and relationships with Anglos and their institutions that were so important not only to the old population but to the new, as well. In 1910 when the Mexican Revolution sent a million Mexicans over the mythic border created only 62 years earlier, cousins joined cousins, *conocidos* joined *conocidos*, job seekers used local networks, and many voluntary associations worked overtime to ensure their support. In Tucson the Revolution increased its Mexican-born population by 100 percent; and like their ancestors before them, they reinforced the cultural and class structure developed before their arrival.[32] Thus throughout the Northern Greater Southwest, these patterns were repeated and accelerated until now 14 million or so of us joined as kin or conocidos visited the north with the same ease as Elízar Herrera's relatives and friends. We are found in New York, Florida, Washington, and many other states; and it almost seems that the Northern Greater Southwest, where Mexicanos live, die, and work, will become historically moot as the central place to establish cultural space. However, the process, accompanied by continued "cultural bumping," is filled with pitfalls in the form of Americanization of a most particular kind, in which populations are defined as a sort of commodity to be bought, sold, and sent back across the border. This idea of regarding a population as something of a commodity is not unlike the perception of my father's foreman who saw him as just someone to be replaced by another person who would work for less. In this manner, two opposite cultural identities have developed: the first described in the barrioization process; the second which follows.

The Americanization of the Region's Mexican Population

» » »

There is an underlying idea about Mexican communities and culture that work defines the population. In permitting their bodies to be sapped in the mines, exhausted in construction, left bent by age 35 from the fields, made rheumatic in low-paid housekeeping, and stigmatized by assembly-line trauma, Mexicans reach the endpoint of employment prematurely. However, this idea also serves as the U.S. template for the cultural identity of the population as either an undervalued or devalued commodity to be purchased and sold as "cheap" labor, whether within American borders or outside them into Mexico. Mexicans are thus reduced culturally to being a labor reserve on hand to plug up sudden capital opportunities. This common American commodity identity is imposed on indigenous Mexican cultural systems, distorts the human worth of the population, and reduces its cultural value to a statement of low wages. Commodity identity attributes pejorative linguistic, economic, intellectual, and cultural characteristics to the population, and even denies that the word "Mexican" is a positive descriptor but rather one to be erased or changed to the cultural prisms created by others. This commodity identity is fictional in cultural terms, by the pejorative characteristics assigned to the population, and in economic terms as well, because it also assigned a negative market value to its labor.

Usually couched within racial and cultural idioms, commodity identity is in fact the underlying conceptual platform upon which layers of other ideas are added like "un-American," "minority," "disadvantaged," "culture of poverty," "limited English proficient," or "underclass," all so often attributed to the Mexican population of the United States. These terms seek to explain the manner in which Mexicans do not fit either American institutional or cultural norms and prisms. The cultural referent "Mexican" becomes further negatively layered with seemingly legitimate stereotypes that make it impossible for the term to be used except to mean "commodity"; it is a term to be erased and not envied. In a sense, it is then understandable that for many Mexicans, it is only within the privacy of their neighborhoods that they find a positive cultural referent; for others it means holding on to mythic creations like "Spanish" or Hispanic as a preferred public self-identifier.

This layering was buttressed by a plethora of educational practices and social science studies from 1912 through the 1970s, which not only repeated the devalued definition of Mexicans but used available social scientific and educational constructs to support stereotypes. Varying between biological and cultural determinism as the cause for Mexican children's lower school performance on I.Q. tests, lack of achievement, and poor work habits, this literature often identified genetic admixture as the cause for school problems and also assigned to Mexican culture the underlying mechanisms that created poverty, unequal education, illness, disability, criminality, and extreme forms of self-destructive *machismo*.[33] In the 1990s the terms "underclass" and "limited English proficiency" are used more frequently than others but without consideration of the unintended consequences that add contemporary layers to historical pejorative platforms.

Thus through this "Americanization" process Mexicans became not only strangers in their own land but strangers to themselves. These imposed American identities are not of recent vintage; their precursors emerge from the earliest stereotypic version of Hispanics in general: the Black Legend and the alleged mongrelization of genotypically mixed populations.

Pre-Commodity Contact Stereotypes

In the United States one stereotype of Mexicans stems in part from the Black Legend in which Spaniards were depicted as cruel, indolent, and rapacious—an idea often repeated in the 1777 *History of America* by William Robertson. However, just as important were eighteenth- and nineteenth-century American attitudes toward phenotypic mixtures, which most Anglo-Americans, according to D. J. Weber (1992, 337), regarded as a "violation of the laws of nature." One of our own vaunted anthropological predecessors—Henry Lewis Morgan—wrote about such mixture between Indian and European in the following manner:

> The Indian and European are at opposite poles in their physiological conditions. In the former there is very little animal passion, while in the latter it is super abundant. A pure-blooded Indian has very little animal passion, but in the half blood is sensibly augmented and when the second generation it reaches with a cross giving three-fourths white blood, it becomes excessive, and tends to indiscriminate licentiousness and decay, which it will be extremely difficult to overmaster and finally escape. (Harris 1966, 139)

Describing mestizos in 1840s California, Thomas Jefferson Farnham, a successful Maine lawyer, wrote: "The half-breed, as might be expected, exhibits much of the Indian character; the dull suspicious countenance, the small twinkling piercing eye, the laziness and filth of a free brute, using freedom as mere means of animal enjoyment."[34] According to Farnham, the Mexican is cowardly, intellectually limited, slothful, dishonest, and linguistically disabled because Mexicans speak both native languages and Spanish, which then permits them to become familiar with "the ignorance accompanying the one, and the arrogance and self-conceit inherent in the other."[35] Yet for Farnham like for many early Anglo American explorers and commentators, the question of gender had a slightly different connotation because Mexican women were looked upon as exotic creatures or as Farnham stated it, "The ladies, dear creatures, I wish they were whiter."[36] Mexican women, however, were usually depicted as persons of questionable morality in American puritanical terms and are described by Richard Henry Dana as having "but little virtue [while] their morality is, of course none of the best."[37] Given the opportunity, Mexican women would be quite prone to infidelity if "the extreme jealousy and deadly revenge of their husbands" were not intervening factors.[38]

Early pictorial representations of Mexicans were offered as contrasts to American values and characterization. American miners in California were depicted as industrious in a kind of individual cooperativism, while Mexicans were usually seen observing fiestas, holding fandangos, men performing tricks on horses, and women in low-cut blouses selling tortillas or flirting.

Besides being prone to emotional licentiousness, the Mexican women and men in California were also, "scarcely a visible grade, in the scale of intelligence, above the barbarous tribes by whom they are surrounded." Similarly, California was protected with Mexican soldiers who were "heartless creatures, headed by a few timid, soulless, brainless officers, . . . [and with] these semi-barbarians intend to hold this delightful region, as against the civilized world."[39]

Such attitudes were not restricted to California; in Texas, Arizona, and New Mexico different versions of similar stereotypes became manifested. Mexicans were, in the words of Noah Smithwick, who settled in Texas in 1827, "scarce more than apes."[40] In Texas, in keeping with this animal metaphor, the killing of Mexicans became sport because Mexicans, as Paredes notes (1973, 16), were mythologized by Anglo-Texans in the 1830s in the following manner:

1. The Mexican is cruel by nature and only understands cruelty.
2. The Mexican is cowardly and treacherous and no match for the Texan and can only get even by stabbing the Texan in the back.
3. Thievery, especially of cattle and horses, is second nature to the Mexican.
4. Mexican degeneracy is the result of blood mixture or mongrelization of second-rate Spanish Europeans and substandard Indian Mexicans.
5. The Mexican has always recognized the Texan as superior.
6. The Texan has no equal, and the quintessence of this is the Texas ranger or "rinches" as Mexicans refer to them.
7. The word for "Mexican" is correctly pronounced "Mesikin" (my contribution).

Similarly Stephen Austin characterized the conflicts between his slave-holding colony in Texas and Mexico as a "war of barbarism and of despotic principles, waged by the mongrel Spanish-Indian and Negro race, against civilization and the Anglo-American race."[41] Carried out to its logical extreme, there is little wonder that six years after Austin's pronouncement Texas historian Henry Stuart Foote suggested that the "extermination [of Mexicans] may yet become necessary for the repose of this continent."[42]

Accompanying such views were further deeper psychological rationalizations which Paredes (1973, 20) eloquently describes.

> The picture of the Mexican as an inveterate thief, especially of horses and cattle, is of interest to the psychologist as well as to the folklorist. The cattle industry of the Southwest had its origin in the Nieces–Rio Grande area, with the stock and the ranches of the [Mexican] Rio Grande rancheros. The [Anglo] "cattle barons" built up their fortunes at the expense of the Border Mexican by means which were far from ethical. One notes that the white Southerner took his slave women as concubines and then created an image of the male Negro as a sex fiend. In the same way he appears to have taken the Mexican's property and then made him out a thief.

This mythology of Mexican inferiority, treachery, thievery, and immorality provided a rationale for the killing of Mexicans by Texas

Rangers, whether they were guilty or not or simply perceived as accomplices; and this became a standard procedure even into the modern period (Paredes 1973, 20). During the Mexican uprisings of 1858 and 1915 in Texas the murderous practice peaked, when according to one estimate as many as 5,000 Mexicans were shot or hung, including all the adult males of one small ranching community who had not even participated in the 1915 revolt (Paredes 1973, 26).

Thus, Mexicans as a cultural group in Texas, as well as the designation "Mexican," came to be contrasted negatively to the prevailing positive dominant cultural prism of "Americans," including the more vociferous "white" Southerners, who had been welcomed into Texas and the Southwest by Mexicans. However, this is but another layer that provided part of the language but not the grammar for the simultaneous creation of the negative class and cultural designation of the group and its referent—"Mexican."

In Arizona, J. Ross Browne describes Mexicans of Tucson and Sonora as living in the "Greaser" style with nothing beating "Sonora . . . in the production of villainous races. Miscegenation has prevailed in this country for three centuries. Every generation the population grows worse; and the Sonorans may now be ranked with their natural compadres—Indians, burros, and coyotes."[43] Passing "forty-niners" expressed similar attitudes. Asa Bement Clarke wrote in a disdainful manner of the abandoned ranches and groves, "It must be a miserable race that could deliver up such a valley with its delightful climate."[44] What he could not have known was that the desolation he attributed to low personality characteristics was in fact the result of raids carried out with the superior arms sold to Apaches by American traders in the regional illegal market.

Most Anglo newcomers to Arizona shortly after the Mexican war "considered Mexicans lazy, dirty, violent and immoral."[45] For the most part and except for Anglos marrying elite Mexican women, the consensus on Mexican women's "morality" was negative, because they danced openly, protected themselves with pistols, and generally were a strong and nonsubmissive group who pretty much disdained traditional patriarchal roles and especially so when the death rate among males was so high.

The political economy of land acquisition and mining in Southern Arizona rationalized the negative attitudes and the commodification of

Mexican labor. Very telling also were the many private treaties that Arizona mining and ranching interests successfully negotiated in the 1860s with local Apache bands in exchange for permission to raid to the south in Sonora. As Apache chiefs in one of the bargaining sessions of the period indicated: "They wanted to be friends with the Americans, and would not molest us if we did not interfere with their 'trade with Mexico.'"[46] Similar attitudes toward Mexicans and Sonora were expressed by Sylvester Mowry in a speech before the Geographical Society in New York on February 3, 1859:

> The Apache Indian is preparing Sonora for the rule of a higher civilization than the Mexican. In the past half century the Mexican element has disappeared from what is now called Arizona, before the devastating career of the Apache. It is every day retreating farther south, leaving to us the territory without the population.[47]

Mining interests, which depended solely on Mexican labor, were opposed to these agreements because the transfer of labor to the mines on the Arizona side of the border was made more difficult by Apache intrusions into Sonora. However, underlying this concern was both the profit motive and a much larger sense of innate racial and cultural superiority in which the Anglo owners concluded that Mexicans were unfit to control the mining wealth of the area given the previous Hispano/Mexicano abandonment of the mines, ranches, and poor conditions of the populace due to the incessant Apache raids. In 1859 Herman Ehrenberg, a local mining engineer, described these conditions:

> If we hate the Mexicans, or if we want to take their country, we want no blood-thirsty savages to do the work for us or to injure them. The United States is strong enough to fight her own battles. No quiet and industrious Mexican will venture himself and family in our midst under the circumstances, to live for work; and if any hands at all come up, they will be the outcasts, the lazy, the desperadoes, in fact the worse than good for nothings. How can mining prosper under such circumstances and how the whole country![48]

The 1835 observations by an American army officer in New Mexico also repeated equivalent observations of Mexicans by characterizing Mexican agropastoralists as "the meanest looking race of people I ever saw, [and] don't appear more civilized than our Indians generally. Dirty, filthy looking creatures."[49] New Mexico was the area that had the most intensive ethnic interaction with Anglos, including marriage, alliances against attacking native peoples, and "thick" trade relations east to Missouri. However it is also New Mexico that is described as "bleak, black, and barren," and its population "peculiarly blessed with ugliness."[50] In the same year (1840) New Mexicans are described by another commentator as "debased in all moral sense [of whom most are] swarthy thieves and liars."[51] As a final judgment of Anglo attitudes toward New Mexican phenotypes, one of the members of the boundary commission, created shortly after the Mexican war, remarked that the "darker colored [peoples were invariably] inferior and syphilitic."[52]

Thus with a panoply of ethnic and racial attitudes readily expressed within the region, the next step to the creation of a substitute identity was contextually possible. While certainly considered a commodity under Mexican rule, Mexican labor became that and more under U.S. rule—a commodity upon which would be visited an ethnic and racist fetishism already developed and distributed through the public forums of the day. These attitudes would not only foster the usual unequal and discriminatory practices but would, as well, stimulate an ongoing redefinition of the population. This redefinition becomes most apparent in the manner in which Mexican labor became segmented by a combination of occupation, class, and ethnicity, all of which were buttressed by the idiom of racism and ethnocentrism and received differential treatment both economically and legally.

Regional Migration and Development:
The Third Entrada
» » »

As has already been described, the Texas revolution, Mexican war, and the purchase of the Mesilla Valley at gunpoint, known as the Gadsden Purchase, reduced the Mexican nation by half by 1857.[53] However, in the mid-nineteenth century continued small- and large-scale migration of Mexicans from the south to the California gold fields, the developing cattle market in Texas, the silver mines of Arizona, and the emergent commercial and trade activities and ties from Santa Fe, Albuquerque, and Tucson to the east produced a countervailing process. Emulating their much earlier migrating brethren, these populations of Mexican men and women in the nineteenth and twentieth centuries moved throughout the region, whether north, east, or west. They were enlisted or attracted by farming, mining, and railroad recruiting agents and contractors or were pushed out of Mexico by the Mexican Revolution, depressions, natural calamities, and economic changes. This in fact was the beginning of the third great Mexican entrada from the south to the north and back again.

All those factors mentioned above stimulated lineal and cyclical migrations of Mexicanos between border states (Vélez-Ibáñez 1980, 218). By 1848, only a year after the Mexican war, 25,000 Sonorans had already moved to California to work the newly discovered gold fields. In the period 1917–1921, 72,000 Mexican farm workers were admitted to the United States without the restrictions of the Immigration Act of 1917 (which included an $8 per head tax, literacy test, and prohibition of contract workers). Such restrictions were also waived for nonagricultural workers from Mexico for employment by the railroads, mines, and construction companies. In that period, Mexicans worked in iron and auto works in the Midwest, building trades in Arizona, railroad building in Southern California, and in slaughterhouses in Kansas and Chicago (Vélez-Ibáñez 1980). Although the population was recruited to work in the United States, they were, nevertheless, confronted with discriminatory wage practices, legal restrictions, period expulsions, and a hardening of the commodity identity of the Mexican population.

Commodity Identity in Practice

The commoditization process of Mexicans began very soon after the Mexican American War. In California, as early as 1850, the Foreign Miners Tax, which demanded that foreigners pay $20 a month for the privilege of mining, was exacted primarily from Mexicans who only two years earlier had been Mexican citizens of California and Sonora. Accompanied by other legal measures such as an antivagrancy law, which was openly referred to as the "Greaser laws,"[54] Mexicans had become, as D. A. Weber (1973) has described them, "foreigners in their native land." Sonorans and Californios alike were taxed, arrested for vagrancy, and even suffered lynchings, murders, and beatings. Thus, many Mexican miners were driven south of the newly created U.S-Mexican border. When not driven away, most Mexicans were treated unkindly by the juridical system; for example, only Mexicans could be executed for capital offenses, and even Manuel Domínguez, a signer of the California Constitution of 1849, was not allowed to testify in court because of his Indian blood (D. A. Weber 1973, 152).

In Arizona, New Mexico, and California rapidly industrializing silver, copper, and gold mines congealed stereotypes into the commoditization process by equating the word "Mexican" with the lowest-paid labor and the most difficult and menial jobs. The word became articulated through the infamous dual wage and labor structure—on the one hand was the "Mexican" wage, and on the other, the "laborer's" wage designated for Anglos. In the mines, such wage and labor structures persisted until after World War II and only ceased with pressure from Mexican unions organized by veterans. In Arizona in the early 1870s, Mexican miners received $12 a month to $1 a day depending on the occupation, while Anglo miners received between $30 to $70 a month for the same job.[55] In the 1890s the lowest daily wage for Anglos in Arizona mines was $3.00, while for Mexicans for the same ten-hour-day work the wage was $1.75 to $2.00.[56]

Even in Sonora and with the support of the Mexican president, Porfirio Díaz, one set of wages for Anglos and another for Mexicans became established. Anglo workers were generally given preferential treatment by being hired for administrative and overseer positions despite the more extensive experience of Mexican miners. The Cananea Consolidated Copper Company, organized in 1899, Amalgamated Copper (Sonnichsen 1974, 26), and Phelps Dodge all either owned or controlled vast tracts of land, minerals, and even the people who worked for them on both sides of the border; and the Mexican and U.S governments supported these companies' labor structures and practices. Such practices extended to the railroads from the late nineteenth through the early twentieth century. A combination of labor stratification in which Mexicans were employed in the lowest-paid occupations and were excluded from Anglo unions, such as the Operating Brotherhood of the Southern Pacific Railroad, made Mexicans permanent laborers despite their qualifications, the quality of their work, and their labor union activities. Even now, there are U.S. Mexicans in Tucson, Arizona, who were railroad workers during the 1950s and 1960s and recall training their Anglo coworkers on the *traques* (those men who would later become their track foremen).[57]

With regard to agriculture, in 1907 Mexican men and women in west

Texas were paid a daily wage of $1.00 to $1.25 while Anglos were paid $1.75 to $2.00,[58] and this pattern extended into the 1940s throughout Texas, California, and Arizona. It is also insightful to note that such laborers were considered a necessary though backward commodity. To counter nativistic fears of impending invasions by Mexican agricultural labor in that period, W. H. Knox of the Arizona Cotton Growers' Association stated:

> Have you ever heard, in the history of the United States, or in the history of the human race, of the white race being overrun by a class of people of the mentality of the Mexicans? I never have. We took this country from Mexico. Mexico did not take it from us. To assume that there is any danger of any likelihood of the Mexican coming in here and colonizing this country and taking it away from us, to my mind, is absurd.[59]

Despite the numerous strikes, work stoppages, and walkouts sponsored by U.S. Mexican labor unions, most gains were very limited and did not change the placement of the Mexican worker in the lowest paid positions and in the most occupationally stressful agricultural jobs. Agricultural mechanization in the 1950s accentuated such stratification, with Anglos running machines and Mexicans running after them. The prevailing attitudes of Knox's time can be seen to extend into the era of César Chávez during the late 1960s and early 1970s.

The dual labor structure in the 1920s extended across the occupational spectrum throughout the Southwest, and Mexican women were not excluded.[60] Mexican women in laundries, factories, department stores, and cigar-making shops earned less than their Anglo counterparts. For example, in laundries, Mexican women earned a weekly wage of $6.00, and Anglo women, $16.55 for the same occupation. In department stores, Mexican women earned half as much as Anglo women and were placed on floors that not only reflected a dual wage structure but the hierarchy of the system. Mexican women worked in the "basement" departments, and their Anglo coworkers, on the upper floors.[61] Thus Mexican women who worked as saleswomen for the Popular Dry Goods department stores in El Paso in 1919 were paid $10.00 to $20.00 a week working in the basement while their Anglo counterparts earned $37.50 to $40.00 working on the main floor.[62] In spite of labor unions, in each of these occupations, and their activities (they organized their first strikes in 1919), most Mexican women continued to occupy the lowest rungs of the double-wage structure, the worst occupational categories, and were paid the lowest income for piecework production. Given that many Mexican women working outside the home also supported large families as single parents, they were especially exploited.[63]

Even language has been used as a means either to dismiss Mexicans from their jobs or to prevent them from gaining employment. In the early twentieth century various legal measures were passed, which prohibited anyone who was "deaf, dumb or could not speak English" from being employed underground in the mines, operating mining machinery, or running any sort of motor, vehicle, or locomotive driven by steam, electricity, cable, or any other source of mechanical power (Sheridan 1986, 170). These measures were supported by both Anglo labor unions and mining companies as a means of insuring job safety in the Southwest; however, Mexicans suspected that they were simply attempts to prevent them from either being employed, gaining promotion, or being hired in skilled occupations in spite of the fact that most Mexicans had long traditions of being mechanically inclined and bilingual (which was more the norm than the exception).

Although many of these laws failed in their attempts,[64] they did, however, stimulate company regulations prohibiting the speaking of Spanish on the job. Some of these continue to this day in Southwestern utility companies with the added curiosity that Mexicans were seldom hired by such companies in the first place. In addition, no empirical data exist nor are references available that suggest that safety infractions or accidents are due to the use of Spanish on the job. Prohibitions of this sort also extend to Spanish-speaking office workers, in spite of the fact that they must translate for Spanish-speaking customers and for their Anglo supervisors who do not have a command of the Spanish language. Last, however, even at this moment while efforts are made by good-willed persons to overturn such prohibitions, some of the companies insist that a "safety" clause be included to prohibit the speaking of Spanish or any language other than English during job operations in the field.[65]

Historically, linguistic prohibitions, dual labor structures, labor segmentation, and job differentiation based on culture and not citizenship seem to support the adhesion of culture to a devalued commodity function and utility. When the fact that until after World War II

Mexico- and U.S.-born Mexicans were not permitted to join labor unions in U.S. mines and railroads is added to this complex, it is clear that even labor organizations reinforced this cultural and devalued labor identity. Throughout the Southwest, debt peonage in the mines, cattle industry, and railroads commonly involved Mexicans, and occupational segmentation like that in the mines extended to agriculture, railroads, and construction. In this manner the practice of identifying "Mexican" jobs with Mexican culture took shape.

The entire situation was reinforced by periodic contract agreements between the United States and Mexico such as the agricultural *bracero* agreements during and after World War II. "Cheap" Mexican labor for agricultural work in the United States numbered in the hundreds of thousands between 1942 and 1964, and in 1960 braceros made up 26 percent of the seasonal agricultural workers in the United States (Galarza 1964, 94). Whether referred to as braceros, *mojados* (wetbacks, wets), illegals, or undocumented, the equating of Mexican culture with little-valued agricultural labor was one more dimension added to the more general cultural stereotype.

Periodic Expulsions, the Reinforcement of Commodity Identity

Among the most important historical measures in rationalizing the fictional commodity identity of the Mexican population in the Southwest were the repatriation and deportation policies and practices specifically directed toward Mexicans. Although it is assumed that this was the case after 1929, in actuality these policies were initiated during the national depression of 1894.[66] As Heyman (1991, 120) points out, the new legal context of visa regulation that was instituted during the heyday of the repatriation period[67] created the differentiation of kin networks into distinct cultural branches and divided Mexican from Mexican American kin in a "form that had not existed before [1929]."

After 1929 legal citizenship rather than cultural context became the hallmark of cultural identity so that for many Mexicans born in the United States, immigration restrictions on Mexican kin created a "they"/"us" differentiation and interrupted the easy flow of kin between extended cross-border familial systems. As American schools under the guise of "Americanization"[68] programs relegated the Spanish language to a secondary position and denigrated the use of the language as well, self-denial processes set in such that some U.S. Mexicans began to change their names, anglicize their surnames, and internalize self-hatred and self-deprecation.[69] Such differentiation was accentuated by systematic deportation, repatriation, and voluntary departure processes; examples are "Operation Wetback"[70] in 1954 and recent immigration sweeps such as "Operation Jobs" in 1982. The Simpson-Rodino Immigration Reform and Control Act (IRCA) of 1986 was created to reduce undocumented immigration. However, it has had no striking impact on the labor sectors of which Mexican undocumented workers are a part.[71] In fact, what it has done is to guarantee permanent settlement of Mexican migrants through legalization and increase the legal flow of individual workers and families back and forth across the border.[72]

IRCA, however, has increased the division between eligible and noneligible Mexicans in the legalization process. Even within the same extended familial network the legalization of one family member sharply contrasts with the illegality of others. Together with immigration sweeps of Mexican workers, which seem to coincide with immigration "reform" bills such as IRCA, further emphasis has been placed on the "foreignness" of the Mexican population in Mexico in comparison to that of the United States and on the mythic cultural differences between the populations.[73] Such demographic and political splitting between Mexico-born and U.S.-born Mexicans establishes the cultural basis for the creation of an ethnic U.S. Mexican and the denial of cultural continuity between separate populations.

The Social Science and Educational Contributions to Commoditization

Nick Vaca's two basic articles (1970) and my own research (Vélez-Ibáñez 1970) in social science and education clearly lay out the foundations for work on commoditization. The eugenics paradigm of the 1920s regarded Mexican children as intellectually inferior because of "blood" admixture, with an "emotional nature" and appearing dull and stupid.[74] They deserved an occupationally rather than an intellectually directed curriculum[75] because they were retarded.[76] Mexican children had a "natural" affinity toward drawing and other mechanical abilities.[77] These researchers pointed to an innate superiority in mental

ability of "white" as opposed to Mexican children, a clear positive cor-
relation between the shade of skin color among Mexican children and
mental achievement,[78] with fundamental differences between Mexican
and Anglo "races." For the purposes of curriculum, Mexican males
were to be trained as skilled manual workers and females as domestic
servants and to do various kind of handiwork.[79] While these studies
could be dismissed as the ravings of a eugenics-influenced generation,
they had far-reaching consequences for educational policy, which
deemed it appropriate into the 1960s to steer Mexican children toward
"activities" courses, such as carpentry, mechanics, woodshop, art,
finger painting, home economics, segregated within "1C" programs.

Studies of the 1960s and 1970s were generally not concerned with
finding a biologically determined cause for Mexican mental inferiority;
rather, an overwhelming number of them depicted Mexican values as
not only opposite to American values but detrimental to achievement
by Mexicans in the United States. According to the studies, these cultural value complexes were well structured, and when they were compared to American values were obviously not only faulted but inferior.

Vaca[80] outlined these cultural value complexes in the following
manner:

Mexican Value System	Anglo Value System
Subjugation to nature	Mastery over nature
Present oriented	Future oriented
Immediate gratification	Deferred gratification
Complacent	Aggressive
Fatalistic	Non-fatalistic
Non-goal oriented	Goal-oriented
Non-success oriented	Success-oriented
Emotional	Rational
Dependent	Individualistic
Machismo	Neuter? [my addition]
Mexican Value System	Anglo Value System
Superstitious	Non-superstitious
Traditional	Progressive
Spanish [my addition]	English [my addition]

Thus from the cultural determinist perspective the Mexican value
complex was the basis for impediments to school achievement, the
causes of social ills, and a traditional system that had to be exchanged

for one providing the true path toward economic success. This meant of course that because Mexican culture was alleged to be a significant drawback, Mexicans had to change, erase, and otherwise divest themselves of language, ritual, values, social relations and, not unlike their caste ancestors, "whitenize." To put it another way, this cultural erasing process was a means of making us all "Americans," for in the minds of educators to be a Mexican was the opposite.

For instructional purposes, new pedagogy and curricula were devised from the 1960s through the 1980s with the newly defined culturally disadvantaged, "at risk," and culturally different populations in mind. Many such programs assumed that the cultural and linguistic differences of Mexican children (as opposed to "American" language and culture) prevented their achieving academic excellence. It was also presumed that U.S. Mexican children had little information, experience, or developed cognitive structures that would allow them to take advantage of instruction. This tabula rasa approach has favored watered down, remedial, and mediocre instruction in "consumer math," "remedial English," and "special" programs, which in time have produced large sectors of our population unable to read beyond a fifth-grade level and with mathematics skills at the most elementary level.

These more recent educational programs, like earlier versions of Americanization programs in the 1920s and 1930s, prohibited the speaking of Spanish in schools through the 1960s, have underfunded less-than-successful bilingual programs, have created an ever-increasing number of Mexicans with largely household-derived oral language skills, fractured literacy in Spanish,[81] and casual English literacy and composition skills. Aside from exceptional bilingual programs in some Mexican neighborhoods, too many of these programs have become the domain of upper-middle-class Anglo children who are bused in for the sake of ethnic balance and who outperform the local working-class Mexican children. The unintended consequences of such programming are the reinforcement of traditional stereotypes of Mexican children and the creation of double educational sectors not unlike the labor structures already discussed.

Hill's "Anglo-Spanish"[82]

Except for efforts by largely Anglo upper-middle-class adults and their children to learn Spanish in order to communicate with their servants and workers, Spanish itself is parodied, mispronounced, mis-spelled, misused, and misplaced; and, as Jane Hill most insightfully and creatively has shown, a new "lingo" of "Southwest Anglo-Spanish" has been created and is exemplified by the now famous Schwarzenegger growl in *Terminator 2*, of "Hasta la vista, baby."[83] Just as sad is "No problemo," which is taught to the steel-headed robot by a precocious 14-year-old, who not only eliminates the needed verb construction but uses the wrong noun ending. Closer to home, an Anglo dental techni-cian, pointing and shaking her finger, recently said to a Latina Phi Beta Kappa, Ph.D. clinical psychologist and director of the Counseling and Testing Center of the University of Arizona, "You all comprendi [*sic*]?" in communicating the importance of proper gum care.

For Hill, such parodic uses of Spanish by Anglos in the Southwest continues to support a broad structure of social and economic domi-nance.[84] She clearly shows that the use of such distorted phraseology is a mechanism for distancing and maintaining racial hierarchy. Thus, taken together with all the other mechanisms used historically for the cultural distortion of Mexicans and their spoken language, it is little wonder that the word "Mexican" is itself a pejorative and that new terms of reference are invented to be used to identify an otherwise un-acceptable, fictionally identified population.

For Mexicans in the United States new terms of reference have been invented, which have attempted to deal with the problem of commodi-tization, such as Mexican American, Latino, Latin American, Hispano, and the latest term of legitimacy and acceptability, "Hispanic." Al-though long used as a self-referent in Northern New Mexico, it is curi-ous that this should be the most acceptable term used by Northern New Mexicans given the obvious geographical and historical designa-tion of the area as "New Mexico" and not "New Spain," which was the historical term for Mexico. In addition, it is an even greater curiosity given the rather insignificant proportion of Peninsulares and Creoles that actually settled in Nuevo México and the long history to the pres-ent of Mexicans from the south as chapter 1 articulated.

Except for the self-referent "Chicano," most other terms are erasing labels that ease the discomfort of both Mexicans and Anglos. The dis-comfort that is raised by the term "Mexican" comes from having to rec-ognize a long and undistinguished history of economic exploitation, occupational segmentation, social segregation, miseducation, political and legal mistreatment, and cultural and linguistic erasure. Ironically, the one label that revives that history is the very word that is denied legitimacy—"Mexican." We now have an even more inclusive erasing phrase: "people of color," which further reduces the human population to a melanin referent rather than dealing with its history, struggles, and reality. It erases at one fell swoop the culture of various populations in the United States, and in so doing Mexicans become the historical "others" without a history.

However, this labeling process has always met with resistance and accommodation. Segments of the Mexican population have struggled against commoditization and ethnic and racial typification. They have struggled at household, community, regional, and national levels, sought to change American institutions, penetrating their ranks, and continue to struggle to this moment with the latest versions of that commoditization and ethnocentrism. The North American Free Trade Agreement (NAFTA) and the anti-immigrant sentiment in the present are large-scale versions of already long-established patterns.

From the past, appeals to racism and ethnocentrism are used to buttress oppositional arguments to both NAFTA and south to north migrants, while proponents consistently appeal to the commodity advantages of "cheap labor" with a type of colonial condescension reminiscent of the "white man's burden," offering its beneficial, civilizing technology to a backward nation. Mexicans on either side of the chain link fence are once again caught in attitudinal, behavioral, and economic processes that reduce them, like Adalberto, to a devalued commodity coupled to a cultural identity created by others.

»   »   »   »   »

PART 2

Political Process, Cultural Invention, and Social Frailty: Road to Discovery

IN 1968, he came to see me with two other persons: one was a small goateed Mexicano while the other Mexicano was larger, robust, and a half head taller than my own six-foot height. Both had vibrant and dancing eyes, and exhibited an energy that partially filled my house in Tucson, Arizona, and he—Gustave V. Segade—filled the rest. He was a former Ph.D. student at Arizona, a classically trained scholar, now associate professor of Spanish at San Diego State College. The other two, Jorge González and Gus Chávez, were students at San Diego State College and the three were "recruiting" faculty.

The students were tapping me because I had written a short story that some had liked, and Gustave knew that I had earned a master's degree in English—one of two since 1883 earned by Mexicans at the University of Arizona. They were looking for culturally congruent faculty for a new program in Chicano studies and knew that I had nominally participated in some of the movement activities in Tucson. I had merely corrected the spelling and a few grammatical errors on some nonnegotiable demands being made by high school and university students. At about that time I had already had an altercation with one of the more conservative members of the high school administration where I taught English. The difference of opinion originated when I called the administration's attention to the student handbook from one of the "feeder" junior high schools that prohibited the use of Spanish on the playgrounds, in the halls, or in the classrooms. Given that the student population was at least 50 percent Mexican in both schools, which were located in the middle of the neighborhood where I was raised, I had thought it inappropriate but was accused of trying to "destroy" the school when I raised the issue. Therefore, I was somewhat positively prepared for the inducement offered by Gustave V. Segade and his two student companions. It was at this time that I began to fully participate in a political sort of "movement" aimed toward understanding and analyzing why and how the Mexican population had long struggled politically, socially, economically, and culturally against its commoditization.

This initial experience led me to explore many-faceted explanations of the underlying forces and pressures that the Mexican population had faced in turning into a type of commodity; and that experience led me to face cultural identity contradictions and paradoxes in explanations of the whys and wherefores of the struggles of the population against these commodity forces. Unsatisfied with some of the answers, I eventually turned to anthropology and central Mexico for partial answers. My initial work in this field and area of the world focused on how a population could survive under conditions in which 75 percent of children between 0 and 4 years of age died. I found the answers in many places, in self-sacrifice, reciprocity, family, and a willingness to take extraordinary risks to survive. I found the Mexicans of Mexico, not unlike Mexicans in the United States, experienced the same social frailties as well as successes. I applied the lessons learned to understanding the U.S. Mexican population's historical and political struggle—our cultural and organizational mechanisms, our struggle to create hearth and home in the process, and our continuing struggle in the present.

CHAPTER 3

» » » » »

The Politics of Survival and

Revival: The Struggle for Existence

and Cultural Dignity, 1848–1994

IN HER HIGHLY PERSONAL and memorable book, *A Beautiful, Cruel Country*, Eva Antonia Wilbur-Cruce described the passing of civility between Mexican and Anglo *rancheros* and migrating Tohono O'odham native peoples in rural Southern Arizona at the turn of the twentieth century. This was a process in which the word "Hispánico" was replaced with "Mexican," "greaser," and "spic." Mexicans became "to some an abomination, something to be annihilated from the face of the earth."[1] Anglos became "gringos," "topos," "basura blanca"; and "racial wars raged like wildfire in our valley for many years."[2] She described such racial hatred as "appalling . . . [and] so prevalent for so many decades—a poison with which we came in contact every day."[3] This poison, however, regardless of context seems to have always marked the struggle of Mexicans to survive as human beings in the everyday actions that constitute social living. This poison imbued the simple issues of survival, of feeding our families, of having recreational time to sit back and look at the sun, and of merely just looking at and playing with our children. This mental poison has been the most pressing overt and covert process for a largely working-class population. This poison has meant economic exploitation throughout these many years of being bumped and bumping into others. This poison also marked how we were able to speak, that is, whether we could speak to our children in the language of the past and present; how we were to act, that is, whether we could join with our relatives and friends in *confianza* and ritual; how we were to earn our daily bread, that is, whether we could work without the terrible connotations imposed upon us culturally by the idiom of commodity and prejudice; and finally, how we were to engage ourselves and each other humanely, that is, whether we could become sufficiently reflective of some of our behaviors and practices that destroy our social, mental, and physical health.

Since the nineteenth century these continuing struggles over physical, social, linguistic, and cultural survival have been generally cast within the context of racial poison. This poison has followed the south to north movement of Mexicans in search of cultural space and place, and it has influenced the varying versions of political action that have partially defined the cultural development of Mexicans since the American *entrada*. Moreover, these struggles, and their cultural and organizational responses, set the stage for what was to become in the late 1960s and early 1970s one of the great convulsive transitional cultural movements in the Northern Greater Southwest: the Chicano movement.

In the following discussion, two levels of political action could be treated, each of which to varying degrees reflects these struggles within the context of racialism. First is the level of "institutional politics," that is, those political behaviors that have much to do with the traditional American notion of electoral and governance politics. Office holding, representative governing, "democratic" institutional participation, and political leadership in a broad sense are part of an unfolding process. The task is relatively simple here but much beyond the purview of this work because it basically involves an enumeration of office holders, political parties, and gauged effectiveness.

For the most part, throughout the Southwest from the 1970s on, with the onset of such drives as the Southwest Voter Registration Drive and processes of shifting demographics, marked changes have occurred in representation, electoral impact, and rising political influence of Mexicans in the United States. However, probably more important are the second-level political struggles against differential treatment in wages, housing, education, occupational opportunities, public accommodation, and medical and mental health care. At times, these differentials are expressed on the first level, but seldom are they part of the normal "flow" of political relations and governance, which could resolve them. If anything, these issues are more likely "forced" into the institutional arenas by rebellion, mobilization and organization, protest, and struggle than by an underlying process that guarantees "fair play," representation, or judicial equality. These protests are of a different sort and most are organized around cultural place, space, and processes not often understood nor detailed. They are filled with contradictions and internal opposition, and sometimes the sheer task of ferreting out claim language from true idiom is exhausting. Nevertheless, the cultural basis of political action is seldom if ever discussed; however, without such a discussion the "Great Chicano Cultural convulsive transition movement" of the twentieth century cannot be understood.

The following discussion is divided into four phases: early cultural rebellions, 1846–1922; unions and labor protests, 1883–1940; benevolent civil societies, 1875–1940; and the "Great Chicano Cultural convulsive transition movement," 1965–1975. The first two phases form the political and cultural platforms upon which the agrarian politics of the United Farm Workers movement of the late 1960s developed and provided the organizational, cultural, and social impetus for what I term "the Great Chicano Cultural convulsive transition movement," which emerged between 1965 and 1975. Although often referred to as the "Chicano Civil Rights Movement," it was, in fact, much more: it will be shown to be a movement of extensive proportions with layers that were international, national, regional, and local in scale. It encompassed a major cultural "revitalization" process in which much of the commoditization identity was rejected, traditional and adaptive forms of political organization used and invented, new learning and academic arenas developed, while old ones were reexplored and reinterpreted; and finally a syncretic blend of ideologies and values was induced. More important, it made specific and overt the cultural and social relations between south and north, which had long been obfuscated by the political definition of the border and citizenship.

Early Rebellions in the Northern Greater Southwest

» » »

From California to Texas, in the mid-nineteenth century following the Mexican war, periodic revolts, wars, border raids, armed and unarmed confrontations, community upheavals, long-term skirmishes, and coordinated rebellions emerged in response to a variety of forces that were unleashed following the Treaty of Guadalupe Hidalgo and the Gadsden Purchase. The economic penetration of large-scale industrial capitalism took various shapes in specific types of technologies and methods of organization. In Arizona, California, parts of Colorado, and New Mexico, the mining of gold, silver, quicksilver, quartz, and then copper created great demand for skilled Mexican labor, which since the eighteenth century had developed mining and extracting techniques, labor methods, and smelting processes for gold, silver, and quicksilver, which was required to separate silver from its ore base in the patio separation process.[4] Soon after their arrival in California (which had become foreign soil only one year earlier), the Sonoran miners were openly attacked, and even the most anti-Mexican commentators of the day felt some chagrin over the frequency and intensity of conflict.[5]

In Texas, the process of industrial farming and cattle raising gave rise to the old feelings of ethnic and racial hatred and was expressed in incessant border raids, ethnic and racial conflict, as well as lynching, murder, and wanton theft of property by bands of raiders on both sides of the Texas-Coahuila and Chihuahua borders. Most such conflicts focused on cattle, land, and the newly created border. From 1836 to 1925 and beyond "the killing of Mexicans without provocation is so common as to pass almost unnoticed."[6]

In each of the subregions of the Northern Greater Southwest but to varying degrees, different versions of intensive capital penetration exacerbated cultural conflict and evoked opposition by segments of the Mexican population. In New Mexico, serious conflict arose over land due to the arrival of Anglo cattle companies with Mexican-hating Texas cowmen, the acquisition of water rights by development firms, and the large-scale nationalization by the United States of thousands of acres of land. Such penetration threatened Mexicano sheepherding, common water use, and individual land holdings, and provoked cultural conflict, which stimulated wars, feuds, and racial hatred almost simultaneous to the Texas process.

Similarly in Arizona, the mining frontier was a center of ethnic, class, and boundary violence in which Mexicans were typified as "vicious Sonorans."[7] In southern Arizona alone, for the period between 1857 and 1861, 172 violent deaths were recorded, of which 111 were Anglo and 57 Mexican. Of those Mexicans killed by personal violence and not accidentally, 5 were killed by other Mexicans, 23 by Anglos, and 26 by Apaches. Of Anglos, 16 were killed by Anglos, 20 by Mexicans, and 62 by Apaches. Because the Anglo population was 50 percent smaller than the Mexican (of the total southern Arizona area), the percentile rate of homicide among Anglos is multiplied to a proportion much greater than in the Mexican population. In 1860 only 871 non-Mexicans and 1,716 Mexicans lived in southern Arizona, with the former mostly made up of males. Therefore, using the 1860 figure as a base, for the 1857–1861 period, approximately 13 percent of the Anglo population died a homicidal death, while less than 5 percent of Mexicans met their end in a similar manner. Forty-five percent of Anglos killed by non-Apaches died at the hands of other Anglos, while 56 percent were killed by Mexicans. On the other hand, 80 percent of Mexicans killed by non-Apaches died at the hands of Anglos while 20 percent were killed by other Mexicans.[8] From whatever position this is viewed, it would seem that Anglos were much more sanguine in their approach to Mexican and Anglo mortality than Mexicans to Anglo and Mexican mortality. The question then would remain open as to who was really "vicious." The record belies the commonly held attitude that Mexicans were sheep who did not defend themselves against Anglos by using the same unfortunate methods of homicide.

Mistreated miners at times killed their mining supervisors and destroyed newly placed boundary markers separating Sonora from Arizona.[9] But the most effective protest that Mexican miners used was to simply walk off their jobs and cross the recently declared international boundary only a few miles south into Sonora. In a sense these constituted the first international "labor walkouts" and are among the earliest known in the United States.

Mexican cowboys suffered whippings by Anglo ranch foremen, vigilante action by errant Texas cowboys,[10] and raiding by Anglo and Mexican outlaws, all of which created great tensions between Anglos and Mexicans of the period.[11] This tension was carried so far that in some areas of Arizona there was segregation on the range with Anglo cowboys riding separate from Mexicans. One "early Anglo pioneer" remarked that Mexicans who "forgot their place lasted about as long as a snowball in Hell . . . [and] the color line was as real as the Hassayampa Highway is now."[12]

The silver strikes in the late 1880s around Tombstone attracted Texas cowboys who sought cheap beef to sell by raiding Mexicano ranches on both sides of the Arizona/Sonora border. Thus, the infamous Clanton gang, of O.K. Corral fame,[13] killed dozens of Mexicans in their raids, and their hatred was so great that they had little compunction about killing the Mexican ranchers they robbed on both sides of the mythical border.

In New Mexico, even animal husbandry was attached to cultural conflict. Because Mexicans were responsible for much of the sheep tending, and many of the cowboys herding cattle were Texans, a strong relationship was established between the type of animal tended and the cultural affinity of the mutually antagonistic groups, leading to range wars and land grant claims.[14] While throughout the region cross-cutting ties and relationships between Anglos and Mexican elites had been normative, the entrance of large scale agricultural, railway, mining, and cattle raising interests and capital created horrific conflicts, which weakened these ties so that Mexicanos of many classes responded in a variety of ways including a great variety of direct actions usually associated with "primitive rebellion."[15]

Cultural Rebels in California: "Zorro Doesn't Live Here Anymore"

Three hundred years before the discovery of gold in California by Francisco López on March 9, 1842, Spanish colonial Mexico had already had its own gold rush in Zacatecas in 1548, and mining as a form of extraction was familiar to Mexicans. By 1850, twenty-five thousand Sonoran miners from Pimería Alta and Baja (Sonora) and Mexicans from New Mexico, Chihuahua, and Zacatecas—many of whom were experienced silver, gold, and copper miners having already worked in the silver mine Arizonac and the gold mines of New Mexico—had entered the California gold fields, following the De Anza trail. By 1865, for example, most laborers and miners at the famous northern California New Almadén quicksilver mine were Mexican.[16]

Soon after their successful entry into the California gold fields, however, discriminatory and criminal actions against Mexicans, who were now foreigners in their own land, included lynchings, claim jumping and murder, robbery and holdups, armed attacks by bands of American miners, and the application of differential legal treatment. Moreover, even before their actual movement from Sonora to California, Sonorans and their communities had most unpleasant confrontations with some groups of Yankee forty-niners who were traveling overland from many points in the United States through Mexican territory before the Gadsden Purchase. As map 3.1 shows, various routes followed by different groups beginning in 1849 took them through and nearby Sonoran Mexican communities.

In June of that year a forty-niner party of thirty sacked the town of Cieneguilla south of Altar. A month later a party of eighty Texans who had captured stolen Mexican cattle from Apaches demanded payment for their good efforts and upon refusal by the Alcalde helped themselves to the beef, butchered it, and then threw the entrails into the mayor's house. Upon reaching San Xavier del Bac slightly south of Tucson, they proceeded to administer thirty-nine lashes to an Indian who had pilfered some items from among their goods. One such party was headed by the naturalist John Woodhouse Audubon; in August the group had gotten lost and reached Ures more dead than alive. They then proceeded to get drunk and obnoxious and began to harass the local townspeople, for which some of the party were thrown in jail.[17]

With these unfortunate incidents, however, the tone for the mistreatment of Sonoran miners in the California gold fields had already been formed. For the most part, Sonorans were treated with contempt. These *gambusinos,* or professional prospectors, traveled the De Anza trail in groups of fifty or a hundred beginning early in the spring from Sonora, and they entered Los Angeles by way of the San Gorgonio Pass. As was the custom for many Sonorans then and now, they traveled with their families on pack mules, horses, and burros so that between 1848 and 1850, ten thousand Sonorans went through Los Angeles each spring on their way to the mines in Sacramento, Almadén, and San José. In the southern mining district of northern California, so many Sonorans and other Latinos, like Peruvians and Chileans, built mining camps in Calaveras, Tuolumne, Mariposa, Stanislaus, and San Joaquín counties that the center of the southern district came to be named Sonora. There the Sonorans built hotels, bakeries, restaurants, and the infrastructure for their almost totally Sonoran camp.[18] (See map 3.2.)

Shortly after the establishment of the Foreign Miners Tax of 1850, whose legislative author had declared that he could "maintain a better stomach at the killing of a Mexican" than squashing body lice,[19] a mob of two thousand Anglo miners invaded Sonora trying to kill all Mexicans within reach, burned down the settlement, rounded up more than

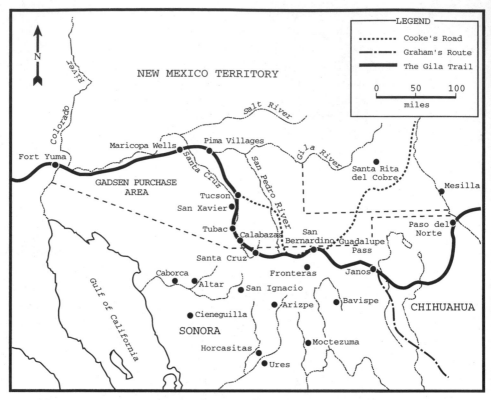

Map 3.1 Yanqui Forty-Niners. Source: Officer 1987, 224

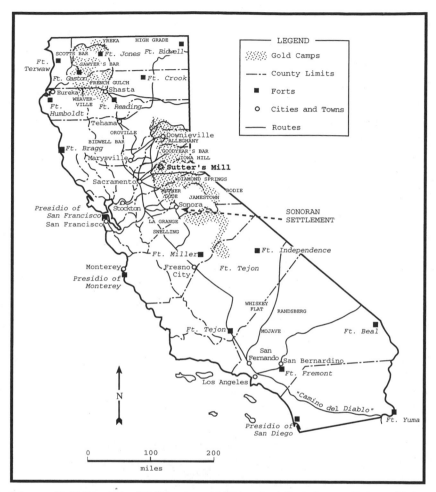

Map 3.2 Gold Districts of California, with Counties (1852). Source: Rojas 1986, 63.

a hundred Sonorans, lynched and murdered scores, and drove the rest to Southern California. Up to 1860, Mexicans were the majority in all the counties in the southern mines, but by 1870 they had mostly been driven out by Anglo Americans. However, among those miners driven out of Sonora was the leader of the first rebellion in California, the former miner and soon-to-be outlaw and mythic cultural rebel—the Sonoran, Joaquín Murrieta.

Cultural Leaders and Independent Heroes

Although it has been alleged that it is not known whether Joaquín Murrieta actually lived or not and that it is the legend that is clearly more important than the man,[20] this has been contradicted by recent work.[21] In fact, as one of five brothers, Joaquín "El Patrio"[22] Murrieta Orozco was born near Altar, Sonora, between 1824 and 1831, the son of Juan Murrieta and Juana Orozco.[23] (See plate 3.1.)

In late 1849 or early 1850 Murrieta, at the age of eighteen or nineteen, together with his new wife, Carmen or Rosa Félix, traveled to California at the request of his brother to assist him on his gold claim. Joaquín witnessed his brother's lynching, and soon he and his wife traveled to take over his brother's claim. There his wife was raped and murdered, and he beaten and thrown off his brother's gold claim.[24]

However, myth, legend, and man make it very clear that the traditional Zorro tale of the dashing Spanish Don fighting for the poor against the *ricos* was replaced by a more contemporary idea of the "cultural hero" of the time, a Sonoran miner who was scarred emotionally by the rape and murder of his wife and materially by his expulsion from his gold claims, who then formed a band of men bent on revenge, theft, and pillage of Anglo resources. Rather than a "social bandit" he should be considered, as others of the period, a "cultural hero and leader," because Murrieta organized resistance with an alternative "auxiliary" political authority and generated community approval and legitimacy for his actions.

He reflected community values in relation to Anglos, expressed in the Mexican ballad form: "El Corrido de Joaquín Murrieta." Although not written until after the middle of the nineteenth century, it is still sung to this day in Arizona and Sonora and defines Murrieta not as a "social bandit" but as one who defended himself and his family;

Plate 3.1
Joaquín Murrieta,
ca. 1890, Cucurpe,
Sonora. Reprinted by
permission from Rojas
1986, 24.

his land was usurped, his wife violated, and he was driven from his home but returned to avenge, protect, and set up an auxiliary authority through organized armed resistance against the imposed Anglo system.

Variously named "Muriati, Murrieta, Ocomorenia, Valenzuela, Boteller, Botello, and Carrillo,"[25] Murrieta became a mythic hero in the minds of Mexicans who needed a hero-myth as much as Anglos needed the mythic villain. The former was composed of all the social values a suffering population needed: innocently wronged, valorous, hard-working, a man of the earth digging out the earth's riches with his hands, able to withstand hardships of the chase by rapacious Anglo sheriffs and rangers, skilled and cunning with the ability to out-strategize superior numbers, and finally never to be caught nor defeated. For Mexicans, this was the hero to be cherished regardless of the reality of the man, and therefore he was a bona fide cultural hero rather than a "social bandit" or "primitive rebel." His Anglo mythic counterpart was the opposite: cowardly, bloodthirsty, lazy and murderous, sneaky, without mercy, and unmanly by striking from well-covered hiding places. Murrieta, his organized followers, and the communities that protected him were to be wiped out, and all Mexicans were equally guilty for whatever Murrieta allegedly committed; indeed, various vigilante groups disarmed all Mexicans along the Amador river.[26] Regardless of the reality of Murrieta's actions, he did serve as a focal point for pent-up anger and frustration for Mexicans, Californios, and other Latinos of the period.[27] What is of importance is that the actions of Anglo vigilante groups crystallized what most Sonorans and others were already quite familiar with: the intense attitudinal prejudice of too many Anglo miners, legislators, and judicial officials who turned a blind eye to the lynchings, murder, and wounding of Mexicans, as well as to the wholesale theft and usurpation of mining claims.

Murrieta, however, was not alone among the resistors of the period. Like Murrieta, Salomón Pico of Santa Bárbara in the 1850s was supported by Mexicans who believed that he had been denied his property and land and generally supported his killing of Anglos without mercy.[28] Similarly Tiburcio Vásquez, cattle rustler, horse thief, and stagecoach robber, was perceived as a hero by Mexicans in California, as he raided, stole property, and killed Anglos for twenty years between the late 1850s and 1875 when he was hanged. He was particularly revered, however, for his statements made to the English-language press whose various reporters interviewed him. According to the editor of the *Los Angeles Star* in 1875, Vásquez rationalized his career by asserting, "A spirit of hatred and revenge took possession of me. I had numerous fights in defense of what I believed to be my rights and those of my countrymen. I believed that we were being unjustly deprived of the social rights that belonged to us."[29] With this rationale he committed numerous robberies, holdups, horse thefts, and burglaries. His closing words were "I believe I owe my frequent escapes solely to my courage. I was always ready to fight whenever opportunity offered, but always tried to avoid bloodshed."[30] As Rosenbaum (1981, 58) aptly described Mexican reaction to Vásquez's position: "Vásquez was a man who fought back against the insults and depredations of the Anglos, and he therefore became a symbol of pride and courage for the people as whole."

However, not all Mexicano resistors were cultural leaders or heroes in the sense of being protected by Mexican communities, organizing resistance, or revered for their courage and upholding of Mexican values. There is also a panoply of others about whom little is known and thus were not as popularized as Murrieta, Pico, and Vásquez. Narciso Bojórquez was evidently a cattle rustler, while Jesús Tejada, Tomasio Redundo [*sic*], and Narrato Ponce, a Chilean, were sought variously for murder, stage holdups, rustling, and prison escapes. Reyes Duarte, Andrés and Agustín Castro, José and Nicolás Sepúlveda, Pedro Vallejo, Ramón Amador, Chico Lugo, and Juan Soto, a homicidal maniac, were also to varying degrees respected but also feared for their acts of robbery and murder especially against Anglos.[31] As in other parts of the Northern Greater Southwest, most Mexicans did not support the robber or thief. However, it may also be the case that in some instances, the need for heroes was so great that some may have been provided with more legitimacy than they deserved.

For New Mexico and Texas, cultural rebels played mythic roles as well. A genuine cultural hero and Robin Hood of Texas—Juan Nepomuceno Cortina—was known for initiating "Cortina's War" on July 13, 1859, after killing a deputy sheriff who was pistol whipping a former servant of the Cortina family while he was arresting him. This conflict congealed all the issues and conflicts of the Texas border region. In a sense, this war was, in fact, based on *cultural* grounds rather than on issues of gold claims, not paying taxes, or personal effrontery. Cortina's War represents true cultural revolt and not merely a process of "social banditry" or a localized version of confronting long-standing issues. Cortina's approval arose from the fact that he represented the cultural expectations and needs of the community and border region from which he emerged. It is in this sense that he is a "cultural leader" organizing armed resistance to combat the arrogance and domination of Anglo law and order, the religious distaste displayed by Protestant bigotry of local-level Catholicism,[32] and economic exploitation and the domineering political control of all facets of the region's resources by non-Mexican politicians and their elite Mexicano collaborators. He like Murrieta also had *corridos* composed to him, and fragments collected by Américo Paredes express the underlying community and political values in this musical dedication:

That General Cortina
Is very sovereign and free;
His honor has increased
Because he has saved a Mexican.[33]

By 1860, Cortina and his army had lain waste to a 150-mile stretch of the country; and even though more Mexicans than Anglos died in the raids he conducted, the former were "friendly" Mexicans who either worked for Anglos on large ranches or collaborated as informers for the Anglo authorities. For fifteen years, Cortina raided the American side of the border and when confronted with superior forces, slid back into Mexico where he was also hunted by Mexican troops. It is instructive to examine some of the manifestos Cortina left for the main issues this cultural rebel had used as his rationale for rebellion. Part of his September 30, 1859, proclamation clearly indicates that his is not a "bandit's" ideology at play. Rather like Murrieta, Cortina created an "auxiliary authority" to the Anglo system, which served only Anglos.

> Our object . . . has been to chastise the villainy of our enemies, which heretofore has gone unpunished. These have connived with each other, and form, so to speak, a perfidious inquisitorial lodge to persecute and rob us, without any cause and for no other crime on our part than that of being of Mexican origin, considering us, doubtless, destitute of those gifts which they themselves do not possess.[34]

The auxiliary authority he created is further elaborated in the following statements:

> To defend ourselves, and making use of the sacred right of self-preservation, we have assembled in a popular meeting with a view of discussing a means by which to end to our misfortunes. The assembly . . . we have careered over the streets of the city in search of our adversaries, inasmuch as justice being administered by their own hands, the supremacy of the law has failed to accomplish its object.[35]

Cortina congeals much of the quest to which Mexicans aspired by stating:

> Innocent persons shall not suffer—no. But, if necessary, we will lead a wandering life, awaiting our opportunity to purge society of men so base that they degrade it with their opprobrium. Our families have returned as strangers to their own country to beg for an asylum. Our lands, if they are to be sacrificed to the avaricious covetousness of our enemies, will be rather so on account of our vicissitudes.
>
> We cherish the hope . . . that the government . . . will accede to our demand, by prosecuting those men and bringing them to trial, or leave them to become subject to the consequences of our immutable resolve.[36]

Thus, Cortina is certainly not a "social bandit" but rather a cultural leader and hero attempting to set right the political, juridical, economic, and cultural imbalances resulting from American control and hegemony. Because he organized armed resistance to carry out these goals, Cortina is one level above all the rest of the cultural heroes of the time.

At the local and regional level, great issues are not settled by reference to ideological treatises, but rather to the basic issues of survival in all its forms. To expect Mexicans without resources and power to somehow structurally change what had already been determined by American armies and then refer to those who do seek to protest and combat their conditions as "social bandits" is somewhat of a naive fantasy.

Others who did not form organized groups or carry out raids of resistance were similarly supported and appreciated by regional Mexican communities. These "independent" cultural heroes, like Gregorio Cortez of Texas and Elfego Baca of New Mexico, also represented the cultural values admired by Mexican communities. Cortez and Baca were similar in that their lives follow almost the same course of events: the initial confrontation with Anglo cowboys or lawmen, the chase or confrontation in which the independent cultural hero, although greatly outgunned, outnumbered, but not outfoxed, reveals the cultural weaknesses of the opposition, and finally their demise by six-gun.

Born on the Mexican side of the border between Matamoros and Reynosa, Texas, in 1875, Gregorio Cortez and his brother Romaldo worked as farmhands and *vaqueros* (cowboys) until they rented farms within one mile of each other and grew corn.[37] In 1901, an altercation arose between Cortez brothers and Sheriff W. T. "Brack" Morris of Karnes County, where the Cortez families resided. Mostly due to Texas racism and ethnocentrism, a small but significant cultural and linguistic misunderstanding over the sale of a mare led to an exchange of gunfire in which an armed Morris shot and seriously wounded an unarmed Romaldo Cortez, who later died under mysterious circumstances in jail. The sheriff took a second shot at Gregorio but missed; Cortez, also armed, returned fire and killed Morris. Chased by posses, hidden by friends, and walking barefoot, Cortez was forced to kill a second sheriff who was known to shoot Mexicans first and asked questions later in the usual Anglo manner. After receiving a little brown mare from a friend, Cortez fled for the border, chased by literally hundreds of possemen including Mexicano lawmen even though he was still held in sympathy by most Mexicans.

Nevertheless, ten days later, after having walked, sometimes barefoot, for over a hundred miles and having ridden for more than four hundred on a series of mounts, Cortez was captured, tried, and found guilty of killing the second sheriff. Cortez served twelve years of a life sentence in Hunstville prison and was pardoned on July 14, 1913. As Paredes so movingly described his release: "At thirty-eight [Cortez] had spent almost a third of his life in prison, and all because he had traded a mare for a horse, just as the legend says."[38] However, the *corrido* composed in his honor represents many of the Mexican sentiments from the border region when it is sung with this refrain:

> Of America her nation
> Has suffered this setback,
> For our brother Cortez
> Has honored his flag.[39]

A second "independent hero," Elfego Baca, emerged from a conflict known to Mexicans as the Batalla de Frisco and to Anglos as the Mexican war.[40] The context for this conflict should be understood as an aftermath of the invasion of Texas cowboys, which occurred at the time of the railway penetration into the Socorro, New Mexico, region and southeastern Arizona. When the Texans entered the area they shot up towns and terrorized Mexicans, many of whom abandoned their homes and ranches and crossed into Chihuahua and Sonora, in some cases for the first time.

The town of Doña Ana alone lost sixty New Mexican families, and this emptying of Mexicans by Texan cowboys was basically designed to control the rich pasturelands of western New Mexico and southeastern Arizona.[41] Like their counterparts in California, New Mexicans fought back, and Elfego Baca of Socorro, New Mexico, was one of their group. At the age of nineteen, in October 1884, Baca accompanied a friend who was a Mexican deputy sheriff in the town of Frisco, New Mexico, to help him deal with the influx of Texas cowboys who had the penchant for shooting up the small town. Specifically, however, the cowboys had castrated one Mexican man, had hanged another who had protested, and generally carried on a series of terrorizing actions against Mexicans.

After a slight fracas with one of the cowboys, Baca made a citizen's arrest of one of the rowdies, but word soon reached his companions among the John Slaughter outfit, which had become aroused because a mere "greaser" had arrested a white man. Eventually after a second "face down," eighty Texas cowboys faced Baca who took refuge in a mud hut where after thirty-six hours of combat he killed two Texans and wounded six more. After the next day, most wandered off not willing to face Baca's accurate solitary armed response, and after a parley and truce, Baca was arrested, stood trial for the altercation, but was acquitted in Albuquerque. After many similar altercations with Texas cowboys, Baca eventually became a lawyer and much later was elected sheriff of Socorro County. He died of old age. For Cortez and Baca, the status of independent hero emerges from a deep level of cultural recognition. All the negative attributes heaped on Mexicans are reversed by the clear recognition of the psychological frailty of the powerful. By the simple act of resistance of one alone against many, of refusing to surrender, of overcoming impossible odds, and of defying the entire array of authority, the independent hero momentarily overturns the hegemony of the Anglo cultural system and its agents. This reversal empowers the weak with "suppressed insight" and gives life to the idea that it is, in fact, better to die standing than to live kneeling down. For Anglos, the fear used to dominate, to suppress, and to control is reversed, and overwhelming numbers and resources are brought to bear to stamp out the individual hero as quickly as possible, before their own fear of the Mexican consumes them and that "suppressed insight" is allowed to grow. For Mexicans, especially the rural and urban working class, this "suppressed insight" has been expressed in a variety of actions including recognizing cultural leaders and heroes but also in their organized armed rebellions, such as the very violent but short-lived Plan of San Diego of 1915, which will not be further elaborated here.[42] However, the development of organized labor strife from the nineteenth century to the present and indicators of important cultural expressions of "growing insight" were of extended duration.

The Cultural Basis for Strikes, Protests, and Labor Strife

» » »

As has been emphasized in previous chapters, the continuous migration of Mexicans from the south into the newly created Southwestern United States emerged as the aftermath of large-scale industrially organized developments in mining, construction, railroads, and agriculture and ranching. This process in California was directly associated with the gold fields, in Arizona mining and cattle, in Texas agriculture and cattle, and in New Mexico a combination of the three. In Arizona, for example, the reopening in 1857 of silver mines in and around Tubac used skilled and unskilled Mexican labor, made up of men and women, as well as the Mexican and Spanish technology associated with silver extraction. Mine operators attracted not only Mexican males and Mexican women who worked in camp as cooks, washerwomen, tailors, and housekeepers, but also Mexicans who had been former presidial soldiers, and their families in the Presidio of Tubac returned to cultivate lands they abandoned after the Gadsden Purchase.[43]

Wages to miners were paid in Arizona silver mines, but a system of peonage also developed in which the "company store" earned from 100 to 300 percent profit on goods sold to Mexican workers, which guaranteed that mines operated basically on free labor. This system of peonage was secondary when compared to the dual wage structure paid Mexican and Anglo miners. Similarly, farms, ranches, and businesses of various sorts used similar methods of employment. When Mexican workers fled these conditions, they were chased and when captured were whipped, and in some cases their hair was sheared off.[44] Eventually between 1900 and 1940, 60 percent of the labor in the mines of the Northern Greater Southwest was Mexican.

Despite their unfair treatment, between 1900 and 1930 more than a million Mexican workers were contracted, visited periodically, and settled in the Northern Greater Southwest. As table 3.1 shows, the increase in Mexican workers migrating to the United States was such that it equaled almost 10 percent of the total population of Mexico. Industrial farming in Texas and especially of cotton drew Mexicans from 1887 on, and by 1940, 300,000 Mexicans worked during the picking and planting seasons throughout the middle and west parts of Texas.[45] Beginning in 1900 with hardly any production, by 1929 the Northern Greater Southwest produced approximately 400,000 carloads of vegetables and fruit, which accounted for 40 percent of the entire output of the United States, a development owed mostly to Mexican labor. Seventy-five percent of all labor used throughout the entire production process was Mexican.[46]

TABLE 3.1
Mexican Migration to the United States, 1900–1930

	1900	1910	1920	1930
Arizona	14,171	29,987	61,580	114,173
California	8,086	33,694	88,881	368,013
New Mexico	6,649	11,918	29,272	59,340
Texas	71,062	125,916	251,827	683,681

Source: McWilliams 1990, 152.

However, whether in the mines, in the fields, on the *traques* (railway tracks), or in the cities, labor conditions were such that they created the basis for work stoppages, strikes, and protest. At times, Mexicans were used to break strikes and to replace protesting workers. At others, Mexicans led and organized labor efforts. Even in the present, as a later discussion will illustrate, some of these conditions have changed little for the new cohorts of Mexican workers. What change did occur arose in the aftermath of great struggles, defeats, and small victories at very large costs.

A cultural basis is evident in the manner in which Mexicans led, organized, and conducted their labor activities. In many instances, Mexicans used existing social organizations such as mutual aid societies as the cultural platforms upon which to establish a union and recruit members and its leadership for labor activities; these organizations also served as a social and economic safety valve in times of extreme stress due to strikes.

These mutual aid societies were usually organized along gender lines, so that women's "auxiliaries" became the main mechanism for organizing Mexican households into the major material basis of support for strike activities. When such aid societies did not exist, and if the industry such as the mines were gender selective, Mexican women organized "auxiliary" branches of the union around their households and provisioned the actual material needs of many of the strike activities, as well as provisioning households in need. During labor activities, such as strikes, in which women were either the main labor force, such as in food processing, or part of the labor force, to whatever degree they participated, women held "double duties": leading, organizing, and conducting strike activities but in addition being mainly responsible for organizing and provisioning the strikers through the organization of households. Mexican women used extensive kinship networks as communication and material conduits to transfer information, food, money, and assistance to parts of the labor community that lacked them. These are the cultural bases for the early and later struggles of Mexicans in the mines, fields, processing industries, railroad, and urban production activities.

The Early Struggle in Ranching and Agriculture

Among the first reported organized protests by Mexicans was the cowboy strike of 1883 in west Texas in which Mexicans participated with Anglo cowboys, even though the latter thought it anathema to have Mexicans participate. The strike of seven Panhandle ranches was preceded by an ultimatum signed by Juan Gómez among others, even though Mexican *vaqueros* and Anglo cowboys were in segregated labor groups and paid differentially.[47] However, such grouping did have a cultural basis because Mexican *vaqueros* organized themselves in teams, from which they selected one of their own as their spokesperson, negotiator, and leader as was the case in much of Texas, New Mexico, Arizona, and California. It is also probable that most if not all were related by either fictive or consanguineous ties, which crosscut their specific labor duties. In this manner, "thick" social relations of kinship served as the template upon which to rely during either strike activities or labor negotiation.

However, among the earliest of major labor disputes are the series of efforts in the sugar beet industry of Oxnard and Ventura, California, in which over a thousand Mexican and Japanese workers went on strike on February 28, 1903, after forming the Japanese Mexican Labor Association (JMLA).[48] Like their cohorts in mines of Arizona and Colorado, agricultural workers were paid in script that could only be redeemed at the company store. In addition, their labor was contracted by an intermediary, not unlike present conditions in many parts of the agricultural industry, so that a large percentage of their wages were taken as a contract fee.

After the death of one Mexican striker at the hands of armed guards hired by the Western Agriculture Contracting Company, brief negotiations ended in the JMLA achieving a modest victory.[49] This was not the last strike, however, because the JMLA did not become established as a bargaining agent with the growers themselves.

Of interest are the sources of ideological and cultural influence that buttressed these small strikes and the massive ones that were to follow in the ensuing periods through the late thirties. For the most part the workers were either residents of the communities close by or were relatives of people in those communities; or the communities themselves were strongly attached to the workers through commercial relationships. However, the actual organizing experience sprang from two other sources: first, from skills learned in Sonora and Chihuahua where strikes and working-class action had been articulated especially by syndoanarchists, and second, from the creation of mutual aid societies that cemented community relationships with common community objectives. In some cases, different union organizations shared the same buildings for their meetings, the same leadership, and many times the same membership.[50] While mutual aid societies were not unions, in many cases, especially in California, these organizations served as the training ground for Mexican political leadership and for union organizers.[51]

Ideologically the strike leaders and union members had been highly influenced by the anarchist syndicalist Flores Magón, who was extremely influential in Mexico and the United States in that period. Smiley Rincón, one of the strike leaders, was so influenced that he later participated in the Spanish Civil War as part of the Abraham Lincoln Brigade and died in combat.[52] As was the case throughout the Northern Greater Southwest, "Magonista" ideology was articulated through its Partido Liberal Mexicano (PLM) in varying forms: as mutual aid societies, labor unions, self-help volunteer associations, and in the many benefit functions for the poor and infirm. The labor union was another more organized form emphasizing liberty (for people to free themselves), communal organization, and elimination of oppressive government, all of which appealed to workers suffering from just the opposite.

The PLM ideology in Mexico, and for significant reasons in the United States, strongly emphasized the true participation of women in revolutionary activity in realizing PLM goals to create a utopian society in Mexico, in which government and church would be destroyed because of their oppression of Mexicans.[53] It rejected nationalism and national boundaries and emphasized the commonality of interests between different national populations who were involved in the same basic struggle, and it rejected any form of racism. Flores Magón articulated the final goals of humanitarianism and the actions of PLM revolutionaries as "the only ones capable of transforming all countries into a single large one, beautiful and good, the nation of human beings, the country of men and women with only one flag: universal fraternity."[54] Thus influenced, many agricultural labor activities and strikes took on a utopian cast; and as further discussion will show, Mexican miners in other areas of the Northern Greater Southwest were similarly influenced, and union actions and organizations had a much broader ideological base than simply striving for better wages and civil rights.

Armed ideologically and with community resources in hand, the first union of Mexican agricultural workers was established in 1927 in California under the banner of the Confederación de Uniones Obreras Mexicanas (CUOM), which organized twenty locals for 3,000 agricultural workers.[55] Between 1928 and 1933 four large strikes were called by thousands of Imperial Valley, San Joaquín Valley, and Los Angeles County Mexicans. Strikes were broken up by wholesale arrests, deportations, tear gas attacks, and by violent goon squads, who as the deputized armed guard of growers, terrorized and beat Mexican strikers.[56] During the 1934 lettuce strike in Brawley, California, the sheriff broke up an attempted meeting of workers, and 9 were tried and convicted of violating the 1919 Criminal Syndicalism Act. Braulio Orozco, a Brawley carpenter, and another Mexican, Eduardo Herrera, were among those convicted, together with seven Anglo organizers.[57] This pattern of intimidation and terror was often used during the following periods against all working-class attempts to organize in a number of industries. On January 9, 1935, during a strike call, state, county, and city lawmen ambushed a caravan of cars leaving a workers' meeting in El Centro and arrested 87. Three days later in Brawley, another meeting of workers was tear gassed, killing one child, and a number of arrests were made. By February 19, workers' temporary housing was burned to the ground, and 2,000 strikers were evicted including Mexican, Filipino, and Anglo workers.[58]

In California, thirty-seven strikes were called in 1933 alone, twenty-four of which were led by the Cannery and Agricultural Workers Industrial Union (C&AWIU) composed of 95 percent Mexican families with a leadership of largely Anglo women, who formed a radical cadre identified with the Communist Party.[59] While winning wage increases in twenty-one of these strikes, during the San Joaquín Valley cotton strike of 1933 in which 15,000 Mexican, Filipino, and Anglo workers walked off their jobs, violence, threats of deportation, and terror strongly influenced the small gains made, such as partial increases in wages.[60] An especially prominent part of the opposition was the farmer-organized Associated Farmers, which specialized in union busting and dispute resolution at the end of pickaxes, rifles, and clubs and used its considerable resources to indict union leaders under the 1919 Criminal Syndicalism Act. The association succeeded in eradicating the union, which was replaced two years later by the United Canner, Agricultural, Packing, and Allied Workers of America (UCAPAWA).[61]

Similarly, in Texas as early as 1912 Mexican onion clippers organized strikes in Asherton, and although they were broken up by a strike-breaker, five years later they rose up again. Zamora (1993, 59) cites one of the newspapers of the period:

> Some Asherton Mexicans got the idea that onion clipping was skilled la-
> bor, and that they ought to be fashionable and strike. Likewise they
> thought they had the onion growers where they couldn't kick. . . . The
> onion growers couldn't see the raise. They offered to come through with
> half the extra money, but the clippers said it was a whole loaf or no crust,
> and they were pretty crusty about it too. The onion men simply sent out
> for more Mexicans, and now the former clippers are in the soup, no
> money, no job, and no strike fund in the treasury.

In both cases, attempts to link strikers directly with criminal syndi-calism was used as the means to discredit legitimate issues of wages and working conditions.[62]

In agricultural labor through the thirties, strikes by Mexican field-workers and other nationalities, such as Filipino and Japanese, were re-peated throughout Arizona and Texas, as well as in Idaho, Washington, Colorado, and Michigan. Allied production lines were also struck so that in 1934, 6,000 Mexican pecan shellers, most of whom were women, struck the San Antonio, Texas, pecan shelling sweatshops.[63]

Until World War II, Mexicans led, organized, and participated in na-tional and local labor unions of agricultural workers such as the Agri-cultural Workers Union of Texas, C&AWIU, the Catholic Workers Union, CUOM, or its later version CUCOM (Confederación de Uniones de

Campesinos y Obreros Mexicanos), the Farm Laborers Union, the Mexican socialist Land League and Renters Union in Texas, the Texas Agricultural Worker's Organizing Committee, and the UCAPAWA.

With the coming of World War II, the Bracero Program in part undermined the activities of labor organizing, but in addition, thousands of Mexican agricultural workers joined the armed forces, began to work in war-related industry, or migrated to the cities mushrooming with the new industrial war structure. For those remaining in the fields with the *braceros,* Ruiz (1987, 56) reports the experience of María Arredondo:

> In 1944 we camped in Delhi under trees and orchards in tents. We made a home. We had rocks already or bricks and cooked our food and got boxes for our table . . . Mart [her son] suffered, he remembers. Picking peaches was the hardest job—I used to cry because my neck [hurt], the big peaches were heavy. I [could] only fill the bag half way because I couldn't stand the pain. . . . We lived too far from [the] bosses and that is where we used to get our water. Restrooms—they were under the trees, in the field, or by the canal.

After World War II, the labor organizing, strikes, foment, violence, and repression began again as a means of gaining limited wage and organizational advantages;[64] and twenty years after World War II, the red flag with its black eagle and white background of the United Farm Workers organizing committee, led by César Chávez and Dolores Huerta, again raised the hopes and dreams of Mexican farm workers.

"The Mines Eat You Up"

This statement was made by a former union organizer of the 1930s and 1940s, Maclovio Barrazas. He described what working in the mines was like in the early 1900s and into the 1950s, when Mexican miners were not only part of a dual wage structure, did the dirtiest and most dangerous jobs, were frequently injured, and suffered from miner's disease and other lung diseases, but also felt the effects of the traditional violence of strike breaking.[65]

Much earlier in 1893 and 1926, outside of San Antonio, Texas, Mexican miners from Thurber took part in a series of strikes sponsored by the United Mine Workers. In response, mine operators killed the Mexican union organizer sent in 1903 to recruit miners and to assist in the organization of a planned strike. It seemed that the brotherhood of unionism was stopped short when in 1926 the organization was weakened by a strike and a tightened production schedule; all of its 162 Mexican union members and their families were sent by rail to Mexico by the union because they were the most superfluous.[66] How many of these families were U.S. citizens is unknown. Nine years later, several thousand Mexican coal miners went on strike against the Gallup-American Company of New Mexico; the mine was placed under martial law, and those miners who had settled on company property were soon evicted and their housing burned down. After a series of confrontations and bloody battles, over 100 miners were arrested and some were charged with criminal syndicalism. Like his cohorts in Texas, Jesús Pallares, the leader of the Liga Obrera de Habla Española (which organized some 8,000 members during the strike), was arrested and deported to Chihuahua a few miles south of Gallup.[67]

Such confrontations were especially extreme in Arizona; for example, in 1917, 1,200 Mexican and non-Mexican strikers of the Phelps Dodge Copper Company were rounded up by "Arizona Rangers," deputized company goons and vigilantes, placed in boxcars, and sent to Columbus, New Mexico, where they were not permitted to detrain; then they were dumped in the middle of the desert without water or food. It seemed that the president of Phelps Dodge extended his executive authority in supporting and ordering these extra-legal measures (known as the "Bisbee Deportations"); and although he was indicted in federal court, the charges were dismissed.[68]

Labor union activity in Arizona, however, is filled with contradictions created by Anglo unions, the Phelps Dodge Company, and other organizations. For example, the first Arizona local of the Western Federation of Miners founded in Globe in 1896, as a protest to a wage cut and to the employment of Mexicans even though the double wage structure was in place.[69] The union had the specific goal of preventing the mine owners from replacing Anglo miners with Mexicans from Mexico rather than U.S.-born Mexicans.[70] Anglo miners, however, supported the double wage structure and protested strongly if Mexican miners—U.S. born or not—received pay increases that jeopardized their own positions.

Mexicans, however, were also quite willing to join in strikes and to organize on their own and, in fact, were successful in staging the Clifton-Morenci strike of 1903 (of the 3,500 strikers, 85 percent were Mexican). As in the agricultural strikes previously discussed, benevolent and mutual aid societies and social clubs, as networks of relationships and platforms for organizing by Mexicans, played a crucial role in the strike's success. A newspaper of the time reported: "The Mexicans belong to numerous societies and through these they can exert some sort of organization to stand together."[71] The organizations in question were actually the Alianza Hispano Americana, which was founded in 1896 as a chapter of the main lodge of Tucson, as well as the Zaragoza Society and Obreros.[72] The same source described the effectiveness of this culturally based strategy:

> The strike is now composed almost entirely of Mexicans. Quite a number of Americans have left the camp. These men are taking no part with the Mexicans. . . . At Metcalf, where practically all the men employed are Mexicans, the tie up of operations was complete from the start. The men prevented the loading of any ore on the cars which haul it to the Arizona [Copper Company] reduction works at Clifton. . . . It seems that the Mexicans are being led by one or two prominent leaders; they gather two or three times a day in Morenci and listen to speeches from the leaders who are very industrious [and] have used harsh language concerning "gringos". . . . This morning at 5 o'clock, more than two hundred Mexicans were already gathered at the mouth of the Humboldt tunnel, listening to the harangues by the leaders and music by the band. . . . This will probably be the end of Mexican labor in the District.[73]

After a period of heavy rains, great torrents of water rushed down the entire length of Clifton, washing away fifty people, breaking dams, washing out the homes along Chase Creek, where most of the Mexican families lived, and also washing away the first great mining strike of 1903.[74] With the declaration of martial law, the presence of federal troops, six companies of national guard, and the destruction created by the flood, resolution to the problems would have to wait for further strikes and further confrontations. More prophetic, however, was the second great Clifton-Morenci strike of 1983.[75] Almost eighty years after the first Clifton-Morenci strike, this series of events would destroy a union and split whole communities into opposing factions.

Thirteen years after the 1903 strike, the same issues remained: the hated double wage structure, peonage of Mexican workers by the company store, selling of jobs, raffling of worthless trinkets to workers who were compelled to buy them, and mistreatment by foremen and managers. On September 12, 1916, three unions made up of 5,000 Mexican miners again struck Phelps Dodge, the Shannon Copper Company, and the Arizona Copper Company. For 19 weeks they closed the mines.[76] However, the mine corporations had hundreds arrested and the national guard was sent in to break up the strike.[77]

Twenty-eight years later, the National War Labor Board found that three major copper companies classified employees as "Anglo American Males" and "Other Employees," which meant females, "Latin Americans," Blacks, Filipinos, and Indians. Pay differentials were such that if an inexperienced Mexican (an other) was hired, he was paid $5.21 a shift as a "common laborer," and an equally inexperienced Anglo was paid $6.36 a shift as a "helper." Equally onerous was the fact that no Mexican was paid more because of longevity, so that a miner could work for fifteen years and not earn any more than someone who had been hired to work an hour before. This pattern of discrimination, exploitation, and double standards was quite revealing of the systemic nature of discrimination described by the National War Labor Board: "The problem . . . is one which is woven into the fabric of the entire community, indeed of the entire Southwest. Unions and employers alike have had a part, and a significant part, in its creation and continuation."[78]

It was not until World War II in El Paso that Mexican smelter and refining laborers received union recognition[79] and not until after World War II that Arizona Mexican miners, many of whom had returned to the mines after having fought in World War II campaigns such as Iwo Jima or the Battle of the Bulge, were able to secretly organize their own unions in the Arizona copper mines and eventually become recognized as bargaining agents. In previous attempts to join Anglo unions, such as the plumbers and carpenters craft unions, Mexicans were told that they could only belong to the laborers union, the International Union of Mine, Mill, and Smelter Workers, "with the other Mexicans."[80] Thus, they joined up, and in 1946 the "Mexican Mine Mill" led a 107-day strike that concluded with an official contract and company recognition as bargaining agents; with this recognition the infamous double wage system also ended exactly one hundred years after the Mexican American War. Ironically, most of the Anglo craft unions then joined

"Mine Mill," but it was never lost on Mexicans that they had been the "fighters."[81]

After enduring red-baiting during the McCarthy era and fighting for better housing, living conditions, and so-called separate-but-equal working conditions, and the hiring of women, in 1983 the Mexican union was practically destroyed once again by corporate opposition, national guard intervention, and another disastrous flood. But this is another story.

Urban Conflicts and Important Mexican Gender Events

Although the Mexican population was an important labor commodity in agriculture and mining, Mexican energy and labor were also used as central resources for profit and capital success by the entire gamut of industrializing enterprises in the region. Among the enterprises that relied on Mexicans for their success were the railway companies upon which agriculture and mining depended to move products to eastern U.S. and world markets. What is of historical significance as well is that the basic exploratory and trade trails used by the first and second indigenous and Hispano/Mexicano settlers became the basis for American railways.[82] The first settlers, it will be recalled, used south to north and east to west trails to transport shell, scarlet macaws, turquoise, and buffalo hides, among many other products carried by women and men as well as by dogs, serving as mules. In a similar manner monumental ideas and practices were transported from Chalchihuites to Paquime and from Hohokam to La Quemada. The second settlers with their pack trains pulled by mules and oxen moved from Santa Fe to Mexico City carrying furs and hides and from Magdalena to Tucson carrying carriages, surreys, and silver (some of these followed the De Anza trail to San Diego from Tucson, from Santa Fe to El Paso, and from Tucson to Guaymas),[83] again transporting ideology and practices.

Following these ancient trails the railroad companies depended on Mexicans for laying down their rail system. Extensively used in the construction of the Southern Pacific and Santa Fe lines in the 1880s, Mexican labor made up 70 percent of the section crews and 90 percent of the extra gangs on the main southwestern railway lines, which employed approximately 40,000 Mexican railway workers, who settled wherever a railroad camp was established. Eventually, Mexicans began to buy lots around the camps where they lived for a dollar down and a dollar a week, so that many communities along the railway systems of the region originated as Mexican labor camps. Present-day Watts of Los Angeles riot fame was originally named Tajauta by the Mexican railway workers who formed the *colonia*.[84]

According to the 1930 census, over 70,000 Mexicans worked in the categories of "transportation and communication," which consisted basically of Mexicans working as trackmen and laborers on the railway and as maintenance men on street cars, where these existed.[85] Here, too, Mexicans had to face the prospect of discrimination, the double wage structure, and living in boxcars and tents.

In 1920 the Tucson city directory listed the Southern Pacific Railroad ("el SP," as Mexicans termed it), as employing 102 Mexicans, 91 percent of whom were railroad laborers, while only 4 Anglos were similarly employed.[86] Just the opposite in their distribution in the occupational hierarchy, Anglos were employed in the best-paid skilled jobs, occupying the following percentages of each position: 86 percent of railroad foremen, 74 percent of railroad inspectors, 71 percent of railroad machinists, 96 percent of switchmen, 91 percent of timekeepers, 99 percent of brakemen, and 100 percent of railroad conductors, the most socially prominent of categories.

It is ironically tragic that in 1942 in Tucson, when many Mexican railroad workers left for war, Mexican women were hired in some positions that paid better than laying tracks. From carrying out maintenance duties to firing up locomotive engines, these "Susanas del SP"— the Mexican version of "Rosie the Riveter"—took the first important steps in breaking down some of the "color" occupational barriers on the railroad, as well as in the struggle against sexual harassment in general.[87] They successfully had men fired for sexual harassment and may have been among the first women in the United States to do so in the workplace in 1943! Some of the women stayed on after the war although most were laid off in favor of the returning veterans. However, as in the mines, Mexicans were kept out of labor unions until they created their own, because the Operating Brotherhoods of the Southern Pacific did not knowingly admit Mexicans until 1960.[88] The union controlled all occupational access, with entrance denied except for the occasional trickle up of one or two Mexicans a decade. As Manuel González stated, "We [Mexicans] used to train them [Anglos] for everything. They didn't know how to handle tools, how to use a wrench, they didn't even know how to read the gauges or know the difference in pressures that you needed to fire up an engine. Yet when wage time came or promotion—¡*olvídate!*"[89]

This situation forced Mexicans to periodically attempt organizing their own union; and like their agricultural and mining cohorts, they used the voluntary association as a place to organize a union in 1919. Meeting at the Alianza Hispano Americana in Tucson, Mexican workers organized a strike that demanded their complete wages, when the railroad company cut them off, as it did periodically.[90] Those who suffered most were at the bottom of the wage scale and were the first laid off without the representation of the Anglo union. This strategy of wage cuts, as much as 30 percent, and periodic layoffs were protested many times by Mexican workers in 1921, resulted in a strike of 1,800 workers in 1922, and provoked continued unrest through the 1960s.[91] Mexican railway workers in Texas and California suffered similarly and in some cases worse because strikebreaking was met by the immediate firing of railway workers and replacing them with contract replacements from Mexico.[92]

Mexican women like men had similar experiences in labor sectors that were primarily occupied by women, such as agriculture, food processing, cigar and tobacco rolling, laundry work, clothing factories, restaurants, and department stores; and they fared worse than most Mexican men with a "triple" discrimination of occupation, culture, and gender. Thus, Mexican women not only earned less than Anglo women in comparable employment within the same arena of work, such as department stores, but in addition, Anglo women earned less than their male counterparts. The third layer of discrimination, however, was in the spatial hierarchical arrangement, in which Mexican women were located physically. Thus, Mexican women who worked in S. H. Kress department store in Tucson up to 1960 were seldom if ever promoted to head saleswomen jobs even though the store depended on the Mexican population both locally and from Sonora for its business. It is not known whether there were pay differentials between Anglo and Mexican women but it would not be surprising given the double wage structure in most commercial and industrial businesses in Arizona. However, Mexican women were not docile and did not accept the firing of two of their number in 1936 and did stage a slowdown and walkout in the process.[93] The manager of the store had fired two young Mexican women for no cause and hired two Anglos to take their place.[94] Nevertheless, it was in the often-hated laundries that the greatest exploitation occurred in the most extreme circumstances. If the mines ate up Mexican miners, large-scale laundry businesses into the 1960s dehydrated its women workers in an exterior temperature of 110 degrees in the summers and an interior temperature of 130. In some cases, 90 percent of the work force were women of which 90 percent were Mexicans. In Tucson, Arizona, a number of strikes by Mexican women were held to protest these conditions, but they were never organized into a permanent labor union.

Women were represented by the Amalgamated Clothing Workers of America (ACWA) in the copper mines during World War II, when they, like their sisters on the railroad, replaced men who went off to war.[95] Highly respected by their male co-workers, women were hired and worked in the most difficult occupations but were allowed to organize within what was considered a "women's union." This imposed genderized representation, however, did not deter women from conducting a number of wildcat strikes to protest poor working conditions and the firing of two women for supposedly "flirting with the floorwalkers." In reality, as is the case in most repressive contexts in which the powerful accuse the victim of a wrongdoing, it emerges from a kind of psychological legerdemain, which in this case actually concerned the sexual harassment of women by the foremen rather than the other way around. After two days of strikes, the women gained their demands.[96] After the war, unlike most of their sisters on the railroad, women continued to work in the mines, even though the company tried to harass them into quitting.[97] However, the women joined the Mine, Mill, and Smelter Workers of America, which by the end of World War II had been recognized as a bargaining agent for most Mexican workers.

Corporate Benevolent Voluntary Associations and
Other Forms of Organized Cultural Creativity
» » »

Although it is beyond the scope of this work to describe the literally hundreds of labor organizations, strikes, protests, and stoppages from the nineteenth century to the present, it is imperative to note the underlying cultural and ideological resources used to organize and support labor, civil, and community protests and conflicts. At the forefront of such actions were the most culturally basic of Mexican cultural inventions and creations: the benevolent and voluntary associations. These functioned as the most important organizationally resistant forms to economic exploitation, civil discrimination, and educational inequity. They played a crucial role in many of the urban protests and strikes of the nineteenth and twentieth centuries, as well as serving as important precursors to educational organizations important to the reform and protest activities of the 1970s. However, culturally they stand out as the most obvious example of Mexican social formation that is not only "traditional" but in fact highly transformative and adaptive to changes in economic and social circumstances.

The cultural and ideological basis for these social organizations is most obvious in the case of the hundreds of voluntary societies that were used as the platform on which labor activity was organized throughout the Northern Greater Southwest. The historical menu is rich in mutual aid societies, protective associations, fraternal lodges, religious associations, women's legal assistance groups such as the Sociedades de Madres Mexicanas, Masonic orders, patriotic organizations, and rotating credit associations that covertly and overtly supported and continue to support the basic goals of Mexican working-class people: community integration and Mexican civil rights. Although it was the case that the political orientation of these groups was heterogeneous or variable according to leadership and members, for the most part such organizations in one form or another did not directly address workers' issues. They provided religious instruction, death benefits, space for community meetings, some unemployment relief, funds for the poverty-stricken, funds for legal relief, resources for small businesses and economic crises, and organized "patriotic festivals" and public events celebrating El Cinco de Mayo, Mexican Independence Day, founders' and community saints days, and even the Fourth of July. In their entirety, however, such organizations and their functions reflect deep underlying social and cultural values that emerge in part from deep religious convictions and the household values of mutuality, assistance, and support.

La Cofradía de Nuestro Padre Jesús Nazareno: The Prototypical Cultural Case

As was the case throughout Arizona, California, Colorado, New Mexico, and Texas, voluntary organizations began to emerge in the late nineteenth century in relatively large numbers. Their precursors had already been established as offshoots of religious institutions such as the Catholic Church. The famous "Penitentes" (Penitents) or Cofradía de Nuestro Padre Jesús Nazareno (Confraternity of Our Father Jesus of Nazareth) of New Mexico and Colorado was a lay flagellation organization, which may have been carried north from Mexico with the *entrada* of De Oñate in 1598 or with De Vargas a hundred years later. The first reference to the Order of Penitents was made in church documents in 1794 and again forty years later by Bishop José Antonio Zubiria of Santa Fe when he disapproved of the self-inflicted corporal punishment practiced during Easter rituals; however, the Penitentes were not a homespun organization specific to New Mexico as some have thought.[98] It is known that a church dedicated to the Nazarene Christ was built in the 1750s in Morelos, Mexico, by the brotherhood, which existed in northern Mexico where representatives of the New Mexican order periodically visited their brother and sister chapters.[99]

This "traditional" religious organization in reality took root in the late eighteenth century when church institutions throughout the Northern Greater Southwest were in an unsteady state. With few priests to perform rites of baptism, confirmation, matrimony, and burial in the midst of great conflicts with indigenous peoples as described previously, the Penitentes emerged as an extremely important organization to take up the religious and material gap created during the "secular period" (ca. 1790–1850).[100]

Membership in the organization was generally reserved for men, but women created their own Auxiliadoras de la Morada (Auxiliaries of the Chapter), which performed specific duties such as tending the ill and infirm, organizing benefits for the poor, caring for the homes and families of those unable to, and serving as a kind of adoption agency for children without parents. Not unlike the unions, these auxiliaries bore the most important community responsibility in organizing activities other than the actual rituals that the Penitentes conducted. That is, as in most Mexican ritual events, women organize the mobilization of resources, relationships, and exchange and "keep tabs" on who has engaged in reciprocal behavior or not.[101] Men in the Penitentes did, however, carry out the actual rites, which consisted of self-flagellation, cross bearing, and other extreme forms of self-denial. These acts were manifestations of greater social sacrifices centering on the care of each member of the group and their families in times of illness or distress. In addition, however, like their later benevolent *mutualista* (mutual aid society) versions, death benefits, such as the actual funeral arrangements, survival benefits for the survivors, and for the actual care of widows and orphans, were provided to members of the *morada* (chapter).

Nevertheless, beyond these specific charitable acts, the Penitentes like their later *mutualista* counterparts played important economic and political roles in their communities. The entire Penitente community cooperated in planting, tending, and harvesting crops and formed economic cooperatives, which loaned money to their members. These functions were not unlike those developed by European Jews in "free loan associations" later in the nineteenth century in the United States and based on similar social values of providing for the needy but preserving their dignity without almsgiving per se.[102]

The Penitentes played an extremely important political role in the resistance against Anglo authority during the Taos Revolt of 1847 when they joined in armed resistance to the newly established American government. However, it was in the new Anglo politics that the Penitentes became quite adroit; most *moradas* were registered as Republicans and were represented in great numbers in the state constitutional convention of 1910. They were instrumental in making the state of New Mexico a bilingual state with the passing of Article 7, providing training for teachers in both languages in order to qualify them to teach Spanish-speaking students with Article 8, and in prohibiting school segregation and providing free access to public education with Article 10.[103] Although waning in political influence and economic importance in the late twentieth century, except in more isolated rural areas, the Penitentes did function to manifest "traditional" cultural resistance to encroaching non-Mexican political and economic forms, while simultaneously adapting to new social and political realities.

At the cultural level the Penitentes are the prototypical organization, and two important conditions, inherent in most Mexican social formations and central to mutual aid societies like the Penitentes stand out: first, ritual and social density[104] are the "glue" for maintaining and reinforcing deep-felt social values of reciprocity, mutuality, and exchange; and second, these organizations are "grounded" in the more fundamental social repository of women and their networks and households as chapter 4 will illustrate. Suffice it to suggest here that it is within the households that the underlying value of *confianza* (mutual trust) is articulated and then given further elaboration by both circumstances and formations such as mutual aid societies, which serve a variety of protective and adaptive functions.[105]

THE *MUTUALISTAS* AND OTHER BENEFICENT SOCIETIES:
THEIR DISTRIBUTION AND FUNCTION

Every subregion of the Northern Greater Southwest originated mutual aid societies, or *mutualistas* and other beneficent societies especially in the late nineteenth and early twentieth centuries. Most emerged from the south in Mexico and had long been participated in by workers and the middle class before their appearance north of the border. However, important economic and political considerations stimulated their emergence. First, the widespread poverty of working Mexican populations was a major condition for *mutualista* development and the need for the few resources it could distribute. Second, the cyclic "business process" of depression and boom stimulated periodic population movements north to work and their periodic expulsions south in the late 1890s and in the Great Depression (1929–1939), so that within this dynamic adaptive forms of assistance were developed to reduce hardships. Third, the continuing economic, labor, civil, and educational rights abuses of Mexicans whether born in the United States or not created a strong impetus for either using or forming the *mutualista* organization as the basis for protest and action. Fourth, the need for an alternative authority to Anglo government, business, and institutions had been created by the prevention of most Mexican participation in these arenas. Last, periodic Mexican revolts and the French Intervention in the northern Mexican border states, in the mid- and late nineteenth century, and the Mexican Revolution of 1910 also provided the stimulus for the continued formation and development of the *mutualistas* as new populations associated with the old.

In Texas alone, the earliest *mutualistas* were the Club Recíproco organized in 1873 and the Sociedad Mutualista Benito Juárez founded in Corpus Christi, Texas, in 1879, both of which focused on the needs of workers. By the late 1920s at least seventy-two *mutualistas*, Masonic lodges, and beneficent societies had been formed, some with as many as twenty-five lodges or chapters and some with international and regional scope.[106] Thus, approximately three hundred craft or specialty oriented organizations were functioning in a variety of ways: examples are La Unión de Pintores (painters); El Club Centenario de Carpinteros y Albañiles (carpenters and masons); La Sociedad Unión de Jornaleros (day laborers), Protección y Trabajo; La Unión de Impresores (typographical workers). El Club Cooperativo Mexicano, with 1,300 members, in 1922 established a food cooperative; Los Amigos del Pueblo and La Sociedad Benefactora focused on educational, legal, and job-related issues. La Unión de Agricultores Mexicanos—an independent labor federation with locals in Guadalupe County—in 1915 in Seguín, Texas, demanded minimum wages of $1.50 per day and having Mexican sharecroppers refuse a third of their crop as rental. All-female organizations supported women's issues in Pearsall, Kingsville, and Brownsville, Texas; examples are La Sociedad Mutualista Benito Juárez, wow, No. 1003 Ignacio A. de la Peña, and La Sociedad Carmen Romero Rubio de Díaz Señoras y Señoritas. La Liga de Protección Mexicana, founded in 1914 in Austin, specialized in legal services and contracted lawyers to assist its members especially on tenant laws, interest rates for loans, rights of assembly, and due process. Similarly, La Orden Hijos de América, founded in 1921 in San Antonio, specialized as a politically oriented pressure group and won the right of bringing suit against Anglos, the use of public beaches in Corpus Christi, and the right to serve on juries. Although restricted to U.S.-born Mexicans in its membership, it nevertheless championed civil rights for all Mexicans regardless of birth.

Arizona, among all regions, was home to one of the most important *mutualistas* in the Northern Greater Southwest—the Alianza Hispano Americana—but it is also representative of many similar *mutualistas* in California, New Mexico, and Colorado.[107] Founded in 1894 in Tucson, Arizona, and incorporated as a *mutualista* in 1897 until its demise in 1965, the organization focused on redressing civil rights violations, on educational equity, capital punishment, and the support of Mexican labor especially in the copper-mining regions. Although the organization had been founded by Mexican men of prominence, its membership was mostly working class, expanding to 320 cities throughout the region. It achieved political importance especially in the state of Arizona with a total membership fluctuating between a low of 1,171 in 1907 to a high of over 13,000 in 1929. By the mid-1960s the organization had faltered under a cloud of embezzlement charges.

The activities of the Alianza went far beyond supporting legal and political issues for Mexicans. In addition, it became a center for the training of cadres of young men and women in political organizing. It brought together stratified class and age groups in common causes such as generating benefits for the needy, stumping for political votes; but more importantly it created a series of clubs directed toward specific age groups. These clubs, such as the Club Mavis, Twenty-Teens, Club Esmeralda, El Centro, Monte Carlo, and the Gaylords, all focused on the young, unmarried, high-school-educated Mexicans.[108] While ostensibly these seemed to be only social clubs sponsoring dances, benefits, and food booths, they in fact became politically important organizing tools for the Viva Kennedy campaigns of the 1960s. For thirty years these clubs produced important cadres for political, educational, business, government, and community organizing.

These cadres established the same sort of "dense" relations that are analogues of familial "thickness," in which multiple relations are common, intermarriage the mode, and intense interaction and exchange the norm. In all, they created a network of what seemed to be "elites" but in actuality were the progeny of working-class families with a sprinkling of middle-class business offspring who became influential in the state of Arizona and strongly supported the welfare of less fortunate community members. In part, this network also provided some of the leadership for what was to become the Chicano movement of the 1960s and 1970s.

Thus, for Mexicans in the Northern Greater Southwest, the *mutualistas* and other benevolent associations up to the 1950s served as the main agent of local and regional social change, legal justice, labor organizing, and the creation of future cadres. The *mutualistas* and similar organizations, as will be recalled, originated in the south, were developed under very terrible economic and political conditions, and were made adaptive to the North American reality, in which most Mexicans were denied equal opportunity, provided with racist and commoditized identities, and made second-class citizens without first-class recourse. For Mexicans, the *mutualistas* and other benevolent societies functioned in multidimensional ways and in multifaceted forms to balance this asymmetry.

"The Great Chicano Cultural
Convulsive Transition Movement"

» » »

For ten years, between approximately 1965 and 1975, the Chicano movement swept like a fresh wind across the fields of California, the rural areas of Texas, the educational institutions of Arizona, the northern lands of New Mexico, and the cities of Colorado. What occurred in each state was replicated in the others to different degrees. This cultural, political, social, and psychological movement of protest, rebellion, creation, and determination set in motion changes toward cultural pluralism in the nation and the region, which have yet to be recognized.

I have termed this movement of persons, ideas, and action as "the great Chicano cultural convulsive transition movement" because, in fact, it was part of a worldwide convulsive transitional movement of poor and culturally subordinated peoples seeking determined resolutions to their conditions in light of rising expectations.[109] For Mexicans of the United States four basic elements were pregnant with meaning and ready for determined efforts toward resolution. First, the issue of the traditional quest for land, space, and place was expressed in either historical or mythic renditions of the loss of Mexican territory as an aftermath of the Mexican war and judicial and legislative manipulations. Second, labor conflicts and lack of representation in the fields, orchards, and vineyards of California continued. Third, the effect of cultural and linguistic erosion and the identification of the population as a commodity continued. Coupled to these last issues was the forced assimilation of the Mexican population especially through educational mechanisms and the rejection of Mexican culture as a viable adaptation of American values and practices. Fourth, and coupled to the other three in a symbiotic manner, was the continued quest for judicial redress, democratic representation, and the elimination of discriminatory and racist practices on the job, in schools, home purchase, public accommodations, acquisition of loans, and in sundry other daily activities.

Associated with these major factors was the emerging contrast and disparity between those who had managed to survive the many obstacles and were relatively successful educationally and economically and those in much greater need. As Navarro (1995) shows, a sense of "relative deprivation" was central to the emergence of the entire movement and specifically to youth versions of the movement.[110] The contrasts had become accentuated in the aftermath of long betterment drives in the many creative and oppositional activities organized by Mexicans already discussed.

Gómez-Quiñones (1990, 86) points out that between the late 1940s and the early 1960s, Mexican communities had been responsible for landmark legal decisions that made more equal education possible. The *Méndez v. Westminster School District* case (March 2, 1945), which was filed by the League of United Latin American Citizens (LULAC), challenged the segregationist practice of placing Mexican children in separate schools in Southern California; and by 1946, the court in the case had ruled that such practices were in violation of the equal protection clause of the Fourteenth Amendment.[111] In Texas, two years later, *Delgado v. Bastrop Independent School District* was filed by the G.I. Forum on the same basis as the California case; and the U.S. District Court ruled in favor of Delgado by prohibiting the physical segregation of Mexican students on the basis of culture and language.[112] These were the legal precursors of the *Brown v. Board of Education* (1954) decision outlawing separate but equal facilities for all. *Hernández et al. v. Driscoll Consolidated Independent School District et al.* (1957) eliminated forcing Mexican children to enroll in the first grade for two years in Texas.[113] Unfortunately new educational strategies were employed that functioned to accomplish the two year requirement by placing children in "1C" programs such as those that were developed in Arizona.[114]

Formal legal discrimination in employment in this period was ended, formal school segregation eliminated, legal restrictions for serving on juries were struck, the poll-tax was declared unconstitutional, prohibitions of segregated public accommodations were instituted, and property restrictions were prohibited.[115] Nevertheless, the social, economic, cultural, and social effects of discriminatory practices continued. Coupled with the continued urbanization of the Mexican population in this period 1950–1960, the realistic expectations of World War II and Korean War Veterans, the continued development of community based organizations like the Community Service Organization (CSO), the participation of Mexicans as voters in the Viva Kennedy campaign, and of entire communities in the Johnson War on Poverty campaign, many Mexican populations throughout the Greater Northern Mexican region gathered together to develop strategies, tactics, objectives, goals, and myths to combat the myriad issues confronting them.

The Chicano movement encompassed all these elements, which were expressed in specific terms and at times in indistinguishable combinations of issues: educational equality coupled to cultural representation in subject matter and the elimination of "culturally disadvantaged" stereotypes; fair wages and recognition in the fields tied to the termination of discriminatory hiring in factories; young men and women not graduating from secondary schools, while the former were overrepresented on the casualty lists of Vietnam and the latter relegated to early domestic traps with few career opportunities; continued immigration raids on Mexican communities, while issues of nationalism, internationalism, localism, sexism, self-determination, and racism were debated.

The discussion of the issues led to the creation of centers of action throughout the Northern Greater Southwest, and from this process their organizational analogues were developed: among many others these included the Brown Berets, a militant defense group in the cities; El Partido de la Raza Unida, the political party that took political control over small towns in Texas; the student group Movimiento Estudiantil Chicano de Aztlán (MECHA) and its various antecedents like MAYO in Texas, MASA in Arizona, and MAYA in California, which mobilized thousands of Chicano students to action; the community action organization, the Mexican American Political Association (MAPA), which defended local interests and confronted immigration issues before they become fashionable; the Crusade for Justice of Denver, which strongly defended the educational and legal interests of poor people everywhere; and the Reyes Tijerna–led Alianza de Pueblos Libres, which fought to reclaim land and water rights in New Mexico with direct armed action. Of all of these efforts the seminal movement, and in many ways the most culturally congruent of all, was and continues to be in a more modest form, the César Chávez and Dolores Huerta–led United Farm Workers organization (UFW); its manifesto (the Plan de Delano), reminiscent of historical Mexican declarations like Zapata's Plan de Ayala or the Texas Plan de San Diego of 1915, articulated in impressive and impassioned language the injustices visited on farm workers and made stirring declarations for equitable and just solutions. This single document, read or not, served as the rallying cry not only for farm workers, but for students, urban populations, business persons, teachers, young and old, women and men, and certainly cadres of children from not only rural areas but from urban centers who would help their parents picket supermarkets carrying nonunion grapes. Regardless of the segmentation within Mexican communities of ideological convictions and class and occupational distribution, "La Huelga" mobilized thousands of Mexicans to support the farm workers' cause.

Among the most culturally significant and important mobilizations was the student/faculty movement that emerged out of the high schools, universities, and state and junior colleges; it greatly influenced important segments of the Mexican population, educational institutions, and the gestalt and worldview of many Mexicans. It also influenced how Mexicans were to interact with dominant institutions, with majority and minority populations, and how as Mexicans they were to regard themselves.

Although it is much beyond the purview of this work to discuss these aspects of the movement in their entirety, a personal case study is presented of the cultural and social underpinnings of one small but important segment that arose at San Diego State University in the years 1968–1971. It is representative of actions, relationships, and issues that confronted most such developments especially in California, and to varying degrees it was characteristic of the region.[116]

I chose to interpret this case from a bioethnographic viewpoint in order to "reconstruct a literate" text, if not a literary text,[117] while admitting that my view of the experience is not only colored, but that I participated in its creation, as did all my colleagues and friends.[118] This entire book is a reconstruction that has been strongly shaped and influenced by these events, by the ideologies we confronted, by the emotions and passions we articulated, by the relationships we established, and just as important by the failures of all of these as well. The south to north theme, the search for cultural space and place, the unmasking of the "Spanish" colonial tradition, and the pointed criticism of racism and ethnocentrism were all given life and "born" not only of events prior to my participation in the *movimiento* itself but strongly by the *movimiento*. To pretend for the sake of "objectivity" that emotional states, intimate relationships, and exhilarating events do not shape our entire being is naive. Therefore, for this most personal, most important, and searing period, I choose to pretend to combine a highly personal and a semi-anthropological view toward events, persons, and text and discuss the San Diego style of politics.

The San Diego Process

The San Diego process refers to the cultural and political pattern of relationships, exchange, and density that operated during the periods with which firsthand knowledge best provides an insight into the dynamics of the movement. This is not a historical or periodic description or analysis but rather an insight from the inside out of the manner in which perfect strangers became closer than kin, in which regional cultural differences became erased, and the manner in which intense learning, development, and action took place. This process may not be different than that which was developed in any other region of the movement, but from an informed participant-observer's perspective it surely seemed so at the time.

The San Diego process had temporal, spatial, and relational dimensions that gave it shape. First, San Diego was just next to the border. In fifteen minutes we were where we thought it all began culturally. We did not have to go to Germany, Ireland, Scotland, or Irkutsk to look for origins. There were Vélezes in Ensenada, Rosario, and Tijuana. They had moved there in the forties from Arizona and Sonora. The same was also true for many of the students and faculty. Kinship relations were plentiful and could be harvested at will. Second, rural areas were nearby. South of San Diego and National City, only a few miles away from the campus, tomato fields adjoined the San Diego Naval Base and its fleet of mothballed destroyers. Only sixty miles or so east, in the rich Imperial Valley, thousands of resident Mexican farm workers, rural workers, and land owners resided. In that region there was even a Punjabi-Mexican community, mostly made up of farmers and landless laborers whose progeny attended San Diego State and became part of the Chicano movement to search for their own cultural identity. The children of Filipino/Mexican farm workers, whose parents had walked out of the fields with Mexicans from the same area, invisibly joined as well. Third, there was a mix of experienced organizers from different realms who had not been academics all their lives or who had come from privileged classes. René Núñez had been the director of the Chicano Council of Higher Education before joining the faculty, two of us had been former military officers, while others of the faculty had taught in all-Mexican schools in racist contexts. Ruth Robinson, who joined us later, had worked directly in farm labor organizing and had established theater productions with Luis Valdez of Teatro Campesino fame. As a faculty most were seasoned veterans of the region without a great deal of confidence in the fairness or justice of any American institution. We simply had seen them fail too many times, or worse, ignore the obvious and heed the stereotype that reinforced their ignorance.

At San Diego State College, the students had done much of the basic work to create the curriculum and the various programs. The historian Juan Gómez-Quiñones had created some of the first high-quality courses on Chicano history and provided crucial leadership, while Gustave Segade created some of the first courses on Chicano literature at a time when much of it was still being written, and in fact he intellectually founded the Department of Mexican American Studies. In addition, David Weber had used his fine scholarly mind to contribute to a growing bibliography with his original research on Mexicans of the Northern Greater Southwest.

But it was the rip-roaring, no-holds-barred, take-no-prisoners students who gave life, intelligence, strategy, and unwavering commitment to make the San Diego process what it was. They were a mix of urban, rural, Mexican-born, U.S.-born, working-class, middle-class, literate, illiterate, secure, questioning, and critical groups of young women and men between the ages of 18 and 28 or so who simply never gave up. There were among them some of the first of the returned Vietnam vets who, suffering terribly from post-traumatic stress syndrome, faced their own potential destruction on a daily basis and who had to be soothed and stroked so that they would not take out their Colt .45 automatics and use them on themselves. There was Poli Gloria, former *pinto* and *pachuco,* who had worked in the fields, in communities, in the unions, and was Brawley born and nurtured. Brawley, California, in the Imperial Valley had been the scene, as will be recalled, of some of the worst anti-Mexican labor violence of the thirties. Poli was special. He was killed in an auto accident recruiting more Chicana/o students.

But probably what gave the San Diego process its character and its intensity was the emergence of an extremely strong and persistent core of Chicana feminists. While it had been simple to be critical of "Anglos," "the system," the "power structure," racism and ethnocentrism, most of us Mexican males suffered deeply from our own highly internalized sexism that had been learned early and often. As a case in point, it had been quite customary for women students to be elected to political office within student organizations but usually as the recording secretaries or treasurers, hardly ever as presidents or in the nonelected designation of "heavy." A "heavy" was regarded as such because of his/her political reputation in action or in thought. Most of the women faculty and students turned these conceptions on their head; and in an organizer's dream they mobilized themselves and proceeded to refuse election to such posts, created lists of "sexist pigs," confronted sexist commentary and behavior, and placed the burden of change on males in the same way all the students had placed the burden of change on institutions. Women, in fact, became the heavies so that Enriqueta Chávez, Caléxico born, and Felicitas Núñez, Brawley born, and many others banged our heads when they had to, convinced us when they were able to get through our own stupidity, taught us all the values of true respect for women, and more important for us as men, showed us that we were not really that important or needed. Their protests, confrontations, and patience taught me much. They not only became the heavies but shaped many of the political ideas, events, activities, and actions taken locally and statewide.

More important, however, these women reshaped the cultural underpinnings of our expected relationships. They freed most of us from the pretentious expected patriarchy that we held on to for dear life and used as the means of denying humanity to others and to ourselves. Women forced off our masks of civil sexism in which soothing and romantic words covered up our quest for control of female bodies and minds because we couldn't seem to control much of anything else. In addition, however, in becoming unmasked we probably truly learned to love with generosity and acceptance beyond gender.

There were two other ingredients, however, that made possible the San Diego style: first was the amazingly strong influence of the priest/poet Alurista; and second, the highly critical and sophisticated strategies and ideologies generated and learned during the formative phases of the style's development. As I have suggested, Alurista was both priest and poet. He was priestly only in the sense that he had a presence of self, which projected a long familiarity with realms of the spirit, the soul, and the intangible. He had created his own mythology of the Toltecs, Aztecs, and of Mesoamerica as the reference point for Mexican values. He "looked" south for inspiration and to the ancients for the basis of cultural survival and reawakening. He convinced students that what was of value was not necessarily the process of modernity in which people were bought and sold as commodities, but rather that the ancients somehow were tied to the earth, the sun, and the moon and mythically and ritually articulated the answers to some of the deep mysteries of existence and origins.

He certainly avoided the more imperialistic, sanguinary, and hegemonic political realities of many Mesoamerican peoples, but he did focus on the Toltec-inspired Mesoamerican priest/king/poet Netzahualcoyotl from whom he borrowed the concept of flower and song—the analogue of what constitutes poetry and creativity. Thus armed, Alurista composed hundreds of inspired "flowers and songs," which articulated so many feelings that many of us held about police brutality, the Vietnam War, men and women of the streets, farm workers, strikes, politics, students, almost every conceivable interest, idea, and feeling that so many of us had but never articulated.

He cast all of these within a lineal connection to the past that had been disrupted by the reidentification process of the Mexican population as a commodity, or as "disadvantaged," lazy, poor, miserable, and stupid. He countered the terrible costs of acculturation and assimilation, forced or not, with works and words of hope and violent confrontation. However, what he communicated best was his important declaration for self-determination and freedom: "I do not ask for Freedom, I am Freedom." In this manner, he intellectually licensed many of us to throw off the yoke of conventional politics.

With this "all-bets-are-off" premise ideological experimentation and combinations rushed forward. Marxist versions of dialectical materialism were frontally assaulted by a yearning cultural nationalism; socialist worker "Third World" amalgamation developed and struggled toward self-determining strategies; and finally organizational experimentation created a student-faculty governing body, which tried to administer the Chicano Studies Department and the overall umbrella—the Centro de Estudios Chicanos. This structure, made up ideologically of study groups but given organizational expression through a shared administration, simply could not be realized within the confines of a hierarchical academic state structure. By the mid-1970s the department became very much a traditional version of most academic departments. By 1971, I had already left.

However, the movement did not die. It created the impetus for the literal explosion of creative politics in the eighties, the growth of Mexican academics with a conscience, and of literary and social scientific work expressive of all the concerns that had been taken up during the period of the movement. The region would never be the same nor would the quest for homogenizing and culturally erasing the Mexican population remain unchallenged. However, the struggle continues in our minds, in our hearts, in our schools, and in our homes. The San Diego process was but one of literally hundreds throughout the Northern Southwest region.

CHAPTER 4

» » » » »

Living in *Confianza* and Patriarchy:

The Cultural Systems of U.S.

Mexican Households

ULTIMATELY IT IS WITHIN Hispano/Mexicano households of the Northern Greater Southwest that the poison of racism, cultural ideology, an exploitative economy, and political struggle emerge simultaneously attempting to control allegiances, cultural practices and expectations, and labor and energy.[1] As Wolf (1988, 108) points out, "By treating kin relations precisely as a battleground in which cultural contexts are fought out, we may gain a more sophisticated understanding of how 'indigenous peoples' may so often survive and cope in political and economic environments hostile to their continued identity." The position adopted here is that these struggles are part of the normal operating procedure of appropriation that all complex systems of extraction seek to establish regardless of their purported ideology.[2] At the household level, the main struggle of the members is to defend themselves against repeated attempts by the state and/or "market" to exert complete control over their labor and productive capacities. This attempted control is inherent in complex industrial and advanced technological systems; local households respond culturally, socially, and at times politically.[3] The Northern Greater Southwest region is a highly charged and dynamic arena in which new versions of labor and energy-extracting technologies are developed.

In concert with such development, a constant struggle emerges

within Hispano/Mexicano households over control of values and attitudes in regard to work, family, and self. For the working- and middle-
class Mexican households, the struggle focuses on the avoidance of indebtedness and the tempering of the acquisition of what J. Henry (1963,
13) has termed "driveness," the push for achievement, competitive-
ness, profit, and mobility. In the middle-class Mexican household, the
push toward "driveness" creates a struggle over cultural reference, a
conflict over historical and cultural identity, and a resistance against
the loss of children to consumptive and self-absorbed attitudes.

Although dealing with some of the same struggles, Mexican working-
class households, in addition, are often required to support more kin
and friendship relations within and outside the household, to maintain
ritual and dense "multiple" social relations, and to mobilize cooperation, reciprocity, and interdependence with others.[4] Such action occurs
while the household is bombarded with electronic, occupational, and
interpersonal messages as to the efficacy of greater consumption, and
the importance of individualism and self-gratification.

Across class, however, there is a central gender question that emerges,
as well, and that is, what type of restrictions, boundaries, and definitions will be more than likely to also arise in what may be termed
male-centered strategies of familial development. Sometimes known as
"patriarchy," the idea, and relations upon which it rests to varying degrees, defines women subtly and/or obviously as objects of men, as
humans of lesser ability and innate values than men, whose labor and
work within the household or outside of it are valued less than that of
men, and basically as women standing in subordination to men within
and outside of the household. The totality of these relations and characteristics, it is argued, guarantees the inequality of women in comparison to men in all situations and guarantees women's subordination and
devalued utility. This male-dominated and woman-subordinating relation is multiplied in countless human interactions daily, and more important is the fact that it is replicated for and by following generations.

From the position adopted in this work, such patriarchy is "distributed" by conditions, economy, struggle, and the on-going political experience of the households in question; or to put it another way, patriarchy, as persistent and invasive as it is, is neither monolithic nor can it
persistently stand the battering that it receives by the micro and macro
actions of women. In the most extreme forms, patriarchal men seek to
control women's ability or "labor power" by limiting either learning or

work opportunities and thus maintain women's psychological and economic dependency upon them, but the degree to which this behavior is expressed is an empirical question. On the other hand, patriarchal men may require more subtle expressions of their privilege such as requiring women to work "double" and "triple" days of household duties while creating privileged gender lines for themselves. This may even extend to what household chores men will undertake, i.e., those usually related to supposed "knowledge" tasks such as the repair of appliances, construction, or strategic decisions regarding expenditures and investments. Again, this is an empirical question "on the ground" as to the degree such behaviors are expressed.

Certainly, the flip side of this formula is the way in which these elements are distributed for men. Patriarchy at the relational level is seldom a legitimate enterprise; therefore, men must have a cultural basis for demanding such a relation. Men have made the necessity of such a notion, the relationships that it entails, and all of its attending expectations internal to themselves. How this is acquired is much beyond the questions asked in this work, but it begins early, is often repeated, and has much to do with economy, occupational niches, the alienation of work, the kinds of educational and political institutions and references that reinforce already acquired attitudes and learned behavior from within their own household of origin.

An important issue emerges in that these relations, behaviors, and attitudes are "grounded" in the structure or platform of the family and the networks of which women are a part. The idea here is that the kinds of roles that women are limited to, as well as the overwhelming double duties they carry out at home when they are employed outside of the household, are directly tied to the rewards that women receive "culturally" within kin networks.[5] Women are "expected" not only to be excellent caretakers at home and to work in an exemplary manner on the job, but also to fulfill both simultaneously, and be admired and rewarded in a cultural sense by other women, certainly by men, and emulated by children.

There are a number of central factors that lead me to believe that in part how these relations, characteristics, ideas, and associated behaviors do become "distributed" has much to do with how dependent an individual household is on joint incomes above subsistence requirements, the kind of occupations women are engaged in, the level of income a woman receives, and probably more important in an economic sense than all, the level of indebtedness the household has created. In a pernicious sort of way, it may be that the greater the indebtedness, the lesser the strength of patriarchy within the household since it depends in large measure on the income derived by both the women and men of the household. However, all of these factors are further complicated by where and when the "analytical" snapshot is taken. That is, when is the analysis of households occurring: at what stage of the development cycle are they in and what phase of the aging process of its constituents is being described.[6] In addition, great differences will become apparent when generational factors and the location where these unfold are considered. These issues, however, must be contextualized within structural and class characteristics, without which discussion is reduced to differences of opinion.

Structural and Class Characteristics[7]

» » »

The ideological struggle for control of households can be understood by the fact that most Mexican households are supported through working-class occupations. In 1980, only 22.5 percent of the Mexican labor force in the U.S. Southwest was in upper white-collar and upper blue-collar occupations; the largest percentage (75 percent) is concentrated in the secondary and tertiary labor sectors: low white-collar (21.3 percent), low blue-collar (32.5 percent), service (15.5 percent), and a small portion as farm workers (5.8 percent).[8] Such occupational participation is reflected in per capita income. In 1980, the ratio of Mexican to non-Hispanic white per capita income was .55, and of mean household income it was .78.[9] Therefore, individuals in Mexican households earned slightly more than half as much income as Anglos; and at the mean household level, Mexican households earned three-fourths as much income as did Anglo households.[10]

In 1992, 27.4 percent of all Mexican families were in poverty in comparison to 22.5 percent ten years previously, but it is also the case that in 1992 63 percent were not.[11] Slightly more than 13 percent of all Mexican households earned $50,000 or more while the median was $22,477. When compared to Anglo populations these figures show the same disparity of income as that in 1980, but accentuated in 1992 with Anglos having only 10.2 percent of all such families below the poverty level,

28.4 percent of households earning $50,000 or more, with a median household income of $32,311. Similarly in mean income, Mexican families earned only $27,968 while Anglos earned $46,715.[12] Whether compared by "family" (two or more persons that are related) or "household" (all persons who occupy a housing unit), the results are the same: Mexicans in poverty are more than twice the number of Anglos; more than twice as many Anglos earn more than $50,000, and the average income of Anglo families is almost twice that of Mexicans. For the most part, most Mexican households derive their income from working-class occupations, with only slightly more than 12 percent occupying managerial and professional statuses in comparison to 29 percent of Anglos in the same categories. Thus 78 percent of employed Mexican men and women are primarily engaged in lower blue-collar, service, lower white-collar, and agricultural labor with only 3.1 percent of that number in upper blue-collar occupations.[13] In addition, income is also derived from employment by several household members, members having two jobs, and using scarce resources in innovative and creative ways. Also more Mexican households contain more adults than non-Hispanic white households; thus, there are potentially more earners per household.[14] This advantage, however, is offset by a larger number of children per household, greater unemployment than among the non-Hispanic white population, and, probably for the first ten years of a household cycle, intermittent employment.[15] Last, one in five households is largely part of the primary labor sector in income, stability, and security of employment.[16] Thus, there is a significant percentage of middle-class households for whom scarcity is not of primary concern but rather indebtedness due to ease of credit.

However, there are some significant gender differences that may provide an insight into the manner in which patriarchy in any of its forms may be distributed within households. First, 51.6 percent of Mexican women are in the labor force, which is only 7 percent less than the number for Anglo women. Second, 14.0 percent of Mexican women in the labor force are in upper white-collar occupations as managers or in a professional capacity, while only 9.3 of Mexican males are similarly occupied. In addition, almost 30 percent of employed Anglo women are in the same category, and Anglo men are a close second with 29 percent. In terms of income, almost 19 percent of Mexican women earn between $25,000 (16.7 percent) and over 50,000 (2.1 percent), while slightly over 32 percent of Mexican males earn an income in the same range (28.4 and 3.8 percent respectively).[17]

The differences in the percentage between Mexican females and males earning less than $25,000 is significant, with slightly over 82 percent of females and slightly less than 68 percent of males earning less than that amount. Among Anglos, the difference between females and males is more significant but at lower percentages: 62.4 percent of females and 35.1 of males. In terms of distributed income at this level, Mexican males are more like Anglo females, but both are significantly higher than Mexican women although neither approaches the low percentage distribution of Anglo males.[18] From these data it is not obvious that at the upper end of the occupational scale patriarchy affects the participation of Mexican women. In addition, given the unequal percentage of labor force participation between Mexican women and Mexican men (51.6 to 80.5 percent) the difference in the percentage of Mexican women earning over $50,000 is not significantly different than that of males (2.1 to 3.8 percent).

However, if only income and wealth of households are used as indicators of household stability, gender relations, cultural strategies, and the distribution of "patriarchy," little can be understood about the manner in which households develop, their historical resistance to structural conditions, and "on the ground" characteristics that may illuminate the processes of Mexican household formation. The general household strategy employed has been to struggle for cultural and social survival in the face of racist poison and political and economic policies designed to homogenize the population culturally and to separate its members physically from their points of origin.

Before 1929, the south to north movement of persons between border communities was relatively uninterrupted. Cross-border families in fact were common, with portions of large extended kin networks residing on both sides.[19] It still is not uncommon for children to attend elementary and secondary schools in the United States while their parents reside in a Mexican borderland town or city. Such cross-border kinship systems, as Heyman (1989, 7) points out, were really "a series of bilaterally related households and networks scattered between similar types of neighborhoods on both sides of the border." Certainly Alvarez (1987) clearly shows this creation of cross-border networks in the Baja/Alta California region since the 1880s.[20]

Border Balanced Households

» » »

Historically the relations and networks described above have not been distributed in the same manner throughout the border region; the closer to the border, the stronger the probability that a border bicultural identity will emerge. I have long known of the existence of a particular form of family not discussed in the literature until Heyman (1989) termed it the "border balanced" household. This type of household balances its source of income from the United States with its social residency in Mexico. Made possible by possession of the green card, which allows Mexicans to work in the U.S., the border balanced household takes advantage of access to dollars that are spent in Mexico on housing, services, foodstuffs, and repairs. Culturally, most members of the balanced household are functional bilinguals, participate in recreational activities on both sides of the border, and attend schools on both sides of the border (through the sixth grade in Mexico and junior high school and high school in the United States). It is highly likely that intermarriage with U.S.-born Mexicans will result from such balanced households. The ease with which members of such households move between cultural contexts in the United States and Mexico is truly impressive.

An associated phenomenon that arises in both the "border balanced" and in the "cross-border clustered" households is what may be termed generational "hopscotching," in which one or more members of a given household are born in Mexico and others are born in the United States. Alternately, one generation may be born in the United States, a second in Mexico, and a third in the United States. Such hopscotching has both negative and positive consequences for members of a given household, but in general the phenomenon provides the advantage of legal access to personal or institutional resources on either side of the U.S./Mexico border.

The Cross-Border Clustered Households of Tucson, Arizona[21]

» » »

One important type of variant,[22] further removed from the border, is the familial clustering of households or extension of families beyond the nucleated household, which increases with each succeeding generation. I have termed these "cross-border clustered" households, because 77.1 percent of our sample have relatives in Mexico, and a significant proportion (61 percent) organize their extended kin relations in the United States in a clustered household arrangement of dense bilateral kin and maintain kin ties with their Mexican relatives.[23] Studies (Keefe et al. 1978; Keefe 1979, 360; Keefe et al. 1979; Griswold del Castillo 1984, 129–32) have shown that regardless of class, Mexican extended families in the United States become more extensive and stronger with generational advancement, acculturation, and socioeconomic mobility. Although an assimilationist perspective would indicate that the opposite should be true, this has not been the case. In fact, Sena-Rivera (1980, 75) suggests that the "modified extended family" in the United States is more the norm than are nuclear families. The former, he suggests, is characterized by a series of nuclear families bound together with a strong emphasis on maintaining extended family interactional communication bonds. However, in the Mexican case, we have found our sample to be strongly bi-generational and tri-generational but without the attending authoritarianism associated with such familial forms (Litwak 1960, 9n).

Even though our sample was composed of 74 percent U.S.-born residents and was largely working class, this pattern of extension in clustered households was significant and extended with each succeeding generation. Such extended familial networks cross borders and class, are dynamic in composition, and increase in following generations. Keefe et al. (1979, 146–47) and others (Arce 1982; Ramírez 1980, 2) point out that first-generation Mexicans generally have established extended family networks in the United States. Such networks become highly elaborated in the second and third generations and are actively maintained through frequent visiting and the exchange of mutual aid. Even acculturation, as measured by language scales, seems to strengthen extension, and, extended familism is greatest among those who are likely to be English speakers. In addition, the higher the economic and educational status of the household, the higher the extended familial integration. These findings are supported by preliminary findings in a national study,[24] which revealed that the "clustered residential households" I will describe for Tucson, Arizona, were more common among U.S.-born Mexicans than among Mexican immigrants or Anglos.

Of theoretical interest, given these findings, are the parameters that are likely to make ethnic culture a fruitful analytical and descriptive category. If language as a cultural marker is neither necessary nor sufficient, then the intensity, duration, and multiplicity of relations define ethnic culture. We might surmise that the basis of ethnicity lies in the qualitative differences in social relations between populations rather than only in language or custom.

This finding of a relation between a preference for English and familial extension is not borne out by our study. In fact, Spanish in some combination with English is the preferred language within our sample. The results from our study of Mexican/Hispanic households in Tucson, Arizona, show that though the nuclear household is not the primary locale for social life, it is in that setting that *confianza* (mutual trust) is most likely to emerge.[25] Like Keefe (1979) and Keefe and Padilla (1987), we have found that the U.S. Mexican populations operate within a cluster of kin relationships connected to other local households as well as to households across the Arizona-Sonora border. Our data in Tucson, Arizona, show that over 61 percent of our sample have localized kin groups made up of a number of related households involved in extended social and economic exchange relations.

Usually focused on a "core" household of active and largely employed middle-aged-to-older adults, the peripheral households carry out their life cycles very much in relation to a centrally located grandparent or parent. The core and peripheral households create social "density" in that members of such networks are kin, and in their daily lives they add layers of relationships based on other contexts. The person to whom one is cousin is also the person with whom one exchanges labor assistance, has a fictive kinship relation of *compadrazgo* (co-godparenthood), shares in recreational activities and visitations, participates in religious and calendric activities, and in many instances may live nearby. That cousin will either recruit or be recruited by a network member to work in the same business or occupation.

Such networks function differently depending on the situation; which of their many functions will dominate in a particular instance depends upon the circumstances of the people involved. In the recruitment process mentioned above, our findings indicate that such networks function not only as a reliable defensive arrangement against the indeterminacy and uncertainty of changing circumstances but also to "penetrate" the single strands of employee and employer relations and entangle them within the multiplicity of relationships of the network. In an interesting, but not often understood sense, such "entanglement" is a type of social insurance against the vagaries of the employer-employee relation, which is often asymmetrical at best and exploitative at worst. Especially in the informal sector, which is marked by the lack of protection, security, and above-minimum wages, the network penetration also serves as the only means of minimum insurance against sudden firings.

The Tucson household sample shows these networks in remarkable continuity despite constant disruptive pressures. Most of these clustered households engage in frequent exchange relations such as child care, house sitting, ritual participation, visitations, and caretaking of persons outside of the household's biological unit. Very few of the clustered households relied in any appreciable degree on non-kin network members for child care, recreation, and other emotive functions.

Our data show that there is significant residential clustering of one type of all household clusters, which we have termed "primary." Primary clusters are those in which exchange relations of kin groups (of the interviewed household) occur within a residential area of less than a mile. Secondary clusters are those in which exchange relations of kin groups are maintained but are not centered on the household interviewed but more than a mile away. Half of all household clusters were primary and the rest were secondary. There was little significant size difference between the two types: the median was 4.12 households per cluster, and all other socioeconomic characteristics remained constant. For analytic purposes both types may be collapsed for the rest of this discussion except where noted.

Generally, the most frequent exchange within clustered households was babysitting for daughters and daughters-in-law. The differences between clustered and unclustered households was statistically significant at the .005 level of probability, with unpaid child care in clustered households being provided by grandparents of both sexes. There was no statistically significant median age difference between clustered and unclustered households (52 and 48 respectively), and the median yearly income from all sources for all households was $25,164, with a per capita income of $4,934.

However, both figures mask sources of income. Gross monthly income for a sample of forty interviewed and observed clustered and un-clustered households was $2,097 with a mean of 5.1 persons per house-hold. Approximately 80 percent of income was earned from wages or salary with 20 percent earned in the informal economy from weekend labor, bartering, selling of tortillas and tamales, paid child care, and used-article sales at swap meets. Income was generated by two or more household heads and other members in 40 percent of the households (40 percent by male heads only, and 20 percent by female heads only). The percentages of male and female heads does not represent single-parent households but only that only either a male or female head was employed. Eighty-four percent of the Tucson sample were mar-ried, 5 percent were single, 5 percent divorced, and 5 percent widowed. The percentage of true single parents with children was only 5 per-cent. Thus, the overwhelming number of all households were *working* working-class households, with multiple jobs and revenue-producing activities, with a significant number of working persons other than the female and male heads of households, and even in those households with one working female or male head, almost a quarter of their in-come was derived from the "informal" economy.

Nevertheless, such characteristics are only statistical aggregates, which do not indicate the qualitative manner in which such clustering is distributed in historical context. By being attentive to the manner in which the life cycle partially determines such distribution, as well as the effect of the penetration of economic and political forces into the household, an understanding of the viability and limits of household clustering is gained.

The question remains as to how clusters reinforce or debilitate what is known as "patriarchy" at the behavioral, attitudinal, or structural level. In each of the three case studies presented, little evidence sup-ported any of the indications of patriarchy. If anything, Mexican house-holds are mostly in the control of women; expenditures are made jointly; funds of knowledge are divided by gender but distributed in an even-handed manner; most Mexican children are made responsible very early on for each other regardless of gender; and in fact, it is women, especially in the late stage of development, upon whom the entire structure of the household cluster rests or falls in economic and political terms. As will be seen, single Mexican males especially are emotionally dependent upon mother love and support.

However, men most generally expect a "privileged" position in regard to housework even though both adults may be working outside of the household. This phenomenon, however, is directly associated with occupation and class, with the probability of lower blue-collar men more prone to seek privilege and women permitting it, while the opposite is true as income rises and the dependency of the household on the woman's income also rises. There are other intervening factors like men's labor required for house maintenance, car repair, and labor in exchange for favors returned. Thus, the adult males of any household during the week may be engaged in a series of labor tasks apart from their main occupation, be engaged in a "nighttime" job in addition to the day job, provide assistance to and within the household cluster such as repair, maintenance, and construction of housing for either parents, kin, children, or many times neighbors and friends. If the question during the course of interviews of any Mexican sample only directs its attention to men either carrying out cooking or house chores as an indication of "patriarchy," the response may reinforce this indication as an artifact of men doing other work after their own eight- or ten-hour days and thus not being eligible for added labor, as could be surmised at first glance. Thus the distribution of "patriarchy" at the behavioral, attitudinal, or structural level is a bit more complicated than has been suggested by other works but is certainly present and negotiated by both men and women.[26]

Clustering in the Life Cycle: Three Case Studies in Social Exchange Formation and Cultural Emergence[27]

» » »

Household clustering is usually centered around an ascending generation in which kin live close to children and their families of orientation, and in which exchange relations are maintained and mobilized. Once death occurs in the ascending generation, then there is a likelihood of partition along lateral dimensions. In addition, unmarried siblings move out, and although their kin ties seem to wane, this only occurs superficially. There seems to be an initial process of choosing kith over kin, but as their children are born and grow, the kin networks are mobilized to meet occupational and experiential demands.

For the emerging unmarried young adult there is peer preference over kinship ties,[28] a situation that seems to dominate until marriage, at which time the new household becomes attached to a parental household. These household clusters begin to become tri-generational and transformed, and a "core" appears once the birth of grandchildren occurs during late middle age. Such dynamics are the basic characteristic of the assembly process of clustered households, and the "American" version of dispersal seems to be valid only for a limited amount of time within the life cycle of the life of the total household cluster. In fact, as the following case studies illustrate, the preference for density of relations whether parental, consanguineal, or friendship becomes more important than occupational stability in some cases. In addition, given the density of relationships as the second case study shows, intermarriage with non-Mexicans does little to change either expectations for relationships from the Mexican pattern or their behavioral expression in exchange. I term this phenomenon the "black hole" occurrence, in that Mexican extended clusters seem like celestial black holes that incorporate and consume anything within their relational distance, including non-Mexicans who intermarry.

The third case study is illustrative of the general trend found in the first two; in spite of familial fracturing due to exogenous or endogenous variables, a strong recapitulation process seems to develop and mobilize extended relations and the cluster effect beyond subsistence or other economic functional reasons. Such recapitulation processes seem to be indigenous to the implicit life ways of the population itself and are learned early in the life cycle.

As all the case studies also illustrate, Mexican household clusters emerge in historical circumstances that provide a type of "characteristic" that is unique to the household being described. Thus, in the first case study of the Acosta household, the world of work and recreation singularly mark the activities and relations of the household, in part, because of the place in the life cycle the household head occupies but in addition his generational context, from which such a household emerges. In the second study, the Araiza household is part of a large household cluster made up of upper middle-class, white-collar professionals for whom secular and religious rituals historically and today seem to be the underlying cultural "glue" for many of the exchange relations in operation. In the third case study, the Serrano cluster is a blue-collar "core," which has evolved from a partly fractured setting

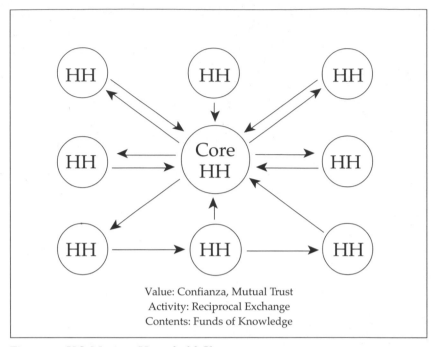

Figure 4.1 U.S. Mexican Household Clusters

and is reflective of the "hopscotching " previously discussed. However, the family is supported by a religious, familial, and nationalistic ideology that provides the underlying rationale for the expansion and development of the household cluster itself. Tragically, such ideology compounds the effects of occupational risk and injury in addition to current trends in the dissolution of young U.S. Mexican households.[29]

The case studies demonstrate that regardless of the historical circumstance from which such household clusters emerge and the specific characteristic focus displayed by each household cluster, all seem to converge developmentally into very similarly organized and structured networks of relationships based upon dense exchange[30] as figure 4.1 illustrates. In other words, each household has a characteristic emphasis—a type of cultural "shape" that differentiates one household from another and is derived from historical circumstances. In addition, each household cluster has accumulated and discarded "funds of knowledge,"[31] which form the basis of material survival and contain within them much of the previous generation's repertoire of information and skills used for subsistence. However, household organization, levels and importance of exchange, and developmental processes are very much the same.

The Early Cycle: Larry Acosta

Larry, at present a single, soft-spoken thirty-three-year-old from Silver City, New Mexico, works as a chemical abuse counselor for a religiously oriented treatment center. He has worked largely in construction since his 1970 graduation from high school where he lettered in football and baseball. The second eldest son in a family of seven brothers and sisters, Larry's now deceased parents were the children of miners who worked in Silver City and in the mining towns of southeastern Arizona. Larry's father, Robert "el Minero" (the miner) Acosta was born in 1928 in the mining town of Bisbee, Arizona, and also worked as a miner in Silver City, where he met Larry's mother. After marriage and the birth of children, the entire family eventually became incorporated within Larry's mother's extended family system, which at one time was estimated to be over 350 members.

After high school graduation in Silver City, Larry, one of his younger brothers, two cousins, and a few close friends from Larry's football team began a ten-year work odyssey in construction, mining, and iron work in seven different towns and cities in New Mexico, Houston, Galveston, and Dallas and later in Tucson and Phoenix. In part, the work cycle followed the usual search-for-work pattern, and in addition, Larry and his cohorts would quit their jobs if any one of the group became dissatisfied with an employer. He with his *compadres* quit by jointly walking off their jobs after disputes with foremen or other employees, or if they were dissatisfied with working conditions. Of interest is that in most cases wages were not as important a determinant for job security as the relationships they had established with each other.

Friendship, however, did give way to crisis or familial problems demanding Larry's attention. During this ten-year work period, he returned frequently to Silver City to visit his brothers and sisters and remained for a period of time in order to ensure that a younger brother was counseled on how to interact with the new roles which his eldest uncle had assumed. Larry's father "el Minero," who had become gravely ill in 1979, had stepped down as titular head of the extended family in favor of his eldest brother. Larry's youngest brother had become embroiled in conflict with the eldest uncle over the degree to which he would observe his uncle's authority.

In fact, Larry returned to his construction work with his second brother, and for the next three years all three brothers and one cousin lived together. Nevertheless, drug use had penetrated Larry's household; and after a period of his and others' intensive experimentation with various chemical substances, Larry's relationship with his friends and brothers began to erode. As Larry states it, "Our paychecks went for one tooting party after another," and conflict emerged over who was to support the drug habits, subsistence and maintenance, and work in an occupation that required a great deal of physical strength and stamina.

For Larry, his brothers, and cousins, the adjustment was, in fact, to break the relationships with their friends and to separate themselves by moving to different apartments in Tucson and by working in various service jobs; yet even with this adjustment, exchange and visitations with relatives in New Mexico remained intense and frequent. Relatives from Silver City visited at least once a month and stayed the weekend, and Larry and his brothers visited relatives and friends during secular and ritual celebrations such as weddings, baptisms, and funerals. As Larry states it, "We find almost any reason to go home and be with real people."

Larry found it necessary to quit the construction trade because so much of it was tied to drug use after and sometimes during working hours. He, his brothers, and one cousin sought help from various treatment centers, the last of which offered to hire him to work with young drug-dependent abusers, a job he accepted as a result of his own successful treatment. Even though this change in occupation also meant a 25 percent reduction in salary from his current yearly income of $16,512,[32] the elimination of pressures to perform difficult physical labor in the midst of a lifestyle of drug abuse compensated for the lack of income. In addition, this change stimulated his return to school, and he completed a business degree in programming at one of the local business colleges; however, he has not as yet had the opportunity to use the degree in the marketplace.

During this period of change Larry has reflected upon the impact on the family of his father's and mother's death. His mother's death, early in 1972, was a shock and a tragedy for the entire family, and his aunts and cousins quickly joined in to fill the gap. His mother's widowed sister moved into their household when he was eighteen and cared for the remaining siblings; he stated that he felt that her presence quickly reduced the sorrow as well as provided continuity. In addition, according to Larry, his aunt was able to reinvigorate the "rhythm" of the household through visitations, assistance, celebrations, exchange, and rituals important to the "clusters" of households of which Larry's was one.

According to Larry, prior to his mother's death there were always occasions for relatives and friends to visit each other's households. Males would go out together to hunt during the season, and both males and females joined in to butcher and dress the animals killed. Holidays were marked by the cooking of large batches of traditional food as well as its consumption in each other's homes; birthdays and baptisms of grandchildren, as well as funerals and weddings, rounded out the year's cycle of events. Even though he and his brothers and cousins were not present some of the time, they did in fact attend many of these events by driving all night after work or on weekends from Houston, Dallas, Tucson, or Lordsburg.

In addition, because most men worked together in the mines in Silver City, their face-to-face meetings were not only frequent but generally marked daily after work by meeting and sitting in their pickup trucks outside one of the local 7-11 stores and drinking six packs of Budweiser. Afterwards it was expected that all would return home to face sometimes irritated wives or a visit with cousins and friends. For Larry, this was the "rhythm" that most men could expect in Silver City, and women played the key role in ensuring that the events described were in fact planned and carried out. However, upon the death of his father in 1980, there was no one to fill his father's household role, and his uncle, in fact, created conflict by trying to assert authority within a basically close-knit family although an essentially bilateral extended kin network. In fact, segmentation of the network occurred along generational lines, so that although the eldest uncle's household did become the "core," connecting some lateral and descending households, Larry's own descending network of brothers, sisters, spouses, and children eventually split off without the existence of a true "core" household. At this point in the developmental cycle of the "clustered" household, no single household had emerged as a "core" because this aspect of the cycle would not occur until the birth of grandchildren.

Larry's own household of brothers and cousins will continue to develop potentially along the same lines. Because there is constant contact with relatives and friends, there is the opportunity for exchange and meeting potential marriage partners within the same class and ethnic context. The probability is almost certain that Larry will create permanency and establish a separate but interconnected household in a clustered arrangement with his brothers and cousins in Tucson, Arizona, while maintaining the cross-state relations with relatives in New Mexico.

What marks Larry's household in special ways is that the worlds of work and recreation are the culturally expected activities at his level of the life cycle, and they both transcend ethnicity. The penetration of drugs into his household and into his network is the result of his participation in a highly mobile occupation, in which physical prowess, faddism, and escapist recreation are relatively normative for his age group. On the other hand, the primary basis for Larry's personal and cultural identity lies in the familial networks of relations that are ethnically and residentially specific to New Mexicans. The introduction of drugs into the household was partially offset by these relations, and his personal decision to seek alternatives emerges as the result of a sense of responsibility not only for himself but for his brothers as well.

The Middle Cycle: The Black Hole and the Electronic Household Cluster

In many ways, the Araiza household seems to be atypical, but it is socially very much like most U.S. Mexican households. Like Larry Acosta, Geraldo "Jerry" Araiza is from a large family and was born in a nearby Arizona border town. His father, Ignacio Araiza Navarette, a child of the Mexican Revolution, was born in 1910 in Tepic, Nayarit, Mexico—a city north of Guadalajara, Mexico. After his father's death, Ignacio, age ten, his mother, and five smaller brothers and sisters had lived for a number of years in coconut fields in shelters made of the fallen palm fronds they could gather. Shortly afterwards, Ignacio was taken in by a priest and became his acolyte. The priest sponsored his entrance into a Catholic seminary in one of the central states of Mexico, and Ignacio became a seminarian until the Cristero Revolt of 1927, at which time the Mexican government closed churches and seminaries in the revolting states.[33] Ignacio himself participated as a courier for the rebellion but after a short imprisonment fled the area for the border. After Ignacio settled in the U.S. border city of El Alamo, on the Arizona-Sonora border, he sent for a cousin whom he married; and twelve Araiza children were born between 1932 and 1946.

For the Araiza family, Ignacio's early experience has been the constant source of inspiration, belief, and continued devotion to both the doctrines and beliefs of the Catholic church. The close association with the church remained, and at present all of the first U.S.-born generation of Araizas and most of the second remain devout Catholics.

The tenth of twelve brothers and sisters, all of whom are high school graduates, Jerry is forty-four years old, a university graduate, whose accounting and investment major prepared him for the controller's office of a large investment bond corporation where he is a corporate officer. Like seven of his brothers and sisters who graduated from one of the state universities in Arizona, Jerry is among the small but significant percentage of professionals who participate in a professional domain largely controlled by the Anglo population, and who live in a largely Hispanic network and context. This is in spite of the fact that his wife Sandy is an Anglo and their three teenage children are basically monolingual English speakers. In fact of all his eleven brothers and sisters, only two married U.S. Mexicans, and nine others have Anglo spouses, and most of their children are monolingual English speakers.

The Araiza occupations vary in range, with one attorney, two child psychologists, two engineers, two teachers, and one occupying an office manager's position in a large department store. The rest are married, have mid-level manager jobs, and live with working spouses.

Regardless of class position, linguistic preference, and intermarriage, the phenomenon of incorporating a non-Mexican spouse within largely ethnic networks and within a cluster of Mexican households is what I have described as the "black hole" effect; the bonds of reciprocity and exchange become so densely operative that most of the relationships and events seem to center on ethnically specific religious ritual, recreational events, and familial celebrations. These compose the cultural "glue" that cement fictive kinship, kinship, and friendship relationships in multistranded networks and associations; and for this house-hold and the adjoining ones, it is clear that regardless of the ethnicity of spouses the "black hole" effect holds true.

In this cluster of households, the density of relations as well as the ritual intensity of those relations seem to counter the effects of inter-marriage, middle-class status, and high levels of mobility. The density is made most apparent in two related behaviors: the ritual cycle and residential and "electronic" clustering of relationships. Two manda-tory participatory rituals divide the yearly cycle: the grandparents' wedding anniversary on June 15 and the celebration of Christmas on December 25. The first is attended by members of the Araiza network from as far away as Norway, where one of Jerry's brothers is a consulate official, and New York, where a sister is a stockbroker. The celebration is usually held in the largest available household, because together with grandchildren between sixty and eighty people attend the two-day festivities, which involve mandatory mass attendance, a ritual blessing of the grandparents by a parish priest, and a communal feast held in the evening of the anniversary date.

The second ritual is operationally much like the first, with manda-tory attendance at Christmas Eve mass, and upon returning home, the opening of presents is the primary event. Thus, it is the children of chil-dren who are the foci of attention rather than the grandparent genera-tion. On Christmas day a slide show of all the year's events is pre-sented, using contributed and representative pictures of major events and news such as births and weddings especially for those family members not able to have attended them.

The secular and religious rituals described in the Christmas slide show fill a year-long cycle of weddings, baptisms, funerals, anniver-saries, high school and university homecoming celebrations, and birth-days. For the most part, such events have a very strong commensal component of gift exchange and a marking function, which incorporate newer generations into the family in very tangible ways. In a sense each new generational member is provided a historical glimpse of the past in different secular and religious forms and is made part of the same process by his/her participation.

Because only six of Jerry's brothers and sisters live in Tucson, the others and their children simply cannot visit and interact with either the frequency or intensity that residential proximity provides. As an adaptive measure Jerry's siblings and their spouses form and maintain an electronic network through modems and personal computers. Jerry's home serves as the central receiving node for communications from out-of-city siblings and spouses, as well as serving as the communications link from Tucson households to out-of-city households. What is of interest to note is that for the most part it is Jerry's nephews, nieces, and his own children who serve as the computer operators. For the most part, Jerry's brothers and sisters are not as computer capable as their own children, so it is the children of children who are the transmitters of important cultural and relational information from parents to parents.

Such a communications link provides all households not only with the latest familial news, but in addition, it forms the basis for the publication of a quarterly familial network journal entitled *El Chisme* (the gossip). Written primarily in English, the journal's contents include articles that always begin with news emphasizing the latest on grandparent health, news of each sibling's family, careers, travel, recreation, romances, recent major purchases, kinship charts, and personal information on each member of the family. Other items in the journal include bilingual jokes, sayings, quizzes, and historical information that may not be extensively known by the various households, such as the personal histories of relatives in Mexico as well as events such as Don Ignacio's Cristero rebellion participation.

For Jerry, Sandy, and their three children intensive and extensive links are very much a function of the ritual cycle in which they engage and are made somewhat possible by the electronic medium used to ensure those links. While there is a "distributional" effect within the Araiza network in which strong preferences between specific siblings are expressed and with whom throughout the year greater intensity is manifested than with other siblings, nevertheless, the ritual cycle described seems to cross-cut personal preferences as well as professional interests. The annual slide show, the quarterly journal, and the intensive electronic communication, all provide a noiseless medium of communication, which keeps the relationships fresh, timely, and appropriate for familial members in the same and in different geographical locations.

The Core Household: Indeterminacy and Uncertainty
in the Midst of Ideological and Household Certainty

For fifty-eight-year-old Hortencia Serrano, the focus of most of her personal and social attention is directed toward the cluster of relations that consist of her husband Tomás, a former aircraft maintenance worker; her four children, three of whom are married and live nearby, and their children; her mother and father, who live fifty yards behind them in Hortencia's old home; and her mother's sister and family, who live next door to her mother. Her job as a bank teller has been her primary occupation since high school graduation in 1954. Even when she followed Tomás to various army bases where they were transferred, Hortencia supplemented their income by working part-time, as well as raising the four children in their rapidly growing family. Unlike Tomás, Hortencia has always had her own stable platform, in spite of the fact that during her early childhood, her father, mother, and his brothers moved from mining town to mining town in Arizona in search of work during the Depression and later when the mines began to dry up. It was only after her father was injured in a mine accident that they moved to Tucson where he and his brothers began a handyman's service. Much of Hortencia's early household experience centered around her paternal relations and households, and she helped to keep the accounting books for the handyman's service.

Tomás's household experience was almost the opposite of Hortencia's. His began in Phoenix, Arizona, the city where he was born, when his parents who had migrated from Mexico to seek work were "repatriated" back to Mexico (see note 19). While attending school only intermittently in Sonora, Tomás sold vegetables with his father on the streets of a northern Mexican border town; the work, although providing a living, barely supported the family of six. A combination of overwork, alcohol, and poor health killed his father in 1945; and at the age of ten, Tomás moved to Tucson by himself and into the storage closet of a grocery store, which the store's owner allowed him to use in exchange for his labor. Soon thereafter, Tomás was caught by police for truancy and placed in a foster home, where he remained until he was of legal age. With only a seventh-grade education, he joined the army and for the next ten years attended a number of service-connected schools in which he trained to become a maintenance mechanic for army planes and helicopters. By 1962, he was released from the service because both he and Hortencia wanted to return to Tucson to be near her family. He joined the Arizona Army National Guard and worked as a maintenance person for 25 years.

For both Hortencia and Tomás, the focus of all of their activities in the past five years has been their grandchildren, children, church, and country. The grandchildren of both the eldest sons and daughter are frequent visitors, and Hortencia and Tomás take care of their four grandchildren at least three times a month, as well as entire weekends at least twice a month. Hortencia especially enjoys being with her grandchildren and mother while preparing the weekly Sunday dinners that are held either in the great-grandparents' home or in hers. During such arrangements great-grandchildren and grandchildren assist in housecleaning, marketing, cooking, and table preparation.

In addition, Hortencia has devoted a great deal of effort to working with each one of her children and now grandchildren on computational skills, in which she excels after being employed as a bank teller for so many years. Almost nightly, Hortencia presented her children with simple problems, becoming progressively difficult, and had them compete with her and the others until someone made an error, at which time he/she dropped out. Hortencia has begun the same process whenever her older grandchildren stay in the household.

Tomás, on the other hand, takes the grandchildren to recreational and entertainment functions, as well as allowing them into his well-stocked wood shop directly behind his home to observe and occasionally experiment on the repair or construction of household items. For Tomás there is no better exercise than hard manual labor, as well as labor in which one's hands form an object from scratch. Such pride was clearly manifested when Tomás and Hortencia moved into their present tract home; he expanded the house from two to four bedrooms and added a dining room and two full baths. With assistance from his sons and daughter, they were able to convert a small plasterboard home into a spacious brick-faced house, which serves as a model to many other families in this predominantly Mexican neighborhood.

In addition, his well-honed mechanical and electronic skills learned in the service have allowed him to purchase rather decrepit automobiles and transform them into almost perfectly restored cars with fully working antique radios. This process of repair and restoration has always occurred in the full view of his children and grandchildren, the consequence of which is that both sons and his one daughter acquired similar skills very early in their development. Both sons and daughter are employed in highly technical, high blue-collar occupations,[34] and all three attribute their abilities to the entire family participating in Hortencia's computational games, in restoration repairs, as well as in assisting their father in the construction of the addition to the home. For each, the familial "funds of knowledge" have been important bridges toward occupational stability.

For Hortencia and Tomás, however, their perception of the "kids turning out right" is credited to the importance of religion emphasized within the household and the reverence for the ritual activities of the church. Tomás is a member of the Knights of Columbus, and Hortencia is a member of the auxiliary. Both of them have participated intensively in the movement through the hierarchy that constitutes the organizational structure of the association, and faithfully Tomás attires himself in full regalia for important ecclesiastical events in which he serves as part of the honor guard for church dignitaries. The highlight for both was the visit of Pope Paul to Phoenix, Arizona, in 1987, in which both Hortencia and Tomás served in different capacities. Attendance at Catholic mass and the observation of holidays and days of obligation are made mandatory for visitors and relations alike if they are present in the household.

This ideological commitment to Catholicism is equaled by their investment in national and local conservative points of view regarding national defense, the importance of a strong military, and the support for political figures like Ronald Reagan and Evan Mecham, the impeached governor of the state of Arizona who is politically more conservative than Barry Goldwater. Tomás, for example, has created an altarlike wall in one of his storage rooms to display myriad plastic emblems of army units, air force squadrons, and models and pictures of astronauts, aircraft, and tracked military vehicles. In addition, he has a large collection of military caps and emblems displayed in glass cases, together with his own military awards. Although Hortencia sometimes considers the display somewhat expensive and exaggerated, she does not disagree with their military tenets, given her own voting record and political preference for conservative issues. Nevertheless, most recently both Hortencia and Tomás appear to be somewhat shaken in their willingness to accept events considering three unforeseen and uncertain developments: the possible blindness of their oldest and favorite son, the divorce of their second son, and the probable destruction of Tomás's immunological system.

The first son, Tomás, seemed to have fulfilled their fondest wishes. A handsome and intelligent young man, soon after his marriage he presented them with their first grandson, "Tomasito." He received advanced technical training in communications from the local telephone company and had been quickly promoted for his diligence and focused work. Unfortunately, his attention to detail also caused a serious injury to his eyes when he ventured too close to a wire-wrapping device used in the maintenance of telephone wires. Two operations later, Tomás Jr. has lost most of his sight in one eye with some certainty that the remaining one has begun to deteriorate.

Their second son Robert, married with two small preteen children, was recently divorced when his wife left him for one of the neighbors. For Tomás and Hortencia, divorce as a possible alternative to marriage has always been something other people have done because of their lack of religious resolve, and they judge divorce to be in the same negative category as abortion. Both are culturally shocked, although they were very familiar with other examples from members of Hortencia's family of orientation who had also divorced. However, the greatest shock for both is the inability to see their grandchildren with the same frequency as before and the great chasm between them and their former daughter-in-law, who remarried shortly after the divorce.

The last negative development is that Tomás has only recently been diagnosed as suffering from the immunological breakdown of his biological system. After his having suffered incessant headaches, nausea, fainting spells, and imbalance, doctors had originally diagnosed his symptoms as due to high blood pressure. Such symptoms continued in spite of medication until tests revealed a high concentration of toxic chemicals in his body fat. Tomás had never informed his physicians that as an aircraft maintenance man in the Army National Guard for almost twenty years he had been responsible for spraying strong industrial cleaning solvents on aircraft engines and airframes without gloves or respiratory protection. When he was asked the obvious question as to why he did not wear protective clothing, his response was that such bulky gear interfered with his efficiency and productivity, and he did not want to be seen as a "lazy Mexican."

However, neither Tomás nor Hortencia have been lazy or lacking in motivation; they have worked hard and sacrificed, committing themselves to the notion of nation and support for individuals and issues that espoused conservative points of view. The military occupation representing that commitment is also a factor leading to Tomás's eventual demise in the not too distant future; neither their prayers nor their devotion can stop the process of physical degeneration.

Commentary

In spite of the obvious differences in class, generation, place in the life cycle, and occupation, all three case studies demonstrate the manner in which households both support and protect themselves from the effects of political and economic penetration in the region of the borderlands. The cases provide an insight into the way in which each household is unique and at the same time similar in its limited ability to incorporate as well as resist destructive aspects of regional change. For Larry Acosta, kinship and clustered relations were both supportive and conflictive, and his occupational participation had to be radically changed in order for him to retain his ethnic identity and cluster. Interestingly, occupational specialization provides the means of escape from possible destructive drug involvement. For the Araiza cluster, their investment in ritual and communications guarantee opportunity for exchange, this in spite of the fact that the transmitted "funds of knowledge" from the past do not include practical means of survival and are reduced to performance, history, and exhibition. For the Serrano cluster, in spite of the tragedy of illness and accident, the same basic process of network construction based on exchange and ritual emerges, and a very much intact fund of knowledge seems to have been maintained.

In addition, each household cluster has an accumulated and discarded fund of knowledge, which forms the basis of material survival and contains much of the previous generation's repertoire of information and skills used for subsistence. Thus, each case presented here has at its core either historical or contemporary rural experience important to the formations of the fund of knowledge particular to each household and cluster. Such funds also have the borderland region as an important historical and contemporary cultural reference point. What provides such funds with the potential for expression is that they are rooted in daily, useful skills and information of a very broad nature and include mechanical, historical, creative, computational, and design mastery.

Such funds are not only reposited within nuclear settings but are also part of the repertoire of information contained within the clusters of households, in which younger generational cohorts learn the substance of the corpus of information and have the opportunity to experiment with it in a variety of settings. They are, in fact, the currency of exchange not only between generations but also between households, and they therefore form part of the "cultural glue" that maintains exchange relations between kin. Such funds are dynamic in content and are altered according to changes in empirical reality, and they may even mitigate the more pernicious effects of household poverty.

The Emergence of the Mexican Child in Social Density[35]

» » »

There is one other dynamic aspect that should be considered in understanding the evolution of expectations for household clustering and the acquisition of funds of knowledge. The probability of such clusters being constructed and for their attending funds of knowledge continuing rests partially not only on an appropriate economic and social context to which they become rooted but also on the early expectations learned by children in such contexts. It is highly likely that, based on the findings on social density described in the case studies, the empirical evidence presented from our Tucson studies, and the substance of various works cited in the literature, U.S. Mexican children will emerge within social platforms in which they will learn and internalize analogous "thick" social expectations.

In regard to early childhood socialization, the empirical record on Mexican children is scant, and the emphasis has been on nonobservational attitudinal studies. The study by Vélez (1983) of mother-infant interaction, however, has provided an insight crucial to understanding the possible genesis of Mexican expectations and potentialities. Her work provides the probable link between early childhood experience and the formation of these expectations in clustered household settings and establishes the theoretical basis for understanding the phenomenon. The original postulate of the work asserted that there would be significant variations in the mothering styles of Mexican American and Anglo women, which could be attributed to cultural expectations including the probability of Mexican mothers' providing more proximal stimulation to infants, being more responsive to their infant's signals, and expressing such differences about infant rearing in their beliefs and values (Vélez 1983, 11).

In her findings, the actual interaction between mothers and infants showed little significant difference in frequency and quality. *"Yet of greater significance for the emergence of the social personality of the Mexican infant was in the social context in which such interaction actually took place and the role of others in the infant's early social experience"* (italics added; 1983, 80). Vélez found that even though she introduced a variety of social and economic controls to match her sample, the Mexican mothers' social density was much greater, contact with the infant and mother by other relatives was significantly more frequent, and greater stimulation of the infant by others was also statistically significant. Thus, the Mexican infant had a social context packed with tactile and sound stimulation, was surrounded by a variety of relatives, and at the behavioral level was seldom really alone. This last finding was also supported by the fact that even though Mexican children had their own rooms available, 92 percent slept in their parents' room, while 80 percent of Anglo children slept in their own room.

Although this was a working-class sample, we have the impression from our present study that the same phenomenon extends to middle-class Mexican American households. If this is the case, then it appears that the early "thick" social contextual surrounding may lead to the emergence of social expectations and dimensions different from non-Mexican populations that do not have equivalent social characteristics. Such differences, I would suggest, include the internalization of many other significant object relations with more persons, and expectation of more relations with the same people, and expectations of being attentive to and investing emotionally in a variety of such relations. The cultural expectation of *confianza* is cradled within such psychodynamic and psychosocial processes, and from these anticipations for exchange relations emerge. Such early experiences give cultural expectation its substance, verification, and reinforcement throughout the life cycle, as conditions select for its possible emergence.

These "thick contexts" are the social platforms through which the funds of knowledge of the cluster of households are transmitted. Thus, some understanding of their models of transmission gives an insight into the possible basis of cultural conflict with formal educational models that seek to shape Mexican children culturally and socially to the appropriate industrial model for the region and the nation.

Fund Transmission and the Basis for Cultural Conflict[36]

» » »

Further analysis of the manner of informational transmissions to children among U.S. Mexican households suggests additional support for the probability of culturally constituted methods; reveals emotive implications for children and their self-esteem; and identifies possible sources of cultural conflict for U.S. Mexican children in the schooling process.

Ensconced within "thick," multiple relations, Mexican children have the opportunity to visit and become acquainted with other household domains as well as the interior relationships. Such clustered households provide the opportunity for children to become exposed to an array of different versions of funds of knowledge. However, what is of particular importance is that the child is exposed not only to multiple domains but is also afforded the opportunity to experiment in each domain. From our findings in current and past studies,[37] the transmission process is largely an experimental one in which specific portions of the fund may be manifested by an adult, but the manner of learning is in the hands of the children themselves. Children will be expected to ask questions during the performance of household tasks; thus, the question-answer process is directed by the child rather than the adult. Once the answer is received, the child may emulate the adult by creating play situations of the learned behavior.

Another important aspect of this learning process is the wide latitude allowed for error as well as encouragement given for further experimentation. For instance, a child's observing and "assisting" an adult in repairing an automobile leads to attempts by the child to experiment on other mechanical devices as well as on "junk" engines that may be available. The usual adult direction is to "finish it yourself and try your best, no matter how long it takes." Even when the child is stuck at one point, the adult usually does not volunteer either the question or the answer. In such a sequence children are taught to persevere, experiment, manipulate, and to delay gratification.

Because of multiple occasions for experimentation, there are also multiple opportunities to fail and to overcome that failure in different domains. It is highly probable that the child may observe a variety of domains and become able to perform tasks adequately in one or more in which he/she has been successful.

A major characteristic in the transmission of funds of knowledge is that multiple household domains provide an opportunity for the child to be part of a zone of comfort that is familiar yet experimental, where error is not punitively dealt with and where self-esteem is not endangered. Multiple domains increase the probability of nonstressful and generally neutral zones of comfort where little criticism is expressed and a child cannot be faulted. When an adult is impatient and judgmental, the child often has the opportunity to experience other adults in different domains where such behavior is not present. The child thus learns very early to use a comparative approach to evaluate adults and to avoid discouraging or punitive persons because there are others available who are not.

Such zones of comfort also allow self-evaluation and self-judgment because the feedback process is in the hands of the child. The only exception is when the child is in danger or cannot physically perform a task. However, the outstanding characteristic that eventually develops for the child is contextual familiarity that is predictable and manipulable. If the probability of error may be great, the child is not encouraged to experiment. The child learns quickly that there are constraints, but these are so obviously in his/her favor that such an understanding becomes the underlying basis for zones of comfort. In emic terms, such zones, as well as the relationships that support their expression, become the basis of *confianza*[38] and place the child within the appropriate cultural frame for adulthood.

Zones of comfort and their cultural frame are threatened by the introduction of the traditional pedagogical approach to learning. From our observations, female children's play is very much marked by the emulation of teacher-originated-and-directed "playing school" sequences, in which there is little student-controlled interaction, but greater expectations of rote or noncreative responses to instruction.[39] In addition, the school model of learning and transmission is emphasized by parents during homework periods, with strong punitive measure either threatened or carried out if tasks are not completed. This use of the schooling model created one of the few sources of adult-child conflict in observed households. Such basic cultural conflict becomes further exacerbated when understood within a larger cultural framework of human emergence. For the U.S. Mexican adult, who has maneuvered through both culturally constituted zones of comfort and formal educational settings, self-doubt, negation, and cultural resistance will emerge together.

Ritual Cycles of Exchange

» » »

An important feature among others within household clusters is the development of ritual cycles of exchange and the many accompanying cultural expressions and emotive states. By ritual cycles of exchange, I mean a series of calendric and life cycle events, which are partially sacred and partially secular and seem to operate with some regularity throughout the calendar year among many households.[40]

The ritual cycles themselves are culturally "Mexicanized" in the sense that these events are largely part of a broad system of social exchange in which labor, assistance, information, and support are reciprocated between persons usually part of Mexican household clusters and their constituent social networks. The actual activities and exchange processes are in the hands of women, and men play a less important role in both the ritual processes themselves and in maintaining broader relations of exchange between clusters. Men are generally more involved in dyadic exchange between individuals rather than in multiple exchanges between clusters as are women. This condition cannot be related solely to a strict division of labor nor to a culturalist explanation;[41] for, in fact, among all Hispanic women, Mexican women have the highest percentage of their number in the paid labor force and

only slightly below that of all U.S. women.[42] They participate as productive wage earners outside the household,[43] and much of an entire
household's survival depends on women's income from informal and
formal economies.[44] Decisions regarding major expenditures are usually decided jointly rather than in the stereotypical manner supporting
a macho-dominant interpretation.[45] In addition, many Mexican households depend on joint income to mobilize resources between household
clusters, and the expenditures made in exchange activities are a part of
ritual events and behaviors.

Thus, the joint labor and limited income of both women and men
support individual households as well as broader networks within
household clusters. Because individual households depend on these
broader social networks to cope with the borderland's complex political and changing economic environment, members are willing to invest considerable energy and resources in maintaining good relations
(Vélez-Ibáñez and Greenberg, forthcoming).[46] One way they do this is
through family rituals: birthdays, baptisms, confirmations, quinceañeras (fifteen-year-olds' coming-out rituals), showers, weddings, Christmas dinners, outings, and visitations. These events not only bring
members of networks together ritually to become involved in exchange
relations, but staging them often requires members to cooperate by investing their labor or pooling resources. Moreover, such rituals broad-
cast an important set of signals both about the sponsor's economic
well-being and the state of social relations with other members—both
through lavishness and attendance. They signal the range of acceptable, socially approved relations and mark the changes brought about
by those who leave them and/or enter them.

Theoretical Framework

Ritual cycles of exchange cannot be properly contextualized
unless we place their performance within broader theoretical frame-
works and take into account the material and economic struggles of
U.S. Mexican households in the borderlands region. Theoretically, I con-
cur with Leach's long-held axiom that not only is ritual a symbolic representation occurring in "sacred" situations, but it also expresses patterns of symbols that reveal the system of socially approved "proper"

relations between individuals (1979, 15). However, socially approved proper relations are neither homogeneous or unstratified, nor are they shared in other than an "equivalent" manner. Such relations are distributed according to class, gender, and age and are learned and discarded according to the particular individual needs of participants. Therefore, all rituals, symbols, and emotive expressions are structured as equivalences rather than as duplications, and in the circumstances described here they emerge in processes tied to struggles of cultural identity, household maintenance and stability, and economic viability and survival.

U.S. Mexican Household Exchange and Support

Additionally, most households are often required to support more kin and friendship relations within and without the household, to maintain ritual and dense multiple social relations,[47] and to mobilize cooperation, reciprocity, and interdependence with others. Depending on kin or friends, however, is problematic. Besides the uncertainty experienced in the search for work, the frailty of having to depend on others for assistance for child care, household maintenance, and transportation leads people to make very determined efforts to enter primary labor markets. Such formal sector jobs are prized not just for better pay, but because they provide formal benefits that help underwrite the household's reproduction and lessen dependence on others.

Friends and kin, nevertheless, often provide a safety net and substantial aid in time of crisis, as well as in "normal" times, that is in the daily activities that constitute the life cycle. Exchanges occur in such a routine and constant fashion that people are hardly aware of them; and they take a variety of forms: labor services, access to information or resources (including help in finding jobs or housing or dealing with government agencies or other institutions), and various forms of material assistance besides money, such as putting up visitors.

Small favors are a constant feature of exchange relations. However, because they are reciprocal, they balance out in the long term and so are less important economically than the exchange of information and special funds of knowledge. Indeed, help in finding jobs, housing, better deals on goods and services, and assistance in dealings with institutions and government agencies are of far greater significance to survival than are the material types of aid these households usually provide each other.

Calendric Cycles and Their Social Functions

» » »

The repetitive yet syncretic series of sacred and secular calendric and life cycle rituals that operate throughout the year and are largely planned, implemented, and controlled by women in the household clusters can be thought of as the cultural "glue" that provides a type of consistency to the exchange process. These rituals are the basic templates for all other variations, distributions, and actual operational activities of exchange; and whoever is willing to help stage such family rituals is the person on whom one can count for other things.

In their simplest form these rituals unfold as they appear in figure 4.2. They are structured around two major calendar rituals: Christmas/New Year and Easter. The former is a terminating and initiating winter ritual, and the latter a summer activity punctuating the beginning of the second half of the entire cycle; many times both rituals are cross-border in function. The life cycle rituals, such as baptisms, confirmations, quinceañeras, weddings, and funerals, mark a secondary or minor level and fit between the cultural space of the major rituals. Interspersed throughout the year are myriad other smaller celebrations, such as birthdays, anniversaries, housewarmings, houseware parties, and ritualized visitations. As figure 4.2 shows, the secondary rituals serve as important spatial and temporal punctuation—something like semicolons—while the rest serve as types of commas, also serving as punctuation of and for events.

The Christmas/New Year Complex

The initial major ritual is a model for most of the social, cultural, and emotive processes essential to the rest. In one manner or another, the Christmas/New Year function sets off most of the characteristics of the other major ritual, secondary life rituals, and minor presentations throughout the cultural and temporal life of many U.S. Mexicans.

The initial Christmas/New Year "arena," from a process point of

Ritual Cycle of Exchange

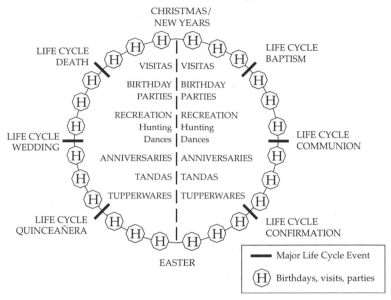

Figure 4.2 Ritual Cycles of Exchange. Source: Vélez-Ibáñez 1993: opposite 127.

view,[48] begins and ends the yearly cycle almost simultaneously. For most U.S. Mexicans, the Christmas ritual although focused on children and the "core" household heads is meant for most members of the cluster regardless of age; whereas the New Year celebration is generally for adults and consists of the individual nucleated households either attending or sponsoring parties or dances. Most of the Christmas expenses incurred are directed toward and support cluster activities, and great stress is placed on cooperating in the raising of proper funds for a sizable presentation gift to the core heads. In addition, gift exchange between cluster members is "tabbed" mostly by women; that is, an accounting of gift values and their evenness is noted. However, just as important is attention to detail in regard to the appropriateness of the gifts according to gender and age of children. This accounting process details whether adult members of the cluster are fulfilling their broader responsibilities of reciprocity. In this manner, the initial ritual also begins the "tabbing" process for the rest of the calendar year.

Christmas is also the ritual in which relations are emotively or psychologically reinforced in a distributive manner for the rest of the year. The specific parameters of the relationships of grandchildren, children, cousins, sisters, brothers, and in-laws are all laid out. Because it is impossible for all members of a household cluster to emotionally, psychologically, and socially invest in the same specific manner for every person, this is also the time when an individual's favorites are noted, preferences are displayed, and confirmations of the strongest and the weakest of relationships are noted and somewhat cemented. Relationships are then evaluated and further defined and changed as other major, secondary, and minor rituals unfold.

This "distributive" process, however, also allows individuals, who by personality preference are identified, social "breathing space." That is, the nonreciprocal, individualistic, and more egocentric person is somewhat "tabbed." In this manner, such persons are given their social due; and although participants in aspects of both ritual and social exchange processes, they are identified with different sets of expectations.

MAKING TAMALES: FREEZING RELATIONS FOR THE FUTURE

Among the most important social expectations illustrated during this period are those that children learn contextually. In keeping with other mechanisms that accentuate the expectation for multiplicity and density, children are exposed to participation, gift-giving, negotiating social preferences, and learning the "have to" of exchange during the preparation of tamales.[49] Tamales are steamed, corn husk wrapped, thick Indian corn dough crepes filled with red chili and meat, green chili and cheese, or a "dulce" of raisins, cinnamon, and sugar. Part and parcel of the importance of the dish is that recipes are the special province of older women, and great pride is taken in the entire preparation. Usually prepared two to three evenings before December 24, tamales are a labor-intensive activity requiring manual labor in the mixing and preparation of the corn paste, the cleaning of corn husks as the covering for the tamale itself, the cleaning and cooking of fresh chili pods, and the cooking of meats, fillings, and other dishes that accompany the main course. Each tamale is handmade with the corn dough spread on the leaf, the filling applied, and then the entire thing folded neatly into elongated crepes.

The actual number of tamales made depends on the size of the household cluster, the number of friends that eventually will be visited prior to Christmas, and the general finances of the cluster itself. It would not be unusual for six to eight women to make fifty to eighty dozen. During the tamale-making process, "heads are counted": i.e., who has been reciprocal during the year, the reputation of various household heads, statements of the peccadillos of men, and the "state" of various exchanges; and important for the purposes of this discussion, children are apprised of all these conversations. It is not unusual at this time for eighteen to twenty-four children from various households to be running about licking spoons, sticking their fingers in the corn dough, and using tortillas to make burritos from available fillings. Children are exposed to conversations, value judgments, and commentaries, which set up for them a context for evaluation of others and reinforce whatever expectations are articulated.

Women recapitulate a basic corporate memory and account for changes, provide new interpretations, and redefine relations. During this period cross-border relations are discussed: relatives tallied as to who has recently arrived, as well as general discussions about the need of gifts for less fortunate relatives in Sonora, Mexico. In addition, at this time relatives from Sonora may also visit and participate in events. They usually drop off a younger or marriage-eligible member to spend the Christmas holidays. Thus, during the tamale-making process a range of activities occurs, reinforcing social exchange among those present.

Men meanwhile play largely secondary roles. They are usually restricted to the heaviest labor such as carrying tubs of corn dough and heavy pots of meats and other fillings, and only sporadically are present while the actual tamale-wrapping process occurs. Very seldom do men actually ever wrap, cook, or otherwise function in any of the preparatory processes. They may gather to participate in other activities such as helping on some repair job within the household, drinking a beer or two, or watching a football game on television. Most men perceive the cooking activity as largely women's work and the conversations as "gossip." However, men in fact participate in their own "gossip" activities, exchanging information about the repair of automobiles and homes, leads to employment possibilities, and some discussion of cross-border events and relatives.

The tamales are distributed to each individual household belonging to the cluster; but in addition, a number of dozens are set aside and frozen not just for the future use of each household, but to distribute as part of the general exchange network that unfolds throughout the rest of the year. In an interesting sense, frozen tamales are the one currency that has no commodity value, only social value. In their frozen state they are distributed to those outside the immediate clusters and tend to broaden relations both outside and within the cluster. They remind those present of the labor, effort, and willingness to exchange labor for a share of food.

What is of crucial importance is that the entire process is in the hands of women and centrally important to the older women of the household cluster. They are the keeper of the tamale recipes that sometimes have been handed down by generations of other hands; and, in fact, each cluster has its own favorite specialty, and much is made of the origins and normative character of the recipes. In a way they are the lineal script by which entire households and their descendants may be recognized. Thus, some women will have inherited recipes emphasizing sweet tamales, others pork, others beef; and even the kind of chili that is used stands as a cognitive marker for specific families, their location of origin, and their degree of acculturation. Casting individual variation aside, most women will judge the degree of how spicy the chili is associated with how "Americanized" a recipe will be. Thus the older the recipe, the more Mexican and thus will mark how original and legitimate the tamale maker is as well. Therefore, older women prize their recipes but even more so pride themselves on handing down "un-Americanized" versions to their children.

The Easter/Semana Santa (Holy Week) Complex

Four months later, a series of transborder Easter activities emerges as the stimulus for the unfolding of the second half of ritual cycles. This major ritual is especially important in that of all the rituals throughout the year, this is the most likely one to include large numbers of relatives residing in the Mexican border states of Sonora, Chihuahua, Baja California, and Coahuila. Although many exchanges occur between relatives on each side of the border throughout the first half of the calendar year including the Christmas/New Year complex, the Easter ritual changes the exchange and focus from gifts to reviving relations across the border and within the household clusters them-selves. The northern Mexican relatives will celebrate Semana Santa in the United States by taking advantage of ten days or so of vacation time to participate in Easter rituals and to vacation with their U.S. rela-tives.[50] The women in the households on each side of the border are re-sponsible for initial communication, preparation of some of the foods, time scheduling, and sleeping arrangements.

Like the functions of the Christmas / New Year ritual, Easter is filled with opportunities for social tallying, rekindling reciprocal relations, the articulation of statuses for women and men, and more important, the continued preparation of children for future obligations. While the traditional Mexican observances include adherence to a series of Catho-lic rituals and restrictive dietary habits throughout the Lenten season, the U.S. versions are strongly influenced by commercialized American cultural practice. This becomes most apparent in the preparation of Easter food and its serving.

EASTER EGG PRODUCTION AND FOOD PREPARATION

Whereas tamale making is functionally important to children and older women, the Easter complex is not only focused on children once more, but men seem to play a more important role in the actual food prepara-tion. Older women are not in charge of the major food preparation activities that require intensive labor but usually do provide a single large dish, which everyone has enjoyed in the past. Much of the com-mensal preparation revolves around members of satellite households preparing different foods according to agreements between women, while men largely have their cooking roles confined to the preparation of barbecued and broiled meats. At times, leftover frozen Christmas tamales are brought out as extra dishes.

For the most part, the household clusters will meet either at a satel-lite household or will gather together at one of the local recreational parks on Easter Sunday, usually after having attended church services. Prior to their gathering, each household will prepare Easter eggs, give Easter baskets to children generally under seven or eight years of age, and mobilize the responsibility for specific dishes brought to the gath-ering. However, meat that will be cooked by men is not made part of the communal pot, but rather each individual male will make the pur-chase for their individual household members. Although this segmentation may actually break down when the cooking and eating begin, the purchase of meat, the preparation of the grill, and the actual cooking are in the hands of individual males rather than being a common responsibility of the entire cluster. Interestingly, individual food preparation by males is much more in keeping with the values of American individualism and nucleated households than with more reciprocal and communal Mexican values. In a sense, male roles are more like the labor market roles of fulfilling an instrumental function than the affective and instructional behaviors displayed by women. Men seem to reproduce their labor roles in the commodity domain rather than in the social domain of exchange relegated to women.

There are, however, instrumental roles carried out by women from Mexico during Easter. They will generally be integrated into the household routines, such as helping with child care, attending to spouses, and preparing food; they do serve a valuable labor function for their U.S. women relatives who are employed outside of the household. In part, they relieve their relatives from double labor tasks—those associated with paid wage production and those with nonpaid household production. In a sense, these relatives from northern Mexico provide relief to their U.S. counterparts for a short two-week period. The Mexican women also function to maintain the cross-border characteristic of U.S. Mexican households and contribute Mexican cultural funds of knowledge in a highly commercialized "American" process. Spanish is the primary language spoken, attendance at Spanish church services is encouraged, and even more important, social exchange and resulting expectations are transmitted from these relatives to U.S. Mexican children and adults. They balance out the effects of more American individualistic and commercial acculturation. Obviously, though, this process is a two-way exchange, and Mexico-resident children are very early introduced by their U.S. Mexican cousins to the practice of the U.S. egg preparation and celebration complex and demand an equivalent practice where they permanently reside. Indeed, many Mexican stores in the borderlands make Easter bunny piñatas for Mexican customers. Thus, among many other cross-border practices this work cannot discuss, this seemingly unimportant and innocuous "Easter bunny" practice contributes in a small way to the creation of a regional culture of the borderlands.

Discussion

The Christmas/New Year and Easter events are the major calendric ritual templates on which U.S. Mexican culture emerges and is socially displayed. They mark the two halves of the yearly cycle and are carefully monitored by the households involved and give meaning to the social relations articulated through other events. The terminal and initiating complex ends and sets off the energies and behaviors of exchange by processing and tallying who owes what to whom in a general reciprocal sense.

Between this beginning and end of cultural space and time and the next major marker, lie a series of life cycle rituals, as well as more secular practices incorporated as "normal" and expected behaviors into daily life. They fill out the entire first half but are "distributed" within and among household clusters and individuals according to the indeterminancies and uncertainties of daily life and according to the manner in which individuals and clusters are arranged in concurrent developmental cycles. Accidents, job losses, immigration raids, addictions, unintended love affairs, the tragedy of the unexpected death of a child—all those vagaries of living may make impossible and sometimes shape the best of intentions and expectations for exchange and for the quality of ritual participation of families and individuals. Coupled to a constantly emerging human developmental cycle, the first half of the calendric process merges into the second with the Easter complex functioning to give new meaning and life to the remaining series of minor secular and life cycle rituals.

The constant buzz of social activities that make up the entire calendric cycle are actions by which exchange and reciprocity are carried out in relatively uncertain and indeterminate economic and material conditions. In addition, however, the exchange activities, embossed within the major rituals and the dozens of minor life cycle versions, are the actual behaviors that articulate the shape and content of what constitute their "socially approved" dimensions.

Women's cultural transmission, discussion, and articulation roles, which are part and parcel of both major rituals and their food preparation activities, define them as the interpreters, carriers, and creators of Mexican culture in the United States and the borderlands. If women's

labor and their income are crucial to the maintenance of household stability, their ritual control is central to the maintenance and development of much of the operational and management behaviors that constitute Mexican culture and its exchange activities. Thus, Mexican
women of the Northern Greater Southwest on both sides of the imaginary border are primarily responsible for the planning, organization,
and implementation of not only the activities within household clusters but their cross-border versions as well. If, as Leach has indicated,
ritual expresses "socially approved" relations, then it is apparent that
women define what constitutes "approval," their social exchange relations, the roles that need to be fulfilled including those carried out by
men, and the articulation of the approved versions to children. Nevertheless, such roles, relationships, and their reproduction are not merely
reflections or cheap reproductions of relations of unpaid labor to a
wider capitalist economy. Rather, these are the best methods of thwart-
ing the worst features of economic and political appropriation. These
are thinking, active, creative human beings who have negotiated, ex-
perimented, and transformed in the best manner possible a series of
mechanisms, including the rituals described here, to mitigate and
"cushion" otherwise destructive and destabilizing political and economic pressures.

Rituals are largely managed by women, thus reflecting the central
contributions women make to household cultural and social stability.
As has been described, the border area is a dynamic region of rapid
economic and social development and dysfunction for Mexicans. Cultural appropriation, economic exploitation, and physical expulsion
have been not unusual pressures that Mexicans have had to face. The
cultural templates women operate have been important mitigating factors to these pressures. In this context women from both north and
south of border transcend nation-state definitions of cultural identity.
Rather than to simply accept what constitutes an "American" or "Mexican" according to state myths, women negotiate and manipulate social
relations crucial to the formation and articulation of Mexican cultural
identity regardless of border.

Women, in fact, negotiate multiple dimensions of cultural meaning
within their household clusters through ritual. They define the contexts
and operations for gender relations with men and the use of their labor
as that of peripheral personnel. They expose children simultaneously

to women's versions of social reality, including the ability to negotiate, transform, and tally important reciprocal exchanges with relatives and friends. Children learn early on to begin the tallying process themselves and to discover what constitutes "socially approved" relations.

Lastly, women as the central figures within Mexican cultural practices may serve as the key informational sources for larger social and cultural change. What language women use, whether they keep up or fail to keep up exchange relations, whether they participate or not in the expected rituals, and whether they manage or not the operational activities that constitute them will determine the efficacy of Mexican cultural life in the United States and particularly the borderlands region. If this proposition is correct, then future research must concentrate not only on the meanings and defined parameters of ritual but more important in whose hands they reside.

Conclusions
» » »

This chapter has illustrated that U.S. Mexican households in the borderlands have long been part of the emerging and dynamic economic and technological transformations in the region. That part has usually involved households in the mobilization and creation of exchange relations that serve as the basis for resistance, defense, and acceptance of political and economic pressures. Even though it is accurate to suggest that increasing specialization threatens the funds of knowledge upon which such relations rest, nevertheless, the same basic construction and reconstruction of exchange based on social density seem to emerge. However, such emergence seems to take different forms depending on the life cycle stage.

As has been indicated, the structural and class complexity of the population, as well as proximity to the border, partially influences the "shape" and character of the household clusters described, such as the "cross-border" and "balanced" households with their generational "hopscotching" phenomena. In some ways, U.S. Mexican households occupy a positive position in relation to sudden changes in economy and policy. They are able to bring to bear more members of larger households to generate income. They are able to mobilize relationships and skills in order to support household members who need technical assistance. They are also able to cross political frontiers to take advantage of available economic opportunities to offset limited income. The negative aspect is that blue-collar occupations are dangerous and place men, especially, at occupational risk. Ideologically such households may also become hypnotized by national cultural prisms that accentuate patriotism and reduce regional cultural history to self-destructive ethnic reference. The Americanization educational programs of the past and the monocultural Anglo-dominant schooling of the present create an ethnic situation of cultural conflict, self-doubt, and uncritical acceptance of destructive ethnic stereotypes. In this sense, even the positive survival values of clustered living are offset by national stereotypes and educational values, which accentuate individualism and self-serving vertical mobility. These deny the cultural efficacy of the population by framing them within derogatory stereotypes so that U.S. Mexicans are reduced to being "lazy Mexicans" who have to compensate for apparent deficiencies by working harder, in more dangerous occupations, or even being willing to give up their health. The paradox is that some part of the population comes to believe what has been fabricated and denies its own cultural validity.

Cultural conflict is certain when educational institutions have constructed very opposite operational and pedagogical principles that may not take advantage of the cultural and practical skills based on an industrial form of instruction that Mexican children carry to the schooling process. Nevertheless, children in household clusters have the opportunity to emerge surrounded by dense relations and contexts, in which zones of comfort for learning and experimentation exist. The zones of comfort provide children with the opportunity to learn by trial and error, without much negative reinforcement, and broad arenas of social and historical funds of knowledge not probable in nuclear families.

Finally, Mexican household clusters of the Northern Greater Southwest in Tucson, Arizona, and probably in equivalent regions, are not dependent upon residential contexts for exchange but upon consanguineous or affinal relationships. Unlike the highly mobile, nuclear-based familial systems of the U.S. middle class for which neighborhood and institutions are the major means of social and economic articulation outside of the immediate nuclear family, for Mexican middle- and working-class household clusters, exchange is primarily focused on expanding familial consanguineous and affinal networks. These provide the social platforms that help develop much of the Hispano / Mexicano population into creative, nonpassive, resistant human beings. In spite of being part of every change in industrial technology and form of organization, of being unsettled and resettled by need and deportation, and of being pushed into an assimilationist perspective regarding language and cultural identity, Hispano / Mexicano households remain vibrant and creative units because of their ability to mobilize relations in time of need and to reinforce relations through ritual; and Hispanas / Mexicanas are the primary agents of change and stability.

The question of patriarchy is not denied, but its complexity must be discussed within much broader empirical contexts than single gender studies or studies of households in Tucson, Arizona. Regardless of context, the issue is too important to leave to opinions, ideological positions, or gender posturing. Hispano / Mexicano households of the Northern Greater Southwest are too important and fragile and are in such stressful economic, political, social, psychological, and cultural conditions that the issue cannot be left to academic hallways to be solved. The "distribution of sadness" among Hispano / Mexicano households, as chapter 5 will describe, is simply too overwhelming.

CHAPTER 5

» » » » »

The Distribution of Sadness:

Poverty, Crime, Drugs,

Illness, and War

WHAT I MEAN by "the distribution of sadness" is that there is no doubt that Mexicans throughout the Northern Greater Southwest into the next half century (to 2050) will face great sadness because of the effects of miseducation, poverty, physical and mental illness, crime, drugs, and overparticipation in wars. All of these are disseminated and will continue to be disseminated to varying degrees within the population, despite clusters of exchange and the great investment in social relations, children, and a sense of place and space.

Such sadness will be distributed among U.S. Mexicans who numbered over 13 million of the total Hispanic population of almost 22 million in 1990; and it is highly likely that the U.S. Mexican population will more than triple that figure by the year 2050, given that it increased by more than 50 percent between 1980 and 1990 (see figure 5.1), and the various versions of sadness will be distributed accordingly. As figure 5.2 illustrates, the annual rate of growth of all "Hispanics" is approximately 10 percent per year; so that the "browning" of the Greater Northern Southwest is not only inevitable, it is in process as this is written, and all Hispanics will number over 80 million by 2050.[1]

By subgroup, as figure 5.3 shows, growth is dramatic, with the Mexican population of the United States almost doubling between 1970 and

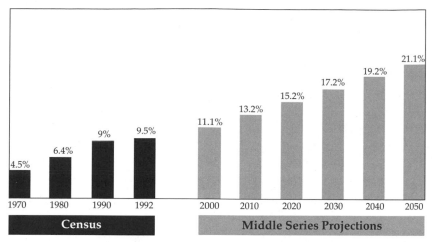

Figure 5.1 Hispanic Population: 1970–2050 (Percent of Total Population).
Source: U.S. Bureau of the Census, Current Population Reports, *Hispanic Americans Today*, 1993: 2.

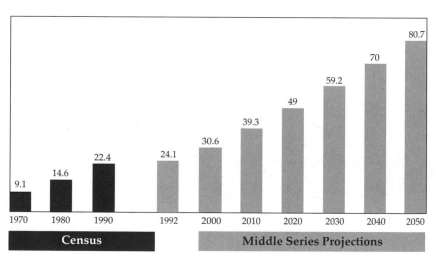

Figure 5.2 Hispanic Population Growth: 1970–2050 (In Millions). Source: U.S. Bureau of the Census, Current Population Reports, *Hispanic Americans Today*, 1993: 2.

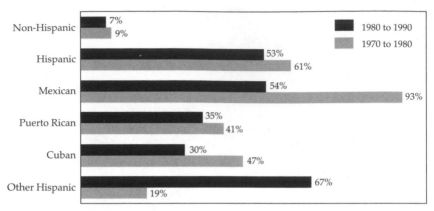

Figure 5.3 Hispanic Population Growth by Type of Origin: 1970–1990 (In Percent). Source: U.S. Bureau of the Census, Current Population Reports, *Hispanic Americans Today*, 1993: 3.

1980 and increasing by half of that again between 1980 and 1990. Similarly but not as dramatically, the Puerto Rican population increased by 41 and 35 percent respectively during those periods, while the most dramatic increase other than Mexicans are the Central and South Americans who increased 67 percent between 1980 and the present. Given the political conditions of Central American countries in general, with Cuba on the brink of dissolution, and indigenous peoples no longer willing to bear governmental inaction, it is safe to suggest that these trends will not lessen.

Mexicans are the youngest at 24 years of age among all groups, with Puerto Ricans at 27 and Central and South Americans at 28.5, with quite a percentage of those between 0 and 14. It does not take a great deal of statistical knowledge to know that large cohorts wait in the wings to enter schools. As the "population pyramid" of figure 5.4 illustrates even more dramatically, when a bar for "Mexican," aged 0 to 5, is added, the bar percentage jumps to 12 percent of that cohort, which is almost 75 percent larger in proportion to the "other than Anglo" population of the same age, in large part due to birth rates almost twice that of the Anglo population.[2] Finally, figure 5.5 shows the present size of the "Hispanic" population in thousands.

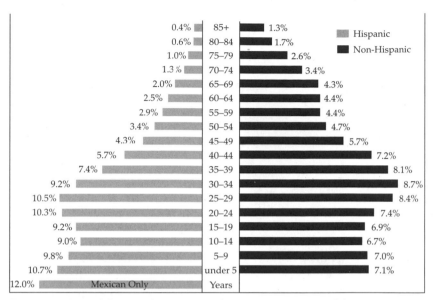

Figure 5.4 Age of the Population: 1990. Source: U.S. Bureau of the Census, Current Population Reports, *Hispanic Americans Today*, 1993: 7.

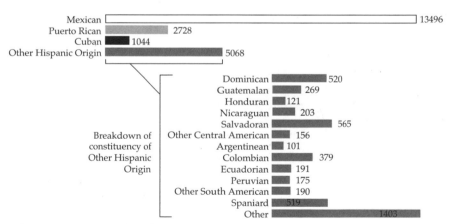

Figure 5.5 Hispanic Population by Type of Origin: 1990 (In Thousands). Source: Bureau of the Census, Current Population Reports, *Hispanic Americans Today*, 1993: 4.

The increase in population over time, the youthfulness, and the large numbers of children either waiting to enter school or already in the "pipeline" are central to understanding the distribution and effect of the various "sadnesses" from which the population suffers and in some cases suffers more than other populations of the region. From every reputable demographic source available, there is no doubt that the single most important predictor of the population's mental, physical, economic, social, or cultural well-being is the acquisition of a high-quality educational experience.[3] While there are too many other factors to exclude out of hand, such as structural factors like plant closings, "restructuring of the economy," English language acquisition, the opportunity structure, ages of the cohort in question, recent immigrant status, and commoditization and ethnocentrism, these by themselves are not as successful at predicting the well-being of most of the Mexican population either born in or having migrated to the United States.

Therefore, it is important to consider that each of the ills (poverty, crime, drugs, the lack of mental and physical well-being, and overparticipation in wars) is directly associated with high-quality educational success. I stress high-quality for the simple reason that even though educational attainment may provide the road to economic well-being, it may also create such cultural conflict that it leads to less than successful emotional adaptation. Individuals who are told to erase themselves culturally in order to be "good Americans" may very well suffer from extreme internal conflicts that do not portend mental well-being. Thus, a high-quality educational experience does not deny the efficacy of language and culture but utilizes their strengths as resources for instruction.[4]

In addition, the "quality" of the school is directly associated with the expectations for success projected to children, the type of community relation that will be created with the children's homes, and the emotive and intellectual support teachers provide to students. Thus, "poor" neighborhoods in which Mexican children live are frequently buttressed by "poor" schools with poor equipment, physical plants, and less-than-adequate hardware needed for instruction. Coupled with endemic low expectations subtly and unsubtly projected by teachers and administrators, who depend on "normative" national tests for instruction rather than normative expectations for success, the precious talents, creativity, and intelligence of too many Mexican children are wasted and seldom enhanced in poor schools.

The Population and Educational Gap

» » »

In California and Texas, over 50 percent of the K-12 public school enrollments are minority students and in both states overwhelmingly Mexican.[5] In every region of the Northern Greater Southwest this same trend in school demographics is similar, with Arizona, New Mexico, and Colorado all showing an increase in the number of Mexican children in public schools.[6] What is worrisome is the fact that perhaps as many as 50 percent of this large potential "bump" of students will not complete high school. Although high school completion will not necessarily assure economic well-being, it is more than certain that without a high school certificate Mexican students are more likely guaranteed economic failure.

The "bottom line" for the Mexican population is that we suffer a lack of educational attainment. In 1990 almost 50 percent of this population aged 25 years and over had not graduated from high school.[7] At the other end of the continuum, only 20 percent of the Mexican population had any education beyond high school.[8] When compared to the fact that Anglos have an 80 percent high school completion rate and more than 45 percent with education beyond high school, these differences become quite stark, and their implications for economic well-being obvious.[9]

There are, however, other mitigating factors that have to be sorted out. Of the total 13.4 million Mexicans in the United States, 67 percent are U.S. born, while 33 percent are not.[10] When high school graduation rates are sorted out between the two groups of those between 18 and 24 years of age, the latter fares much worse, with 32 percent of the U.S. born graduating from high school and only 19 percent of non-U.S. born.[11] The last group will then be at the highest economic risk. This is shown in part by the fact that U.S.-born Mexican families have a mean income of over $32,000, while non-U.S.-born Mexican families have a mean income of over $26,000. Although it is not possible to disaggregate naturalized from non-naturalized, those who entered between

1980 and 1990 will be less likely to be naturalized, and this group has a mean income of only $21,415.[12] This is further illustrated by the fact that non-U.S-born families suffer a 27.4 percent poverty rate, while U.S.-born families suffer a 20 percent rate. Those Mexican families that arrived between 1980 and 1990 have a poverty rate of almost 35 percent, while those arriving before 1980, a rate of 22.7 percent, which is especially meaningful when only 9 percent of all Anglo families suffer poverty.[13] The question will remain open if the most recently arrived will be assured the same opportunity structure as those who arrived prior to 1980 (the latter having already almost matched the U.S.-born Mexicano in poverty rates). In a sense, if there is an "even labor playing field," the most recently arrived for the most part will emulate previous cohorts, and most will neither remain in poverty circumstances nor will they be subject to their negative implications.

However, non-U.S.-born Mexican children may be at greater temporary risk in that a formula for failure for a portion of the cohort is created, combining poverty, problems in school, and occupational insecurity. That is, the most recently arrived cohort of children will live in much more precarious economic circumstances and, therefore, be subject to greater stressors than earlier cohorts. If economic structures remain stable, in the year 2000, 80 percent of the 1990 cohort will not be in poverty and will be more than likely to match the 22 percent discussed above. Meanwhile, however, in 1990 these children will be more susceptible to greater stresses than their U.S.-born counterparts, and a portion of these children may be selected for failure.

A study of 849 U.S.-born and 312 non-U.S.-born Mexicans (aged 14–21) found that problems with school, participation in the work force, and poverty-level family income were compounded for a segment of non-U.S.-born Mexican youth and led to a more devastating formula for failure. However, one-fifth of the U.S.-born youth also failed to complete high school, one-fourth were unemployed, and one-fifth lived in a poverty income household.[14] For a segment of both groups, the same formula for failure was "structured" into the fabric of their economic, social, and cultural platforms, and a portion of their cohorts entered into a poverty/miseducated/underemployed formula. What must also be kept in mind is that the great majority of both groups within this sample did complete high school, did become employed, and did not live in poverty in spite of the formula.

In the long run what is more important is that while there have been significant improvements in educational attainment in the last twenty years, these are continually set back by the horrendous dropout rates of 45 to 50 percent in many areas where our population resides, including the Midwest. Fifteen percent of the Mexican population have less than a fifth-grade education and half as many a bachelor's degree or more.[15]

Thus, whatever social ills are present now will more than likely worsen for selected segments of the Mexican population, given the present distribution of educational "sadness," which recycles poverty, undereducation, crime, violent death in wars, from drugs, and from illness for a portion of that population. All of these are closely associated one to the other, and they arise from poor economic and social conditions that lessen the probability of mechanisms and values like clustering, exchange, and *confianza* (mutual trust), which would alleviate those conditions among the 75 percent or so of the *working* working-class population of Mexicans. They are all, however, closely associated with the lack of a high-quality education.

In almost every "sad" category, in the Northern Greater Southwest, Mexicans are overrepresented in proportion to their percentage of the total population. Essentially we are underrepresented in educational attainment and overrepresented by inordinately high rates of overage status in schools and dropout rates from primary, middle, and secondary schools.[16] The saddest indicator, however, for Mexican children under 18 years of age is their overrepresentation in poverty rates of almost 40 percent compared to 13.1 percent of Anglos.[17] This single indicator illustrates the almost circular relationship between youth, poverty, and educational inequity.

Gangs as Sadness
» » »

A behavior sensationalized in much of print or electronic media is the tendency of some youths to join "Hispanic" gangs. Movies, television programs, newspaper and magazine articles, as well as scholarly work, all seem to emphasize the increasing violence, deviant behavior, drug-related crimes, and loathsome behavior of gangs. However, what is not emphasized is that they constitute an important though small segment of young people, between 3 and 10 percent in

Mexican barrios; most of the gang members come from poorer homes than those youths from the same neighborhood who are not gang members.[18] In addition, some children who join gangs come from households with female heads, with more children in the family, and in more dire economic circumstances than other comparable barrio households.[19] Given that single female heads of household below the poverty level with young children under 18 years of age constitute only 7.5 percent of all Mexican families, this source accounts for very few gang members, and it must be assumed that other sources provide greater numbers.[20] In fact, most gang members emerge from families with both parents.[21] For the most part these families are in poor economic circumstances, unemployed, with six or seven persons per family, and poorly educated. Only about one-third of the fathers have a high school education, and parents who were born in Mexico have received less than four years of schooling. Of this last segment, 20 percent of the fathers and 14 percent of the mothers have received no schooling at all, and only 19 and 22 percent of the fathers and mothers respectively have finished high school.[22]

Regardless of nativity and depending on which generation of gang members are discussed (because they emerge hierarchically and chronologically according to different cultural characteristics), the most recent "cliques" are characterized by coming from families in which large numbers of mothers enter the workforce even when fathers are present.[23] This illustrates the increasing necessity for dual incomes in an economy of ever-decreasing opportunities. However, this characteristic is not essentially different from that of many of the poor households in the same barrio whose offspring do not belong to gangs. Therefore, regardless of the strains of nativity and poverty, economic factors by themselves are insufficient to generate gang membership.[24]

There are other factors that most recently seem to be necessary for gang membership, one of which is the appearance of internal negative dynamics associated with spousal abuse, adult dissatisfaction with life's course, and emotional instability especially of fathers, many of whom are alcoholics who act out their own occupational, educational, and social frustration.[25] Another factor, according to one study, is that 38 percent of the homes of young persons who joined gangs had someone in the home who was disabled, usually one of the parents.[26] Also associated with this characteristic, over 50 percent of the homes in which members of gangs were growing up suffered a death of one of its family members, with 30 percent of these the loss of the father and 26 percent the loss of a sibling.[27] With such disability and morbidity "distributions," usually due to occupational dangers, it is little wonder that "acting out processes" become normative in such households.

This "acting out" by parents, however, leads to shoving selected individuals out of the household; these young people then join up with other versions of themselves. The "streets" with all of their attending ecological dangers, become the "public home" of these young males and females. They create their own sources of emotional satisfaction, release pent-up anger and frustration created by outside sources, and then are reinforced, buttressed, and maintained by the "streets." Theirs becomes a peer group based on *confianza* (mutual trust), sibling feelings of reciprocity, reliance, and expressive styles. These are, in fact, the only sources of emotional satisfaction in a largely unsatisfactory emotional platform of psychological and social danger.

The *cholos'* (self-defined term for gang member) insistence on defending turfs with *placas* (gang signs and graffiti), attacks on nonresidential youths, and the return attacks as retribution are not unlike some of the expected behaviors of adults who find their homes under siege by seen and unseen forces. For *cholos*, however, theirs is a double bind in that the "streets" are not theirs to own, and they are rejected by the institutions that control them including police, businesses, schools, churches, community service agencies, and most private and private corporations that could employ them. Thus, as gang members, a maladaptive set of behaviors, mind-sets, and created cultural mappings emerge that take a life of their own and introduce younger members into *la vida loca* (the crazy life) and violence. As one member of a girl's gang described what she did to make her "homeboys" and "homegirls" happy: "Anything, go up to a person and stab them, rob a store, come out with the money, and party down with my homegirls and homeboys."[28] This is the essence of *la vida loca*.

Sadly, happiness is expressed as destruction: physical, psychological, and cultural, for this very small but important part of the Mexican population. Nevertheless, many interventions other than police suppression do in fact have positive impacts on gang members; and the one overriding intervention that does function is the availability of occupational opportunities and community-based activities.[29] Continued reliance on the police force and suppression as the major means of eliminating gangs creates conditions for further duplication and extended violence. Arrests and convictions "glue" the thirteen-year-old into a cultural system whose only honorific is recognition received from newspapers for his arrest and the "time" done in jail or prison. In a kind of insane spiral of actions intended to be in opposition to its outcome, police suppression further brutalizes an already brutalized youngster who responds with more violence and expressed rage.

One outcome is that gang members join with drug-based or prison gangs, then the emotional and psychological need-based rationale for group membership is taken over by economic relations of profit and its concomitant violence and homicide having to do with the protection of drug turf rather than residential territoriality. These sub-groups then are no longer emotional cohorts but become highly dangerous, effectively "flat," and tragically disengaged social outcasts whose main occupational commitment is the support of various versions of drugs such as marijuana, heroin, PCP, crack, cocaine, and the newly invented "designer" drugs.

It does not have to be this way. In a moving conclusion to his memories of *la vida loca*, Luis J. Rodríguez says, "If there was a viable alternative, they would stop. If we all had a choice, I'm convinced nobody would choose *la vida loca*, the 'insane notion'—to 'gang bang.' But it's going to take collective action and a plan."[30] So far there is neither; and as long as there is no place or space, cultural or social, from which our youngsters can receive recognition, affection, and feelings of value, there can be no respite for either those that join gangs or those that suffer their responses.

Crime as Sadness

» » »

Tied to *la vida loca* is crime, but not all crime among Mexicans can be tied to *la vida loca*. Crime, which is central to contemporary American concerns, has always been an issue for Mexicans but of a double-edged sort. First, for Mexicans there has been, and for the most part continues to be, an "uneven judicial playing field," in which the likelihood for arrest, detention, conviction, and extreme sentencing is much greater than for other segments of the population of the Northern Greater Southwest. Second, an overwhelming number of Mexicans are very conservative regarding crime and the moral underpinnings of law and justice. How these two obviously contradictory conditions can exist in the same time and place is closely associated with the process of criminalization of some behaviors.

For example, the criminalization of marijuana and its association with Mexicans in the United States emerged in the aftermath of the development of the Federal Bureau of Narcotics (FBN). With the passage of the Uniform Narcotics Law in 1936, the bureau decided to make use of newspaper articles published in the 1920s, which had previously been ignored, concerning Mexican marijuana use and arrests. Prior to 1934 the bureau had denied there was a marijuana problem and that the newspapers of the time had exaggerated both use and linkage to the Mexican population. After the rise of the FBN's new director, Harry Anslinger, the organization shifted its position to that described. He and others argued that Mexicans had introduced marijuana smoking via the Southwestern United States and that it had victimized the nation's youth. The culprits specifically responsible for this victimization were Mexican farm laborers.[31] What is most curious about this claim was that among 90,000 Mexicans in California in the period 1928–1932, an average of only seventy-five cases per year of drug-related charges were made against the Mexican population according to the California Narcotics Commission. The same statistics were not only available to the Federal Bureau of Narcotics, but in fact they used the California Narcotics Commission reports to substantiate their insistence on criminalizing the use of marijuana.[32]

However, almost fifty years later narcotics had become the most important single rationale for Mexican incarceration. Most other offenses were associated and continued to be associated with drugs, so that by 1975 more than 50 percent of all Mexican prisoners were addicted to heroin use.[33] At California's Lompoc prison alone, more than 70 percent of Mexican prisoners were addicted to heroin; and given the state's harsh minimum sentences for narcotics offenses, Mexicans serve longer time for narcotics-related offenses than any other group.[34]

What can be said of the Mexican prisoner population is that for the most part addiction-related criminal behavior has little to do with morality and law breaking per se but does have a great deal to do with the underlying pain—emotional, psychological, social, and cultural—

that a segment of the population suffers.[35] Marijuana, heroin, PCP, crack and contemporary cocaine use have their direct association to overriding psychic pain rather than to legal inattention. For much of the Mexican population, drugs are symbolic of social ostracism due to racism, ethnocentrism, miseducation, and economic suppression rather than of a different set of moral precepts.

In 1970 the United States Commission on Civil Rights conducted an analysis of the administration of justice in the Northern Greater Southwest, after receiving numerous complaints by Mexicans of physical and verbal abuse and harassment by police; exclusion from grand juries; lack of defense counsel; discriminatory use of bail; and few or no Mexicans in law enforcement.[36] In every one of these categories, the commission found serious police abuse, violence, discourtesy, excessive use of force, few or no resources for these conditions, no representation on grand juries, bail abuse, lack of counsel, and lack of Mexican law enforcement officers.[37]

Fifteen years later, studies conducted by various researchers concerning the dismissal, convictions, and sentencing length of Mexicans did not agree as to whether there was so-called ethnic bias against Mexicans or not. What becomes even more important but was not mentioned by the researchers was the overrepresentation of Mexicans arrested and incarcerated and their eventual impact on the population itself. For example, in a 1984 study of 10,000 cases, researchers looked at differences in treatment of Mexicans, Anglos, and African American defendants in Los Angeles County. They found little difference in judicial treatment, but the most curious part of this study was the number of defendants these represented: over 2,500 Mexicans, 2,300 Anglos, and over 5,000 African Americans.[38] The researchers never asked the most important "up front" question, why the disparity between the percentage of those arrested and that of the demography of the general population: in 1980 Mexicans and African Americans combined represented a total of only 30 percent of the total population of Los Angeles County. Why was there overrepresentation in the cases selected when they did not select overrepresentation for statistical reasons?

Such conditions, of course, are not new, and the overrepresentation of Mexicans in prison over a hundred year period is easily substantiated. Between 1876 and 1909, 50 percent of the prison population of the Arizona Territorial Prison was Mexican, while only 30 percent of the general population was Mexican; and by 1973 with only a very small percentage of the U.S. population composed of Mexicans, the percentage in federal prisons was 18.4 percent.[39]

In another study of over 10,000 cases of a random sample of first, second, third, and fourth arrests of individuals, and from a population of fifth or later arrests, the "breakout" by population was almost evenly distributed, with slightly over 50 percent Anglos and 50 percent Mexicans and African Americans.[40] Similarly, in yet a third California study of sentencing of felons in a Fresno, California, random sample, 41 percent of the sample was Mexican, 22 percent African American, and 37 percent Anglo. Given that the city of Fresno is only 18 percent Mexican and the county population 30 percent, the same overrepresentation becomes apparent.

The most pressing and undoubtedly distressing statistics, however, are those associated with youths. In 1993 the California Youth Authority reported that 15.3 percent of their incarcerated population were Anglos, African Americans 33 percent, and 44 percent of the offenders were Mexican youth largely between 16 and 19 years of age. Ten years earlier, in 1983, Mexican youth had constituted slightly over 31 percent of the incarcerated population, while African Americans made up 38 percent, and Anglos, 28 percent. In 1970 Anglos were 40 percent of the incarcerated youthful population, African Americans over 30 percent, and Mexicans only slightly over 18 percent![41] Thus, while already overrepresented in 1970 in relation to the general population, twenty years later the incarceration of Mexican youth had increased by over 100 percent while the Anglo population had decreased by half.[42]

Similarly for all the adult felon population of California, new admissions in 1991 consisted of over 37 percent who were Mexican, 29.3 percent Anglo, and 27.8 percent African American. Ten years earlier, in 1981, the percentage of newly admitted felons consisted of 25.7 percent Mexican, 38 percent Anglo, and 35.2 percent African American. In 1971 only 16.8 percent of newly admitted felons were Mexican, 28.3 percent African American, and 53.5 percent Anglo! Like the distribution for youths, the percentage of new adult Mexican felons in twenty years had increased by over 100 percent, while Anglos had decreased by almost half.[43] It is highly probable that these percentages reflect a created "tracking" system that guarantees an almost lineal prison career for California Mexican youths.

What then do these various percentages mean in relation to the Mexican population as a whole, not just for California but for the region? These data are more than likely repeated throughout the area but in an exacerbated manner in California primarily due to the economic restructuring of the state, the loss of employment potentials to the population, and the strict narcotics-associated sentencing laws. For the past half century, the Mexican population has always been in the most precarious of economic positions, so that the initial overrepresentation of the population in the prison population a hundred years ago reflects basically the same rationale in the present. When the specter of racist and ethnocentric attitudes overlies the economic conditions faced by Mexicans in the region, these selective factors have a tendency to choose parts of the population most in need and susceptible to possible criminalized or criminal activity.

However, what seems most apparent is that there is a painful and emotional injury present for these segments of the population that are not amenable to punishment, further incarceration, or police suppression. Even though small portions of the general Mexican population become part of this dynamic of pain, drugs, and incarceration, the increase over the last twenty years is more than sufficient to stimulate the thinking out of carefully articulated plans to mitigate the results of crime and incarceration and to enhance opportunities for this segment of the population, so they can find the cultural and social place and space that support their needs.

Mental Illness as Sadness

» » »

How and why mental illness is "distributed" among Mexicans are important questions. The reason is very simple, and the response provides an insight into the "cultural places" and "psychic spaces" that Mexicans have found. "Epidemiologic" studies, which provide an answer to the questions and give a comparative base from which to gauge that answer, use very large samples selected for "representativeness" of the characteristics of the population; and the selection of respondents is such that the responses are probably valid for the region's population as a whole, and the same questions can be asked again with almost the same reliable responses.

So far much of the best work shows that the distribution of "depression" among Mexicans can be divided between those who are English dominant and those Spanish-language dominant. The latter group "scored" significantly higher in depression than either Anglos or English-dominant Mexicans.[44] In addition, within the Spanish-dominant group females had much higher scores than males; and although educational attainment was not statistically significant, those with lower depression scores had higher educational achievement.[45]

By and large, however, Spanish-dominant Mexicans as a group had significantly greater levels of other types of symptoms such as anxiety and scored higher than either Anglos or English-dominant Mexicans. Divorced Spanish-dominant women had the lowest scores of any marital category within the group, but here education was directly related to anxiety scores, with those with less than nine years of school having very high symptoms. Among English-dominant Mexicans, those with less than four years of education had the highest scores, and females had much higher indications than males. Nevertheless, both males and females with the lowest educational attainment had the highest average scores.[46]

Education continues to play a very significant role within the Spanish-dominant group in that the highest level of psychosocial dysfunction "scores" were found among those with the lowest educational attainment, and those with the lowest scores had more than a high school degree. Females within the group again had higher scores, but married couples had higher scores than either the divorced or widowed. Similarly among the English-dominant group women had higher scores than men, and women who had less than nine years of schooling had the highest scores.[47]

All these scores, however, do not indicate "mental illness" but rather are indicators of the distribution of mental health characteristics within segments of the population that have a propensity toward or express anxiety, depression, or psychosocial symptoms. The data from these studies do show the inverse relationship between formal education and mental health scores and demonstrate that higher rates of disorder are found among those lowest in educational attainment. The reason the educational attainment relationship is so important is that income and education are more closely associated for Mexicans, and especially the Spanish-dominant segment, than other cultural groups.[48]

Similarly other studies have shown the same relationship between depressive symptoms among U.S. Mexicans and the lack of educational attainment.[49]

The greater question, however, seems to be whether Mexicans suffer greater mental health problems than other segments of the population. Most studies show that, in fact, Mexicans have higher depression rates, higher levels of depressive symptoms, and a higher rate of diagnosed mental illness than Anglos or African Americans.[50] Within the population, farm workers, first-generation Mexicans, those with low educational attainment, and those in maritally disrupted relationships are in greatest jeopardy.

A sample of youths was tested for symptoms of depression, its relation to the use of inhalants, and its effects on their self-esteem. For the most part youths using inhalants had a high prevalence of depression and suffered high levels of familial conflict and low self-esteem.[51] Their mothers especially also showed high levels of depression, high levels of anxiety, learned helplessness, and suicidal tendencies. In turn these mothers' symptoms were related to lack of educational attainment, alcohol and drug use, little familial support, unemployment, and their child's depression. What was central to understanding childhood depression was the importance of the relation of the mother's depression and that of their children. The greater the depression of the mother, the more their children used drugs, were more depressed, and made more suicide attempts.[52] When combined with the effects of perceived racial discrimination, which is related to depression, lack of self-esteem and lack of self-worth, there is a high probability that depression, anxiety, and feelings of worthlessness will also emerge in selected segments of the Mexican population and especially among the unemployed, under-educated, first generation, and maritally disrupted.[53]

Physical Illness as Sadness

»   »   »

In the same way that we understand the "distribution" of symptoms regarding mental illness, so too this approach gives us an insight into the way in which Mexicans are susceptible to specific physical illnesses and disabilities. There is enough evidence to show that Mexicans have higher death rates than non-Hispanic populations from cirrhosis of the liver, tuberculosis, diabetes, infectious and parasitic diseases, circulatory diseases, certain types of cancer, and accidents.[54]

In addition, Mexicans have a propensity for obesity, higher levels of blood glucose, cholesterol, and triglycerides than Anglo populations.[55] Type II diabetes mellitus, which is closely associated with these conditions, appears at greater rates among the Mexican population than among Anglos. This condition probably arises from a combination of dietary associated factors like the intake of fats, simple carbohydrates, and other "low-income" foods, but there may also be a genetic predisposition because of an Amerindian "admixture" (there is evidence that among Native Americans this a genetically predisposed condition and Mexicans are partial inheritors).[56] This inheritance consists of either a "thrifty gene" or the "New World Syndrome," both of which describe an ancient genotype that allowed the efficient storing of nutrients or their efficient breakdown, but in the present with the advent of fast-foods, available food resources and high carbohydrate intake contribute to the emergence of metabolic diseases.[57]

Within the population, women again are at greatest risk for other diseases. Mexican women have higher mortality rates from cervical cancer than other populations due to late detection and treatment when survival chances are reduced.[58] In addition, Mexican women have double the rate of Anglo women for gall bladder disease, also in part due to genetic "admixture" and perhaps dietary preferences, although there is some conflict as to the contribution of dietary practices.[59] Mexican women seem to suffer a slightly higher mortality rate from liver cancer than Mexican men but both are twice as high as Anglos. Even though cirrhosis of the liver is usually associated with liver cancer and cirrhosis is alcohol related, this does not explain the appearance of liver cancer especially among Mexican females because they have been shown to be the least likely to consume alcohol of all populations.[60] Rather, both men and women may be suffering from high liver cancer rates from exposure to hepatitis or to pesticides especially in Texas where some of these studies were conducted.[61]

Mexican men as well seem to have worse "cardiovascular disease profiles" than Anglo males. That is, of nine factors which combine to create a profile of possible cardiovascular risk, Mexican males fared worse in all but two: hypertension and the amount of daily cigarette smoking, even though there were more Mexicans who were current smokers.[62] Mexican males were higher in triglycerides, cholesterol, systolic and diastolic blood pressure, body mass, diabetes, and, as mentioned above, the current percentage of cigarette smokers. Nevertheless, Mexican coronary heart disease mortality is showing the same downward slope as it has for non-Mexicans.[63]

What then can we surmise from these various studies of physical health? First, women for the most part are at a greater disadvantage than Anglo women in some areas such as cervical cancer and related conditions. Second, males are at a distinct disadvantage in relation to cardiovascular disease and liver cancer than their Anglo counterparts. Third, both Mexican women and men suffer higher rates than Anglos of the associated diseases of obesity, diabetes, renal failure, gallbladder diseases, and related problems like limb amputations. All of these conditions and others, however, are directly associated with socioeconomic status and education, and there is a probability of each of these being appreciably reduced by early intervention. However, most of us simply cannot afford to intervene because 37 percent of the Mexican population is uninsured in comparison to 16 percent of the Anglo population.

Wars as Sadness: Trading Souls

» » »

Since World War II, Mexicans have overparticipated in combat units and suffered casualties in inordinate numbers. War from just about any point of view is problematic. It is probably not a "naturally aggressive" activity for our species in general or for Mexicans specifically, even though various anthropological works have thought the opposite.[64] From most accounts, in war the one underlying instinct of survival that is constantly being tested and suppressed is the instinct to flee. Most combat veterans support the idea that relations to peers, taking care of your "buddy," or *camarada*, and an acquired reflexive "combat" mode are the most important reasons for not fleeing when every indication strongly suggests the opposite. These are just about the only factors that keep a person alive when everything is created to do just the opposite. In this vein, in almost every war, the quest for the "million dollar wound" assumes almost mythical proportions and is explained through elaborate rationales.[65] The "million dollar wound," a minor wound that allows an individual to escape the certainty of death, is one improbable way that doughboys, dogfaces, or "grunts" of every war have thought an unembarrassing way out.

For Mexicans, war has presented the most paradoxical of situations. For some, war is the only way out of some of the conditions already described. International conflicts present an alternative to the war in the streets, and the chances of survival may even be better on the battlefield than in the streets. For others, war is the only way to regain the dignity lost because every other institution suggested a Mexican should not have any. Of course, in the past there was the chance that the draft number was such that it was simply your turn, except for the fact that a Mexican was not eligible by class or education for deferment, so the chances of ending up in a "line" company after the draft were much greater than for other populations. Even within the military services, most drafted Mexicans ended up in combat units because of a lack of educational achievement or simply because that was where most Mexicans were expected to be. It may be that Mexicans were "tracked" not unlike in school systems, which placed Mexican children into slow learning tracks as opposed to Anglos. Except that the war track was much more deadly.

As mentioned above, Mexicans are "distributed" in casualty lists from World War II to the present in inordinate numbers. Sometimes the distribution of members of Mexican households in war is so great that it includes most male and some female members of generations. In one family of fifteen, for example, ten had joined the armed services between 1941 and 1965, five served in World War II, and one returned wounded, scared, and scarred for life. The sixth and seventh sons served in Korea, and the latter, a marine, was killed two weeks after celebrating his eighteenth birthday. The last three sons also served in combat but returned safely; yet their safety was illusionary, for from these ten brothers, ten more sons were born who served in Vietnam with all of the resulting scarring of that war. In addition, a daughter of one of these sons served in Operation Desert Storm.[66]

In Silvis, Illinois, just west of Chicago, on a block-and-a-half-long street, sons and grandsons have gone to war for more than 40 years; they are Mexicans who originally worked on the *traques* in the double wage system of the early 1900s. From World War II through Vietnam, eighty-four young men from this tiny street went to war; eight did not return, and many more returned maimed. In two of the families with the same surname, thirteen went to war and three were killed.[67] Such distribution seems inordinately unbalanced for the population, a fact that is borne out by other statistics. In 1993, over 20.6 percent of the U.S.-born Mexican male population were veterans when compared to 16.6 percent of Puerto Ricans and 13.8 percent of Cubans.[68] However, it is not among the living where Mexicans are the most overrepresented but rather among the dead, the casualties who in their youth died in old men's wars.

In World War II, among the twelve Mexican Medal of Honor recipients four were honored posthumously; in Korea, of seven, four were awarded posthumously, all to marines; and in Vietnam of ten honored, four also were given posthumously and all to marines.[69] Thus, of the twenty-nine Medals of Honor given to Mexicans since World War II, 41 percent were awarded posthumously and most to marines.

As these numbers indicate, large segments of the Mexican population joined either elite units of the army like the paratroopers or the marines or were drafted into combat units. In World War II, many combat units were made up almost exclusively of Mexicans; an example is "E" Company of the 141st Infantry Regiment of the 36th Division from Texas, many of whom fought in Italy, France, Germany, and Austria with division casualties (killed or wounded) in the thousands. In addition, in Europe Mexicans filled the ranks of the 30th Infantry Regiment of the 3rd Infantry Division; the 22nd Infantry Regiment of the 4th Infantry Division; the 23rd Infantry Regiment of the 2nd Infantry Division; the 313th Infantry Regiment of the 79th Infantry Division; the 7th Infantry of the 3rd Division; and the 142nd Infantry Regiment of the 36th Division.[70] All of these units fought from Italy to Austria.

Likewise in the Pacific, from Arizona the 158th Combat Team "Bushmasters" was initially 25 percent Mexican, members from two dozen indigenous tribes, and rest from other populations. General Douglas MacArthur called them the "greatest combat team ever deployed for battle," and their casualties reflected this characteristic.[71] They fought bravely in the Philippines, where earlier in the war New Mexican coastal artillery units, made up of mostly Hispanos/Mexicanos, had been captured and forced to walk in the infamous "Bataan Death March," which many did not survive. In addition, Mexican marines distinguished themselves in every battle in the Pacific from Pearl Harbor to Okinawa, and Mexican sailors were in every major Pacific campaign (Mexican air force fighter and glider pilots and ground crews participated mostly in the European theater of operations). For some marines the Pacific was not to be their last field of battle: they became three-war marines.[72]

This disproportion of Mexicans fighting and dying in wars continued through Korea and Vietnam. "E" Company of the 13th Infantry Battalion, United States Marine Corps Reserve of Tucson, Arizona, was composed of 237 men of whom 80 percent were Mexicans when it was called into active duty on July 31, 1950, and two months later landed as part of an invasion force in Inchon, Korea. Of this number, many were seventeen and eighteen years old, but others like sixteen-year-old Mickey Ríos returned to Tucson to graduate from high school after being wounded and decorated. Largely untrained and inexperienced, these young men landed on Inchon with many of them having learned how to fire their M-1 rifles and machine guns aboard ship and with only two weeks of infantry training in Japan.[73] From the Inchon landing, through bitter fighting for Seoul and the frozen battle of the Chosin Reservoir, and beyond, these young men fought and died with 10 of the original 231 from Tucson never returning, having sometimes "traded souls," as one survivor explained.

I was then a machine gunner perched up on Ammo Hill outside of Koto Ri on our way back from the Chosin. We were keeping the Chinese off the roads so that the other units could slip in behind us. We had just destroyed a bunker, our officers had all been killed, and our sergeant was in back of us and not available. Two guys were bringing up a Corpsman who had been hit trying to bring up a guy who had been shot beyond the slope of the hill. As I passed them in that direction they told me not to go over there since the guy who had been shot was being used as bait. The Chinese had zeroed in on him and they were hitting anyone who tried to get him. He was yelling for us not to try to get him and to stay away. But hero me, I said "fuck it" and crawled down to him and it was damn hard work with all the snow and litter around. I got to him and he still insisted on my leaving him. I couldn't so I told him to crawl up on my back which he did with great pain since he had been hit in both legs and one of them was in really bad shape. But I grabbed a hold of him and stood up and he was really heavy since he was a big guy by the name of Polaski and he was soaked from the blood and wet snow. The rounds were going all around us but I didn't notice them much and I managed to get us up and over the ridge and I tried to set him down but I had forgotten that his legs were broken so that one of them folded back under him and he used his foot as a pillow. I picked him up again and straightened him and gave him some morphine. Two guys dragged him down the hill and I never saw him again.

Just about then I decided to see if there were any other guys down where Polaski had been and I asked some of the others that were around to go with me. Nobody volunteered but just then "El Bobby" was coming up the hill. He had been held up spraying foxholes. He said, "Vamos" and I said no, don't go with me. I wanted to protect him. His wife was expecting their first. But he said, "Vamos, para que sepan que los Mexicanos saben como morir donde quiera." (Let's go, so that they learn that Mexicans know how to die anywhere.) So we went down, and Bobby covered me by keeping the Chinese down. I collected some weapons but there was nobody else around.

We went up over the ridge again, when I looked back, Bobby was curled up on the ground shot in the chest. Another Machine Gunner was crying over him and I couldn't quite figure out why since they had not been good friends, but I figured maybe he felt something for him. I picked up Bobby in my arms and tried to shake him awake, but it did do no good. By that time we started getting hit pretty good with phosphorous shells and between the smoke and me crying I thought I saw Bobby going to heaven. But it was time to go and that was the end of Bobby. I grieved for Bobby, I still do.

Only years later did I find out the reason why the other Machine Gunner had been crying so much. He had killed Bobby by mistake. I guess "El Bobby" and Polaski just traded souls.[74]

For Vietnam, the trading of souls from both "friendly" and unfriendly fire was a common occurrence, but again in disproportionate numbers. Without college deferments, without educational advantages to stay out of combat units, and with the willingness to engage in combat, too many returned in body bags or maimed psychologically or physically.

An analysis of the distribution of Mexicans in combat units, the casualty rates, and the aftereffects of that war on the Mexican population has not yet been done. What is known is that between January 1961 and February 1967, slightly less than 20 percent of those killed in Vietnam from the U.S. Southwest were Mexicans, and between December 1967 and March 1969, 19 percent were Mexicans.[75] In 1960 only 11 percent of the population was Mexican, which indicates the magnitude of the "distribution" of Mexican casualties in that war.

As further evidence indicates, Mexicans were distributed disproportionately in the elite combat units and suffered casualty rates accordingly. In the first period 1961–1967, 23.3 percent of all Southwest Marine Corps casualties were Mexicans, while 19.4 percent of all army casualties had Spanish surnames and were predominantly Mexicans.[76] In the second period 1967–1969, the latter percentage was reduced to 17.5 percent. Data are not available for the Marine Corps in this last period, but I would suspect that the rates would not have decreased but increased given the greater intensity of combat during that period.

Of the 58,000 casualties in Vietnam between 1961 and 1973, I would estimate that at least 20 percent of all those killed from the Greater Northern Southwest were Mexicans who will never have the opportunity to travel north, south, west, or east. For Arizona alone, 80 Mexican youths were killed in the two-year period December 1967–March 1969, which represents over 24 percent of all casualties in the state. For this same period, almost 40 percent of all casualties from New Mexico were Mexicans. From Texas, of all casualties 25 percent were Mexican, and from Colorado and California, Mexicans constituted 19.1 and 14 percent respectively. For this period alone, the total percentage of young Mexicans never returning was 19.6 percent. Given the intensification of the war up to June 1969, the total estimated percentage of 20 percent is conservative.[77]

Of the survivors who were maimed physically and psychologically, Mexicans suffer high rates of posttraumatic stress syndrome (PTSD) because a high percentage of the population served in combat. In addition, there are some indications that the effects of discrimination both within and out of the service and the consequences of low educational and economic experience enhanced the PTSD effect.[78] Whatever the source, deep pain was distributed among these young men and their families, and it continues for many to this day.

> When I was living at my sister's house, I would still get up in the night— still thinking I was fighting—dreaming that I was still yelling for my men. I still get flashbacks as if I was still in action and in Viet Nam. I see persons I knew and relive when they got shot. I still think back of men dying and asking for the last rites. Mostly *raza*, Catholic-religious guys would ask me

for the blessing because there weren't any priests out there during the battles. . . . [W]ar is not a good thing, it's a lot of hatred and people getting hurt. And after the war, there is no way to erase the pain and suffering.[79]

Conclusions

» » »

For Mexicans, our participation in each of the categories of sadness is overrepresented. What stands out is that the lack of high-quality education is directly associated with low income, which itself is associated with various expressions of sadness. Gangs, crime, physical illness, mental symptoms, and overparticipation in war all share the same sources.

It does appear that these conditions may worsen with the "economic" restructuring of the U.S. economy. This restructuring, which is replacing relatively high-paying skilled jobs in construction, mining, and industry with low-paying service employment, will only exacerbate present conditions. For young people, hope of "getting a good job," particularly when they have dropped out of school, will probably fade, as it will for those with a high school diploma. When new American wars, interventions, police actions, humanitarian efforts, interdictions, and other assorted rationales emerge, Mexican youth may be in worse condition—in larger numbers—with all the corresponding tragedy for the dead and maimed, and for those who survive.

Thus, new cohorts will face the ever challenging present whose future indicators are not too beneficial for either sound minds or sound bodies. Nevertheless, this population has always faced the difficulties of economic inequality, commoditization, discrimination, miseducation, and all their attendant ills with ideas and behaviors adaptive to becoming human and humane. However, even these have to be buttressed by educational institutions and opportunities that support them. Unless these appear in significant numbers, there is no doubt that more of us will fall by the wayside to become the next casualties of all the "ills" present in the Northern Greater Southwest. In so doing we all become casualties.

PART 3

» » » » »

So Farewell Hope and with Hope

Farewell Fear, Coming Full Circle

in Words and Pictures: Finding

a Place and Space

TWENTY-FIVE YEARS AGO, I wrote a piece with basically the same title. It was among one of the first pieces published by Quinto Sol Publications, and its publication and the hundreds that were to follow began an avalanche of works that no one thought we could create but did. The story itself is like the process that led to its publication in that it concerns cultural creation without the necessity of either requiring the cultural blessing of an authority or recognizing its necessity. Octavio Romano-V, the founder of Quinto Sol, scoured the region for poetry, short stories, and narratives of any sort to "tell the tale." He found them in hidden places and as a literary sleuth brought their meanings to light. His search for those texts was like the existential search so many of us had been undergoing, wrote about, but did not dare put in anyone's hands to reveal. He enabled us to transcend our many fears and induced us to hope by gently and sometimes not so gently showing us our commonality in the region's shattering experience.

The protagonist in the piece "So Farewell Hope and with Hope Farewell Fear" had embarked on a journey for meaning and searched the hidden places of a shattered soul. Its title was taken from Milton's epic poem, *Paradise Lost*, in which Satan has battled God's archangels and has been thrust down to Hades. There with his fellow angels, Satan announces that their fall is but a way of recognizing that all hope for getting back to heaven is lost but so also lost is the fear of ever losing it.

Ricardo (Ree-car-do as pronounced by Anglos), the protagonist, narrator, and "voice" in "So Farewell Hope," had never been able to penetrate Anglo cultural heaven even though he strove mightily to achieve it, to the extent of joining the Marine Corps and fighting for respectability in Vietnam. Previously he had often been spanked by Anglo teachers and principals for speaking the only language he knew and for refusing to change his name in favor of the "Other"—the very force that repressed him culturally, linguistically, and historically. All of these experiences left him physically shattered, psychically maimed, and socially alienated. The experience set him off on a quest to the south for self-discovery, meaning, and connection because his past had been erased, his present distorted, and his future left without hope.

As he progressed on his journey, his memories of himself emerged as distortions not of reality but of reality distorting his self. In the midst of Southern Arizona irrigation fields, peopled by sweating Mexican farm workers, he peered down into a tank of swirling water, which normally distorts faces, but his was clarified. In so doing he was able to "see" beyond his individual injuries to those collected around him, and he adhered to them so that he was able to continue his trek south as a partially connected cultural being, and partially without fear. In this manner, he said farewell to the false hope of becoming recognized by that which rejects his humanity; but in abandoning that hope, he also bid farewell to the fear of nonacceptance and to the necessity to be legitimized by that which oppresses the self into the distorted image of versions of Mexicans.

This distortion was equally clarified by the mural movement of the same period, and fortunately I was present when this process began. In 1969, the first time I saw Queso and Guillermo's murals hanging from the roof of the old round Ford Building in Balboa Park in San Diego, I thought they were like huge, dark and speckled bat wings dipping down from the girders.[1] The speckles were painted symbols of hope, the past, and the present. Also sprinkled about were figures and places of the locality, region, and Central Mexico. All these expressive panels seemed constrained by the building's walls, not unlike the population itself—bottled in, culturally cryptic, yet resurging and looking for life.

At the time when I first saw Queso and Guillermo's murals, Logan Heights, a small but long-present Mexican community just south of San Diego, had been dissected by Interstate 5, and in 1969 the Coronado Bay Bridge, which connects San Diego to Coronado Island, was being completed. The bridge cut another large piece from the community and replaced homes, businesses, and gathering places with huge concrete pillars holding up the brightly lit serpentine bridge that now connects active-duty navy admirals and marine generals with their retired counterparts on the island. The island has long been used as a retirement haven for the navy, for amphibious training for marines, and for the training of UDT and SEAL teams.[2]

Logan Heights also fared poorly because it had been zoned an industrial area, and the rapid development of junkyards practically enveloped the community with rusting automobiles and parts, brown, oil-stained railway tank cars, and huge discarded ship boilers plus thousands of aged mechanisms, tools, and sundry other piled up artifacts.[3] Logan Heights like hundreds of other Mexican communities during the 1960s had either been "removed" by urban renewal or more than likely dissected by freeway construction. All over the Southwest, Mexican communities were dissected by freeways, razed by well-meaning but destructive "War on Poverty" strategies, and in the Logan Heights case suffering further dissection by a bridge.

However, "La Logan" as it was affectionately called by residents and nonresidents alike, was also the site of La Tortillería, a favorite of us all for its flour *gorditas* and hot tortillas that were served with piping hot and piquant *posole* and *menudo,* gingerly carried to the long wooden communal tables by elderly Mexican women in *nana* (grandmother) aprons and long, faded print dresses. The flavors, aromas, and sights in an interesting way blended culturally for us with the Aztec calendars with the feathered, muscled warriors holding moribund princesses. Tiny businesses like these had been the norm and to a much more limited extent served a still vibrant community of beautiful brown children who skipped to school, straining mothers carrying too many infants to the store, and young men old before their time going off to low-paying jobs while a few stuck needles in their arms to erase the pain.

However, the year of 1969 came in the midst of the "Chicano Convulsive Transition Movement," described previously, in which U.S. Mexicans sought cultural and political renewal. The penetrating concrete pillars of the bridge and the on and off ramps seemed to stab into the heart of "La Logan" and seemed to be the concrete manifestations of the harm and ill visited upon so many Mexican communities both historically and contemporaneously. Just as important, for many the concrete pillars and ramps reflected the continuous stabbing of Mexican culture by "Americanization" programs, miseducation, commoditization, and overrepresentation and distribution of "sadnesses" in war, crime, drugs, and illness.

For some of us, the concrete pillars represented the penetration of historical capitalism into the Southwest, the exploitation of Mexican populations, and they seemed to be like huge jail bars that imprisoned the population into communities fractured geographically, economically, culturally, linguistically, and socially. Finally these concrete pillars seemed to form huge mental cages that encapsulated Mexicans into an Anglo prism of culture and reference. The on and off ramps went nowhere. What Logan Heights represented for many of us was us. Thus combined these perceptions, emotive states, political expectations, and cultural frustrations; and local dynamics resulted in the physical takeover of what eventually came to be known as "Chicano Park" and simultaneously the Ford Building at Balboa Park, which had been scheduled for demolition. Led by MECHA students from San Diego City College, San Diego State University, and Mesa College, high school, junior high, and elementary school students, and community members, the land under the bridge was finally designated in 1970 as a city park site for its residents, and its stabbing pillars became the walls upon which would be painted more than nineteen murals between 1973 and 1981.[4]

At almost the same time, Queso had chained himself to the doors of the Ford Building, fearing its scheduled razing. Eventually, it too became a Chicano possession, known as "El Centro Cultural de la Raza," and continues to function as a center of expressive muralism, dance, poetry, and plastic arts in the present.

It is from such contexts throughout the Southwest that the mural movement of the seventies and eighties and into the nineties exploded on bridge pillars, river canal sidings, building walls, and in almost every conceivable place that declared the same type of "basta" echoed by creative literature. Like the literature, the mural movement emerged in the midst of struggle, discarding the prisons of conventionality of an imposed culture. New forms were invented unfettered by traditional gender specification and internal repression of feelings and ideas. The common thread for words and pictures was the unleashing of creative forces that not only explored avenues and byways in the search for place and space, but found meaning, expression, and finality in the process. In so doing we came full circle and found many places and many spaces.

» » » » »

CHAPTER 6

The Search for Meaning

and Space through Literature

THE SEARCH FOR CULTURAL PLACE and psychic space is an ancient theme transcending the Mexican literature of the region; it has been central to many literary works all of which represent different versions of this archetypical narrative. However, as recent scholarship has shown, the literature of the region and of the contending forces for cultural place and space have much earlier progenitors.[1] Lomelí argues convincingly that Alvar Núñez Cabeza de Vaca's *Relaciones* (1542), Don Pedro Baptista Pino's *Exposición sucinta y sencilla de la provincia del Nuevo Mexico,* and Fray Gerónimo Boscana's *Chingchinich* (1825?) "as integral written parts of early Hispanic regionalistic writings, clearly constitute a part of the written tradition from which Chicano literature would eventually emerge."[2]

This argument is based on identifying works by region rather than by nation, and I would add that within each region there emerge subregional literatures that wax and wane like the cultural systems that emerged prior to the European inundation. These regional literatures may be composed of "folklore," letters, reports, broadsides, newspapers, and historical documents detailing water, land, and nuptial disputes—all of which create the basis of a historically lengthy written tradition and provide some basis for articulating regional identities over time and place. Thus Cabeza de Vaca's rendition of his trek is not merely about the wanderings of a lost and shipwrecked Spaniard and his struggle for survival in an unforgiving region but of a *curandero* seeking to find his way home and being changed, transformed, and acculturated by native peoples. He may be considered the first Chicano author.

At present, poetry, novels, "pieces," and expository narratives by the hundreds dot the Mexican literary landscape in the search for and expression of place and space—internal and external. Sometimes these are moving expositions of women creating new spaces and places away from the confines of Mexican patriarchal definitions, "canons," and expectations. Sometimes, it is the *cholo* celebrating his possibilities and potentials and decrying the destructiveness of created realities. At times, it is a lesbian poet looking for connections to a mythic past and creating mythic potentials for the present. In others, works of biting irony and sardonic commentary on the foibles of us all fill their pages and pierce our pretensions, especially of those of us who continue to seek legitimacy from the "authority" of whatever ilk.[3]

What each of these creators qualitatively invent and induce is "experience" of multiple domains, of multiple relations, of multidimensional levels of paradox, and multiple solutions of one population and region. This experience forms multiple voices not unlike the acquisition of the multiple voices and expectations Mexican children gain in clustered Mexican households. These are voices of creation emergent from a struggle that is simultaneously internal and external. In their entirety these voices express the many visions of one geography, one region, and one world. Like the population of the region who themselves are multiply gifted, the literature of the region is multifaceted.

Nevertheless, the common thread that unites them in much of the literature is the basic existential search for place, space, and connection, and just as important cultural creation and invention. Whether it is Mexican women simultaneously expressing ancient and generating new and innovative modes of writing or Mexican men struggling to deconstruct their own inventions, much of the Mexican literature of the region defies easy classification, pigeonholing, or categorization, because it is born of struggle and creation within a region of struggle and creation.[4] This is not a world of easy categories.

There is one inalterable element in this struggle and that is the presence of millions of Mexicans on both sides of a political border. This is the base of the created literary canon. These millions, our class struggles, our gender awakenings and conflicts, and emergent regional, racial, and commodity identities are the inducers of creativity as well as its producers. The Mexican canon cannot be based on an abstracted national, politically created identity of a "truly integrated American literary history."[5] This is not an even playing field but rather one in which inequality defines all relations.[6]

Like the literature and people themselves, the canon is borderless, collectively self-determined, and defined without regard to legitimization by others. Its legitimacy lies in the ongoing struggle to survive in the midst of gross inequalities and emerges within the multiple dimensions of experiences and their limitless expressions. It decries easy comfort in the cushion of victimization but rather expresses resistance, creation, and invention. Victimization is for those seeking moral justification for restitution. The literature and the people have seldom sought such an easy formula and generally express its opposite: human creation based on the right to live without repression, victimization, or degradation. If it is accurate that "history [is] the decisive determinant of the form and content of the literature"[7] then that history must be inclusive of the relations of inequality. Inequality cannot be reduced to "differences" nor to an imagined "dialectic of differences" between a dominant and subordinate literature. It is not likely that a "dialogic" system between dominant and oppressed literatures is very probable except between elites.[8]

For the most part, what unites many U.S. Mexican writers is the quest for substantive and endearing space and place and cultural solutions in the most unequal of circumstances. This process many times has taken place at the local level in relation to others unlike ourselves, or like ourselves sometimes respectful, subordinating, dominating, submissive, oppressive, and egalitarian.[9] For many Mexicans of the region that quest has been problematic, conflictive, creative, and generative but always occurring in the midst of inequality of resources, influence, and control. Much of the history of the region consists of just such tensions, and the struggle, emergent for many of us, is expressed in a variety of forms, forums, and methods. What seems germane to this discussion is a Mexican canon expressing struggle, invention through struggle, and invention in the midst of class, gender, and cultural asymmetry. The region's literature is focused in part on the millions struggling in the midst of inequality to survive in a history of mostly survivors and creating and inventing many visions of a literature.

In discussing U.S. Mexican literary invention, I purposely focus on writers that not only create, criticize, propose, discuss, and analyze but obviously struggle sometimes in solitary and at others in collective ways with the multiple dimensions of Mexican experiences. Each author provides an important insight into a tiny slice of the creative experience of Mexicans as well as a glimpse at a few of the hundreds of creative works written in the present by Mexicans in the United States. As a group, the authors selected represent many but not all of the dimensions of the experiences themselves, and for that reason they write in traditional and innovative forms about their connection to those experiences.

I have limited the discussion to narrative or seminarrative works because this form provides easier access to a nonspecialist like myself. In addition, the works discussed do not represent all narratives written by the authors because this is not an exercise in literary history. Rather, this discussion concentrates on the expression of the multidimensionality of experiences and visions and their relation to the ancient search for cultural place and space. I make no claims about approaching this discussion as a literary critic but rather as an anthropologist whose political values emerge from a limited but important experience within the Chicano movement. That movement provided the impetus for the creation of much of the literature and was attentive, sometimes successfully, to the class, cultural, and gender struggles of the Mexican population that gave it birth. Therefore, this chapter is an essay of exploration, not definition; of appreciation, political and cultural judgment; and an attempted biased explanation, not a definitive statement. I doubt that for any literary endeavor like this there is any other characteristic that is reasonable.

Among the first group of writers are Gloria Anzaldúa, José Antonio Burciaga, and Richard Rodríguez, who are part of what I would regard as a narrators' collective, as singular as each may be. For each, art is a form of political activism, sometimes overt and at other times covert; but each is a political activist, sometimes in opposition one to the other and sometimes within themselves. Most are poets, but even those who are not are poetic.

The second group are the novelists and poets Ana Castillo and Miguel Méndez, who are generational contrasts in so many ways, but with experiential dimensions that separately or combined provide deep insights into the politics of art and present grand searches for meaning and place. Castillo's *The Mixquiahuala Letters* (1986) and Méndez's *Los Peregrinos de Aztlán* (1974, 1992) engage us in marvelous discoveries and creations, making us believers in the unbelievable. Both move across generations, across gender and specificity, and separately tell a full story and a fuller one together.

All five authors represent not only themselves but the many visions of ourselves in literary place and space. For those who have been able to understand their process of creation, the result, as Rosaldo has suggested, "is not identity confusion but play that operates within, even as it remakes, a diverse cultural repertoire."[10] For those who have not, what awaits is coming to terms with their visions of an experience that can be imagined as one looking in the mirror repeatedly, seeing the singularity of one's self over and over again.

Gloria Anzaldúa, José Antonio Burciaga, and Richard Rodríguez

» » »

La Gloria

Each narrative created by Gloria Anzaldúa touches on a created space between disaffection and resolution. The sources of disaffection are internal to a rural South Texas version of Mexican Tejano and Anglo Texan culture close to the Mexico/U.S. border, in which women are presumed to be submissive objects and in which their silent resistance is expressed in wailing. Machista, domineering, hurtful, and demeaning, a masculinized Mexican world of submission was created for Mexican women. In this agricultural setting, the Anglo, who is dominant, hurtful, and supports a demeaning "white" world, reigns supreme over Mexican men. This hierarchical structure was a source of Anzaldúa's disaffection and provided her with a genuine insight into this masculinized version of machismo. For Anzaldúa, this machismo is created by a loss of dignity and respect, thus generating a "false machismo which leads him [the Mexican man] to put down women and even to brutalize them."[11] This understanding, however, may never allow or support such behavior in spite of historical and structural sources; it promotes action not acceptance.

At the same time, Anzaldúa's insights define her recognition of a non-masculinized version of "machismo," which counterbalances the masculinized version. The former is defined by a father's love of family as he struggles to prevent the racist, ethnocentric, exploitive, and suppressive forces that not only endanger him but destroy the family itself. Unlike the brute who "takes to the bottle, the snort, the needle, and the fist," Mexican males in this "other" version of machismo provide succor, protection, support, love, tenderness, and gentleness. These gentle values exist, though not sufficiently distributed except in men like her father.[12]

However, rather than seeking retribution for masculinized machismo, Anzaldúa seeks resolution for Mexican women and men. Although the struggle for Mexican women is a feminist one, its resolution lies partially in upending men's own fixed gender expectations, which allows gentleness to emerge and the men then to "expose themselves to the woman inside them and to challenge the current masculinity."[13] Only gay men, gentle fathers, and a few isolated individuals seemed to have succeeded, but all men need a cultural movement in order to become gentle in a less haphazard way.[14]

To expand her understanding, Anzaldúa chose to leave the South Texas region of Mexican and "White" masculine machismo. Culturally she chose to extract herself from the double-binding rural versions of a suppressed cultural system, which ironically also inadvertently provided the basis for her decision to leave. What Anzaldúa describes as the "Shadow-Beast"—the source of rebellion—may emerge from the same source that gave impetus to the hundreds of strikes, resistances, and rebellions Mexicans throughout the region have historically mobilized.

For Anzaldúa the source of rebellion lies in myth, yet there is a much simpler source, which Mexicans refer to as *basta*—enough. As a child shut up in her room reading, writing, inventing, and painting, this version of basta was exactly the counterpoint to all that was expected of her: obedience, silence of speech and suppression of thought, submission, and worse, labor in the fields and labor in the home as a requirement, not as a choice. Anzaldúa silently shouted "Basta" as a child and loudly shouts it as an adult in her work. For thousands like her and us, "Basta" and the Shadow-Beast may be the same holograph from different prisms.

Between her escape from the rural version of Mexican culture and hearth in the south and her establishment in her new environment, Anzaldúa declared her identity as a Mexican lesbian. The declaration itself was a liberating act by means of which she conducted her ultimate rebellion against a culture of sexual control and rigid prohibitions against homosexuality.[15] "Being lesbian and raised Catholic, indoctrinated straight, *I made the choice to be queer*" (Anzaldúa's italics). This choice for Anzaldúa created the path that allows her to slip between and within the multidimensional Mexican experience and ultimately provides a way of crosscutting such multidimensionality as well. She refers to the lesbian path as a way of "mitigating duality," that is, a way of dealing with the *loquería* (the crazies) that arise in moving between various dimensions.[16] Anzaldúa's choice, although obviously involving rejection and opposition, also created the impetus for a clarity of vision, in which the fear of rejection and the convenience of submitting were themselves rejected out of hand and in their place an understanding of the fallacy and source of an "other" defined identity. This clarity allows "woman" to respond without the masked features of patriarchy and the shackles of dependency and submission.

Equally transformative for Anzaldúa was her entrance into the mythic past as a bridge to the present. She created an "in-between" myth, which adhered to her declaration. Given the four-tiered jeopardy of homophobia, cultural ethnocentrism, sexism, and geographical disassociation, she also had to glue her path with that which provided the emotional and political strength for her to survive. She chose an amended Middle American pantheon as the basis for that adhesive and an ideological and structural mythos. She claimed a premilitaristic Aztec state in which a balanced opposition between the sexes favored a solidarity between men and women whose duality was expressed by the deities Ometecuhtli and Omecihuatl. For Anzaldúa, this pantheon and its attending mythic structure provide a geographical connection to and ideological base for the south. She invokes and uses as referents a number of female deities, such as Coatl, Tonantzin, and Cihuacoatl, all of whom serve as apical ancestors and provide lineality from the past to the present throughout her works.[17] Simultaneously, she recaptures the La Malinche/La Virgen de Guadalupe complex by denying the traditional patriarchal view of La Malinche as a betrayer and the postconquest definition of La Virgen de Guadalupe/Tonanztin as a "denatured" earth mother.

Utilizing cultural heroines and their appropriate myths which provide her symbolic strength, Anzaldúa silently invokes them in her devastating criticisms of masculinized machismo, white racism, bourgeois Mexican rejection of the U.S.-born Mexican, homophobia, cultural alienation, "other" defined personal and social identity, linguistic imperialism, suppressed women's voices, and white feminist "blank spots" in which women of color are excluded from theory but are referred to in footnotes. However, in her stream of philosophical and cognitive explorations and inventions, she develops a cultural understanding of our potentials, possibilities, realities, and the emergence of a new cultural population. She frames that cultural understanding by declaring:

> When not copping out, when we know we are more than nothing, we call ourselves Mexican, referring to race and ancestry; *Mestizo* when affirming our Indian and Spanish ancestry (but we hardly ever own our Black ancestry); Chicano when referring to a politically aware people born/or raised in the U.S.; *Raza* when referring to Chicanos; *tejanos* when we are Chicanos from Texas.[18]

Whether this mix of cultural, phenotypic, political, residential, and geographical categories is analytically accurate is less important than its synergy to find a way of forging connections within the population and to other groups. For Anzaldúa, they constitute the multidimensionality of a new single Chicano population. Such dimensions are not singular and separate; together they formed the cultural and social material for a new self-recognized population after 1965.[19] While it is problematic that Anzaldúa refers to "race" or "common blood" as the basis of some sort of racial memory connecting Mexicans to progenitors, the phenotypic categorization of populations does have and continues to have "social value" of the most negative sort, which Mexicans, Anglos, Indians, and African Americans have yet to resolve.[20]

For Anzaldúa, this emergent mix of phenotypic and cultural properties struggles for expression. Inwardly the struggle combines gender, racial, cultural, and social categories that create multiple selves. In her essay, "La conciencia de la mestiza," she invokes Vasconcelos to provide the intellectual basis for the new "mestiza" consciousness—a consciousness of the borderlands.[21] She poetically transforms the Vasconcelos synthesis by writing,

Because I, a *mestiza,*
continually walk out of one culture
and into another,
because I am in all cultures at the same time,
alma entre dos mundos, tres, cuatro,
me zumba la cabeza con lo contradictorio.
Estoy norteada por todas las voces que me hablan
simultáneamente. (Anzaldúa's italics)[22]

Such identity forms the basis by which ambiguity and contradiction become a "normative" state. For mestizas, the ability to shift from one set pattern of perceiving to another (from perceiving reality from a holistic perspective to a more lineal one) is within the range of possibilities.[23] She is not sure how these multiple possibilities function nor is she sure of their specific source, but she does identify these possibilities as that which she calls "soul." It is in the soul that these possibilities work out, where their assembly takes place and a new element is formed—the *"mestiza consciousness"* (Anzaldúa's italics). For Anzaldúa, it is this consciousness that connects the straight mestiza to the lesbian mestiza and creates a special circumstance for the creation of a new epistemology, which both share and which crosscuts the categories of straight and lesbian.

Within this consciousness new "paradigms" are created, erasing the duality of subject and object, of races, of males and females, of the other and the same. The resolution for Anzaldúa lies in eliminating duality and bipolar models of the universe. Such resolution then provides the basis for an "unethnic" position in which national imperialism, ethnic superiority, cultural primacy, and an "un-Other" position replaces an imposed righteous "Other." Otherwise, it is too simple to "retreat to the safety of difference behind racial, cultural, and class borders."[24] To rage within these walls and categories is to ". . . rage and be contemptuous of ourselves. We can no longer blame you, nor disown the white parts, the male parts, the pathological parts, the queer parts, the vulnerable parts."[25] She seeks what physicists may term "a unified theory" of the universe; yet for Anzaldúa, this unified theory rests on an understanding of "process"—"Whatever the -ing, the gerund is . . . changing"[26]—in which change is normal, transformation is "natural," and social fields and human events are not classified to be changed; or to use her metaphor, a serpent that sheds its skin and metamorphoses.

Although she locates this process within feminism, her referents are either Mexican or Native American cultures, which she characterizes as those that do not "try to fix and define and rigidly keep . . . everything in their little cubbyholes." This multiple potential replaces the singular historical interpretations of Chicano historical discourse, which Anzaldúa considers an essentially male-dominated template, itself fixed on fixity.

A lack of fixity, however, also allows Anzaldúa's "retorno," her return, from that which she left—the tragic valley of south Texas from which she had previously shed old skins. Nevertheless, here her vision is the clearest not only of the on-going exploitation of Mexicans but more poignantly of the basic tenet of the region, of the Mexican population, and of humans in general. That tenet is the struggle for survival and the search for place and space.

> Today, I see the Valley still struggling to survive. Whether it does or not, it will never be as I remember it. . . . Here every Mexican grows flowers. If they don't have a piece of dirt, they use tires, jars, cans, shoe boxes. Roses are the Mexican's favorite flower. I think how symbolic—thorns and all. Yes, the Chicano and Chicana have always taken care of growing things and the land. . . . Below our feet, under the earth lie the watermelon seeds. We cover them . . . to keep the freeze away. . . . They survive and grow, give fruit . . . We harvest them. The vines dry, rot, are plowed under. Growth, death, decay, birth. . . . A constant changing of forms, *renacimientos de la tierra madre* (rebirths of mother earth). (Anzaldúa's italics)[27]

For Anzaldúa, this is the immutable movement which gives meaning to the struggle for survival.

El Tony

Shifts, change, movement, and emerging "situations" form the baseline for José Antonio Burciaga's biting prose, whose tone masks its character. In works of commentary and remembrance, Burciaga explores primarily a male Chicano world of contradictions, paradoxes, and double binds. Like the world held up by Anzaldúa, this Chicano world is multidimensional and laced with interstitial roads between main avenues. For Burciaga, the universes surrounding him are filled with puzzles, misunderstandings, undiscovered layers and dimensions, all of which are tinged with his "awe." It is as if every topic, idea, person, experience, or event is part of a sea of many others—that is, an ocean of many-chambered nautiluses which he shares with the reader in a shell of Chicano wit and humor.

Burciaga shares a commonality with Anzaldúa of which neither she nor he may be aware. For Burciaga like Anzaldúa what largely marks Anglo perspectives, whether radical, conservative, feminist, or liberal, is their insistence on "fixing" things. From his perspective, Anglos are constantly fixing events as points in time and seeking to create categories for those fixed points. Burciaga finds little seasonality in the Anglo world, little appreciation for the sound and movement of change, and too much insistence on immediate repair instead of evolution. For Burciaga, "flow," movement, change, flux, and shifts are normal, and human intervention is possible, even probable, but not predictable. There are grander designs than Homo sapiens' plans.

The overall design and the sometimes comic way in which we seek to fix our indeterminate selves are the "stuff" of Burciaga's work, which is tinged with seasoned pain. Arturo Islas pinpointed the core of Burciaga's visions, "[He] knows that we laugh the hardest when we are in pain."[28] Central to Burciaga's work is pain but not out of rage. It is a hurt accumulated from the denial by Anglos and other Mexicans of the cultural efficacy and legitimacy of the Mexican population of the United States. It is pain accumulated but expressed not through the medium of a formal ideology or created myth but through a series of *navajazos*, knife slashes of sardonic wit, which touch our Chicano funny bone.

These are not random slashes; they have form and shape and are representative of his works *Drink Cultura: Chicanismo* (1992) and *Weedee Peepo* (1988, 1992), from which the commentary that follows originates. An insight into the form begins with his dedication to *Drink Cultura*, where he refers to a whole: first, Cecilia, his spouse, his children, Rebeca and Toño, and then moving up a generation to his mother and father, María Guadalupe and José Cruz. Laterally, he includes his extended family, his brothers, "Pfias," "Rulis," "Big Norm," "Clete," Joe, and his sisters Lupe, Margie, Connie, and Marty; then down one generation to his nephews and nieces, Oscar, Michael, and Marisa.

Within this network and circle of *familia* with their *apodos* (nicknames), generational and cultural signposts are placed providing the basic clues to the form and shape of the work. His mother, a former Mexican school teacher, refused to allow her children to be erased culturally; she taught them language, history, poetry, and their expression as a "good thing" to have. However, this history was not just the Mexican or Spanish side of the equation; his mother was evidently the source for an added appreciation of indigenous people, such as the Aztecs, and their culture.[29] This knowledge base was taught him within the context of principles derived from the fact that his mother was forced to quit teaching after she refused to sign a constitutional prohibition in Mexico that forbade the mention of God or religion in the classroom. Thus, his underlying impetus for writing is to communicate the "good thing" in the midst of all the silencing of language and culture.

His father, for forty years a custodian of a Jewish synagogue in whose basement the Burciaga family lived, polished the menorah for Hanukkah and made sure its eternal light remained lit. His ecumenicalism went beyond material custody, for he risked his life in protecting the synagogue against burglars and guarded the sacred Torah against anti-Semites who threatened the congregation. At Mr. Burciaga's funeral mass in 1985 while a priest said the service in English and his nephews sang in Spanish, the B'nai Zion Congregation said prayers in Hebrew.

To different degrees his father's Mexican love, charity, wit, moral principle, and good will formed a partial basis for the expressive aspect of Burciaga's cultural being, while his own internality emerged simultaneously from his mother's Mexican intellect, formalism, morality, and deep language structure. These unambiguous but rich cultural platforms are the basis of Burciaga's perspective, but it is the puzzling and overdetermined contrasting ambiguities of Anglo and Mexican cultural life that become points for his wit, topics of discovery, and his subject for thematic and linguistic experimentation. With a little added training from the Christian Brothers, border city adventures, the U.S. Air Force, the university, *y la vida en general* (and life in general), he honed what he had already learned, and from all these sources he developed his major interests.

Two basic functions underscore Burciaga's work: first is intention to instruct the uninformed Anglo and Mexican and to divest the misinformed Anglo and Mexican of erroneous ideas. The second is to influence and unobtrusively change images, meanings, and symbols that have caused or continue to cause pain and suffering for the Mexican population. "And this is one reason why I write—to express those beliefs and to teach what was once a silent sin. These words etched in black ink are made not from individual letters but scars that perforate the paper-like open wounds to the soul of a young Chicano who sought the truth in his own reflection." [30] Burciaga would agree that his method involves placing "situations" before the reader without categories of solutions and interventions; [31] and certainly he chose this method, for he is Mexican rather than Anglo and multidimensional not lineal. As it is most appropriate to a literature of movement and orientation rather than of fixity, Burciaga's method is to create a holography of borders rather than a representation. [32] Hicks describes this approach as indigenous to border situations—literary, territorial, social, cultural, and psychological.

> A model of analysis of border writing must be multidimensional. If we imagine the "real" to be a matrix of interactions between "subjects" and "objects" that can be partially translated, but . . . resists symbolization, then border reality might be conceived as a framing of certain crucial interactions: nature and technology; humans and nature; popular culture and mass culture. . . . Just as one part of a hologram can produce an entire image, the border metaphor is able to reproduce the whole culture to which it refers. [33]

Burciaga creates the metaphor that produces a holographic image of the original subject—language, political action, personalities, ideas, or criticism—so that he is able to project the relationship to the subject rather than the subject itself and therefore produces an interaction between and within the various dimensions of that subject. [34] It is this ability that substantiates his emphasis on "situation" rather than solution, presentation rather than representation, flux rather than fixity, and multidimensionality rather than singularity. Thus, in one of his most holographic of essays entitled "Let Pete Live," he begins with a plea for understanding from the "Gods": "The Gods are getting very demanding and not only to television evangelists. On April 1, Pete Duarte, executive director of La Fe Medical Clinic in the poor south side of El Paso, announced that Xochitlisquatl [pronounced so-cheet-leetz-quatul] would have to be appeased with a cool half million bucks for the restoration of the medical clinic or Duarte would be sacrificed according to ancient Aztec tradition." [35]

In this single paragraph Burciaga provides us with an extended metaphor in holographic shape by providing varying prisms of light that fundamentally change meaning, dimension, and cultural space. In the first line "Gods" control the fate of monotheistic electronic evangelicals. Then follow the prisms of time, space, a condition, culture and class, human need, solution, and reference to a mythic persona whose appeasement demands the ironic sacrifice of the clinic's director. This last prismatic twist of irony prepares us to engage in comic mythic time and space and "on the ground" simultaneously. In the next ten paragraphs, Burciaga creates twists and turns of irony and imagination, each of which creates varying prisms of meaning, shades of different insights, and virtual realities.

Burciaga captures the multiple dimensions of experience in which Mexicans participate and which they manipulate. These multiple dimensions are like wide-scale murals except that in the stead of colors and forms, these are more like fields of relationships that undulate, move, and change depending on the strength of the twist of irony. The entire work breathes of the multiplicity of experience to which Mexicans have access—talking to the gods, dealing with desperation, caring for the needy, building programs—and all the while thoroughly enjoying their ability to do so. He concludes this piece with a typical Burciaga ending: "A group of concerned citizens for La Fe Clinic has set up a fund called the Let Pete Live Fund. 'The contributions would not only be tax-deductible,' said Duarte [as if quoting the director], 'but contributors also would receive a green card for legal residency in Aztlán, the mythical promised land.'"[36]

His ending like his beginning provides an equally multifaceted prism of combining what is "on the ground," what is "above," and what is possible. He is able to crosscut these dimensions by twisting the ironic strand and thus connecting each dimension. For Burciaga, place and space are to be found in the holographic images displayed, turned, and gazed at through his prisms and our own in spiraling motions. These combined images refract the possible experiences of the Mexican and their various visions and versions. There is no return, but rather a continuity of movement through space and time, and the places he has created are metaphors and their holographic presentation united at different levels of spirals.

His ability to make a carnival of all the mispronunciations or reinterpretations, whether by Mexicans or Anglos, gives pleasure and celebrates a people. The book's jacket with the title *Drink Cultura* printed on a Coca-Cola bottle with a red background set on Mexican-flag green creates a holograph of a deeply Mexican set of ironic twists. These poke fun at consumption, of bottled culture, and of the necessity, as well, for Mexicans to take some nourishment from what he will present between the covers of the book. In an almost perverse way he is a linguistic and visual guerrilla making light of the serious and making serious what is perceived to be light.

What seems to be equally absurd at face value is *Weedee Peepo,* which is, of course, a Mexican pronunciation of "We the people"—that most sacred American pronouncement of democracy, representation, and republican ideology. Set within the confines of a dialogue between his parents in which they were preparing for a test to become "Naturalized" (a contradiction in terms), Burciaga reveals that "Weedee Peepo" mispronounced, fractured, and taken advantage of, was his parent's code for challenging those who would make them less than human, and it would serve as a reminder to themselves to do the same to others. However, as Burciaga points out, his parents did not need to learn "Weedee Peepo" because regardless of pronunciation, they had always been "We the people." So for Burciaga the spiral of living continues on.

El Richard

Pobre Richard. "Tan lejos de Dios y tan cerca de los Estados Unidos" (So far from God and so close to the United States.) Richard is as much part of the search for place and space as any Mexican. He is a kindred soul, a brother, a likeness of ourselves, and a holographic presentation of ourselves, as genuine as any of us. His is the triple tragedy of class, culture, and unvalued physiognomy—the first giving him a sense of conscious exclusivity, the second largely captured and cocooned in the stereotypes of commodity, and the third a constant unwanted reminder. All, however, push him to seek out places and spaces; for these have created a dissatisfaction in him, which he did not and does not know how to resolve.

Two works form the basis of this commentary: *Hunger of Memory* and *Days of Obligation: An Argument with My Mexican Father.* The first, his autobiography, is a poignant and troubled search for cultural place and space. The second is a type of extended narrative that seems to be the beginning of a return to that which he lost but is not yet convinced that he lost.

His autobiography details his emergence in the midst of a middle-class Anglo neighborhood with nobody to speak to but his parents. He listens in shame to the alleged cacophony of his parents' apparently fractured English and finds respite only in the private world of the Mexican and Spanish. From this awareness of the unacceptability of his home's "private" Spanish-language world and the "public" world of English, Rodríguez embarked on a road toward recognition by the *gringo* public world. In addition, he looked at his own reflection in the mirror, and unable to cope with the rejection because of his indigenous physiognomy outside of his home, Rodríguez suffered from an almost terminal psychic *empacho*.[37]

Richard in part reminds me of Ricardo in the short story that began part 3. It is, in fact, totally serendipitous that the two are named the same but not that each was pushed by the same forces to seek a place, space, and connection. Both suffered from being culturally and psychologically mauled and maimed. Richard was scarred by all the Anglo messages of nonacceptance, illegitimacy, racism, commoditized expectations, negation, and cultural erasure. His response was to become a "public middle-class scholar" and travel his denial through the primary and secondary schools, elite Stanford, and the hallowed halls of the British Museum. He was often reminded that he was different in spite of the prices that he had paid in submitting to the erasure processes.

His experimentation with the "Other," which rejected him, really began with the visit to his home by well-meaning teachers who urged the family to cease the only real means of human communication they knew—Mexican Spanish. From then on, it was a short hop to the total denial of home, kinship, language, relationships, and ultimately of his identity as being unfit for the American "public world." His ultimate fate was to become trapped in an existential cultural warp—a psychological catch-22 of a social isolate caught in an ideological impasse. His only real acceptance came from his temporary utility in serving whatever forces of cultural repression were in current fashion in the United States.

Ricardo in the story, on the other hand, never allowed his name to be changed, even though he had his hair pulled and even though he was swatted by the school principal. He never accepted the Anglo caricatures of his parents even though his parents were more willing than he to accept the gringo dictums, because "they had more education than they did." For Ricardo there was no difference between an Irish brogue and his parents' Mexican accent. Unlike Stanford, British Museum, and graduate school–bound Richard, Ricardo went down a different avenue, which too many have taken—the overrepresented avenue of the soldier, marine, sailor, and airman.

Ricardo's experience did not set him against his parents, his cultural community, and his working-class background. These were the referents that allowed him to return to sanity and overcome the insanity of his shattered and shadow self. There was nothing innately different between his parents and the schools, between the private and public worlds, between himself and Anglos. There was nothing different except the overt and covert markers of racism and ethnocentrism from Anglos and their institutions that tumbled down on Ricardo often, consistently, and cumulatively.

Ultimately, Ricardo found solace not in a mythic past but with equivalent communities from which he had emerged. The irrigated fields, although almost Elysian as they are described, are filled with the green of growth but tended by "sweating stoops." For Ricardo, there is no return to the past but only to a future road that would not allow him to be defeated or to quit. He had acquired optimism about growth and development. His face reflected in the distorted pool of water became clarified and something to be looked at and not denied.

On the other hand, Richard became a part of one aspect of the literati, appeared on the *MacNeil/Lehrer Newshour,* and traveled as a celebrity. But he always had to look in the mirror and see a big beautiful brown Indian face, which he found distorted and rejected by those he admired the most. Even the "public" words of admiration for his physiognomy were masked—a clerk in London asking if he had been skiing, a bellhop in New York if he had been tanning in the Caribbean, or an undergraduate at Berkeley wondering if he were an Aztec. Unlike Ricardo, Richard returned to the silence of his isolated self, cut off, and unlike most of us not rejoicing in much of anything.

Even the Christmases in his home sadly ended in the realization that he and his father had been silently present all day with no words and culture to exchange. What he was left with was the Anglo public adulation by individuals and groups that agree to the silencing of Mexican culture, Spanish language, Mexican accent, and the innate conflict between a devalued Mexican culture and an Anglo super-prism of superiority. Ironically what was left for Richard, as well, was perhaps a way home.

This seems in fact the process in which he is engaged at present. He has come about a bit from his previous certainties; so that ten years after his autobiography, it is not by error that his second work is published as *Days of Obligation: An Argument with My Mexican Father.* Unfortunately still caught in his own time and cultural warp, Rodríguez states that the objective of this work is to reconcile the differences between California comedy and youth and Mexican tragedy and antiquity; that is, between himself and his father. He begins his reconciliation work with his parents who had left the ancient tragic land to come to the new world of optimism and television sets. "I will present this life in reverse. After all, the journey my parents took from Mexico to America was a journey from an ancient culture to a youthful one—backward in time."[38]

This ahistorical view of Mexicans in California belies the fact that Mexicans had been traveling to California long before television sets were invented to join with others like themselves in Sacramento, Sonora, San Francisco, San Jose, San Leandro, Los Angeles, and San Diego for the same reason as his parents. The fact that Mexicans had already "bumped" into ancients as well does not deter Rodríguez from constructing California in the Protestant American prism of newness. It is not that Rodríguez is ignorant of history, because, in fact, he is quite knowledgeable; but he fails to connect the past with the present and therefore restricts his existence to a bipolar metaphor of either/or, public or private, a past and a present, and gringo and Mexican. He really does think that Mexicans are just another set of immigrants rather than pretty old migrants—part of transmigratory processes begun long before the word Mexican was invented.

His view is a product of his own historical nakedness presented to the reader at the beginning of the book in the form of vomit, which he spews into a toilet bowl while on a "recapture culture" trip to Mexico for the British Broadcasting Company: "I am on my knees, my mouth over the mouth of the toilet, waiting to heave . . . I have forced myself to sound (Spanish words) during the day, bits and pieces of Mexico spew from my mouth, warm half-understood, nostalgic reds and greens dangle from long strands of saliva."[39]

With such a psycholinguistic purging, Richard then begins his long narrative of pieces and places rather than of peoples and spaces. He is at times able to become gently attached to those nearby, to actions and to places, as well—his friend César, feeding the poor in Tijuana, and looking at a severed head in a jar purported to be Joaquín Murrieta's. But he seems to waver most in his discussions of his father by referencing him not as "father" but rather his "Mexican father." It is almost as if countries can claim his paternity so that the United States and perhaps George Washington seem to have equal claims on his creation.

In fact, he repeats the same basic theme as he did in *Memories* of seeking his public identity within the classroom and its memories of the names of British kings, dissident Protestants, and the eighteenth-century white men with powdered wigs who shaped the United States and shaped his life.[40] The United States for Richard is a huge father—only its Puritans and kings can explain the reasons for rebellion and iconoclasm. Mexican rebellions, strikes, and protests in the United States are ignored by Rodríguez because they did not emerge from the characterological and intellectual structure of the United States.

As he explains, Thomas Jefferson, Samuel Clemens, the public school system, Protestantism, individualism, cowboys and Indians, Benjamin Franklin, Andrew Jackson, Shakespeare, Arthur Conan Doyle, and Judeo-Christian ethics created American "public culture"; and he ultimately connects "Thomas Jefferson to Lucille Ball to Malcolm X to Sitting Bull." "The panhandler at one corner is related to the pamphleteer at the next, who is related to the bank executive who is related to the Punk wearing a FUCK U T-shirt. The immigrant child sees this at once. But then he is encouraged to forget the vision" by ethnic studies, bilingualism, diversity ideology, and well-meaning cultural nationalists like Chicanos.[41]

Even Rodríguez's brand of Irish Catholicism is threatened by the onset of "bilingual masses." Having been nurtured by Irish Catholic Christian Brothers, pastors, nuns and all of their accompanying brogues, Rodríguez does not regard his Irish acculturation as "un-American" but rather only a slight variation on an American theme. Before a meeting of Catholic priests, he asserts that "the Church is setting itself against the inevitability; the inevitable Americanization of the grandchildren. You are going to lose the grandchildren; in fact you've lost them already. You are papering your churches with poverty. . . . A foreign language liturgy should be a mere strategy, a temporary appeasement that should not distract us from our goal—the Catholic knowledge of union, the mystical body of Christ."[42]

The Irish Catholic is the quintessential American model for him and, he avers, for Mexicans. White, redheaded, iconoclastic, realistic, rebellious, charming, anxious, and individualistic, the Irish Catholics and their St. Patrick's Day parade counter American Protestantism. In so doing they have filled the judicial, political, and legislative halls of the United States with their membership. For Richard, the Irish represent a compromise for becoming American and an American Catholic—preferably with an Irish brogue but not a Mexican accent. What Rodríguez, of course, does not detail are the Molly McGuires, the strikes, the rebellions, the riots, their overparticipation in wars, their insularity of religion, and the basic chauvinism of a newly found American Irish Chicanoism, which they could not celebrate in Ireland against either Protestants or the English.

What seems to be somewhat contradictory to his Irish model, however, are some important ingredients: first is Richard's homosexuality, which the Catholic Church in general condemns. There is little room in "Holy Mary Mother Church" for what it fears the most—a priesthood stripped of its celibate rules, of men in love with men, and certainly of a Marian dominated ideology that is countered by a lesbian and/or feminist identity. Second, Rodríguez ignores the unabashed patriarchy and chauvinism of aspects of Irish American culture and church. Richard's Irish and Marian convictions do seem to become problematic when redheaded Kathleen Quinn of South Boston appeared on CNN News on March 12, 1994, to protest the exclusion of lesbians, gays, and bisexuals from the annual St. Patrick's Day parade in Boston and its subsequent cancellation at the behest of the Allied War Veterans of South Boston.

Such historical matters Richard ignores. He creates a type of vague, contradictory, and indeterminate "national character" outline of American culture that is simultaneously Protestant, Irish Catholic, individualistic, democratic, and most definitely English only. Chinatown in his own San Francisco does not exist, Little Italy in New York and Boston do not coincide, the Punjabi/Mexican farmers of Imperial Valley, California, never appeared, and the Filipinos who inhabit the Protestant churches described in his book, all seem to be figments of others' imaginations.

For Rodríguez, Mexicans are basically just another immigrant group; the fantasy border to the south is the Atlantic Ocean, the various versions of Mexicans extending into prehistory are myths, and Mexicans using organized methods of individual and collective betterment in spite of exploitation, discrimination, and cultural repression seem curiously excluded. Unlike Rodríguez's attempt to characterize reactions to economic and political repression as "Chicano self-victimization," Mexicans have seldom ever considered themselves victims. Mexicans have never claimed some sort of moral superiority based on a false notion of victimization. Instead, Mexicans have fought in wars, initiated landmark court cases, learned English, fought discrimination and Jim Crow laws, and have organized and mobilized themselves to better communities, build Catholic churches, and more importantly improve the lives of Mexican children. For Richard it was just a matter of reading Milton, erasing the Mexican accent, and perhaps picking up the Irish brogue.

Richard concludes his work as he began: to pit what is ancient and Catholic—Mexico—against what is new and Protestant—America—but in a more personal form. "Who is more right—the boy who wanted to be an architect, or his father, who knew that life is disappointment and reversal?"[43] In following this line of inquiry of contrasts, Richard corners himself into a monologue of differences that are not multidimensional but ahistorical and bipolar. There is nothing to crosscut the multiplicity of experiences of his life because he has not given them their due nor made any connection to choices he has made between his many "public" and his many "private" lives other than a political one based on shame. He has constructed a two-dimensional space of opposites instead of unfolding the multiple dimensions that are part of all Mexicans of the American Southwest and of himself. This binary universe seems to be occupied by a few stars, with only occasional travel to nearby barren planets that make him vomit. Pobre Ricardo y siempre te queremos. Que Dios te bendiga.

La Ana

The Mixquiahuala Letters is an epistolary novel consisting of forty letters written by a thirty-something Chicana—Teresa—to a thirty-something Puerto Rican—Alicia. Although the form is traditional, this is a nontraditional work generated from a very nontraditional mind. In a method not unlike Burciaga's holographic metaphor, Ana Castillo begins with a choice for the reader. Castillo asks the reader to take a chance in selecting which letter to begin reading depending on the reader's personality and preference: for the "Conformist" those from 2 through 27, skipping 29, 32, and 33, going on to 30, 31, 35, 39, 40, 37, and 34. For the "Cynic" the reading should include 3, 4, 7–33 while skipping 13 for a time, skipping 2, 5, 34, then reading 35–36, 13, and 37–38. For the "Quixotic," skipping 1 for a time and reading the rest in chronological order, although skipping 34 and 36. Castillo finishes her instruction by saying that for those who particularly like short fiction, all the letters should be read as separate entities, and she wishes good luck on whichever journey the person has selected.

In a sense Castillo asks us to choose which avenue to explore and not necessarily either hers, her narrator's, or even those suggested in her directions. Underlying this work is a process of description and emergence of thoughts, personalities, events, and actions, most of which do not necessarily have to "fit" together, and, in fact, they should not. That is, whatever we seem to perceive as fitting is a choice that is often made unconsciously, chaotically, and serendipitously. In a similar kind of way, she has given the reader the option of making a choice but in addition, and probably closer to her notion of the way the world works, to choose to not make a choice. The reader could put the book down and say, "Blazes with your notions—that's too uncomfortable." Or equally well, the reader could create his or her own choices randomly or systematically by choosing odd or even epistles, or even more quixotically, by following sheer unconscious "whim."

The work is like a circular puzzle that seems to be composed of discrete parts but in mythic terms admits of different shapes other than those that would fit. The end is the beginning, the middle is the beginning, and the beginning is the end. This is "mythic time and place," as

Segade terms it,[44] but with a searing conscience that especially targets the foibles of weak men, oppressive cultures, racism, Mexican and Anglo sexism, and stupidity. Nevertheless, these are categories that do not do justice to the affection, love, tenderness, and kindness that is woven through the many circles composing the work. This is a love affair of hope.

My reading of *The Mixquiahuala Letters* for the purposes of this work did not follow Castillo's suggestions; rather, I began with one of the letters most often skipped: 34, because its importance to the writer might be gauged by its frequent absence. By whim perhaps, 36, the other equally skipped epistle, was my second choice. This proved fruitful because 34 seemed to establish this as a work based on the search for cultural places and spaces and on finding self in community, connection, painful self-awareness, and security in the elimination of life's many ghosts. The rest of the novel seemed to be the revealing of the manner in which this process occurs.

Beginning with letter 34, Teresa, the narrator and commentator, writes to Alicia, a Puerto Rican intimate, and relates that after visiting Alicia's one-woman art show in New York, the series entitled *La Casita* had provoked in her "a disturbing response."[45] The exhibition is composed of a number of angry papier-mâché dolls with hair from the artist's head. "They stand at the dock with disproportionate dimensions and wait; black eyes stare at the viewers haunted by loathsome trickery. Their arms hang inanimately at their sides. One angry doll inside the house, before a lopsided table with real . . . copper utensils . . . The other drowns in the ocean, visible from the window of the little house."[46]

These two dolls, the former Teresa and the latter Alicia, illustrate in one dimension their temporary conclusion as to the many dimensions of these women, their relationship to each other and to others around them, their experiences, their travels. Teresa writes, "The series goes on this way, variations of the memory in surreal honesty." That memory is their memory, and she recalls their first meeting in Mexico where Teresa and she began their long journey together, meeting danger, experiencing failed love affairs and cultural imperialism, and most important sorting out the many contradictions of class, culture, gender, and sexuality.

Now the memory of that intense experience is beginning to wane.

Teresa writes that she is home, with her son and her husband, reading student writing assignments and settling down to a seemingly placid life as conventional as Richard Rodríguez would have us believe all Americans experience. "There is something I have yet to tell you, Alicia. We're going home, Vittorio and I. . . . In Cuernavaca, Vittorio's grandfather will take naps with him in the garden on the hammock tied to two tamarind trees. He will tell him stories he never told me. Magi will call him 'hag,' rolling a warm tortilla sprinkled with salt and wrapping his little fingers around it." She ends 34 with "God bless and keep you, Alicia. I hope your upcoming trip to Europe will lead you to a place you'll want to go back to and call home."[47]

However, this innocuous ending/middle/beginning initiates a journey as provocative and as holographic as that described for the art show. On her novelistic journey Castillo traverses the often created limitations of Mexican, Anglo, paternal, and maternal cultures, which she disassembles in order to find her own road. Like so many Mexicans before her, Castillo invents identities in order to confront the pain of all those limitations. The manner in which she does this is to partially eliminate past human compromises and then create new potentials and possibilities. She in fact twists from the inside out, like Burciaga using irony as the main *navajazo,* except for Castillo it is the protagonist Teresa who is being twisted from the inside out. This is accomplished by means of the physical, psychic, and cultural journey of Teresa and Alicia within and between the United States and Mexico. In Mexico, Teresa confronts the basic stereotypes of herself as a Mexican from the United States—an unzippered and promiscuous being bereft of substance; a cultural "mongrel" neither one or the other; an unlettered and unintelligent *pocha*.[48] The supreme irony is that she is none of these, and indeed she sought freedom from these stereotypes in the very culture that so categorizes her.

In the United States, Mexican males also strip Teresa of her humanity so that she can only be deemed "a wife," while Anglo women are considered the most desirable because of their characteristic physiognomy of blue eyes, straight blond hair, straight noses, and pouty lips— a kind of mythic Kim Basinger overwhelming Mexican Batmen. For Teresa, Anglo women themselves use this advantage to relegate Mexican men to the subordinate status of Latin lovers. Such a situation then reinforces the subordinating dynamic of Anglo women over Mexican women. However, Anglo feminists are the standard bearers of women's liberation and have served as intellectual sources for Tere's own feminist position.

In letter 10 Teresa writes of her salad days in San Francisco when she and other women appear on a radio program entitled *Somos Chicanos*, and in a stream of consciousness she makes associations that are a take-off on a Joan Baez tune:

> Alicia, do you remember?
> Not just names, but names of long, lost kin
> husbands lost to immigration officials taken on a bus
> and never heard from again.
> they were cousins
> The eloquent scholars with their Berkeley Stanford
>   seals of approval
> all prepped to change society articulate the
> social deprivation of the barrio
>   starting with an
> Anglo wife, handsome house, and a Datsun 280Z in the drive-way. . .
>   and we formed a society of women a sacred triangle
> an unbreakable guard from a world of treason deceit and
> weakness.

Out of this cultural, gender, and class morass, Teresa tries to forge aspects of a new identity over a two-year period spent in travels between Mexico and the United States and in a ten-year period of experiences, sometimes with Alicia and sometimes without her, in Puerto Rico, New York, Chicago, and California. Teresa/Castillo creates a set of ironic exceptions: most Mexican males are predators, yet Ponce is a protector against ghosts; Anglo males are too distant to perceive, yet they never appear; white beauty and class unconsciousness are pernicious, yet they are embodied in Alicia the Puerto Rican companion who is drowning in the Atlantic; and a person cannot go home again, but epistle 34 begins the work with the homiest of metaphors. Therefore, for Teresa/Castillo there are identity solutions in which each of these aspects as they are struggled with, are turned and examined, and their many variations recognized and discarded. For Teresa/Castillo, the "hers," the forging of a new identity, more human, caring, and loving, is the temporary but definite solution. For "hers" the path in part consists of her grandfather and her son in a hammock telling stories, with mother nearby, and with the "hers" always present, vigilant, and secure in the knowledge of herself. For Castillo, the search for place and space begins and stops with self and freedom from all the Others' cultural impositions.

El Miguel

Some have suggested that *Peregrinos de Aztlán* (1991, *Pilgrims in Aztlán,* 1992), as well as other works by Miguel Méndez, is a novel of the grotesque[49] (that is, an artistic form that purposely deforms a character or situation to make it congruent with a deformed and deforming social context).[50] *Peregrinos* focuses on the most deformed of settings for Mexicans: the border (a deformation that, though created by war, continues to be misshapen by the asymmetry between the two countries) where the chain link fence from the Mexican side appears open but from the American closed.

For Méndez, the border is crosscut by the great Sonoran desert, the killer opportunity track, which all aspiring poor Mexican pilgrims from the south must cross to reach the waiting fields of plenty in the north. It is beautiful, beckoning, magical, and inviting—something like a brown siren except that the pilgrim has no mast to be lashed to. The pilgrim traveling north can only depend on others just like him to travel the long road to pick cotton in Marana, cantaloupes in the Imperial Valley, and lettuce in Yuma, Arizona, and as well to bury those who die along the way, sometimes insane from thirst, hunger, and overexposure.

Although majestic and pure, the desert kills not because of any anthropomorphic characteristic but because the border made it into an assassin; one-way rules were established and fences were erected under, over, and around, which the poor skirt and avoid. The border for Méndez is the grotesque creation of Mexican and American politicians, of expanded capitalism, which knows no borders, and of failed revolutions on both sides. The border fractures language and culture and worsens the already formidable poverty of Mexicans in Mexico. The border creates cities like Tijuana, Juárez, Nogales, and Brownsville that are not only the disembarkation points for Mexicans heading north, but in part are northern creations for American sybarites heading south. The distorted nature of the area allows Méndez to comment not only as one narrator but as various narrators and speaking characters of varying points of view in various settings; he offers these multiple voices to explain, comment on, and express the grotesqueness of the border.[51]

In Tijuana, old Loreto Maldonado, a poor Yaqui and former Mexican revolutionary who is the centerpiece for all the voices in the novel, recalls the heroic actions of the Yaqui Colonel Cuamea of the Mexican Revolution, although he fully understands that after the revolution all Yaquis became "indios" again to be exploited and oppressed by rapacious mestizos. In Tijuana Loreto, with dignity and "correctness," has been reduced to washing cars, guarding them for tourists, and refusing handouts from Mexicans and Anglos alike.

It is through Loreto/Méndez that the desert's neutrality is revealed, while the border's avarice and moral degradation is brought into the comparison. Loreto/Méndez's presence, either in the background or in the forefront of the work, serves as a moral standard, an ethical baseline, and mystical platform around which all the grotesque characters and situations are presented. Loreto/Méndez's mythical and sorry circumstance is best summarized in the following:

> *I saw in my pilgrimage many Indian peoples reduced by the torture of hunger, and the humiliation of plunder, traveling backwards along the ancient roads in search of their remote origin. They ended up downcast, ceremonious in their gait and with the ritual gestures of beings who know the depths of human secrets. They came to seek life and the worthy embrace of the graveyards . . . and I saw that through the wide doors of the unploughed lands there entered multitudes of Chicano brothers who made paths and roads to peace and tranquility from the immense sandy plains* (Méndez's italics).[52]

This seemingly inviting expanse has its price because it not only invites but also kills those uninitiated or inexperienced. *"Their backs were bent and there was bitterness on their faces and the infinite weariness of slaves. They embrace their Indian forebears, and together they all cry in silence, burying those who have been killed, who are so many that no one can ever count them"* (Méndez's italics).[53]

These pilgrims, however, shine in comparison to the bourgeois Dávalos de Cocuch family of Tijuana who give alms to the poor in order to buttress their moral legitimacy, because they themselves are ostracized by their own class cohorts. Loreto Maldonado and the other characters like Doña Candelita, the poor herb seller, La Malquerida, the prostitute, El Buen Chuco, the alcoholic, Lorenzo Linares, the poet, and Kite, the crazed comic, seem to have a social web of greater humanity than that of the Cocuches, the Mexican politicians, killer police, bourgeoisie, coyotes, bartenders, and most gringos.

Jesús of Bethlehem (Belén in the Yaqui territory of Sonora) arose from such humanity; he was a Yaqui medicine man, healer, drunk, and tragicomic hero, who in Tijuana tells his tales of trying to redeem the poor in Sonora, only to be scourged by the rich landowners for daring to say that workers should receive just pay. Jailed in a hundred different jails for naming politics as the eighth deadly sin, Jesús is born with the *"tragic destiny of redeemer without having been sent by the Supreme One"* (italics, Méndez).[54] His end like that of most of his fellow poor is tragic—beaten by police rifle butts, kicked like a dog, and tied up and whipped.

Across the border in the United States, the Foxye family fares less well. Their only son, Bobbie, had become a hippie and attached himself to Loreto as if he were a kind of Don Juan of Castañeda fame. Méndez describes the Foxyes as an archetypical American

> couple [who] worked around the clock trying to put their projects on a good footing, saving every penny in total abstinence from anything that meant spending a cent on having fun. They even ate poorly in order to save money. The precepts of religion were a great help to them in their economic goals, since they were forbidden to drink or smoke or do anything that meant spending money without income. But that did not keep them from accumulating wealth, even wealth based on the suffering of others.[55]

Joyless and alone in the world, the Foxyes set out on a binge, she joining social clubs and he creating a legitimate genealogy that somehow would link his "presentless" present with a cutoff past, but only if those linked were passengers on some ship "with a springtime name." Sterilized to avoid further children because Bobby had taken so much time away from their business concerns, both Foxyes lived a daily grind of material existence without spiritual or carnal touch. Bobby's 1970 reaction was negation of both and a search for connection to his parent's despised Other—Loreto the poor, destitute Yaqui.

The intertwining of the different versions of each Mexican persona provides a holographic image that twists and reshapes our view as well as our understanding of them. Not unlike Richard Rodríguez who captures himself between the public and private worlds of his existence, Méndez uses a technique of creating various versions of each persona—some public, some private. La Malquerida (unloved one), the grotesque prostitute as her public world would have her be, is in her private world Rosenda Pérez Sotolín, who had been a typist but had been fooled into traveling with a couple who sold young women to Mexican brothels. Raped, beaten, and psychically dismembered, she became La Malquerida. "But who helps out a poor girl with no money or political influence? Like a tiger, he [the rapist] broke my membrane, tearing me apart body and soul. My soul too!" [56]

Kite, a crazed street beggar, had been a famous comic the Great Tolito, who after his death is described by officials as "nothing but a bum, one of those useless men who don't even have a history." [57] Likewise, El Vate, the poet and drunkard who has composed an elegy to another poet, Lorenzo who died on his trek north, commits suicide by casting himself down into a rocky ravine. At the inquest, the lawyer Espíndola Fernoch seeks to establish El Vate's identity: ". . . we are trying to clear up, out of pure formality his name." [58] After calling a number of cursory witnesses, the officious Fernoch declares the nameless El Vate a suicide after a declaration reminiscent of the double-talk of PRI politicians parodied by the Mexican comic, Cantinflas. As an afterthought Fernoch reads El Vate's elegy to his poet-friend Lorenzo, who has died in his arms in the desert. The elegy buries not only his friend but El Vate himself: Alive "he wished to make the desert flower with poems. Ecstatically, he went forth to plant metaphlowers and fountains with jests of polychrome letters, his red blood, lakes, jungles, and the vivid irises of his fantasy." [59] Dead, he is "now a bony smile that rises above the shining stars, singing with the wind, caressed by the sand dunes, lulled by small voices in cathedrals that will never again stumble in memory." [60] After reading, Fernoch has no comment. It is as if neither Lorenzo, El Vate, or their poetry had ever existed. Their "public" and "personal" selves thus become extinguished by a society that quickly discards the former and disregards the latter. [61]

The most wasted character is the protagonist/narrator/multiple-voiced Loreto Maldonado. He was seen as nothing but an old, large-nosed, decrepit Yaqui who mumbled about Colonel Cuamea. He could do nothing in his old age but wipe off the dirt and mud from "Misters'" windshields and hope for a tiny wage for watching their cars. He was seen as an inordinately proud beggar who never begged and was insulted when an offering was made him without his selling his labor. No one knew until his death that he was a revolutionary colonel who, having fought many battles, was rewarded for his sacrifices with nothing but hunger and betrayal. Dying alone in shack by the river bed, Loreto lay there like a dog until his stench was too great for neighbors to ignore. Later *bichis* (garbage men, literally, "the naked ones" in Yoemi) picked up the body and discovered a small chest nearby, which contained a picture of Colonel Loreto Maldonado, General Cajetes, and Colonel Cuamea. He too became erased and unrecognized in the present.

For Méndez, however, Loreto's is not a quiet voice. He screams for action and for resolution. The resolution for Méndez is not his personally constructed identity or individual recognition as a writer. His resolution is not personal salvation nor self-aggrandizement; rather, resolution lies in the writer revealing the public and private identities of those unheard, the voiceless, those ostracized or limited by social conventions of class, gender, and culture. The writer's task is to ensure that Loreto's, El Vate's, and La Malquerida's search for meaning, space, and place are documented and that their surreal existence no matter how grotesque is placed and spaced.

Méndez concludes:

When amnesia began to sow shadows in our memory, we went to our ancient lakes, seeking in the depth the faces we had lost. We saw through the mist of the ages that they were blurred and no longer the same. We reached the ancient bed of a river, facing the mountain of granite. . . . We inquired about our destiny but no one wanted to understand us because our signs were so strange. . . . We descended to the bottom of the sea, where the stars descend to their nests, to ask if the heavens know where we are headed or where we come from. . . .[62]

The grotesque and the twisted are clarified in the light of the written word, and the writer, like Méndez, provides the energy, images, sources of vision, and cathode by which we all view, reflect on, and compose the permanency that a people whose history is constantly being erased require in order for them to respond politically and organizationally.

Conclusions
»   »   »

Each creator presents a slice of Mexican reality, fantasy, and mythic time and place. Anzaldúa is explicit in her search, partial resolutions, and commitments. For her, the border is a place and space for experimentation and resolution to the repression of women, Mexicans, and even for the "Other." There is an inherent angry hope in her work which Castillo and Méndez both express. Castillo like Méndez tells a scattered tale on purpose using the epistles of choice like starting/end points and may take the reader as far as he/she is capable. It is only when she describes Teresa's son that the reader is left alone to rest temporarily. Méndez similarly creates starting and end points back to back, and sometimes the end precedes the beginning but without Castillo's choices. He never permits the reader to rest and continually bombards us with the lack of alternatives for the poor he has created. For them there is no search for space and place because there are no choices except the oppression of the Tijuana street, the back-breaking work of the fields, or death in American wars.

Burciaga seems understated in comparison to Anzaldúa, Castillo, or Méndez and that perhaps is the consequence of the form of composition. His images, like those of Rodríguez, seem less packed and simpler than those of either the novelists or Anzaldúa. He fills his pages with history, anthropology, literature, myths, and political satire and irony. He, like Méndez, recognizes the crucial import of the written word, for the people he most cares about he understands are being erased by a cold Coke instead of consuming their own cultural history. On the other hand, Rodríguez does not seek to establish history and lineality. His function is the opposite: to replace private Mexican histories with a public, Irish American rendering and his own interpretation of its meaning.

All the creators are political in their art and their art is political. For Anzaldúa, Burciaga, Castillo, and Méndez, any exploitive or repressive system is to be resisted, and their art is both the means of and the end to that process. For Rodríguez, cultural assimilation is not repressive; it is, in fact, a process for the cleansing of unwanted and nonfunctional cultural baggage. There are many Mexicans who would agree with this position. His too is a political statement and not just an "artistic" position, as if this were possible. For me, however, there is an underlying difference between Rodríguez and the rest of the authors discussed. Rodríguez's political position does support the structure of power that is responsible in part for many of the conditions that give rise to the many distributions of sadness previously described. Therefore, his art, subtleties, ironies, and contradictions do have far-reaching unintended consequences beyond the written word. This must be an awful responsibility to consider in light of the anti-Mexican measures like Proposition 187 in California, anti-immigrant hysteria, and attempts to undo policies, like affirmative action, designed to balance historical inequities.

Each author in his/her own way does provide the imagery of portions of the Mexican population, even though the written word is the most perfect of imperfect means by which to paint pictures. Such pictures to varying degrees mobilize interest and action so that, regardless of the position the reader assumes, that position will be challenged and the viewer is never the same once having become part of the creator's work.

CHAPTER 7

» » » » »

Making Pictures: U.S. Mexican

Place and Space in Mural Art

M EXICAN MURAL ART in the United States continuously fills physical place and space, resurrects symbols and origin myths from the south, and declares a sense of community not only through its representations but also by means of the methods it employs to create its expressions, never relying on any legitimizing authority. Of all the explosive expressions of U.S. Mexican struggles in the nineteenth and twentieth centuries, the mural movement is the most profoundly cultural in its organizational mutuality and *confianza*, its group mobilization and action, and the participation of diverse elements of the U.S. Mexican and other communities. It follows cultural mobilization processes of community movements such as those generated by the labor unions and mutual aid societies previously discussed. The economic and social conditions of the mural in the present are not dissimilar to those of the recent past.

The mural movement spread from California to Illinois, from New Mexico to Texas, and from Arizona to Colorado; hundreds of walls throughout the Southwest have been covered with community-created symbols and themes, as well as with murals sponsored by community and state agencies. In California alone there are more than 1,500 murals still in place, and others continue to be created as new populations from the south join those in the north.[1] Of course, not all representational U.S. Mexican art is in mural form, as recent exhibitions and shows have illustrated.[2]

U.S. Mexican mural art is representative of the entire population rather than being an individualized artistic expression. The U.S. Mexican mural movement has four underlying characteristics that separate it from predecessors.[3] First, murals were frequently located in space vacated by U.S. Mexicans due to historical elimination or "urban removal"; alternatively murals filled "blank spaces" unfilled by others. Second, many murals were placed and continue to be placed on internal and external walls in schools and community centers to express community values and the quest for knowledge and communal support. Third, the U.S. Mexican mural movement has the distinct characteristic of incorporating various cultural populations into the mural statement, and it changes as new populations, especially from the south, become important demographically or politically. Fourth, mural themes and symbols change as larger social and economic issues emerge.

These characteristics, however, are in part defined by sponsorship. If, for example, the mural produced emerges in the aftermath of community dynamics that push the artist to represent such processes, the resulting representation will have much to do with identity loss and formation, economic repression and political misrepresentation, social dislocation and violence, and the ever-present conditions of the U.S. Mexican border. If the works are largely emergent from such dynamics, then the participation of various community groups is assured and "ownership" is not closely identified with the painters but rather with the issues and the community itself.

On the other hand, publicly or privately sponsored works, even though reflecting the same issues as those of the dynamically stimulated mural process, are less likely to be participatory, "owned," or communal in their relationship to the surrounding community. However, even within this framework, sponsorship in and of itself is not necessarily the most definitive factor; sometimes sheer mural aesthetics and presentations are so generative within a community that the work "captures" the community itself and goes beyond it because of its representation. This capturing is a reciprocal process, with the community and mural becoming one, many times, paradoxically, in stark contrast and in opposition to the actual physical or social environment. The murals, like the literature, are multidimensional and holographic and give multiple meanings to community identity.

Much has been written about the themes that many murals depict such as pre-Colombian motifs, emergent cultural birth, exploitation of various sorts, and cross-cultural human connection.[4] Some are internationally recognized, such as Judith Baca's never-to-be-finished *Great Wall of Los Angeles*, which is more than a half-mile long. Feminist, regionalist, nationalist, and internationalist, Baca recruits youths of all cultural groups to paint, and she also recruits academics, community members, informants, and local historians to collaborate in its production.[5] U.S. Mexican murals constitute wide symbolic and cognitive mappings, but their overriding similarity is their underlying created and invented communal emphases.

The following discussion concentrates on two sets of murals: one from Northern California and the second from Tucson, Arizona. These were selected from the thousands of murals available not because of a statistically representative sampling process but rather because they express in the most vivid way possible the general themes treated in this work. They are, however, not unrepresentative of the multiplicity of themes of the mural movement itself. They provide an unending ending and conclusion to processes much larger, older, and continuous than the life of this work and certainly of its author.

Los Murales de Stanford

» » »

Of all the physical sites in the Southwest with murals of not only physical beauty but cultural formation and integration, holography and multiplicity, the murals created by José Antonio Burciaga at the residential hall of Casa Zapata at Stanford University in Palo Alto, California, stand as a continuation of paradoxical dimensions. The university, itself a bastion of the elite and the largely exclusive domain of the very rich and famous, was, but may never again be for reasons to be discussed, the place for U.S. Mexican cultural birth and renewal. Although at present the university is prestigious and influential at the national level, it did have a much humbler beginning. The land on which it was built was farmland and hunting ground of various bands of indigenous Ohlones, who also traded along the San Mateo coast for salt, beads, and obsidian. That population, however, would eventually become extinct due to European diseases and overwork.[6]

Palo Alto (tall wood) was rejected as a settlement by Spanish explorers in 1776, as well by the Sonoran Juan Bautista de Anza and his colonists, as they passed through because of the lack of water in San Francisquito Creek, which defines the northern border of Palo Alto. However, during the Spanish colonial period, the Palo Alto area was used as pastureland for cattle and for growing maize, peas, and beans, with seeds from Mexico, for the nearby Mission of Santa Clara. After mission secularization in 1834, Mexican land grants prevailed over thousands of acres on which cattle were raised for the export of tallow and hides to New England shoe factories. The Robles, Buelnas, and Soto families came to control three large ranchos: Rancho San Francisquito, Rancho Rincón de San Francisquito, and Rancho Rinconada del Arroyo de San Francisquito. San Francisquito—a 1,500-acre rancho granted to Antonio Buelna in 1839—encompassed most of Stanford University. Squatters played a significant role in the final disposition of the Buelna land grant: one Francisco Casanueva managed to acquire title to the land through subterfuge from the widowed María Concepción Buelnas and her second husband, Francisco Rodríguez. By the end of the Mexican American War, Anglo squatters such as Thomas Bevins, Jerry Eastin, William Little, and Sandi Wilson invaded the land, after which George Gordon in 1868 purchased all the land even though the widow's original deed was recognized by the new U.S. governing power. Juan Buelna, the widow's son, died in Palo Alto after a long career working as a gardener on the land his widowed mother had lost to Casanueva and Anglo settlers—even though she been given patent to the land in 1868.[7]

Eventually all Mexican grants passed into the hands of Anglos through intermarriage, when sold for taxes, illegally acquired, and/or purchased outright; and more than 8,000 acres became a perpetual grant used by Leland Stanford to found the University in 1884.[8] In 1876 Leland Stanford had purchased a 650-acre section of Rancho Francisquito for a country home, and he eventually purchased the rest to augment other lands given him as a right-of-way for the Central Pacific Railroad, the western link of the first transcontinental railroad. Since that time, Mexican presence had been confined to streets named De Anza, Portola, and Coronado, to farm workers on university farms, to gardeners and landscape workers for Palo Alto homes, and to university blue-collar maintenance and service workers, until the advent of the "Chicano Convulsive Transition Movement." Student protest stimulated U.S. Mexican student and faculty growth at the university during the sixties and seventies. In 1994, Stanford boasted thirteen U.S. Mexican faculty and a few staff and faculty administrators of low bureaucratic rank; of these, one was a Resident Fellow of Casa Zapata, the residential Chicano house.

The creation of Casa Zapata in 1972 as a "theme house" emphasized a culturally congruent residence for all Stanford undergraduates, with an emphasis on U.S. Mexican students. Its murals represent and reproduce the actual and visual return of Mexicans and the reclamation of space and place (a function of many murals throughout the U.S. Southwest). The land where these murals are situated abuts the bank of San Francisquito Creek—the area used by the Portola expedition of 1769 to camp and which serves today as the boundary of the Stanford campus. Five years after the expedition, Juan Bautista de Anza'a diarist described the redwood tree for which Palo Alto is named: "There is . . . a very large redwood which can be seen for more than a league before reaching the arroyo, and from a distance looks like a tower."[9]

The placement of the murals is most important because they are part of a residential context for U.S. Mexican students, the artist-in-residence, and the adult Resident Fellow(s). By 1985, after the tenure of a number of artists-in-residence, thirteen murals were painted on the interior and exterior walls.[10] Like the San Diego murals, these initial works by various artists express revived and newly invented motifs and symbols of Mayan, Aztec, Native American, Mexican Revolution, student protest, Chicana liberation, and revolutionary movements and figures.

The Burciagas arrived in 1985; and while Cecilia created the social and political context for student success within and beyond Stanford, José Antonio wrote, painted, and exhibited aspects of Mexican culture to a wide community of listeners, establishing the cultural representation of a community much broader than Stanford as well. Together they laid the cultural and social foundation for students and created an in-residence "clustered household" in which they served as the "core" in the same manner that older generation members function in U.S. Mexican "clustered household" communities.[11]

These circumstances reproduced aspects of historical lineality, reciprocal social relationships, cultural mutuality and *confianza*, physical presence, and, most dangerous for any institution, a political potential. Such cultural representations and political potentials are most obvious in Burciaga's three Casa Zapata murals and their connecting panels, which all together form an integrated series of murals: *The Mythology of Maize* (plate 7.1) and a connecting side panel, *Introduction of Maize* (plate 7.2); the well-known *Last Supper of Chicano Heroes* (plate 7.3) and a second connecting panel, *More Chicano Heroes and Heroines* (plate 7.4); and finally, *The Cycle of Life* (plate 7.5).[12]

After Tony Burciaga had conducted an exhaustive study of corn in Mexico, he began *Mythology of Maize* (a 15' × 12' mural) in January 1987 and completed it the same year (plate 7.1); thematically it extends beyond the one panel to two adjoining walls for a total length of 60 feet.[13] The panel is a cosmic composition of genesis and rebirth based on Burciaga's research, which focused on Maya mythology and specifically the *Popol Vuh* (a book of genesis of the Maya people). At the bottom left of the mural a reclining wooden man represents the first human beings created by the gods, who were disappointed that the wooden beings could not give thanks. Therefore, they next made beings of clay represented by a reclining woman at bottom right, but they too could not give thanks. Finally, the gods created nine men and women from maize, but their eyes were clouded until they could give thanks. The two central figures emerging from the central sun are the newly born peoples able to see and to give thanks for life.[14] The various figures seem to represent the emergent Mexican peoples of the United States similarly placed and too long held in wooden or clay forms in speechless and sightless postures. Their emergence, however, is not the result of Mayan gods' intervention but rather the joining of the past with the present—of Quetzalcoatl and the *cholo* seen above the two central figures. Surrounding the two emergent figures are various mythical motifs and symbols, including the origin of corn in the various scenes, one of which is an underground ant colony, and a woodpecker trickster.

Quetzalcoatl, also depicted in Kiva murals discussed in chapter 1, is central to the discovery of corn and with it life. Above the central male figure is a *cholo* or *bato loco* created by the flying Quetzalcoatl—the feathered serpent that is quite a contrast to Michelangelo's Sistine Chapel version of the bearded European god giving life to a white Adam. The *cholo*, wearing a red bandanna and sporting a tear tattoo on his left cheek and a *pachuco* cross and heart on his left shoulder, is holding an almost-spent cigarette. The figures of Quetzalcoatl and the *cholo* ideationally fuse the ancient Mexican creator myth and the *cholo* working class—and do not merely serve as a satire of their European counterparts. Rather, the two figures join in mythic reproduction and recognition of common origins to the south and of the working-class platform from which most U.S. Mexicans emerge. The two joining together generate U.S. Mexican mythic time and place, which then give meaning and "place" to the rest of the adjoining panels; but more important, they make public the hidden historical, mythic, and symbolic presence of the U.S. Mexican population. The mural creates mythic history in which the present and the past are one in the same place and space. It is antiperiodic and nonlineal in form, and simultaneity rather than completion is its norm.

The entire work is surrounded by a bower of green corn plants with each of the four cardinal points represented by appropriate white, yellow, orange, and red ears of corn. Above and to the upper left of the bower is a white moon whose light is representative of an enveloping love that permeates the entire mural with a light silver sheen. This sheen and the orange billowing clouds create an illusion of integration with the other panels. The rest of the panels then "distribute" the mythic statement without lineality, as if this were a history beginning from the end rather the beginning.

In between the major panel and the *Last Supper of Chicano Heroes* is a minor work: *Introduction of Maize* (plate 7.2) shows an indigenous man picking a cornstalk while a Mesoamerican woman and man instruct onlooking Europeans, including a blond and blue-eyed Cortez who has been handed a corn cob by a Mesoamerican woman, about corn's mysteries. A pilgrim from the Mayflower seems to be paying apt attention to a Mesoamerican man, while behind them all stands a partially obscured Father Junípero Serra. Above them white and green ribbons intertwine from the edge of the subpanel.

Apart from the obvious pedagogical statement made in this part of the mural, there is also an ideological vision that specifically declares the manner in which the indigenous populations received Europeans as their pupils. The relationship, which became a deadly one culturally and biologically, as an initial descriptor illustrates that knowledge for U.S. Mexicans emerges from both traditions, indigenous and European simultaneously. It is within this "bumping" context that a connection can be made with the *Last Supper* panel, which too often has been considered apart from the *Mythology of Maize* genesis/ending mural and this subpanel.

A Toltec monolith divides the subpanel from the rest; it is a type of cultural glue that connects the subpanel and its predecessor to the following mural. The monolith interconnects the different aspects of U.S. Mexican ideology as represented in the *Last Supper of Chicano Heroes* with the *Maize* panel.

While the *Last Supper* mural (plate 7.3) seems to be a pantheon of admired personalities of the Chicano movement, it is that and more. Made up of forty-three historical personalities, ideas, and symbols, it is instead an array of ideas representative of the population, its struggles, successes, alliances, relationships, and humanistic bases. Its working-class base is expressed by the multicultural service workers dressed in white uniforms: Cambodian—Shum Roung; African Americans—Esther Phillips, Linda Washington, Bill Davis, John Towns, Richard Swinington, Jeanette Williams; Mexicans—Lalo Magana, Juan Carlos, Enrique Mares, Salvador Mendoza; Salvadoran—José Araña; and Anglo—Laura Herrington.

Overseeing the entire array is the Virgen de Guadalupe, the patroness of the Americas; therefore, the heroines and heroes are from the Americas—the United States into the rest of the continent—and reflect the multiplicity of admired personalities of the entire area, as well as their ideologies and deeds. This selection was actually the result of a survey that Burciaga undertook among students, faculty, and staff at Stanford after he had decided against depicting the actual Last Supper at the behest of students.[15]

Beneath the Virgin stands a smiling *calavera*, a favorite symbol of Mexican mythology, which in this context is a type of reminder of the ephemeral quality of all human inventions, including the mural itself and all the figures living and dead who stand or sit behind the supper table. Resting at the feet of the Virgin is the *angelito negro*, reminiscent of the Mexican song, "Angelitos negros" whose lyrics ask why only white angels are painted by artists.[16] On either side of la Virgen and la calavera sit and stand artists Frida Kahlo and Carlos Santana, writers Gabriela Mistral and Thomas Rivera, revolutionaries Emiliano Zapata and Che Guevara, political heroes Ignacio Zaragoza and Augusto Sandino, civil rights activist Martin Luther King, feminist Sor Juana Inés de la Cruz, and labor organizers Dolores Huerta and César Chávez. Alongside Zapata service workers and Burciaga's mother and father are represented former Mexican and American presidents and U.S. Mexican cultural rebels and heroes: Californian Tiburcio Vásquez and Sonoran Joaquín Murrieta. Curiously, Francisco "Pancho" Villa is not depicted in the mural.

While there may be disputes as to actual ideological positions of the these figures, they are, nevertheless, multigenerational heroes. The public personas of Jack Kennedy and Che Guevara, as opposite as they were to their private personas, in their ideologies and behaviors did reflect community values for multiple generations. Kennedy's persona, his wife Jacqueline Kennedy, Irish Catholicism, and Irish historical relations were direct cultural and political links to U.S. Mexicans. That is, Kennedy represented a period of hope and optimism for Mexicans of the early 1960s and even for earlier generations. "Jackie's" public use of Spanish revealed a cultural recognition of the existence of Mexicans in the public forum; and because the Kennedys were Catholics, they legitimized Catholic religious affinity for a population that was 90 percent Catholic. At the same time, a little-appreciated historical link to the Irish was recalled for the U.S. Mexican offspring of the post-Mexican Revolution and Depression generation. The San Patricio Brigade (composed primarily of Irish U.S. Army deserters) fought against U.S. forces in the Mexican American War.[17]

Kennedy's opposite, Ernesto "Che" Guevara, a Marxist-Leninist revolutionary, was a highly attractive figure for both generations just mentioned, as well as for the post–World War II "baby boomers" of the late sixties and early seventies. For the earlier cohort, Guevara was a response to the failed optimism of Kennedy's "Camelot" and to his assassination. Kennedy was replaced with an equally romantic and romanticized figure—the Argentine-born "El Che"—who projected the bravery and villainy of Villa and the charisma and honesty of Zapata (who in the mural is seated immediately to the right of Guevara). For the later cohort, Cuba was the new Camelot, a brave new world in spite of Yankee imperialism and cultural imposition. Cuba was the successful model of what subservient and subordinated populations could accomplish in common, even against the most powerful of foes. Finally, in the mural Guevara is pictured as a Christ figure and a suitable re-

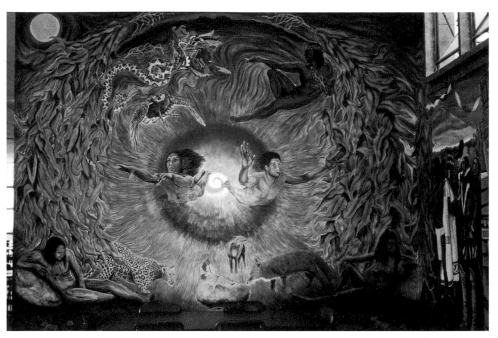

PLATE 7.1
Mythology of Maize,
Casa Zapata,
Stanford University

PLATE 7.2
Introduction of Maize,
Casa Zapata,
Stanford University

"...and to all those who died, scrubbed floors, wept and fought for us."

PLATE 7.3
Last Supper of Chicano Heroes, Casa Zapata, Stanford University. Photo courtesy of José Antonio Burciaga.

PLATE 7.4
*More Chicano Heroes
and Heroines,*
Casa Zapata,
Stanford University

PLATE 7.5
Cycle of Life,
Casa Zapata,
Stanford University

PLATE 7.6
Cuida desierto,
Tucson, Arizona

PLATE 7.7
In Memory of
Eustaquio C. Urrea,
Tucson, Arizona

placement for Kennedy for this generation. The figure of Guevara connects all the figures and ideas in the mural to the theme written on the tablecloth: ". . . and to all those who died, scrubbed floors, wept and fought for me."[18] The entire mural, then, pays homage to the humble, the exalted, the revolutionary, the ideologue, the romantic, the pragmatist, and the philosopher, who in some form or another struggled for the benefit of others.

A second Toltec monolith, *More Chicano Heroes and Heroines*, painted in 1989 (plate 7.4), as Burciaga explains, was created in the aftermath of complaints by Stanford workers, students, and community members about being excluded from the *Last Supper of Chicano Heroes*.[19] It reflects one of the general characteristics of the mural movement itself: "communal" expression. This panel, unlike the *Last Supper*, was created from a survey, as well as from the painter's individual choices and preferences. Although Burciaga regards *More Chicano Heroes and Heroines* as the least successful of the murals, it might be regarded as the most representative of those who participate in the daily struggles that benefit others everywhere. While maintaining the corn theme, this panel includes previously excluded service, maintenance, landscape, and culinary workers at Stanford, secretaries, the poet Alurista, painters, and a woman tortilla maker in the foreground. Andrés Segura, who is kneeling and playing the mandolin, was Burciaga's indigenous Mexican mentor on his field trip to Mexico to research corn. Central to the panel, as well, is Segura's brother, a young man in Aztec headdress sitting in a wheelchair; he was a former Aztec dance performer crippled by degenerative arthritis. He is accompanied in the immediate background by the painter Burciaga, Cecilia Burciaga Preciado, and their two children.

What is most immediate to the mural is the theme of work and the sacrifice represented by corn, made more pressing by the poem attached to a papaya tree in the left foreground. The poem "Work," by Cintia Fitizer, encapsulates the entire panel in the first stanza:

Others did this
better ones than you,
for centuries
On them depended
your sense of freedom,
your clean shirt
and your leisure to read and write . . .

In part, however, this panel is successful because it follows the last panel chronologically. *More Chicano Heroes and Heroines* was painted two years after the *Last Supper* and a year after the last panel, *The Cycle of Life*. It benefited from the mythic expression of the *Cycle* panel in that it forced Burciaga to respond in a more grounded manner to U.S. Mexican reality—the labor and the struggles of its women and men, familial values of love and affection, the tragedy of the unexpected distribution of sadness, and the creative and artistic capacity of its population. Thus, although this panel in chronological terms was the last one produced by Burciaga, there is a freshness and humanity, a sense of community and *confianza*, and demystification present here that is absent from the *Last Supper* and *The Cycle of Life* (plate 7.5.)

The Cycle of Life, in contrast to the first panel, *Mythology of Maize*, has the overriding characteristic of being, as Burciaga states it, "a cool color of blue green" in contrast to the hot-orange, creative, passionate colors of the first.[20] It presents a perduring sense of continuity beginning with the brown mother earth figure connected by the yellow corn sheaves and corncobs to the blue expansive cosmos. Three arching corn stalks on each side accompany the three crownlike corncobs and are symbolic of a more Catholic trinity than its apparent mythological representation would suggest. This image continues in a more abstract way the seeming irony of the Michelangelo figures of the first panel and expresses the synergy and symbolic syncretism of the entire mural.

The trinity icon connects the panel internally and integrates rather than ends the 60-foot mural by connecting it to all the other panels with a sense of overwhelming perdurance by its sheer scale and meaning. This dynamic is reproduced in a physical, historical, and behavioral sense in that the panels are painted within the Zapata cafeteria so that the site becomes a living context within which students, service workers, parents, and faculty may engage in daily commensal behaviors. Because the entire base of the mural is painted to match the color and shape of the actual tiles of the cafeteria's floor, an illusion of seamless continuation between the mural, the cafeteria, and those present is created. Thus, everyone present becomes part of the mural, and the mural becomes part of them, with the latter unaware of this synergy. Those present eat, share, communicate, teach, retell, gossip, laugh, cry, lecture, recite, dance, listen, strategize, study, and interact daily in hundreds of ways with each other, and this process blends into the murals so that the behaviors give human life to a representational mythology. In this manner, the "Other" and the "One" become the same. History is created and recounted simultaneously in the same time and place.

For those present, the past and present are not unlike the end/beginning of the first and last panels, even though neither begin nor end the mural. The past and present become "historical," and space and place—cultural and proximal—become interconnected and alive. Space and place, then, emerge daily, being rediscovered, embellished, and created by those present, in reference to the past and the created present. In this sense, Chicano "mythic" time and place is forced to take human form by human beings participating in its daily creation, and history is given a human reference as well.

Los Murales of Tucson's Downtown and Central Areas
» » »

Almost 220 years after Juan Bautista de Anza had left the same region and traveled in 1776 with his colonists to Palo Alto, Tucson, Arizona, had become the home for 187 extant interior and exterior murals, of which 133 were painted by U.S. Mexican artists.[21] Forty-five murals were painted by Anglos and probably 8 murals were produced by Native American artists and one by an African American.[22] Although this discussion will restrict its description to a few representative murals of Tucson painted by U.S. Mexicans, it should be understood that mural painting antedates the Chicano mural movement and postdates it as well.

The first mural-frescos of Tucson were painted by an unidentified Hispano/Mexicano in the 1790s, and the work still survives inside the Mission San Xavier del Bac—the northernmost religious center of Spanish colonial activity. Of a traditional eighteenth-century colonial baroque style, these frescos depicted a European Virgin holding an equally European Christ child over a stone manger and surrounded by winged archangels; nevertheless, these scenes are interspersed with indigenous symbols masked by gilded scrolls.

In the mid-1950s, this Europeanized tradition was continued by commercial banks commissioning traditional historical scenes of benevolent conquistadors, loving priests, and adoring Indians, all set against the background of soft purple skies, brown desert floors, and long-armed saguaro cacti. These largely muted pastel representations were painted by non-Mexican painters for a non-Mexican audience, for whom the primary intended and multiple unintended functions were to decorate barren bank walls and to continue an ersatz "Spanish" history and occasionally to legitimize a less-than-sterling Anglo historical reputation. The 1955 *Legend of the Seven Cities of Cibola* mural in the interior of the former Southern Arizona Bank was commissioned by the bank whose president ordered the extralegal "Bisbee Mine Expulsions" of the 1920s (see chapter 3).[23]

Between this period and the Chicano mural movement other murals of a decorative sort were commissioned by Farmer John Meats, a sausage and beef packer. The company commissioned a former Australian wrestler and scene painter from Hollywood to cover their building walls,[24] and for almost a quarter of a mile an entire wall that divides Grant Street from the property is painted with spotted cows, happy bulls, an occasional droopy cowboy, languid saguaros, brown desert floor, and blue skies with a few wispy clouds. However, between 1975 and the present, an explosion of bright, lively Mexican murals filled the interior and exterior walls of schools, community centers, electrical substations, housing projects, private residences, restaurants, grocery stores, and bakeries. These range from memorials to more recent "ecological" presentations and from mythological depictions to pedagogical statements regarding education and family. All the murals owe their inspiration to the political and cultural revitalization processes of the late 1960s and 1970s. Like their Los Angeles and Stanford counterparts, the murals express a population's quest to establish definitive cultural statements of identity and to balance the inequities of education, economy, and political representation.

As the specific discussion of two examples will illustrate, the same basic "communal" approach, as well as southern and regional influences, is expressed in these murals. The general discussion will be limited to an analysis of the distribution of the U.S. Mexican murals of Tucson in the "Downtown" and "Central" areas and their relationships to their contexts rather than their thematic and symbolic characteristics. Other murals of the "Greater Tucson" area will be left for a more ample treatment in a later work, but suffice it to say that those works painted by U.S. Mexican painters in this broader area are in most instances painted in educational institutions.[25]

Distribution and Locational Characteristics

Among the first murals created in Tucson were those at the Westside El Río Neighborhood Center painted in 1975 by Antonio Pazos and his group. In the 1970s, at least ten murals were produced, but the actual number is unknown due to the fact that some were left undated. However, they are certainly strongly identified politically and culturally with the "Chicano Convulsive Transition Movement" of that period.

After 1980 and until 1989, fifty-five were painted and many commissioned by artist-in-residence programs, community centers, city and county agencies, and private businesses. At least forty-five more were painted between 1990 and 1993.[26] Another twenty-three murals were not dated, but most were probably painted in the post-1980 period.[27] Such an explosive growth in the number of murals can be appreciated further by the fact that in 1983 only twenty-five murals had been painted in Tucson, according to one analysis; however, because this research does not include interior works, another two may be definitively added.[28]

Murals in the "Downtown" and "Central" areas are clustered as a result of the internal dynamics of the area and as an aftermath of the "urban removal" of much of the Mexican population from the downtown area during the mid-1960s.[29] As the former site of the colonial and Mexican presidio of San Agustín de Tucsón, the downtown area had served as a central place for the clustering of Mexican households until the advent of the War on Poverty (see chapters 2, 4, and 5).

THE DOWNTOWN AREA

In the "Downtown" area, four clusters emerge, as table 7.1 shows. All the murals in Cluster 1 are associated with businesses, and except for one site, none are "group" works or associated with mural movement art; three sites are basically commercial advertisements for a product, restaurant, or bank. The works by Tineo and Pazos on the north walls of the Tucson Museum of Art are canonical murals painted in 1992. Although emblematic of the themes of the mural movement, they are locationally institutionalized and observed by heterogeneous cultural populations rather than lived by any one of them. These fine works, for all intents and purposes, seem to be appropriated and delocalized from

TABLE 7.1

Clusters of Murals in Downtown Tucson

Cluster 1	Cluster 2	Cluster 3	Cluster 4
101	2	1	50
108	11	91	7
18	60	73	81
67	106		43
109			130
32			27
			76

Source: *Guide to Murals in Tucson* 1993, 4.

their political and cultural context, even though the murals have reappropriated the location considering that the site of the museum was part of the presidio and associated Mexican neighborhoods.

In Cluster 2, one mural was a group work directed by a U.S. Mexican muralist and painted by the elderly multicultural residents of the Martin Luther King Jr. Apartment Building in 1993. The inclusivity of heterogeneous populations in this work and in many others of the Tucson area is very much like that already discussed in the Stanford murals and in many others in the Southwestern region. Entitled *A Show of Hands,* the mural was directed by Eddie Domínguez and incorporates Mexican, African American, Indian, and Anglo motifs and symbols not unlike the residents of the apartment complex.

Similarly, another mural situated on a building housing a highly commercialized pawn shop is a symbolic and representative contrast to the function of the shop itself. This group mural *La fuerza de nuestra raza* painted by Pima Community College students is a bold statement of cultural identity and locational license.

For Cluster 3 only one mural by Julio Bernal, entitled *Quetzalcoatl,* can be considered a movement mural. Painted in 1991 at Safford Middle School, the mural contextualizes the new functions of the school in its role as a "magnet school" with a science-oriented curriculum, to which primarily Anglo children are bused for special attention. While serving a local population of Mexican children in a largely working-class neighborhood, Safford suffers from the same stratification problems other "bilingual" magnet schools have in that non-Mexican students are transferred in and dominate the advanced classes, including those in Spanish. The mural is an attempt to balance this situation by providing the children with a mythic connection and cultural reference to their heritage, but in addition, it counterbalances the Anglo mythology represented in an accompanying mural, *Space and Technology,* painted at the same site by an Anglo artist.

Within the central area, Cluster 4 contains the greatest number of sites and is the most representative of movement murals thematically and locationally. It also contains works of the 1990s reflecting concerns not associated with the Chicano movement. This area, especially "Barrio Anita," was the only residential space left partially intact by the urban removal process of the 1960s. However, because of a gentrification process in the area, especially by law offices, the adobe buildings of this neighborhood are housing fewer Mexican residents, even though their protests often appear plastered on walls of newly renovated structures.

A number of murals are located in neighborhood schools and youth centers on interior and exterior walls. The murals depict a wide range of motifs focusing on learning, success, academic subjects, and youthful development; they include an array of pyramidal, Toltec, Mesoamerican, Mexican, and indigenous symbols and figures integrated as cultural references.

Among these, the 1993 barrio and communal mural *Cuida desierto: Take Care of the Desert* is a creation declaring permanency of place, space, and region. Painted by three artists and a host of students from Drachman Elementary School and La Pillita Youth Center, the mural is indicative of a space and place no longer yearned for but rather one to be protected. It is as if the creators of the mural have found the "peace" of having arrived, of stability, of established presence, unlike the other "searching" murals seeking a place to settle. In this mural there is little sense of yearning but rather of integration of the living forces of creation as shown in plate 7.6.

The central pedagogical focus of the *Cuida desierto* mural is the physical environment and its ecology—a trend that began earlier in the 1980s.[30] However, this "ecological" theme is strongly associated with a mystical and mythical emergence and growth. Painted on the south wall of a reconstructed adobe residence, which adjoins an empty lot seen in the foreground, the mural is reminiscent of the coolness of Burciaga's *Myth of Maize.* However, this mural has a kind of "cool heat," which is a result of combining the monumental forms of a mestizo mountain face (right) and a brown mother earth holding the result of a procreated life form in the shape of a moon face from whence emerges a glyph of infinity (left). At the center, an exposed hand rising above the earth is reminiscent of Burciaga's Chicano Adam and Quetzalcoatl creation, except that here the creative force is extended to a female form and symbol. Animals, cacti, and water are themselves connected by the brown mother earth and given life by the yellow signatures of the children who contributed to the mural. Thus, while many other murals throughout the Southwest, including those previously shown, produced balanced female and male figures of various sorts, this mural is essentially a creational and feminist woman. The monumental bearded mestizo figure to the right sits slightly open-mouthed, as if in awe at the sight of the creative act. This creational woman theme is much more associated with the traditional Southwestern genesis myths of the Tohono O'odham, Pima, Apache, and Hopi, which emphasize the motherliness and creational woman aspect of the process rather than a Mesoamerican or colonial male figure. It is also a more feminist treatment in that the power of creation is represented in the hand of the mother image and thus makes a strong yet subtle political statement of the potential and actual power of women.

In addition, the mestizo seems to be a less important figure in two ways. First, although he is an upright figure, he is "rooted" to the earth and seems to serve as an anchor, not the progenitor, of the creative activity to his right and right rear. Second, while the figure is well defined, unlike the female figure holding the creative moon/ovary, the very definition makes him more human and less mythic. The creative hand/force to his right does not emerge from him, but rather it emerges from a space more deeply rooted than his literal and mythic presence to touch the hand of the reclining earth mother. Thus, the mural is much more a product of the nineties than the sixties in integrating mythic and monumental symbols, which are at once creative woman/feminist and attentive to regional ideology and environmental values, with the latter two trends emerging during the 1980s.[31]

CENTRAL TUCSON
There are fourteen blocks of murals in central Tucson, and most mural sites do not adjoin each other. However, the concentration of murals in

the central Tucson area is directly associated with the presence of a high concentration of Mexicans in the area, with some exceptions.[32] For example, the murals on the west side of the city are in the midst of four Mexican barrios: El Hoyo, Hollywood, Anita, and Menlo Park. Consisting of middle-class, working-class, and poverty sectors, this area was also the site of Chicano movement activities, which resulted in the creation of El Río Neighborhood Center and its murals (thirty in all) after a series of protracted demonstrations, sit-ins, and marches.

The area with the densest concentration of murals is a part of central Tucson better known as the Barrio Libre.[33] It includes South Tucson—a one-mile-square city—which is an autonomous Mexican community. Most of the population immediately outside of South Tucson has about the same economic status as do the people living in South Tucson and Barrio Libre.

SOUTH TUCSON

In 1990 South Tucson itself was composed of 6,535 residents, 76.5 percent U.S. Mexican, with a modest mean income of $10,026 and with 38 percent of the population below the poverty level.[34] In contrast, for the city of Tucson's Mexican population (22 percent of the total population), the mean income was $18,241.

Of the more than 2,100 housing units in South Tucson, 43.5 percent were owner occupied, with 3.18 persons per unit; 56.5 percent were renter occupied, with 2.82 persons per unit. South Tucson's tax rate is based on $.16 per $100 evaluation, while the city of Tucson's is $1.00 per $100 evaluation; thus, land values in South Tucson are relatively low, and "start-up" homes are possible.[35] Therefore, the probability of first-generation Mexican migrants from the south living in the area is high.

These general social and economic characteristics, when combined with able political leadership, as I have described elsewhere, may inspire community action. Murals are one expression of this, appearing most frequently in schools, public buildings, service centers, and public housing units.[36] In the case of South Tucson, these circumstances have led to the creation of thirty murals by U.S. Mexican artists, twenty-seven of which are located in public housing units, community food banks, and elementary schools. For the most part, the murals, as celebrations of the communities in which they appear, are multicultural and depict historical figures that include Martin Luther King, Emiliano

Zapata, Pancho Villa, Benito Juárez, César Chávez, and Malcolm X. In addition, farther to the south of the South Tucson area, this same pattern of heroes is repeated with some variation.

Among the most poignant and representative of the murals in the South Tucson cluster (and in some ways of the Southwest) is the untitled memorial to Eustaquio C. Urrea, a neighborhood youth killed in a drive-by shooting. As illustrated in plate 7.7, a scroll at the bottom of the mural lists the "artist" Mario Moreno and young "painters": Henry Cortez Jr., Louie Cota, Victoria García, Tony Gómez, Anna Franko, Lionel Franko, Yovang Moreno, Yanette Moreno and Baby D, Tony Sierra, Christina Singer, Danny Strickle, and Mando Valencia. The mural is a memorial that presents the major figures important to U.S. Mexicans; in addition, it invites the observer to participate in a communally identified place. The mural is painted on the north wall of the Ronquillo Bakery—a bakery that is as much a part of the Mexican community of Tucson as the Flores Pharmacy, the cathedral of San Agustín, Nayo the barber, Safford Junior High, the "Hollywood" barrio, or the Victoria Ballroom.[37] Ronquillo's is synonymous with longevity, durability, and lineality to the past.

La panadería (the bakery) plays one of the single most symbolic roles in Mexican communities. This is the place where Mexican Christmas cookies, Day of the Dead skulls, and sweets and breads after mass on Sundays (whose origins have been long forgotten but are known by their Nahuatl, French, or Spanish names) can be purchased. It is on the walls of such a site that the memorial is painted. The mural is, as are all others, more than what it represents. Reminiscent of so many similar works in which creation is the subject, it also uses the Michelangelo archetype for form; but here similarities cease. In this case, an Aztec figure held up by two angels—one male underneath and the other a small female angel—fuses with the reclining Spanish figure. Their fusion creates the Mexican and American map in the background. While the flags designate nations, these figures represent the cultural congruence and southern and northern existence of the Mexican population on both sides of the political border. It is a recognition of their "place" as one separated by national emblems.

Similarly, the cultural space is mythically defined by the European St. Jude who is also the patron saint of travelers, lost souls, and prisoners, and therefore functions as a protective mantle to Eustaquio C. Urrea on his journey. However, non-European mythology informs the political and cultural ideology of the cultural space of the mural. The Aztec figure emerges out of the sun—the life source for the planets represented and all life. An Aztec priest stands directly beneath the sun, suggesting that his existence emanates from the same source. The priest extends rooted plants from a small yellow vessel to the populations that represent the probable heterogeneity of the painters but more specifically the cultural heterogeneity of the region: the American eagle—the Anglo; the Zulu shield—African Americans; and the Hopi Katsina—the Native American population.

The mural projects many visions of one world and in part the many visions of Mexican populations that live and fill the cultural and social space of South Tucson, Arizona, and the Southwest. As a memorial it reveals disturbing aspects of Mexican life but, nevertheless, is a timeless memory of the Mexican population's origins, myths, existential condition, and relations to others. It underscores the idea that all visions do blend into one and that, regardless of bumping, origin, and symbols used to represent them, all human beings share in the human condition of emergence from the same evolutionary and spiritual source. The mural portrays the recognition of the commonality of human diversity as represented in its multicultural figures. Thus, many visions of one world are ensconced in this mural painted on a bakery wall in the Barrio Libre of South Tucson as a living memory to a child destroyed by other children who have not yet found their place and space.

Conclusions

»   »   »

The U.S. Mexican mural movement continues to be a vibrant expression of local and regional concerns in the universal language of art. At an apex of political consciousness, the murals were not only expressive but created the places and spaces either denied, removed, or devalued by much larger political and economic forces than the communities in which the murals were painted. All murals are a type of pedagogical statement; thus, their presence in schools seems to be especially appropriate for children isolated from a larger community context. Educational institutions seem to have appropriated, like never before, the forms if not the symbols of liberation, self-determination, multiculturalism, and mythic relations. The works highlighted revealed not only profound existential questions of human emergence but also provided a multivisual and multivocal means by which human beings could interact and become objects, subjects, the one and the other in simultaneous processes.

Politically, the murals served as a notice—a type of documentation of cultural persistence and continuance. They opposed a singular means of expression through the communal participation of different voices while simultaneously echoing a single voice by their presentation. The murals also reflected larger political and cultural processes beyond the locality in which they were painted. They were international in scope but expressed specific symbolic versions of global issues. These issues changed as larger forces also changed: for example, the shift from singular cultural concerns to multicultural concerns, from representations of male-configured ideas to creative woman, and from mostly economic and political themes to larger ecological and environmental issues. Nevertheless, the mural movement has captured one truly essential theme that extends from Kiva to U.S. Mexican mural art: the perennial search for place and space.

CHAPTER 8

» » » » »

Conclusions: Unmasking

Borders of Minds and Method

I N   M A N Y   W A Y S, this work has been an attempt to gain a hold on very slippery processes and materials. I have not tried to seek out "laws" of society or great "norms" that might help us adjust our understanding of everyday reality. Rather, I have tried to tell a tale from the inside out and from the bottom up about groups of people who for centuries searched for a place and space to occupy. At the same time, I have attempted to unmask many of the assumptions that create the borders of the mind regarding Mexicans of the region. I have told the tale without the pretense of being "objective" or being so subjective that the narrative turned into autobiography. Rather, in this blend "anthropology" has a constant declared companion—the subjective experience of the writer.

In part, I have tried to provide a context and process to understand the presence over time of this cultural population called Mexican in a national state called the United States, in a region of the Southwest. Each of these terms and categories are unimportant except in what they mean to the populations that refer to or are bound by them. Simultaneously, this exploration served as a means for me and the many others within me to serve as friends, opposition, interlocutors, and negotiators for the emergent word about the many borders of the mind and the region.

For many Mexicans and for me, the border is among the most important ideas in our lives simply because our identities are so tied to this creation. Created at almost ten-year intervals, the border emerged for Tejanos in 1836 through the Texas Rebellion, in 1847 for Californios and Nuevo Mexicanos through the Mexican War, and in 1858 for the Sonorenses through the Gadsden Purchase. The border, however, is like a perpetual creation, and governments have the power to decide when and if Mexicans will be allowed to "cross over"; and for the privileged few some sort of tag, such as a "green card" or, at the highest level of achievement, identity as a "naturalized" citizen. The latter is an especially ironic twist considering that only plants and animals are natural citizens of any space.

The various "fences" through which Mexicans peer when looking north and those through which non-Mexicans peer looking south are all integral to the created and constructed border as defined by their respective national states: the United States of America and the Republic of Mexico. Such a border has not only kept people out and let some in physically but also created cultural and historical views that function in the same manner. When economic times are poor, Mexicans are excluded, and those who remain are resented, and U.S. Mexicans even internalize an assumed identity to deny themselves an association with the "unnaturalized." When times are good, Mexicans are welcomed for their backs and hands. This process of inclusion and exclusion has created in the minds of many a regard for Mexicans as something to be bought and sold—a commodity not unlike an automobile that when no longer useful is discarded.

Simultaneously, this process has created a kind of ersatz history in which Mexicans have to allude to a glorious Spanish or Aztec past for verification of identity and for legitimacy. What must become apparent from a discussion of the "Second Settlers" is that most Hispanos/Mexicanos who migrated north from New Spain after the post-Pueblo Revolt of 1680 were primarily craftspeople and agropastoralists who had more in common with the Pueblo peoples than they did with the upper reaches of the peninsular caste/class sector. Folktales aside, the "Spanish" tradition often used as the cultural reference point for these settlers had already changed due to the impact of the Pueblo Revolt and the fact that the exchange and trade relations with Chihuahua did not cease until the Santa Fe trail was well traveled.

The movement from the south of populations, ideas, and inventions had, in fact, begun much earlier with the introduction of the triad of corn, squash, and beans (and probably chili) from the south. The Hohokam development of monumental forms, such as temple mounds and ballcourts, is a direct result of a southern origin. Their agricultural production through irrigation, which reached sudden complexity in A.D. 900, as has been discussed, may be due in part to an infusion rather than to only a slow developmental process.

In the far-reaching exchange and trade relations between the various waxing and waning centers, a reference to the peripheries of Mesoamerica can be made in the pre-European and protohistoric periods. The trade at different periods among the Casas Grandes complex, Pueblo Bonito, the Hohokam, the Sonoran statelets, and the Chalchihuites and La Quemada complex supports a hypothesis of a long period of constant movement of etched shell, obsidian, turquoise, hides, parrots and scarlet macaws and many other artifacts to the north, south, east, and west. This movement of basically sumptuary items indicates an exchange between different, well-organized political, economic, and social systems from at least A.D. 300 to as late as the sixteenth century in some cases.

Thus, except for territorial boundaries that these various complex systems may have induced, there were no 2,000-mile declarations of exclusivity. In fact, as has already been discussed, it is more than likely that trade during this period was hardly interrupted even by war, and multilingualism was probably the norm among adjacent populations. In addition, the symbolic and ideological worlds of these populations were also not excluded from the sphere of influence; thus, the Kiva complex, their accompanying Quetzalcoatl myths, the Katsina cults, and mortuary practices seem to be directly associated with southern origins and the exchange between populations.

What we may call the border syndrome has created a pernicious view that the development of community life north of the border began with the penetration of American populations and methods of production. Mixed with racist and ethnocentric attitudes, the early descriptions by Anglos of Mexicans and Mexican community life were stereotypically negative especially in regards to the quality of its infrastructure, social system, and religious beliefs. These descriptions could not have included an appreciation of the impact of the American illegal arms trade on many Hispano/Mexicano communities since 1806. As an aftermath of the Mexican American war, many Mexicans were more than willing themselves to welcome Anglos into their midst. Through intermarriage and legal maneuvers even further economic loss was experienced by small and large Mexican landholders.

Such a process, however, did stimulate the creation of a fundamental aspect of the border syndrome: the ersatz "Spanish" reference, which is in part a construction related to relations with Anglos rather than merely the creation or continuation of a mythic tradition. In order for intermarriage between Anglos and the daughters of relatively wealthy Hispano/Mexicano families to have occurred, a social and racist construction called "Spanish" blood as opposed to the "mixed" blood of mestizos became the acceptable reference for Anglos in reference to Hispanos/Mexicanos.

In turn, Hispanos/Mexicanos "whitenized" themselves long after the dissolution of the caste system and except for class differentiation, this type of racialism became a way to designate individual Mexicans as "acceptable" to Anglos. This notion also had an ideological impact on the concept of the border, in that all those south of the border were "Mexicans" not Spanish and thus inferior to the "good" Spanish kind. The word "Mexican" not only became an opprobrium as a commodity reference but acquired a special spatial reference with regard to those "on the other side."

When this idea of a commodity population is coupled to "Americanization" programs, English only, immigration raids, double wage structure, labor repression, the various economically induced pogroms of the 1890s, 1900s, 1930s, 1950s, 1970s, 1980s, and the present 1990s hysteria, a border gestalt of extreme exclusion is created. In this manner, some U.S. Mexicans have come to believe that heritage should be denied and that U.S. citizenship is the hallmark of cultural acceptability and the only means of avoiding border syndrome contamination. In addition, sometimes fashionable terms like "diaspora," which describe the tragedies of human populations and are appropriate for African Americans and Jews, are misapplied to Mexicans, because Mexicans have not been expelled from the south but from the north—in reverse so to speak of the diaspora notion. This idea further accentuates the presence of the border as a reference for analytical departure.

Many Mexicans, however, did not and do not accept the "border syndrome" or their expulsion. Resistance, rebellion, mobilization, creation, and invention continue to be the cultural responses of much of the population. Taking their lead from the nineteenth-century cultural heroes of California, New Mexico, Arizona/Sonora, and Texas and the *mutualista*-organized labor unions of the twenties, thirties, and forties, Mexicans seldom allowed themselves to be either defined or defeated, to be victims or to be victimized for very long without actions such as the "Chicano Convulsive Transition Movement," which continues to this moment.

Such conflicts are also carried out in the appropriation process within the Mexican household. Cultural defense and creation are one and the same; and in spite of the obviously gender-specific issues also present, Mexican clusters operate in a "cross-border" mode, exchange and multiple relations create "density" and the social platforms from which children emerge. All are "glued" by the ritual activities controlled by women. Funds of knowledge emerge and are exchanged in all these actions; and Mexicans constantly create, adapt, discard, and embellish labor-derived as well as household-created information bases. All these conflicts, relations, issues, and activities create the historical life of individuals, households, neighborhoods, and region.

At the household level, there are few borders except those created by institutional oppression and distribution of various kinds: mental illness, crime, gangs, and war. Not all households can sustain the various created borders of the mind or sustain themselves culturally against appropriation processes. Sometimes, as in the case of families from which many gang members originate, the death of a working adult destroys the social fabric that protects and supports youngsters, and they are left to create their own social options. At other times, the border syndrome induces a type of heroic but tragic ending, and "El Bobby" becomes many Bobbies—from the Civil War, World War I, World War II, Korea, Vietnam, and the sundry other little wars in between and to the present.

What becomes apparent in this struggle against oppression is that Mexicans express many aspects of their condition and the multiple dimensions of existence and culture. Such expression is found in literary works and in mural paintings that solidify place and space in living representations. Both the literature and the murals, while creating multiple dimensions of culture, deny the border syndrome as an illness. If anything, the border is something to be crossed, violated, and confronted. The borders of the mind, of cultural boundaries, of marginal

identities are often disassembled and reconstructed in creative episto-
laries, painfully recalled childhood memories, and poignant and solitary monologues. For the most part, the literature emerges out of struggles that lead to synthesis rather than to duality. At times, entire realms
of bimodal perception and contrasts are unpacked and reshaped into
holographic images that change shape and form. Such images take
up the struggles of gender, race, culture, and class and contrast boldly
to the borders created between the "public" and "private" worlds of
Richard Rodríguez.

However, such contrasts are part of the heterogeneity and plurality
of the Mexican population itself. The murals emerged, like the literature, out of a struggle to define places and spaces in the most unequal
of social and economic circumstances. The images have no borders because they produce an instant cultural congruence with the population
itself and its borderless culture. If the murals truly provide a singular
"anthropological" insight, it is that much of U.S. Mexican culture is
community and working-class based, and it is most inclusive in its dynamics. U.S. Mexican culture in spite of its many warts, including a
declining but present patriarchy and sometimes oppressive religiosity,
is like a movable feast in which women and men incorporate rather
than deny, include rather than exclude, invent rather than repeat those
many dishes of ideas, relationships, and expressions of those who are
like them or unlike them. The murals capture this sense of commonality,
easy acceptance, multiplicity, and reciprocity. Despite these dynamics
of relationships, most larger economic and political processes have not
been kind to U.S. Mexicans. Political subordination, cultural repression, linguistic erasure, miseducation, social stratification, psychological trauma, and injury and early death in the workplace are also part of
the historical and social experience that extends into the present in
many communities and in some regions of the Southwest.

Some have suggested that such conditions are seldom total, that no
form of domination over a "bumped" population is ever complete.[1]
From this point of view, oppositional cultures emerge in those spaces
so that optional cultural forms arise and with them optional traditions—a deconstructed "reconstruction" of events, behaviors, and unknown historical relations. This point of view, however, places too
much power in the dominating group and not enough in those being
affected; it licenses without intent an idea that somehow domination

"slips" and allows cracks so that those dominated have the opportunity to invent alternate options and histories that act in opposition. This idea eliminates agency from those dominated and induces a kind of victimization that may provide a morally superior position to those dominated but allows them no agency. Agency is allowed only by the fissures in the "dominating" process and not by the conscious organizational and mobilizing ability of cultural creators.

There were few fissures available to the cultural heroes of the nineteenth century, to the strikers and community mobilizers of the twenties and thirties, to the women of the railroad and mining industries, to protesting university students, to parents creating funds of knowledge, and to the literature and mural creators. Without culture there is no politics, and politics without culture is merely an exercise; and for these "dominated" populations, culture was the basis for struggle and invention.

What then provides the impetus for such a *basta* cultural base to continue, to form resistance, agency, and communality? The conclusion is inescapable: it is the constant movement of the population from the south, replenishing, reinforcing, replacing, and reproducing sets of values, behaviors, relationships, and lineal connections and their contradictions that provide that impetus. As I have shown, this movement is much more ancient than the present culture makers but it has been continuous, with different groups "bumping" into those already present, with revolts and rebellions ensuing, with caste and classes created, with constant warfare as well as cooperation emerging, with conflict and intermarriage, with "Americanization" and suppression, with community constriction and political mobilization and reaction, and with populations creating hearth, home, and cultural place and space. All these processes have been made possible by Mexicans without borders who join one with the other, regardless of birthplace, across a communicating grid of experience and culture. This union of various groups will increase not lessen, and with it the many borders of mind and space will lessen as well.

However, new borders are being erected daily by the governor in California who sends National Guardsmen to the border "to stem the tide"; even though the 2.5 million dollars that it costs the state adds to a 3 billion dollar state deficit. New borders of the mind appear in newspapers that depict a Mexican youth in handcuffs escorted by a border patrol officer to a dark cloudy background while above them both reads a caption: "Holding the Line: The Border Patrol's Deadly Game of Cowboys and Mexicans" (*San Francisco Chronicle*, 7 November 1993, p. 1). Similarly "Operation Blockade" on September 19, 1993, obstructed the El Paso–Ciudad Juarez border crossing thus extending the idea of militarizing the border by a show of massive force.[2] Coupled with a developing internal counter-insurgency doctrine, this event does not portend creative approaches to regional thinking.[3]

From the point of view of the American public, new borders became apparent when in a 1990 poll more than 60 percent agreed that all Hispanics were "unpatriotic," while 72 percent agreed that the population was welfare dependent.[4] Similarly, more than 50 percent agreed that the population was unintelligent and that more than 50 percent were lazy and prone to violence.[5] When such borders are present to be "distributed" among Mexican youngsters, their psychological and cultural impact is tragically felt. Youngsters like Hugo Salazar, a gifted artist and member of a youth gang, continue to this moment to have created emotional borders: "We all die. The question is when: A gang, an accident. It's not important . . . When it's your time, it's your time. That's why I am not afraid. I'm 17 years old. But kids die, and so what? God takes them."[6]

In this dialectic between cultural creation and cultural suppression new borders arise. Cultural identities are shaken, new versions created, and their expression emerges in actual behaviors—political and relational—sometimes lopsided and self-destructive, and at others liberating and self-determining. When that new version, however, stimulates individuals to search out as their existential platform an imploding place of isolation and loneliness, human feelings themselves are up for grabs, and like Hugo they seek out a place to hide under the masks of dismay with others like themselves.

On the other hand, new versions may serve an alternate purpose, as they have for undergraduates Tamara Alvarado, Felipe Barragán, Julia González Luna, Elvira Prieto, and Eva Silva who in May 1994 engaged in a hunger strike in the César Chávez tradition to protest the disrespectful "riffing" of a cherished Chicana administrator at Stanford University. They and the hundreds of U.S. Mexican students who joined them acted politically on a cultural basis of respect, reciprocity, and *confianza*. In answer to a question as to why they would go through a hunger strike when they had often gone hungry growing up, Julia González Luna answered simply: "I feel it in my heart . . . It's a whole mess of things, I can't say in one paragraph . . . It's coming to terms with [the fact that] because of the way I look and the way I speak, I'm not accepted."[7]

For both Hugo and Julia—one in a Mexican barrio in California, the other at Stanford University—the issues of cultural identity emerge from the same source: from the borders of the mind created by others and made part of the self. The difference between the two is that for Hugo his own place and space is self-defeating but for Julia it is self-generating.

Both are our children.

APPENDIX

»   »   »   »   »

Facsimile: Letter of

Recommendation

WHITE TRUCKS   [LOGO]   AND BUSSES
LESTER G. LAWRENCE
GARAGE AND SERVICE STATION
PHONE: WALNUT CREEK 19
WALNUT CREEK, CALIFORNIA

December 21, 1935.
It is my great pleasure for me to note, and pass on to any one who may be interested, some of the fine qualities of the man who has served me best and served me longest in the fifteen years of my business career in Walnut Creek.

Mr. A. G. Velez worked for me from March 5, 1927 to Oct. 12, 1928, a period of one and a half years, at which time he left for his home at Magdalena, Mexico on account of his father's illness. He returned to work for me again on December 28, 1929 working steadily for six years to date. He is leaving my employ to make his home in Mexico and with the understanding that he may return any time as there is a job always open for him here.

Mr. Velez is a first class, all around automobile mechanic. He is strictly honest, very industrious, sober, and shows a fine spirit of co-operation at all times. Anyone who may employ Mr. Velez as a mechanic will find him "up to the minute" and fully capable of doing his part well.
Respectfully yours,
LESTER G. LAWRENCE
[SIGNATURE]
LGL/E

Notes

1. A few ethnographic details of birthplace and dates have been changed in order to mask some familial history. However, the processes are factually accurate and nothing has been changed that undermines the dynamics involved.

2. See appendix 1, "Letter of Recommendation Facsimile."

CHAPTER 1: Without Borders, the Original Vision

1. See Haury 1986a, 28, 41; 1962; and for a revised estimate, see Haury 1986b, 443. The spread of maize southward from the highlands of southern Mesoamerica, where it originated as a mutant of teosinite, reached as far as the Peruvian Andes before 3000 B.C.; and two varieties of Mexican squash reached the Peruvian coast by 2500 B.C. However, for our purposes, eliminating the earlier Bat Cave finding of maize of ca. 3000 B.C. because of materials contamination, maize seems to have been carried northward to New Mexico by 1500 B.C.; and Mexican-derived squash was being grown in Missouri and Kentucky before 2300 B.C.

2. See Reff 1991, 226; and Dobyns 1983.

3. Dobyns 1983.

4. Reff 1991, 45–46.

5. See LeBlanc 1989, 95.

6. Zink (1993, 1) first used the word *inundation* to describe European expansion on the American continent.

7. Dobyns 1993.

8. The debate concerning this issue is complex and obfuscated by the lack of

clear theoretical grounding concerning the economic behavior of human beings as well as by the entrenched assumptions that preclude Northern Mexican and Southwestern U.S. pre-Hispanic peoples from engaging in sophisticated and complex regional interactions with central Mexico. The position articulated here was arrived at from the proposition that even though there is no direct demographic proof of south to north migration, ideas and institutions are transmitted in a variety of ways including by the movement of populations, traders, and by "down the line" transmission from one population to another by indirect means. Currently most archaeologists do not support the Haury thesis; however, there is insufficient evidence that such migrations did not occur especially in light of the close approximation institutionally and architecturally of the Hohokam center and that of Mesoamerican populations. Similarly, the Casas Grandes complex appears to be Mesoamerican regardless of a more speculative discussion by Di Peso.

9. According to Haury (1957) maize plants were carried from the south and introduced into the early Cochise culture, located in the region of the Cienega Creek Valley in Southeastern Arizona on the San Carlos Indian Reservation.

10. Haury 1986, 448.

11. Haury (1976, 5) used the word "Hohokam" to designate "those who have vanished." According to Haury, the term was used by Pima Indians to denote the migration of an earlier group of people whom they called "Hohokam."

12. For Beals (1943, 1974), the "Greater Southwest" is part of North America, but not just the United States, and it includes within this conceptualization the arid environment of present-day Arizona, New Mexico, West Texas, Utah, Nevada and parts of other contiguous states. In Mexico, the Greater Southwest would include Lower California, Sonora, Chihuahua, Coahuila, Nuevo León, Zacatecas, and the humid lowlands of northern Sinaloa and Tamaulipas. Beals suspected that he should also include Durango, Guanajuato, Aguascalientes, Hidalgo, and parts of the state of Mexico.

13. See Fish 1989, 19.

14. McGuire 1993, 96.

15. Doyel 1993, 50.

16. Ibid., 62.

17. Fish 1989.

18. Haury 1976, 343.

19. Doyel 1993, 50–51.

20. Ibid.

21. Gumerman 1991, 8.

22. Fish (1989, 25) states that pollen and plant macrofossil information is available in the Hohokam areas for the Archaic period (500 B.C.–A.D. 300) and contains corn, even though no ceramics have been found for this period. Fish

therefore concludes that the information "demonstrates nonsynchronous adoption of farming and ceramics in southern Arizona."

23. Haury 1976, 346–47.

24. Ibid.

25. Doyel 1993, 52.

26. Jorgensen (1980) analyzed 172 tribes in Western North America, coding 292 cultural and 134 environmental variables, and found that the Southwestern data clustered into four of the major groups represented in the region: Puebloans including the Hopi, Apacheans including the Navajo, Yuman, and Pima-Papago (Tohono O'odham). Also see Bahr 1971.

27. Jorgensen 1980, 273.

28. See Gumerman 1991, 8–9 for chronology.

29. See Wicke 1965.

30. Haury 1976, 93.

31. See the distribution of Sedentary period ball courts in Wilcox (1991, 265).

32. See Haury 1937.

33. See Brand (1939, 100) and Ferdon (1967), who are answered most eloquently by Wilcox and Sternberg (1983, 225–28) and Wilcox (1986).

34. Olson 1933, 414, as quoted in Wilcox 1991b, 101.

35. See Peterson 1959; and Di Peso 1983, 76–77.

36. See Feinman 1991, 469.

37. See Wilkerson 1991.

38. Gumerman and Haury 1979, 86.

39. Haury 1976, 299.

40. Di Peso 1983, 76.

41. Ibid.

42. See Jiménez Moreno 1966, 52.

43. See Lafaye 1976, 146–47.

44. Ibid., xx.

45. See Doyel 1991, 233; 239–41; 249.

46. Ibid., 249.

47. Di Peso (1974, 290) states:

It is believed around the year A.D. 1060 a group of sophisticated Mesoamerican merchants came into the valley of Casas Grandes and inspired the indigenous Chichimecans to build the city of Paquime over portions of an older Viejo Period village. These foreign donors may have been drawn here by specific information supplied to them by their family-affiliated spying vanguards, who perhaps lived with the frontiersmen during the last phase of the Viejo Period. These organizers, who may have come from somewhere along the Pacific coast of Mexico, brought with them an aggregate of technological knowledge such as one might associate with an advanced hydraulic society.

However, this view is extremely speculative as to the carriers of such technological innovation. While attractive, this hypothesis is based on little reliable evidence. See also Foster 1986, 63.

48. See Dean and Ravesloot 1993.

49. See Kelley and Kelley 1975, 185.

50. See Mathien 1986, 232.

51. See McGuire 1986, 257.

52. See Reyman 1971.

53. See Dean and Ravesloot (1993, 91). It is likely that in 1230 this center became the "core" of the Mimbres and San Simon peoples and part of the Jornada.

54. See Hargrave 1970, 10; 53.

55. McGuire 1986, 257.

56. Reyman 1971, 319.

57. The "interaction sphere" idea is part of the center-periphery "world systems model" developed by Immanuel Wallerstein and Fernand Braudel. Baugh and Ericson (1992, 10–11) have succinctly described this idea and its application to archaeology.

The world system model postulates a core consisting of a number of competing systems and dependent peripheries that are subordinate to the center. The social and economic adjustments made by the participating societies in this center-periphery model create a regional economy that changes through time, at least in part, due to structural realignments. Through the process of dominance, a core creates unequal exchange mechanisms with peripheral societies that provide important resources and receive only minimal return for the time and labor invested. This model also takes into account that not all societies enter into the regional economy to the same degree. Some societies may represent minicenters or semiperipheries that acquire substantial resources but remain on the fringe of the core-periphery sociopolitical system.

Baugh and Ericson point out that this approach emphasizes the inequality of exchange mechanisms between polities. There is also the peer polity position, which analyzes the symmetrical interaction between neighboring sociopolitical systems. An important aspect of this analysis is "symbolic entrainment" (Renfrew 1986, 8) in which symbolic, ideological, and notational systems are adopted by one or the other system.

58. The Hohokam traded marine shell especially to the northern Mogollon (Mimbres) and the Anasazi (Chaco) and perhaps received pottery in return, especially from Mimbres and other Mogollon areas (McGuire 1993, 105).

59. See Cabrero 1989, 49–50.

60. According to Weigan, Harbottle, and Sayre (1977, 20; 31), X-ray diffraction analysis is carried out by neutron activation of turquoise samples to ferret out its source elements and then trace the pattern of elements to their geological origins. Comparing various samples found in Alta Vista with those originating from mines in New Mexico and Chalchihuites, the authors conclude that they can exclude all the Mexican mines as sources of the turquoise excavated from the site.

61. Ibid., 19.

62. See Wilcox 1986, 143.

63. Dobyns 1993, 5.

64. See Neitzel 1989, 184.

65. Riley (1982, 1) has proposed, and it makes sense, that at the time of the initial Spanish inundation during the "Protohistorical" Period the Greater Southwest formed a regional "interaction" arena of trade, people, and ideas. The proposition rests on the division of this area into provinces: the Serrana Province of Sonora, the Colorado Province, the Desert Province of Sonora and southern Arizona, the Little Colorado of northern Arizona and western New Mexico, the Rio Grande of New Mexico, and the Pecos of eastern New Mexico. Each was tied to the other in trade and exchange, forming a vast interregional network of population contact.

66. The title "The Second Settlers" seems more descriptive of the sedentary and agricultural patterns established by Hispano/Mexicano settlers after those already founded in Pre-Hispanic periods described in chapter 1. It is in contrast to the title of Frances Leon Swadesh's (1977) fine book. However, I am also quite cognizant of the fact that by using only the male plural ending, the Spanish title, "Los Segundos Pobladores," symbolically filters the text with an underlying covert patriarchal film. Therefore I have chosen to use the English translation in order to avoid this inadvertent possibility.

67. The initial Spanish/Mexican *entrada* or inundation of the North American Greater Southwest was a violent "bumping" process accompanied by attempted cultural erasure, which subsided in the aftermath of the Pueblo Revolts of 1680–1696 in the New Mexico region. Early explorations such as the Francisco Vásquez de Coronado (1540–1542) expedition brutally "bumped" Indians who resisted attempts to make them subjects of the Spanish crown. In trying to extract tribute from the Pta Pueblos near Albuquerque, Coronado managed to incite the Pueblo of Tiguex to open revolt, with the result that not only were hundreds of Tiwas killed, but the massacre established the reputation of the Spanish military as a force not only to be reckoned with but one that was to be resisted at high peril. Coronado, after sending reconnoitering parties as far west as the Grand Canyon and east to the buffalo plains, had to report to the Crown that neither was there the expected return on the investment of

wealth for the three hundred Spanish expeditionary forces and their one thousand Mexican Indian "allies," nor the spiritual conversion of the Indians for the six Franciscans who accompanied the expedition. After raiding the grain storage houses of the Pueblos, destroying some thirteen Pueblos who resisted, and causing the depopulation of other centers whose population rather than surrendering fled into the mountains, the expedition limped back to Mexico City. Except for a few Mexican Indians, African slaves, and two Franciscans who stayed behind, no permanent legacy was left except an extreme suspicion of Spaniards and the enmity of those who had suffered at their hands. Simultaneously Coronado's expedition also became the model from which all views of the Spanish entry into the North American Greater Southwest would be cast into American history books.

68. D. J. Weber (1992, 23) points out that in fighting the Muslims the king of Castile licensed an entrepreneur, or *adelantado,* to push forward the frontiers of Christianity. These military chieftains risked their own capital, knowing that success would bring titles of nobility, land, broad governmental powers over the conquered domain, and the right to share in the spoils of war. Under this arrangement, the rewards for the adelantado could be considerable, so could rewards for those warriors whom he engaged to follow him, many of them villagers whose poverty heightened their ambition and whose experience taught them that honor and wealth could be more easily won through plunder than through manual labor. Because these commissioned bands of warriors enabled Spain's monarchs to add to their realm without risking their own capital, they extended the system to the New World.

69. In Campa (1993, 6), Pedro de Vargas is cited as the person employing the term *españoles mejicanos,* which connoted persons as Spanish colonial subjects and located them within the colonial province of Mexico. See also Swadesh 1977, 21.

70. Swadesh 1977, 21.

71. The figures in Gutiérrez (1991, 171, table 4.5) clearly show that in 1680 there were 426 slaves among the surviving households after the Pueblo Rebellion. Forty-five percent contained no slaves; and while 21 percent of the slave holding households owned 60 percent of the slaves, the rest of the households owned 40 percent. One hundred years later, there were only 132 slaves among many more households with only 6.8 percent of all households owning slaves.

72. Ibid., 305.

73. D. J. Weber 1992, 126.

74. Gutiérrez 1991, 172; 174.

75. *Vecino* (literally, "settler-citizen") described those Hispano/Mexicanos who, as subjects of the crown, enjoyed certain rights, duties, and obligations not extended to Indians and mulattos (Swadesh 1977, 226, n. 4). Indians, however, enjoyed special rights such as inviolate land tenure but also provided

labor (*repartimiento*) at planting and harvest time (Gutiérrez 1991, 174).

76. Simmons 1979, 187.

77. Campa 1993, 50.

78. Johansen and Maestas (1983, 49) cite the 1790 census, which reported that of 1,658 family heads in Albuquerque, 56 percent were farmers and 7 percent stock raisers, with another 13 percent day laborers and 13 percent in the weaving trade.

79. See Sheridan 1986, 14.

80. Johansen and Maestas 1983, 49.

81. The term *paisano* was used throughout the Northern Greater Southwest and although literally meaning "fellow countryman," it usually denoted common cultural or contextual origin as well. Not only used as a past reference, the word also connoted present relationships of reciprocity and *confianza* (mutual trust), especially in a rural or farming environment. Nuevo Mexicanos have long used the term *paisano* in small villages and towns; and the Sonorans of Arizona of my father's generation used it as described above.

82. An added cultural quirk was created during the Mexican period, which began after 1821 and Mexico's independence, not because of greater Mexicanization but because of the success of the removal of restrictive trade policies with the United States. For Nuevo Mexicanos, long having been somewhat isolated from Central Mexico and tied to the Chihuahua merchants, the removal of trade restrictions with the French- and English-speaking traders created the opportunities, if not the actuality, for North American acculturation. Thus even before the entry of American troops on August 18, 1846, Nuevo Mexicanos in Santa Fe had long been accustomed to Yankee traders, trappers, and sundry merchants from Missouri and points east. Eventually, Anglo tailors, carpenters, blacksmiths, potters, shoemakers, gunsmiths, painters, and tinsmiths became familiar sights as well. This familiarity eventually, however, cost many Nuevo Mexicanos dearly, for together with the local elite, land deals with small numbers of Anglos set the stage for huge land grants to be awarded because of these new class alliances.

According to Dunbar Ortiz (1980, 69–70), St. Louis, Missouri, was directly associated with the merchant houses to the east by way of the Cumberland Road and therefore had a decided economic advantage in the acquisition of low-cost and high-quality domestic goods; whereas the Chihuahua traders depended on the port of Veracruz to import and then transport finished goods. Trade increased from 1821 such that 230 wagons employing 350 men were being used each year to transport merchandise from St. Louis to Santa Fe and south to Chihuahua at enormous profits.

83. The author's father, born in 1901, in whimsical moods sometimes referred to Arizona as "La Pimería."

84. Officer 1987, xv.

85. Apaches had been pushed out by Comanches during the seventeenth century and by the Wichita peoples and gradually moved into southern Arizona, New Mexico, and southwestern Texas. With their adaptation to the Spanish horse, they became in effect the finest light cavalry of North America (D. J. Weber 1992, 206).

86. See Schroeder 1979, 247, opposite.

87. Officer 1987, 28.

88. Ibid., 31.

89. Ibid.

90. Ibid., 39.

91. The author's grandmother during an Apache raid in Tubac killed an Apache warrior with a *mano* (hand tool for grinding corn) when he tried to enter the window of their home. Interviews and conversations with elderly aunts definitively indicate that women handled the sword, spear, and firearm with dexterity and accuracy in their combat with Apaches.

92. Officer 1987, 44–49.

93. Ibid., 93.

94. See Dobyns 1976, 74–75.

95. Juan Bautista de Anza the Younger was an exceptional presidial administrator and warrior. The son of a distinguished presidial captain of the same name, the younger de Anza was born in the presidio of Fronteras of the Province of Sonora and followed in his father's military footsteps. He became captain in 1759, served with distinction in the Seris Wars, and spent three years exploring the overland route between Sonora and Alta California where on September 29, 1775, he led 240 Sonoran men and women colonists, with 695 horses and mules and 255 beehives, to Yerba Buena, now known as San Francisco. Three births and one death (in childbirth) later, the colonists arrived in Monterey and shortly thereafter traveled north to San Francisco Bay. On September 17, 1776, the presidio of San Francisco was dedicated, and on October 8, 1776, both the mission of San Francisco de Asís and the city of San Francisco were founded. (See Ives 1984, 4, n. 12; 13.)

96. See Sheridan (1986, 22) for a description of the event and Officer (1987, 332) for the number of presidial soldiers, which fifteen years later had not fluctuated greatly.

97. For an excellent description of early Tucson cultural and production systems, see Sheridan (1986, 14–19) from which these descriptions are cited.

98. "Apache Manso" literally means "tame" Apache and denoted those Apaches who had elected to live near the presidios and who served in important roles as scouts for Hispano/Mexicano forces, not unlike their important and tragic role later for the American army.

99. *Tejas* is a Caddo word meaning "allies" or "friends" (Weber 1992, 153).

100. *Analco* is the Nahuatl word for "on the other side of the river," which according to Simmons referred to the south side of the Río de Santa Fe (Simmons 1964, 108).

101. D. J. Weber 1992, 153.

102. Ibid., 187.

103. Ibid.

104. Ibid., 194.

105. Vidaurrieta Tjarks (1979, 150–51) describes *barraganía* as concubinage, which she states is one of the most important means of "racial miscegenation." In addition, the practice of couples living together provided a false picture of household composition, normally registered with single inhabitants—mostly males. Such a practice may also be responsible, in part, for the high illegitimate rates among the population, which in 1790 reached 20 percent of all births. (The large number of *hijos de la iglesia* is discussed in the New Mexico section.)

106. Johns 1991, 124.

107. Ibid., 124–25.

108. See Johns 1975, 504.

109. See De León 1982, 5.

110. Johns 1975, 735.

111. Ibid., 756.

112. Vidaurrieta Tjarks 1979, 143.

113. Ibid., 148, table 4.

114. See Poyo 1991, 85.

115. Ibid., 91.

116. De la Teja and Wheat 1991, 3.

117. With the removal in 1767 of Jesuit missionaries, who had largely controlled Spanish movement into the lower Californias, the Franciscans took over the seventeen missions and forty *visitas* established there. A combination of secular zeal, represented by José de Gálvez the inspector general, and of religious excitement, represented by Franciscan Junípero Serra, resulted; and an intensive penetration to the north was made by land and sea between 1767 and 1769. After numerous delays, explorations, privations, and near starvation, the mission of San Diego de Alcalá and the presidio of Monterey were established in 1770.

118. See Castañeda 1992, 29–30.

119. D. J. Weber 1992, 127.

120. Castañeda 1992, 27.

121. Ibid., 27–29.

122. Although small tribes raided California settlements during the Mexican period, few Californios actually died; and basically Southern California bore the brunt of such rebellions.

123. D. J. Weber 1992, 247.

124. According to Monroy (1990, 113–15, 134), the number of ranches more than doubled (for a total of fifty) after 1821, if the author's "fewer than twenty" estimate is accurate before this year.

125. See Camarillo 1979, 10.

126. For a description of the social structure of Santa Barbara, see Camarillo (1979, 11); and Weber (1992, 265) for the numerical data on population distribution.

CHAPTER 2: The American *Entrada:* "Barrioization" and the Development of Mexican Commodity Identity

1. See D. J. Weber 1988, 117.

2. See D. J. Weber 1968, 52.

3. See Griswold del Castillo 1979, 22.

4. D. J. Weber 1988, 114.

5. Ibid., 124.

6. Ibid., 120.

7. Ibid., 124.

8. Ibid., 122.

9. Ibid., 128–30.

10. Ibid.

11. See Barrera (1979), Camarillo (1979), De León (1982, 1983), García (1981), Griswold del Castillo (1979), Montegano (1987), Romo (1983), and Rosenbaum (1981).

12. This section relies heavily on the excellent monograph by Thomas E. Sheridan (1986).

13. Personal interview carried out by the author between September 1988 and 1990.

14. Sheridan 1986, 53.

15. Ibid., 267, 264–65.

16. From Cornelius Smith (n.d) *Tanque Verde: The Story of a Frontier Ranch,* Privately Published, in Sheridan 1986, 72–74.

17. Ibid., 264–65, tables B2 and B3.

18. Ibid., 142.

19. Ibid., 129.

20. Ibid., 46–47.

21. Ibid., 227.

22. Ibid., 47.

23. Ibid.

24. Ibid., 102–4.

25. Ibid., 37.

26. Ibid., 149.

27. Ibid., 265, table B3.

28. Ibid., 115.

29. Ibid., 159–60.

30. Sheridan (167–69) cites other associations founded in the early 1900s by organizations including the Sociedad Mutualista Porfirio Díaz, Leñadores del Mundo, Sociedad Mexicana-Americana, the Sociedad Fraternal Moctezuma, the Sociedad Fraternal Morelos, the Sociedad Fraternal Santa Rita, the Sociedad Amigos, the Fraternal de Ayuda, and the Liga Protectora Latina, which was one of the early civil rights associations, founded in Phoenix in 1914.

31. Ibid., 166.

32. See Heller 1966.

33. Farnham 1947, 147–48; 161.

34. Ibid., 141.

35. Ibid., 148.

36. Castañeda 1993, 192.

37. Johns 1991, 223.

38. Pike 1992, 99.

39. Smithwick 1935.

40. D. J. Weber 1992, 339.

41. Ibid.

42. Browne 1974, 172.

43. Officer 1987, 228.

44. Sheridan 1986, 32.

45. Park 1961, 16.

46. Ibid., 19.

47. Ibid., 20.

48. Dunbar Ortiz 1980, 65.

49. González 1993, 81.

50. Ibid.

51. Ibid.

52. Ibid.

53. The Gadsden Purchase was pursued by James Gadsden, the chief envoy for the United States and a South Carolinian railroad speculator, who threatened Mexican negotiators with American armed force if they did not agree to the $10 million purchase price of Mexican territory. During negotiations Gadsden laid down an ultimatum by stating, "Gentlemen, it is now time to recognize that the Valley of Mesilla must belong to the United States [either] for a stipulated indemnity, or because we shall take it" (Park 1961, 27). In Gadsden's

communiqué to Manuel Diez de Bonilla, Secretary of External Affairs, he stated: "El tratado de Guadalupe inculca una lección instructiva, o sea, la de una sabia política que nos enseña que, cuando los acontecimientos son evitables, mejor será resolverlos en cooperación armoniosa que precipitarlos, violentamente, a resultas de una oposición ineficaz." See Quijada Hernández and Ruibal Corella (1985, 128) Translation: "The Treaty of Guadalupe [Hidalgo] provides an instructive lesson, in that it is a wise politic that teaches us that when a series of events are inevitable, it would be best to resolve them in harmonious cooperation rather than violently due to unfruitful opposition."

54. Pitt 1966, 198.

55. Pumpely 1871, 21.

56. Sheridan 1986, 176.

57. Author's interview with Manuel González, Tucson, Arizona, April 21, 1965.

58. See Pumpely 1871, 21.

59. Cited in Sánchez 1984.

60. See García 1981, 92–94.

61. Ibid., 93.

62. Ibid.

63. Ibid., 74–79.

64. According to Sheridan (1986, 170) and personal communication (November 12, 1992), such laws were either declared unconstitutional or were overturned because of Mexican organized political protests.

65. Vélez-Ibáñez, Bernache, and O'Leary 1992, 1–12.

66. Sheridan 1986, 90.

67. During the depression, between 1929 and 1935, repatriation and deportation measures were instituted in the United States, and half a million people of Mexican origin were "voluntarily" deported or forced to go to Mexico. Of interest is that one-third were American citizens (see Hoffman 1974, 126).

68. See, for example, Dickerson (1919); Meriam (1933); and Stanley (1920). Stanley is especially instructive in regard to the rather ethnocentric premises upon which such programs were based. The author contends that Mexicans basically are ". . . handicapped by the lack of home training, by shyness, by an emotional nature, all of which interfere with their progress in the conventional course of study." Equally a problem, according to the author, is that "they appear dull, stupid, phlegmatic . . . restive in school and truant whenever possible." She concludes that "we need to cultivate the creative ability [drawing, penmanship, handiwork] rather than the critical and analytical for . . . the Mexican illustrates as he does in the large what is true only in a lesser degree of most of us" (Stanley 1920, 715).

69. See especially the self-exposition by Rodríguez (1982).

70. "Operation Wetback" was an INS-sponsored program of expulsion of undocumented Mexican labor during fiscal 1954 and allegedly resulted in the expulsion of 1,300,000 "illegals" according to INS authorities. See U.S. Department of Justice (1954, 31).

71. See especially Chávez (1988) and Cornelius (1988).

72. Cornelius 1988, 4.

73. The cultural implication for some U.S. Mexicans is to differentiate themselves as "American Mexicans" from the *mojados* (wetbacks). An analogous process exists for Mexicans in Mexico with differentiations made between themselves as "real" Mexicanos and the despised "pochos" from the United States. The latter term basically derides the linguistic and value systems of the U.S.-born Mexican.

74. See Stanley 1920, 714–15.

75. Ibid., 718.

76. See Dickerson 1919, 293.

77. M. Hill 1928, 98; and Coers 1934, 162.

78. Poepone and Johnson 1933.

79. M. Hill 1928, 101.

80. Vaca (1970, pt. 2) places the following scholars (by order of appearance in his work) within the cultural determinist school: Lois J. Gill and Bernard Spilka, "Some Nonintellectual Correlates of Academic Achievement among Mexican-American Secondary School Students," *Journal of Educational Psychology* (June 1962): 144–48; George D. Demos, "Attitudes of Mexican-American and Anglo American Groups toward Education," *Journal of Social Psychology* (August 1962); and Herschel T. Manuel (1965) *Spanish Speaking Children of the Southwest,* Austin: University of Texas Press.

81. Within household samples studied by Vélez-Ibáñez (1995) and Vélez-Ibáñez and Greenberg (1992), there are high rates of literacy in Spanish, which schools would find advantageous but for important economic and legal functions no longer efficacious. For example, we found that 68 percent read Spanish "well or very well" and an equal percentage wrote Spanish "well" or "very well." On the other hand, 59 percent read English "not at all" or only "a little," while 62 percent wrote English "not at all" or only "a little."

Rather than assuming that literacy and comprehension are found wanting in these households, it is the shift from the Spanish-use context to English that interrupts and "fractures" an extended development of Spanish literacy and comprehension in reading and writing. For parents, most economic functions, as well as legal ones, demand English dominance and use; and except for letter writing and popular literature, Spanish dominance in writing and reading is of limited utility in the English-dominant world. Spanish literacy, and its attendant comprehension, not only begins to suffer from disuse, but its important legal and economic functions no longer are efficacious. Thus there is a marked shift from a reading and writing tradition in Spanish to largely an oral one in which only household situations demand the use of Spanish.

Such fracturing, however, has a number of unintended and intended consequences. First, the parent whose basic comprehension is in Spanish is unable to participate in the "incipient literacy" (Scollon and Scollon 1979) of their children. Because the school demands that an English literacy "script" be followed, the comprehensive abilities of the parents are unintentionally deemed to be inefficacious or are unrecognized as existing. Second, from the point of view of the parent, such linguistic abilities lie unused and unreinforced except in activities such as writing a letter to relatives in Mexico or reading popular magazines. The lack of use and opportunity thus "fractures" parental ability within their own generation and prevents the transmission of a literate tradition in Spanish to the following generation. Third, the children, then, receive only the oral version of the literate tradition, and the transmission of knowledge and language is largely confined to household vocabulary and terms. In this sense, the "literate" world is denied the children of Spanish-literate, Spanish-dominant parents.

The implications of such a process are of enormous significance to the acquisition of literacy abilities, cognitive understanding, and complex organizational thought. In a very specific sense, children in such situations are reduced to learning codes of expression in Spanish that for the most part are devoid of a literary tradition except in the most exceptional cases of which there are a few. The language learned (in this case Spanish) will perforce be largely constrained to an immediacy that excludes broader arenas of application. Children are thus exposed to language directly associated with household functions and relations and not to broader economic, political, social, and cultural activities that provide substantive reinforcement to conceptual and cognitive development.

The English learned within the school setting will itself be largely disconnected to a reinforcing literate tradition because its constraints are directly defined by institutional requirements focusing on skills, coding, and specific problem-solving applications. For other than manipulative, functional, and immediate application, English is unconnected to a previous generation, and in fact children function primarily as translators for parents whose own traditions, both oral and literate, are in Spanish. This "fracturing" process between generations may be partly responsible for the type of negative academic performances too often associated with U.S. Mexican children. In the long run, the cumulative impact of such processes is to create pockets of populations in which the problem becomes not one of illiteracy but rather illiteracy in English and Spanish.

82. J. Hill 1993.

83. Ibid., 146.

84. Ibid., 146–47.

CHAPTER 3: The Politics of Survival and Revival:
The Struggle for Existence and Cultural Dignity, 1848–1994

1. Wilbur-Cruce 1987, 316.

2. Ibid.

3. Ibid., xiii.

4. McWilliams 1990, 127–33.

5. Ibid.

6. Ibid., 98–109.

7. Sheridan 1986, 36.

8. Park 1961, 43–44, 118–19. I have added the Mexican born and 80 percent of U.S. born as "Mexicans" and have combined the figures for "born elsewhere in U.S." and "other foreign born" as "Anglos" from figures in table 1, p. 118, and "Distribution of persons" figure on p. 119.

9. Sheridan 1986, 36.

10. Ibid.

11. Ibid.

12. Hall 1946, 8.

13. The O.K. Corral was the scene of the famous Earp-Clanton street fight of 1881, which lasted thirty seconds but left three men dead and two wounded. The fight pitted Marshal Wyatt Earp, his two brothers, Earl and Virgil, his deputies, and the infamous Doc Holiday, an alcoholic dentist, against the Clanton Gang made up of father, sons, and other hangers-on. The most succinct account of the event comes from a bartender who witnessed the fight and, after retelling the story too many times to bear, reduced the action to: "It all begun over liquor. First came the argument, then the shootin', then the buryin'. What'll you have to drink?" See Edwin Corle (1951, 341).

14. McWilliams 1990, 140–41.

15. Rosenbaum 1981, 59.

16. Ibid.

17. Officer 1987, 231–33.

18. McWilliams 1990, 129–30.

19. Pitt (1971, 60) quotes from Green's *Journals* (1845, 269), in which Green, who held openly racist and ethnocentric views regarding Mexicans and African Americans, is identified as the main author of the law. He was the state senator

from Sacramento who, because he had served three terms as a legislator in various southern slave-holding states, was also held in high esteem by other former Southerners in the state with similar views and thus easily elected.

20. Ibid.

21. Rojas 1986.

22. "El Patrio" is the nickname for *patriota*, or patriot (Rojas 1986, 35).

23. At least five children were born of this marriage: Concepción, b. 1817; Jesús, n.d.; Joseph Anselmo, b. 1823; Joaquín, b. 1824–1831; and Salvador, b. 1832. About 40 km from Altar, Sonora, the now defunct village of San Rafael del Alamito was Joaquín's birthplace and the home of Joaquín's father, Juan, and his two brothers, Josef David and Salvador Murrieta, and their families.

24. Rojas 1986, 35.

25. According to Rojas (1986, 195), Murrieta called himself "Joaquín Carrillo" to Anglos and "El Patrio" to Mexicans. In a letter signed in his pseudonym to the *San Francisco Herald* and published on August 19, 1853, Murrieta wrote to the editor to disclaim his alleged capture and decapitation by California Rangers. (The letter was printed as it appears below.)

18 de Augosto 1853
Senor Editor del Heraldo:
Como mi captura, o supuesta captura parecer ser el topico del dia, yo les informo, gracias a su amabilidad, a los lectores de su valioso periodico, que conservo aun um cabeza, si bien se ha proclamado en la presna de desa bella ciudad que he sido recientemente capturado e immediatamente decapitado.
Sinceramente.
JOAQUIN CARRILLO

18 August 1853
Mr. Editor of the Herald:
My capture, or rather my alleged capture, seems to be the topic of the day, and, thanks to your amiability, I inform the readers of your worthy newspaper that I retain my head, even though it has been proclaimed in the press of this beautiful city that recently I was captured and immediately decapitated.
Sincerely yours,
JOAQUIN CARRILLO

26. Rosenbaum 1981, 59.

27. Ibid.

28. Camarillo 1979, 20–21.

29. D. A. Weber 1973, 227.

30. Ibid., 228

31. Pitt 1971, 257.

32. The descriptions of Gregorio Cortez are based entirely on Paredes (1973, 139–40).

33. Ibid.

34. Weber 1973, 232.

35. Ibid., 233.

36. Ibid., 233–34.

37. Ibid., 57–58.

38. Ibid., 100.

39. Ibid., 152.

40 The analysis and description of Baca are taken from Schaefer 1973.

41. McWilliams 1948, 116.

42. The plan called for reclaiming the territories of Texas, New Mexico, Arizona, Colorado, and California. "Negroes" were to be emancipated from "White control" and a "Black republic" created from six additional states, Indian lands were to be restored, and freedom for all Asians to be granted. All Anglo males over the age of sixteen were to be put to death. Additionally, it called for expropriated lands to be given to tenant farmers and those supporting the plan, while communal sharing and distribution of property became central values. Racial hatred was to be eliminated by everyone having access to communications media and the equal distribution of supplies and tools. Schools would be built for all children and would be governed by "universal love" rather than class or racial antagonism. However, after 120 days of violent raiding and counter attacks in Texas, the San Dieguistas were defeated by the Mexican government under President Venustiano Carranza.

43. Park 1961, 43–44; 118–19.

44. Ibid., 52–53.

45. Ibid., 159.

46. Ibid., 171.

47. Zamora 1993, 56.

48. McWilliams 1948, 174.

49. Gómez-Quiñones 1973, 24–26.

50. D. A. Weber 1973, 309–10.

51. Ibid.

52. Ibid., 322–23.

53. Gómez Quiñones 1973, 43.

54. Ibid., 60.

55. McWilliams 1990, 174.

56. Ibid., 174–75.

57. D. A. Weber 1973, 321–23.

58. Ibid., 323.

59. Ruiz 1987, 51.

60. Ibid.

61. An analogous union sprung up a few years later in 1937 as its replacement. The United Canner, Agricultural, Packing and Allied Workers of America (UCAPAWA) played a crucial role for Mexican women, who composed 75 percent of all food-processing workers, and as importantly the union represented Mexican, African American, Filipino, and Anglo workers in the fields after the demise of C&AWIU.

62. Zamora 1993, 58–59.

63. McWilliams 1990, 177.

64. Galarza 1970.

65. Personal interview, Tucson, Arizona, 1965. Maclovio Barrazas was an early union organizer among Mexicano miners in Arizona's copper mines in the thirties and immediately after World War II. He made this statement to me in 1965 concerning the conditions of the mines during the period in which he worked and organized. His statement is reminiscent of June Nash's 1979 book on Bolivian mining.

66. Zamora 1993, 57.

67. McWilliams 1990, 178.

68. Ibid., 180.

69. Park 1961, 248.

70. Ibid.

71. Ibid., 257, quoting the *Bisbee Daily Review.* June 2, 3, 1903.

72. Hernández 1983, 39.

73. Park 1961, 257, quoting the *Bisbee Daily Review.* June 5, 1903.

74. Park 1961, 258.

75. Kingsolver 1989.

76. Ibid., 266.

77. McWilliams 1990, 179.

78. Ibid., 180.

79. García 1989, 189.

80. Kingsolver 1989, 10.

81. Ibid., 11.

82. McWilliams 1990, 153.

83. Ibid., 154.

84. Ibid., 156.

85. Ibid.

86. Sheridan 1986, 180–81.

87. There is no evidence that this, in fact, occurred, but it may be speculated that "Susana del SP" like Rosie "the Riveter" may have stimulated the creation of opportunities for both Mexican women and men. (See Henry 1992, 111–12.)

88. Sheridan 1986, 180.

89. Personal interview with Manuel González, January 1962, Tucson, Arizona. *Olvídate* means "forget it."

90. Sheridan 1986, 180–81.

91. Ibid.

92. Zamora 1993, 69–70; and Wollenberg 1973.

93. Personal communication from Ursula Bustamante, December 1971, Tucson, Arizona. Mrs. Bustamante had worked for various dime stores for thirty years before her retirement.

94. Sheridan 1986, 216.

95. Kingsolver 1989, 10.

96. Ibid., 11.

97. Ibid.

98. Hernández (1983, 15) makes this claim but it is not borne out by the evidence provided in this discussion.

99. Swadesh 1974, 75.

100. Vélez-Ibáñez et al. 1982, 181–86. This description of the *penitentes* in the report and in this chapter was synthesized from the works of Corbin (1937) and Swadesh (1977).

101. Vélez-Ibáñez 1993a, 133.

102. Tenenbaum 1993, 37.

103. Vélez-Ibáñez et al. 1982, 183–84.

104. By ritual and social density is meant the created networks of exchange that emerge as the result of Mexican familial and friendship reciprocity during the calendar year. These networks comprised hundreds of exchanges involving favors, conversations, and acts of kindness in recreation, work, visitations, ritual activities, and through residential proximity. The resulting quality of the social relations may be described as "dense," in which multiple relations are created between individuals and groups. Each relation is a "strand" that when called upon vibrates with all the other strands to varying degrees of importance. Conflict emerges, as well, over miscommunicated vibrations.

105. See Vélez-Ibáñez 1983 and 1994.

106. The numerical total is compiled from Hernández (1983, 65–74), Griswold Del Castillo (1984, 4), and García (1989, 87). In addition, all three works have been synthesized to include those specific organizations mentioned.

107. Vélez-Ibáñez et al. 1982, 17–20.

108. B. Henry 1992, 35–37.

109. Houghton 1969.

110. Navarro 1995, 5–6.

111. See San Miguel 1987, 119.

112. Ibid., 124.

113. Gómez-Quiñones 1990, 86–88.

114. "1C" programs were instituted specifically for Spanish-speaking children and functioned, in fact, to keep children in the first grade for two years. They were terminated in the late 1950s in Tucson. As a five-year-old student in 1C and even though I spoke both English and Spanish, I can recall having my hair pulled by my teacher and being paddled by the principal for speaking Spanish, which they defined as an offense. This did not create an atmosphere conducive to positive reinforcement of any language, and for many of us a seething anger replaced linguistic competence.

115. Gómez-Quiñones 1990, 86–88.

116. According to Grebler, Moore, and Guzmán (1970, 112), between 1950 and 1960 the Mexican population had become more urban than any other population in the United States. Rural areas in which Mexicans lived showed a net decline in this decade; and even though Mexican rural population decreased only slightly in the entire region, in the states of New Mexico and Colorado the rural population had dropped 23 and 17 percent respectively.

117. See Herrera-Sobek (1993) for an excellent discussion on the reconstruction of literary texts.

118. I chose this method of articulation without the sometimes totally obfuscating jargon of the "de-constructive" method and leave to the reader the job of figuring out when he or she is text, when I am text, and when the text is text. In addition, I leave to the reader the job of figuring out the relationship between her or him and me; me and her and him; and me, him, her; and me and me.

CHAPTER 4: Living in *Confianza* and Patriarchy: The Cultural Systems of U.S. Mexican Households

1. See Wolf 1988, 108; Goody 1983; and Corrigan and Sayer 1985.

2. The socialist state's purported ideological intent, to release social labor from the marketplace, is of questionable utility in practice, considering that the state organizes social labor through conscription and regulation and sets it to work, and wages are set by a privileged centralized management and policy unit. Capitalist systems mobilize social labor by purchasing labor power and setting it to work for wages according to the "market," which is largely asymmetrical, because the buying and selling of labor power is not an even exchange. Under both ideologies the quest for household labor by the state or by market responses is part of a constant struggle against which household members have to balance available labor power, consumption, and exchange in order to meet both culturally constituted "demand" and subsistence needs.

3. The history of Mexicans in the labor movement in the Southwest is replete

with examples of entire kinship systems and households mobilizing against racial discrimination, low wages, poor housing, and the infamous company stores. See the previous chapter for the cultural and kinship basis for mutual aid societies.

4. Density of relationships refers to many stranded or multiple relations described as "the extent to which links which could possibly exist among persons do exist" (Mitchell 1969, 18). These relations also have a vertical and horizontal direction (Lomnitz n.d.). Vertical relations between people of different statuses or power positions are largely unequal, with an exchange of favors and resources tying specific persons to networks of supporting power groups. Horizontal relations are based on generalized reciprocity of basic equals. The horizontal relations with which we are concerned here emerge as central to political coalescence in central urban Mexico, economic cooperation in Mexico and the U.S. borderlands, clustered housing patterns in Tucson, Arizona, and neonate emergence in socialization processes.

5. Baca Zinn 1982, 265.

6. From this point of view, aging is not a passive state. Indeed old age is marked by activity, participation, self-movement, and purposefulness, and it cannot be understood in isolation. (See Simic and Myerhoff 1978, 240)

7. Part of this chapter and the statistical information have been previously published in Vélez-Ibáñez (1993a) and other portions in Vélez-Ibáñez (1993b).

8. See Bean and Tienda 1987, 323. I have taken the liberty of recomputing figure 9.3 and combining men and women in single occupational categories.

9. Ibid., 199.

10. Ibid. Our previous work done in Tucson, Arizona, clearly indicates that mean per capita income in 1980 for 76 percent of the Mexican population was $5,202, and for 24 percent of the Mexican population, $8,398. For the Anglo population the percentages were almost exactly reversed, with only 25.5 percent earning $5,202 and 74.5 percent earning $8,398. In comparing mean household income, 76 percent of the Mexican population earned $14,488 while 24 percent earned $21,994. Only 25.5 percent of the Anglo population earned $14,488, while 74.5 percent earned $24,245. See Vélez-Ibáñez, Greenberg, and Johnstone (1984).

11. Vélez-Ibáñez (1993, 199–201) states that in 1980, the poverty rate for U.S. Mexicans in the five southwestern states of the border region was slightly less than 22 percent—a drop of 4.5 percent from 1970 (Stoddard and Hedderson 1987, 56), although Moore (1988) cites a higher percentage from more current census data for "Hispanic" poverty even though the later figures point to a significant rise to 28 percent (Census 1990). However, poverty was very much concentrated in the southern border counties of the U.S. border region; thus, the probability of higher income is greatest in the western coastal counties and

decreases consistently as one moves east toward the Lower Rio Grande Valley of Texas in areas such as Starr County, where the percentage of families in poverty is 45 percent (Stoddard and Hedderson 1987, 56; 59) but actually raised to 60 percent in 1990 (Brokaw 1993, 8). For the most part, such poverty areas are rural and not urban centers, and the pattern of poverty is very much a consequence of the organization of industrial agriculture in those areas in which sectors of the U.S. Mexican population are relegated to low rural farm wages, which are intermittent at best and non-existent for much of the crop year.

However, in urban situations underclass poverty characteristics are counterindicated. South Texas cities like McAllen, Laredo, and Brownsville, where U.S. Mexicans predominate, are among the lowest for household income, high percentage of public assistance, and high poverty levels. Nevertheless, in these same "poverty" areas, more than 50 percent of the houses are owner-occupied, which indicates stable populations in older housing, with residents living longer in one home. This also points to the importance of low-cost home ownership to improve social stability for Mexican households in poverty circumstances.

Even poverty figures do not support the presence of a U.S. Mexican borderland "underclass" with regard to household structures in which young unmarried women with children under 18 predominate. The Hispanic Health and Nutrition Examination Survey (HHANES) by the National Center for Health Statistics showed that most U.S. Mexican single heads of household were middle aged (45 to 64 years) and that their single status resulted from divorce or separation rather than from widowhood or from never having been married (Treviño et al., 9). This seems to be borne out by the fact that only 12.8 percent of U.S. Mexican householders were composed of single females with children under 18 and no spouse present.

In addition, U.S. Mexican women in poverty circumstances contradict expected marital behaviors of unwed single mothers in underclass situations. It is more likely that single-parent U.S. Mexican women will marry soon after the birth of their first child in a study conducted in Chicago (Testa 1988, 27; James 1988, 14). Of single U.S. Mexican women who did become pregnant, 45 percent married the father of the first child. It is highly likely that for single female U.S. Mexican parents, one of the single most important factors to prevent the development of "underclass" characteristics may lie in the ability of women to mobilize male labor and resources in times of need within household clusters. This seems to be an underlying strength in U.S. Mexican household relations, as James (1988, 27) has shown and as has my own work in the samples of households discussed.

Thus, even single-headed U.S. Mexican households do not conform to the often cited characteristics of female heads of households for the "underclass."

Similarly James (1988) and Moore (1988) question the behavioral, ecological, structural, and processual applicability of the same sort of "underclass" category to U.S. Mexicans, and I would suggest strongly that it is due to available circumstances for the development of viable clustered households. (See García 1993, 19, table 3.)

12. García 1993, 20–21, table 4; 19, table 3.

13. Ibid., 14, table 2.

14. See Bean and Tienda 1987, 199.

15. For data on household income origins, see Bean and Tienda 1987, 199; and 188 for a discussion of household size. From our work in Tucson, Arizona, exchange of labor between households releases labor for the marketplace at some time during the work and life cycle of the household.

16. For Ginzberg (1976) the essential characteristics of the secondary labor market include lack of occupational stability, security of employment, and above-average earnings.

17. García 1993, 16–17, table 2.

18. Ibid.

19. See Heyman 1991. Political and commercial life has always influenced borders. As early as 1890 or so, our grandfather made Conestoga wagons and stagecoaches in Magdalena, Sonora, situated 120 miles south of Tucson, and sold them for resale to Don Federico Ronstadt in Tucson, who had sold my grandfather some of the materials with which to construct the finished products. My own father lived in Tucson with his mother's sister and attended Tucson elementary and secondary schools in order to learn accounting and English, both necessary for the expansion of my grandfather's business in Magdalena and for a branch in Tucson (see part 1 of this book).

20. Alvarez (1987) is the most comprehensive and descriptive work done on the subject of south to north migration, taking into account the many changes of economy and polity in the region.

21. For a complete sample description, see previously published portions of this section in Vélez-Ibáñez (1988, 46–47). However, two points need to be made as to the representativeness of the sample: first, the households were randomly selected and stratified according to three contrasting neighborhood types, which I labeled "barrio," "transitional," and "middle income." I had used a k-means cluster analysis to create these categories from data in the "Neighborhood Statistics Program, 1980, Decennial Census." Barrio neighborhoods ranged from 31 to 93 percent Mexican with median incomes of $13,100, transitional with 6 to 47 percent and $13,400, and middle income with 6 to 43 percent Mexican and median incomes of $20,500. Thirty-six percent of barrio household heads completed high school, while 43 and 72 percent completed high school in the other two categories. We proportioned to the sample the per-

centages of Mexicans living in those neighborhoods to make the sample representative of the distribution of Mexican households among those three types of neighborhoods: 59 percent barrio, 14 percent transitional, and 27 percent from middle-income areas.

We selected 60 households in which the method allowed us to treat each household ethnographically so that a "trade off" was a reduction in "non-sampling errors" for "measurement errors," which are artifacts of randomly selected samples. Stone and Campbell (1984: 27–37) demonstrate that the same amount of total error achieved by the survey method at a sample size greater than 700 can be achieved with sample sizes of less than 50 treated ethnographically.

22. A second type of variant is the Mexican economic elite who have taken up semipermanent or permanent residence in the United States along the U.S.-Mexico border. Although Mexican political elites have long settled in the United States on a semipermanent or permanent basis after revolutionary movements in Mexico in the late nineteenth century and early twentieth, the monetary devaluation crisis that began in 1981 and continued through 1985 pushed out Mexican capital and its owners for the first time. In the period 1981–1985, $34.2 billion left Mexico, of which three-quarters was invested in the United States. (See Murguía 1986).

With the flight of capital, Mexican elites purchased homes in affluent areas of La Jolla, California, Tucson, Arizona, and in parts of Texas and New Mexico. However, the mobilization pattern of migration, as well as their choice of place, seems to be the same as that of working-class migrants (Murguía 1986, 13). Both elites and the working class mobilize kinship, fictive kinship, and friendship and use these as contact points, institutional access, and a residential platform upon which to enter the United States. This is certainly the case in Tucson, Arizona, in which entire condominium complexes have been purchased by Sonorenses who have had long-standing dense relationships with one another. Business investments, ritual and secular activities, and household exchange are basically kept to the inner network of elites.

However, most recently, even semipermanent residence and rather closed elite networks have begun to change due to intermarriage with other Hispanic elites as well as with non-Hispanics. The latter is usually a result of attendance in either a southwestern university or one of the east or west coast elite universities.

23. The work by Keefe and Padilla (1987) shows that for the most part there is a clear disengagement from Mexican relatives and a greater exchange relation with localized kin networks. While the latter is generally true of Tucson Mexicans, their rate and volume of disengagement are artifacts of proximity to the border, economic opportunity of exchange, and relatives remaining in Mexico.

It is not unusual along the border for almost complete familial networks born in Mexico to migrate to adjoining U.S. states so that the remnants left in Mexico are largely the elderly and the very young.

The Keefe and Padilla studies were carried out among nonborderland populations, with a sample of persons largely residing in two California counties (Santa Barbara and Ventura). The case studies they presented were not part of cross-border networks that could be maintained. There is little indication in the quantitative or qualitative material analyzed in this work and others (Keefe: 1978; Keefe et al. 1978, 1979) that attention was directed to this phenomenon. Given the distance from the border and lack of historical connections between the families studied and the border region, it is understandable that Keefe and Padilla should not have found significant cross-border networks.

24. Ramírez (1994) details the vast heterogeneity of border populations and uses a functional topology to help understand the manner in which sets of populations engage in daily economic and social interaction, including important kinship systems.

25. See Vélez-Ibáñez (1983, 10–16, 156) in which *confianza* is defined "as the willingness to engage in generalized reciprocity."

26. Zavella 1987; Ruiz 1987; Segura 1989; and Stark 1984. There is a methodological issue that may arise in these works: the samples from which the data were generated derived in large part from a particular economic niche, which skews the processes and emergence of household development. Because all the samples were purposive, they were of great value in providing insight, understanding, and views of important domestic, public, and labor issues, including the use of networks, patriarchy, cultural change, and gender exploitation. However, none of them used methods that could be useful in determining the generability of "household" formation, the articulation and distribution of gender roles, and the formation of structural, attitudinal, or cultural patriarchy.

27. The case studies use pseudonyms to protect the identity of the informants, as well as to maintain confidentiality. I have also changed some events as well as relationships in order to mask and protect well-known households from public embarrassment. In some cases it was impossible to change the ethnographic details without distorting the substance of the relationships and behaviors described; therefore I have tried to be most careful in balancing appropriate ethnographic detail with the necessity of keeping confidential the lives of our informants.

Of the possible sample of forty households, I have selected three to be most typical of the social and cultural heterogeneity of Tucson's Hispanic community. One case illustrates the early life cycle of a working-class household headed by a single person; the second a middle-class household, in which intermarriage with an Anglo seems to be relatively unimportant in the social and cultural systems in which they participate; and the third a working-class late-cycle "core" household of a retired couple.

28. Testa 1988.

29. The Bean and Tienda study (1987, 186) shows that there is a trend of increasing marital instability among Mexican females aged 15–64 compared to non-Hispanic whites. Comparing the years 1960 and 1980, 15.8 percent of non-Hispanic white women experienced marital instability in 1960, while 18.7 percent of Mexican women experienced marital instability. In 1980, 23.3 percent of non-Hispanic white women experienced marital instability, while 21.2 percent of Mexican women experienced the same behavior. It must be noted, however, that the percentage difference between the two populations varies when based on the southwestern states alone, with 31.6 of non-Hispanic white women and 22.7 percent of Mexican women experiencing marital instability.

30. Other populations in the United States also have to cope with distinctive structural and substantive economic and social disparity, e.g., African American populations throughout the country and Puerto Ricans on the East Coast. As Kennedy (1980), Stack (1974), and Valentine (1980) have shown, such populations develop a number of creative household approaches to mitigate the effects of such conditions, including the extensive use of social networks and helping systems. Nevertheless, the regional context for Puerto Ricans and African Americans differs markedly from that of U.S. Mexicans, so careful analytical distinction should be made of each type of adaptive and coping mechanism in relation to an appropriate economic and political context. Even though similar networks operate among African Americans and Puerto Ricans, most studies seem to locate the necessity of such relations in the effects of racism, economic disparity, and the accompanying large proportion of female-headed households. For African Americans the percentage of households headed by females, 40.6 percent, is almost the same as for Puerto Rican households, 36.5 percent (Bean and Tienda 1987, 192). In comparison, only 18.9 percent of U.S. Mexican households were headed by females, and among U.S. Cubans 16 percent, so that different sets of explanations seem to be required for the emergence of similar cultural and social behaviors.

31. There are significant differences between clustered and nuclear-based households. Clustered households seem to have shared in what I have termed broad "funds of knowledge" (Vélez-Ibáñez 1988a and 1988b), which include a great array of familial, household, neighborhood, and institutional contexts. The funds of knowledge comprise information and formulas containing the mathematics, architecture, chemistry, physics, biology, and engineering for the construction and repair of homes, the repair of most mechanical devices including autos, appliances, and machines, as well as methods for planting and gardening, butchering, cooking, hunting, and for "making things" in general.

Other parts of such funds included information regarding access to institutional assistance, school programs, legal help, transportation routes, occupational opportunities, and the most economical places to purchase needed services and goods. My impression is that clustered households are much more self-sufficient and do not depend as greatly on the market for technical assistance.

The borderlands region has been a particular focus for the complex development of such funds within the dynamic conditions previously mentioned; border populations constantly emerge as creators of experience by adjusting, coping, learning, manipulating, resisting, and experimenting with traditional, syncretic, and novel ways of making a living, using scarce resources and limited skills, and expanding, as well as constricting, the "funds of knowledge" necessary for survival. Such funds are the accumulated and proven information resources and practices used and manipulated by Mexican households; they shape the social platforms upon which progeny emerge as human cognitive and emotive personalities. For the most part, these funds at one time were part of rural or small urban settings, such as ranchos in Sonora, mining towns in southeastern Arizona, and developing cities like Albuquerque or Tucson. What is of note for such funds is that they have provided, and still do for immigrating households, daily utilitarian skills and information associated with making a living in a small-scale productive system.

However, because of rapid technological change in the region, there is a process by which such funds become "commoditized" so that only portions of those funds are useful for the market; and depending on the rapidity of economic and social mobility, they become increasingly constrained. Nevertheless such funds are never static; they are dynamic in the same way that the region is dynamic. Most males, for example, will have held an average of 5.3 jobs during their lifetime, yet the most important characteristic of such change is that individuals shift from low-paying service work in restaurants to high-paying industrial work in the mines in this region, and then back to low-paying work as musical sales clerks in a store once the copper market becomes weakened. What is of importance, however, is that with each job shift there has also been an accumulation in the knowledge base that is required to work successfully. From actual case data in the example cited above, the individual accumulated information about food serving, preparation and storage, and the operational characteristic of the restaurant business. Second, depending on the specific area of mining, it will not be unusual for the individual to learn geological information, hydraulics and mechanics, chemistry and physics, and computational skills. In the last occupation, an individual will gain access to the entire gambit of musical presentation, composition, and knowledge of artists, groups, and musical styles. Such information will not be retained by the single individual, however; and because of the clustered network phenomenon, each job or contact contributes to the larger fund of knowledge. Because of the limited level of income for most U.S. Mexican households, such funds are not easily discarded, are in constant use, and are transmitted to following generations.

32. Bean and Tienda (1987, 198) show that the mean household income for Mexicans in the United States was $16,021, which is only slightly below that earned by Larry.

33. The Cristero Revolt was a response to the repression of the Catholic Church by the new Mexican revolutionary government after 1910. By 1927, a full-fledged revolt by Catholics erupted in armed struggle especially in the western states of Jalisco, Michoacán, Guanajuato, Colima, and Zacatecas. (See Riding 1989.)

34. The occupational classification of "high blue collar" is from Bean and Tienda (1987, 323) in which they classify upper white collar as professionals, semiprofessionals, and managers; lower white collar as clerical, sales; upper blue collar as crafts; and lower blue collar as farmers, operatives, and laborers.

35. Portions of this section were previously published in Vélez-Ibáñez 1988a, 40–41.

36. Portions of this section appear in Vélez-Ibáñez and Greenberg 1992.

37. Vélez-Ibáñez and Greenberg 1986; and Moll, Vélez-Ibáñez, and Greenberg 1988.

38. *Confianza* is a cultural construct indicating the willingness to engage in generalized reciprocity. For a discussion, see Vélez-Ibáñez 1983, 10–16.

39. See Tapia 1989.

40. By cultural expressions and states, I mean actual behaviors such as cooking, repairing, sharing, praying, dancing, singing, observing, joking, story telling, arguing, eating, and sundry other expressed emotive states such as happiness, anger, joy, and sadness.

41. Williams (1984, 114) has a similar discussion detailing how Mexican migrant women, who are usually considered as among the most "traditional," are in fact not only productive wage earners, providing half of the household income, but also are considered by men as crucial to their own well-being.

42. See U.S. Bureau of the Census 1989.

43. See table 2.10 and 11 (U.S. Bureau of the Census 1989). In addition, Williams (1984, 125) points out that the cross-cultural literature shows that "women are most influential when they share in the production of food and have some control over its distribution."

44. From our studies (Vélez-Ibáñez and Greenberg 1984; Moll, Vélez-Ibáñez, and Greenberg 1990) among Mexican households in Tucson, Arizona, 20 percent of household income is derived from the informal economy, of which most was earned by women engaged in swap meet sales, cash-remunerated domes-

tic work, selling tamales and tortillas, embroidery and sewing sales, and caring for others' children.

45. See Baca Zinn (1982), Mirandé (1986), and Williams (1984) for a revisionist point of view regarding the participation of women in both decision making and household income contribution in U.S. Mexican households. In addition, recent stratified studies (for example, Vélez-Ibáñez and Greenberg 1984) clearly show that Mexican women play a major role in management, operation, and decision making in Tucson, Arizona.

46. Portions of this section appear in Vélez-Ibáñez and Greenberg 1992.

47. Core and peripheral households create social "density" because members of such networks are kin, and in their daily lives they add layers of relationships based on other contexts. A cousin is also the person with whom one exchanges labor assistance, has a fictive kinship relation of *compadrazgo* (cogodparenthood), shares recreational activities and visitations, participates in religious and calendric activities, and in many instances near whom one may live. That cousin will either recruit or be recruited by a network member to work in the same business or occupation.

48. Processual analysis emerges basically from political anthropology, in which politics are "events involved in the determination of public goals and / or the differential distribution and use of power within the group or groups concerned with the goals being considered" (Swartz 1972, 9). The ideas of arena and social field emerge from this tradition as important methodological tools, which treat the phenomenon to be understood as always emergent. Human behavior, events, and activities do not have a finality but flow and sometimes emerge from others. However, for the purposes of analysis all social fields are presumed to have come into existence at some point in time. Their functions, characteristics, evolutions, change, continuance, and decline can be understood as sets of arenas that stack up to form the social field. These arenas are made up of cultural symbols, human behaviors, resources, exchanges, goals and purposes, and economic and material interests. Thus, the research social field is composed of various arenas, which must be discovered in order to understand single issues like "ethics." That discovery technically utilizes an "extended case method" (Van Velsen 1967), which identifies a baseline of human behaviors, activities, events, or goals as an assumed starting point and then traces the boundaries of their arenas in time and space.

49. Williams 1984, 117–18.

50. However, this movement north to celebrate Easter has its opposite version with U.S. Mexicans traveling south to celebrate Semana Santa, without the usual Easter egg complex; although the closer to the border, the higher the probability for U.S. Easter artifacts to make their appearance. For the most part, this portion of the U.S. Mexican household population will be first-generation

migrants to the United States or those most recently arrived. In addition, they will most likely come from the central or southern Mexican states.

CHAPTER 5: The Distribution of Sadness:
Poverty, Crime, Drugs, Illness, and War

1. All figures and enumerations in the discussion are taken from the same source: U.S. Bureau of the Census 1993, 2, 3, 4, and 7, except where noted.

2. U.S. Bureau of the Census 1993, tables 1.5 and 5.157.

3. The Rowe 1991 study from a sample of 164 white, 168 black, and 149 Mexican American regular male drinkers supports the hypothesis that education beyond the high school level is related to higher perception of self-worth.

4. Knight, Bernal, Garza, and Cota (1993) illustrates the crucial positive role familial cultural identity plays in the formation of children's ethnic identity.

5. Reyes and Valencia 1993, 260.

6. Ibid.

7. García 1993, 13.

8. Ibid., 2

9. Ibid., 3. I have averaged table A column under non-Hispanic white population from the categories of "some college but no degree" through "doctoral degree. . ."

10. Of the latter 4.5 million persons, only 1 in 4 are naturalized citizens so that a little over 3.5 million are not. Of this sizable group, 2.9 million are under 34 years of age, so this subgroup of the population will have the lowest educational attainment and associated income and will be at highest poverty risk.

11. U.S. Bureau of the Census 1993b, table 3:81.

12. Ibid., table 5:157.

13. Ibid., tables 1:5 and 5:157.

14. Santos 1992.

15. U.S. Bureau of the Census 1993b, tables 1:5 and 5:157.

16. Grade delay is "a measure of the age-grade school achievement which could be determined only for individuals enrolled at the time of the census. This was computed by subtracting respondents' current grade plus six (for the first six years not in school) from their age. Values above zero indicate the number of years delayed." Rates of grade delay among Mexicans in 1980 was 9.8 percent, Puerto Ricans 10.9, and Cubans 5.2 (Bean and Tienda 1987, 261–62).

17. García 1993, 17.

18. Vigil 1988, 240.

19. U.S. Bureau of the Census 1993b, table 5:157.

20. Moore 1991, 86.

21. Ibid.

22. Ibid., 88.

23. Ibid., 89.

24. Ibid., 101.

25. Ibid., 100.

26. Ibid.

27. *Street Gang Guide* 1981, 126.

28. See "L.A. Gangs Bloody Warfare Sets Record for Killings in 1990," *Arizona Daily Star,* December 1990, 14; "Los Padrinos Hopes to Keep Kids off Streets," *Tucson Daily Citizen,* 1 April 1991, 3E; David L. Tibel, "Police Optimistic about Gang Related Crime," *Tucson Daily Citizen,* 1 January 1994, 1A; and Rodríguez 1993, 252.

29. Rodríguez 1993, 252.

30. Ibid.

31. Morgan 1990, 247–48.

32. Ibid.

33. Moore 1978, 96.

34. Ibid., 97.

35. Ibid.

36. Smith, Joe, and Simpson 1991, 274. For children who used alcohol and drugs, home environment especially, reflected by marital status and depression of mothers and unemployment by fathers, was strongly associated. McBride, Joe, and Simpson (1991, 315–23) have two significant findings that come to bear on the issue of drug abuse. First, peer pressures and peer drug problems were directly associated with alcohol, drug, and criminal activity. The second was that self-esteem was directly associated with at least alcohol abuse. What is crucial here, however, is that drug use and criminality are outcomes of peer relationships, which themselves are established in the "streets." All the children in the sample were, in fact, already in a drug-abuse prevention program and therefore not randomly selected.

37. U.S. Commission on Civil Rights 1970, iv.

38. Ibid., 88–89.

39. Welch, Gruhl, and Spohn 1984, 261.

40. Moore 1978, 96.

41. Zatz 1985, 181.

42. California Youth Authority 1993, table 1:3; 1983, table 3:1; and 1970, table 3:17.

43. Department of Corrections 1993, 1–3; and 1985, table 12:29.

44. Warheit, Vega, Auth, and Meinhardt 1985, 13.

45. Ibid., 13.

46. Ibid., 17.

47. Ibid., 17 and 20.

48. The community survey offered in both English and Spanish revealed that 538 Mexican Americans (MAs) born in the United States reported more depressive symptomatology than 706 MAs born in Mexico. Immigration status differences (ISDs) in socioeconomic status (SES), stress, and social resources did not account for ISDs in depression. Low educational attainment and low acculturation were associated with depression for U.S.-born SES but not for Mexico-born SES. Possible explanations for ISDs in depression include selective migration and relative deprivation (Golding and Burnam 1990).

In addition, further analysis by Vega, Warheit, and Meindardt (1984, 822) indicates similar patterns when applied to marital status and depression. However, this was primarily due to the effect of economic stress, as reflected by low educational attainment.

49. See Vernon and Roberts 1982; Radloff 1977; Endicott and Spitzer 1978; and Frerichs, Aneshenel, and Clark 1982.

50. Smith, Joe, and Simpson 1991, 272.

51. Ibid., 274.

52. Barrett, Joe, and Simpson 1991, 293–94.

53. Quesada and Heller 1977; and Robert G. Aranda 1971 (both cited in Angel 1985, 415.)

54. Vega, Sallis, Patterson, Rupp, Morris, and Nader 1988, 194.

55. Ibid.

56. For a complete discussion of this topic of "admixture," concerning the Mexican population, see Cabrera-Mereb 1992, 22–32.

57. Markides and Coreil 1986, 258.

58. Martin and Suárez 1987, 852.

59. Diehl, Haffner, Knapp, Hazuda, and Stern 1989, 1532.

60. Suárez and Martin 1987, 633.

61. Ibid.

62. Table 2 (Mitchell et al. 1990, 428) shows that the percentage of Mexican male cigarette smokers was greater in the age category 25–65; the number of cigarettes smoked was half or more than that in almost every age group. Table 3 (429), however, shows fewer Mexican women than Anglo women smokers; and their daily cigarette intake at least two times, and in some age groups three times, less than that of Anglo women.

63. Hazuda, Stern, Gaskill, Haffner, and Gardener 1983, cited in Angel 1985, 416.

64. Morris 1968.

65. Oral interview by the author of a former marine and surviving member of E Company, 24 September 1993. I have omitted the actual source to protect the privacy of some persons and have changed a few details to protect the identity of others.

66. Kim Mattingly Kelliher, "Memorial Day Is Special for Mother, Her Family." *Arizona Daily Star,* 28 May 1991, p. 2B.

67. Bill Vogrin, "Hero Street U.S.A." *Arizona Daily Star,* 1990, p 1D.

68. U.S. Bureau of the Census 1993b, table 3:79.

69. U.S. Department of Defense n.d., 71–90.

70. Ibid., 42–43.

71. See Arthur 1987, x.

72. Some who had been wounded on Tarawa and other Pacific Islands were later wounded again in Korea, like Corpsman James Fisher (USMCR) of Tucson, Arizona. Some not only served in the Pacific theater, but lived to walk from the Chosin Reservoir and 15 years later into combat in Vietnam. These are called "Three War Marines."

73. Vélez-Ibáñez 1990.

74. "El Bobby" is a pseudonym; Mexicans of the region use the Spanish article before English given names to denote their cultural membership. I have used a pseudonym to protect the privacy and feelings of persons involved.

75. Guzmán n.d., 1–2.

76. Ibid., tables 2 and 3.

77. It is likely that some noticeable decrease would be expected between June 1969 and 1973, but the percentages would have remained the same.

78. Becerra 1982.

79. Trujillo (1990) is the only work done on Chicanos in Vietnam that has captured the essence and variety of experiences of the Mexican soldiers, marines, and sailors.

PART 3: So Farewell Hope and with Hope Farewell Fear, Coming Full Circle in Words and Pictures: Finding a Place and Space

1. "Queso" is Salvador Torres (an artist who studied at the Oakland College of Arts and Crafts and with Guillermo Aranda); as a struggling art student at San Diego State University he took the opportunity to train with Gilberto Ramírez, a former student of David Alfaro Siqueiros—one the "big three" of the Mexican mural movement of thirties' fame: José Clemente Orozco, David Alfaro Siqueiros, and Diego Rivera. In 1969, I was visited by Ramírez at San Diego State College where I had become the chairman of the Department of Mexican American Studies and had been able to scrape a few resources together from unallocated funds and an NEH grant to fund Ramírez's stay. In a 12–14 month period under the direction and training of Ramírez, a group of U.S. Mexican muralists who had called themselves Los Artistas de los Barrios, and especially Guillermo Aranda and Rubén de Anda, developed what gave the area its distinctive "Siqueiros" trademark by foreshortening figures that shot right out of

the wall, as Cockcroft and Barnet-Sánchez (1990, 1) described the master's style. Ramírez and Los Artistas' joint work culminated in a tripartite mural in acrylics; the panels are entitled *Conquest of the Americas, Joining of the Chicano and the Mexican,* and *Birth of the New Man.* The mural occupies the lobby of the student union at San Diego State University.

In addition, in the same period I had the opportunity to organize the "First Symposium on Chicano History and Art," which seemed to have provided some impetus for the formation of the Toltecas en Aztlán, a group that then gave substance to the ideas in dance, poetry, and other expressive forms presented in the former Ford Building. Many of the Chicano Park works, some murals at the Ford Building, and the mural mentioned above were all influenced directly by the Siqueiros-taught Ramírez. Aranda who mostly worked with Ramírez, in turn, developed his style strongly influenced by Ramírez in planning, design, motifs, and declared color contrasts and schemes.

2. UDT stands for Underwater Demolition Teams and SEAL for Sea, Air, and Land. The latter are "special troops" used for reconnaissance and shock troop purposes.

3. Cockcroft (1984, 80) is the most comprehensive treatment of the takeover of the region. I was a mere observer and part-time supporter.

4. Ibid., 87–97.

CHAPTER 6: The Search for Meaning and Space through Literature

1. Lomelí 1993, 230.

2. Ibid.

3. Even the present Chicano "critical literary studies" movement seems to have taken on the same quest, but with an unfortunate tendency toward seeking the legitimacy it never needed and countering that which gives the literature its power: the creative and emergent struggle to survive. The "critical studies" genre seeks in its own dizzying logic to join the literature of Mexicans of the region to the "canon" of American literature, as if the act somehow made the authors, their works, and the literary critics involved acceptable, integrated, and part of the landscape of "majority" literature. It seeks to join the most American, feminist, and African American literatures along the same dimensions of acceptability. That is, "they have made it" so must we. In this sense, the "Chicano critical studies" perspective, although recognizing the so-called uniqueness of the Mexican literature of the region, does inadvertently homogenize it by joining literatures with different histories into the American canon alone. In the most curious ways the "Chicano cultural studies" position, in spite of all of its protestations to the contrary, does not recognize the simple fact of the presence of millions of Mexicans across a political line, in the same

manner that Mexican literary and cultural studies critics do not recognize the opposite.

4. Del Río (1990, 432–33) provides a synthesis of the basic feminist issue in one compressed phrase: "The Chicana's healthy distrust of Anglo culture and ideas has also been used by the Chicano male to put her in 'her' place, indeed to keep her silent and passive when it comes to any criticism of the Chicano and his sexual oppression of her, who very often applies what can only be seen as a double standard of judging the Chicana as a *vendida* or worse, as a *malinchista,* a term which . . . implies treason to her own culture and race."

5. Calderón and Saldívar 1991, 20.

6. Chabram (1990, 234–35) suggests that the role of the U.S. Mexican intellectual is to transcend disciplinary and textual boundaries because of the "pre-institutional histories of Chicano academics, histories that originate in the fields, the border, the family." She adds, "Most of all, we must be willing to recognize . . . that the 'differences' which mark our condition as social beings in the academy are not the product of contemporary literary critical or anthropological discourse, but the product of an historical condition, inaugurated by conquest and domination." This is the struggle to which I allude.

7. Saldívar 1990, 5.

8. Ibid., 217–18.

9. Vélez-Ibáñez 1979.

10. Rosaldo 1989, 216.

11. Anzaldúa 1987, 82.

12. Ibid., 84.

13. Ibid.

14. Ibid.

15. It may be suggested that there are interstices within Mexican culture, even of the rural type from which Anzaldúa emerged, in which homosexuality for men is not entirely ruled out as long as the role of the male is that of the traditional progenitor and not the genetrix. Fixed within this version of Mexican culture is the idea that males are the "sources" of procreation and "plant" their seed into the ready and willing female "ground," who then nurtures and produces a mature being. In this way, Mexican males in prison, in isolation, in adolescent contexts rationalize their homosexual behavior as long as they are not considered the female "ground," and only Mexican males who take on the traditional genetrix definition are considered homosexual. Similarly Mexican lesbians may be perceived by males in quite a respectful way but not because of a sense of acceptance or tolerance, but rather, lesbians fit a sort of male-defined stereotype of what a "strong" woman should be—just like a man. What is derived is a sense of respectful fear of lesbians, which may very well reflect a fear of themselves. It's nutty but it's there.

16. Anzaldúa 1987, 19.

17. Ibid. See especially 21–35; 65–98.

18. Ibid., 63.

19. Ibid.

20. The problem of "race" is compounded not just by its social value but also by scientific work, which analyzes genetic typings to derive an estimate of genotypic mixing. Long et al. (1991, 142–57) have carefully located the ancestral contributions of specific allele frequencies in Tucson, Arizona, among Mexicans; and they conclude that the donors are distributed from Spanish, Indian, and African populations with the percentage genotypic contributions largely from admixture between Spanish allele (or haplotype) frequencies of 0.68 ± 0.05; Indigenous alleles 0.29 ± 0.04; and 0.02 ± 1 African American. In comparison with other samples in San Antonio (Stern et al. 1986), the distribution of frequencies was 0.65; 0.34; and 0.05 and in Los Angeles (Mickey et al. 1983) 0.83; 0.16; and 0.6. Long et al. (152) conclude from these data that Mexicans do constitute a biological entity and therefore are influential genetically. Such works are only specific biological descriptors and have nothing to do with "memory," cultural affinity, or some sort of magical relationship. Nor do they fix a "racial" distribution of "blood" among Spanish, Indian, and African American cultural populations. These are red blood allele frequencies, not socially derived racial markers.

21. Anzaldúa 1987, 77–78.

22. Ibid., 77.

23. Ibid., 79.

24. Anzaldúa 1990, 144–45.

25. Anzaldúa 1993, 82.

26. Lobbiniere-Harwood 1989, 45.

27. Anzaldúa 1987, 90–91.

28. Islas 1993.

29. Interview with José Antonio Burciaga, November 20, 1994.

30. Burciaga 1992.

31. Interview with José Antonio Burciaga, March 3, 1994, Stanford, California.

32. Hicks 1987, 86.

33. Ibid., 85.

34. Ibid., 86. I have paraphrased Hicks, who says of the process: "The border metaphor reconstructs the relationship to the object rather than the object itself: as a metaphor, it does not merely represent an object but rather produces an interaction between the connotative matrices of an object in more than one culture."

35. Burciaga 1992, 124.

36. Ibid., 128.

37. *Empacho* is a Mexican term designating a deep stomachache and alludes

to stopped-up intestines. Rodríguez's work has been commented upon and summarized by dozens of Anglo and Mexican critics. For the most part, Anglo critics love Rodríguez's *Memories* because it is congruent with most stereotypic notions of Mexican culture, which, they suggest, is so different (or so odious) that individuals have to become erased linguistically and socially in order to reach the heights of the rationality of the Anglo upper middle class. Even the most critical Anglo analysis proposes that Rodríguez, as a "modernist," rejects the values and conventions of the historical past. Although agreeing that Rodríguez became isolated and dehumanized, this view cannot assume that "modern American institutions" carry secularized consciousness, reason, reflection, and the intellect to which Rodríguez aspired. Mexican culture on the other hand is its opposite—spontaneous, emotive, instinctive, and so different that it has its own notion of time and space. (See Hogue 1992, 54–56.)

38. Rodríguez 1992, xvi.

39. Ibid., xv.

40. Ibid., 168.

41. Ibid., 171–72.

42. Ibid.

43. Ibid., 230.

44. Segade 1973, 4.

45. Castillo 1986, 118.

46. Ibid.

47. Ibid., 119.

48. See especially Yarbo-Bejarano (1992). Her discussion of multiple subjectivity as the theoretical source for the discussion of Mexican women's works has been invaluable, and much of my discussion is owed to her fine insights.

49. Alarcón 1989, 84.

50. Ibid.

51. Bruce-Novoa's insightful discussion (1976) provided me with the basic road map to read and to discuss Méndez's work. I have followed his lead to each of the characters and especially his idea of the historical erasing process inherent in Méndez's' view of the impact of power and class upon defenseless populations.

52. Méndez 1992, 83.

53. Ibid., 83.

54. Ibid., 94.

55. Ibid., 100.

56. Ibid., 122.

57. Ibid., 128.

58. Ibid., 135.

59. Ibid., 138.

60. Ibid.

61. This is the erasure process that Bruce-Novoa so eloquently describes in his discussion of Méndez (1976).

62. Méndez 1992, 178.

CHAPTER 7: Making Pictures: U.S. Mexican
Place and Space in Mural Art

1. For an analysis of the California mural movement, see Goldman (1990). For a description of the Midwest-Chicago movement, see *Barrio Murals* (1987). For the most complete compendium of all murals in Los Angeles County, see Dunitiz 1993. The work dates the earliest mural to 1912; and at present both extant and extinct murals number over 1,500.

2. See *Antiguas raíces* 1968; CARA 1990; and Chávez, Grynsztejn, and Kanjo 1993.

3. These are from the Spanish colonial tradition, the post–Mexican Revolution, and the 1930s WPA (Works Progress Administration) murals of the Great Depression. Murals are not new to the region; and as chapter 1 illustrated, Katsina mural paintings were part of the south to north influence among the Pueblos in the Mogollon areas of New Mexico and among the Hopis of Arizona. The Mission of San Xavier del Bac in Tucson, Arizona, boasts a number of mural frescos, which were created in the late eighteenth century and have recently been restored (*Murals,* 1993, 1). "Evidently the Mexican muralist movement of the twenties and thirties had a profound impact on the social realist muralists of the Works Progress Administration and the Treasury Section programs of the U.S. New Deal. . . . More than 2,500 murals were painted with government sponsorship during the New Deal period in the United States" (Cockroft and Barnet-Sánchez 1990, 1).

4. See especially CARA 1990; Goldman 1990, 29–34; Organista 1983; and Sánchez-Tranquilino 1991.

5. Mesa-Bains 1991, 133.

6. According to Gullard and Lund (1989, 15), from 1802 to 1822, over 7,000 indigenous people were baptized at the Mission of Santa Clara, but 6,556 of those died due to syphilis, measles, and smallpox.

7. Ibid.

8. As chapter 2 indicated, one of the most successful means of acquiring titles to land for Anglo males was to marry the daughters of wealthy Mexican land owners. This strategy was used successfully by a former Irish sea captain, John Gregg, who married the widow María Luisa Soto Copinger and thereby acquired a large section of the Rancho Rinconada del Arroyo de San Francisquito (Gullard and Lund 1989, 46–47). María Luisa's grandparents in fact had been

members of the Sonoran de Anza colonization scheme in 1775, which founded San Francisco. Leland Stanford founded Leland Stanford Jr. University in memory of his only son, who died of typhoid in 1884 in Italy (Allen 1980, 5, 11).

9. Allen 1980, 5.

10. De Jesús 1982–1983, 10–11.

11. Cecilia Burciaga Preciado has sadly been "riffed," as this text is being written, for her outspoken manner. Thus, both Burciagas who served as resident fellows will no longer fulfill those roles. It is astonishing that in the very month of the riffing, Stanford University hosted the Dalai Lama of Tibet and supported the appearance of Aristide of Haiti, both with focused announcements about their struggle for cultural and political liberation. That both Burciagas, who represent the political and cultural conscience of many throughout the Southwest and who are more important to the U.S. Mexican population than either the Dalai Lama or Aristide, should be riffed summarily because of "budget" cuts at the same time and place is unique even for Stanford. It is highly likely that the fees paid to both worthy guests are larger than the Burciagas' annual salaries.

12. The side and connecting panels in fact were named by Burciaga; but I have taken the liberty to name them only for the sake of chronological description, and they should not be identified as such in reality except that I have Mr. Burciaga's permission to refer to them as such. These include "More Chicano Heroes and Heroines" and "Transitions."

Methodologically, I have taken the opportunity to use an informant's approach by asking Mr. Burciaga to comment on all of the author's interpretations for which he has provided "informed" or insider's views and information to support or invalidate the author's explanations.

13. Interview with José Antonio Burciaga, 10 April 1994; and Burciaga 1988b.

14. Burciaga 1988b.

15. According to Burciaga (1988a), he conducted a survey that had a 70 percent response rate, and the final choice of 13 Chicano heroes, from a total of 60 in the pool, reflected his generation of activists. The students offered candidates from a pool of 240 candidates. For Burciaga, the selection process itself unpacked the mythology of what constituted heroes of any sort.

16. Burciaga 1988a.

17. The role of the San Patricio Brigade is a contested one. Depending on whether Mexican or American writers explain their participation, the San Patricio Brigade is either vilified or mythically described. From the point of view of the United States, these men were turncoats who had only recently immigrated to the United States. From the point of view of Mexico, these were cultural heroes who were righteous knights helping to resist a Yankee Protestant invasion.

From the household point of view, post-revolutionary Mexican parents, who

had fled the revolution, married in the thirties, and raised U.S. Mexican children, often related with warm recollections the heroics of the San Patricio
Brigade. Thus, in the U.S. Southwest when the offspring of Irish-American parents who had moved to work in the war industries in California and Arizona
met the Mexican offspring, a cultural template of admiration had already been
established. In addition, the presence of Irish priests and nuns in largely Mexican Catholic schools and parishes sometimes led to further cultural recognition
between populations. An interactive acculturation emerged at times with the
acquisition of Irish brogues by Mexican English-speaking children and Span-
ish-accented "brogued" English spoken by the Irish priests and nuns. In addition to the mere physical presence of Irish migrants and their children from
Boston, Catholic youth clubs, formed by Irish priests, often led to close cultural
associations and intermarriage between Mexican and Irish young people. In
Tucson, Los Kennedy, Los Daily, Los Murphy, and many others refer to the
Mexican Irish families from these unions and earlier ones as well. Brenden
Flannery was in love with my sister for years, and in the early fifties puppy
love flourished between Sheila Campbell and me.

18. According to Burciaga, the phrase originated with one student who chose
that statement as his hero.

19. Personal communication with Burciaga, 5 April 1994.

20. Ibid.

21. All the numerical information is taken from *Murals* 1993, 9–20; and this
discussion of the Tucson murals is heavily indebted to work accomplished in
this guide. It lists 135 sites, but each has multiple murals, with some having as
many as 9, such as the murals of the Old Pascua Neighborhood Center, which
is a multiservice center focused on the Yaqui tribe who partially occupy a half-
mile-square area of the city of Tucson.

Forty percent of the 133 murals were directed and/or produced by five individuals and their groups. These include the prolific David Tineo, Alfred
Quiroz, Antonio Pazos, and Luis Gustavo Mena, who have painted 50 of the
133 murals; one other artist, Gustavo Rocha, painted 5.

22. The eight murals counted for Native Americans probably include a few
U.S. Mexicans, and the opposite would occur in the U.S. Mexican count. Most
Yaquis have Spanish surnames; therefore, it is difficult to desegregate them
from Mexicans, except that in a few cases some of the artists like Guadalupe
Matus, Feliciana Martínez, Dean Narcho, and Bernabé Tapia are clearly tribal
members. In addition, Alfred Quiroz considers himself a Chicano artist although he strongly identifies with his Yaqui grandmother. It is usual, in fact,
for many Mexicans of the region of Arizona/Sonora to be of Spanish/Mexi-
can/Yaqui/Maya/Pima ancestry.

23. This method of legitimizing the present by erasing, borrowing, removing,
or pasting over previous expressive or historical traditions is not a new process

for indigenous, European, or Anglo traditions. Certainly the Mesoamerican "Mexica" habit of amalgamating their own lineage references in extant codices over those recently submitted is well known. The Spanish colonial practice of using materials from torn-down temples of indigenous populations and building churches on the same sites was common. The appropriation of others' histories, however, leaves those appropriated with little but a faint memory of time or space.

24. *Murals* 1993, 1.

25. Twenty-two murals painted in the "greater Tucson" area were produced by U.S. Mexican artists; of these, twenty are in educational institutions and reflect the demographic movement of the Mexican population mostly toward the south. However, 75 percent of these works were painted by the same artists and while artistically impressive do not thematically add to this discussion.

26. The actual numbers were computed from the list provided in *Murals* 1993, 9–18.

27. The actual dates of undated murals are uncertain, but there are a number of examples of murals that were painted in buildings constructed after certain dates; thus, the El Pueblo Neighborhood Center, which opened in late 1979, has one mural painted by Darlene Marcos probably done in the early 1980s. Similarly, other artists like Alfred Quiroz became very active only in the post-1980 period, and his two undated murals at Mansfeld Middle School are of this or a later period.

28. Arreola (1984) did not include the interior murals like Carlos Encinas's 1982 *Commerce in Space* in the library of Hughes Elementary School and David Tineo's 1980 *Nuestra raza* in the South Tucson Community Center.

29. *Murals* 1993, 4–7. The numbered circles refer to sites where murals are placed, and the glossary provides the enumerated list with addresses and map location according to the area in Tucson. Beneath the locational information are listed the artists, title of work, date if available, and some referential designation (see glossary A).

30. Arreola 1984, 418.

31. Ibid., 419–22. Arreola specifically develops the idea that environmental concerns and local or regional symbols were the new trends at the time of his discussion. He did not develop the feminist and creative woman themes.

32. This characteristic of the relation between the density and the concentration of population, however, is generally valid except in those murals clustered in the northeastern part of central Tucson. Specifically, those clustered between Speedway and Broadway and between 6th Avenue and Campbell Avenue are largely murals painted for or by the University of Arizona, private businesses, or located in elementary schools, which have a high concentration of U.S. Mexican students but not a dense Mexican population in the area.

33. Officer n.d., section 48.

34. This discussion uses as a base the 1986 federal definition of "poor" as a family of four with an annual cash income of less than $11,203. For South Tucson, 34 percent of the population is under age 18, and only 11 percent is over 60.

35. *Tucson Daily Citizen,* 6 January 1988; and Jance C. Berry, "South Tucson," *Tucson Daily Citizen,* 1 April 1987.

36. Vélez-Ibáñez 1993b.

37. The Flores Pharmacy was founded in the early 1920s and has been the main source for herbs and traditional Mexican home remedies. The Cathedral of San Agustín has been the bishop's rectory, but Mexicans often regarded it more as their own in contrast to All Saints Church only four blocks away and until the mid-1960s, the Anglo church. Nayo the barber is a political institution who knows every skeleton in every closet and to whom new aspirants to political office often turn for information. "La Safford" was a central educational location for many Mexican youths and served as a transfer point to Tucson High School, which was the only secondary institution graduating small but significant numbers of Mexican students prior to the construction of Salpointe Catholic High School in 1950. The "Hollywood" barrio, now a largely rebuilt stable working-class area, was at one time noticeable for its fighting spirit. The Victoria Ballroom was (is) a dance hall, which had the reputation of some partygoers giving appendix operations without the benefit of anesthesia during Saturday night fun. In actuality, many *quinceañeras,* birthday parties, and marriage receptions were held there. Today it is known for its *quebradita* dances—a type of cowboy hip hop from the Mexican state of Sinaloa.

CHAPTER 8: Conclusions: Unmasking Borders of Minds

1. Williams 1977, 108–127.
2. Montejano n.d., 31.
3. Ibid., 30.
4. Ibid., 39.
5. Ibid.
6. *San Francisco Examiner,* Sunday, 8 May 1994, p. A9.
7. *The Stanford Daily,* Friday, 6 May 1994, p. 1.

Bibliographic Note

WITHIN THE COURSE OF MY RESEARCH, I have relied upon the works of specialists in various fields. I have listed here the major sources according to the specific area of expertise.

In the archaeological arena Emil Haury has contributed significant studies, especially Emil W. Haury (1976) *The Hohokam: Desert Farmers and Craftsmen* and (1986) "Thoughts after Sixty Years as a Southwestern Archaeologist." More contemporary works are Steven A. LeBlanc (1989) "Cultural Dynamics in the Southern Mogollon Area" and Paul R. Fish (1989) "The Hohokam: 1,000 Years of Prehistory in the Sonoran Desert." For a final determination of the Di Peso pochteca hypothesis for Casas Grandes, the standard is set by Jeffrey S. Dean and John C. Ravesloot (1993) "The Chronology of Cultural Interaction in the Gran Chichimeca." The "protohistorical" period (between the demise of many of the complex cultural centers of the Southwest and the European influx) is surveyed by Carroll Riley (1982) *Frontier People: The Greater Southwest in the Proto-historic Period*.

The Spanish colonial period is well covered by two sources: David J. Weber (1992) *The Spanish Frontier in North America* and Ramón A. Gutiérrez (1991) *When Jesus Came, the Corn Mother Went Away*. The second work is especially informative on Pueblo-Hispano/Mexicano relations even though we do not share the same interpretive template.

For the Mexican and American periods an invaluable source is Thomas E. Sheridan (1986) *Los Tucsonenses: The Mexican Community in Tucson, 1854–1941*. His work is absolutely imperative for any remarks concerning eighteenth-and nineteenth-century Arizona, while James E. Officer (1989) *Hispanic Arizona, 1536–1856* is the basic work for anyone interested in the preceding centuries as well as the same time periods. For deep insights into Spanish- and Mexican-Indian relations, Elizabeth Johns (1975) *Storms Brewed in Other Men's Worlds* serves well as an overall study. The essential work for New Mexico is David

J. Weber (1987) *Myth and the History of the Hispanic Southwest;* and for Texas,
David Montejano (1987) *Anglos and Mexicans in the Making of Texas, 1836–1986.*
For the history of Mexican labor in the United States, the most lasting and
helpful studies are found in Rodolfo Acuña (1981) *Occupied America, A History
of Chicanos* and Carey McWilliams (1948, 1990) *North from Mexico: The Spanish-
Speaking People of the United States,* while the seminal work of Arizona mining
labor is in the unpublished text of Joseph F. Park (1961) "The History of Mexican Labor in Arizona during the Territorial Period." For insights into and original material on Texas border labor history, see Mario T. García (1981) *Desert
Immigrants: The Mexicans of El Paso, 1880–1920.* For California labor history as it
applies to U.S. Mexican labor history, the works by Juan Gómez-Quiñones
(1972, 1982) and Devora Weber are important; especially crucial is Weber's most
recent (1994) *Dark Sweat, White Gold: California Farm Workers, Cotton, and the
New Deal.* They with a few others initiated contemporary Mexican labor history in the United States. Most recently the fine work by Gilbert G. González
(1994) *Labor and Community, Mexican Citrus Worker Villages in a Southern California County, 1900–1950* follows Walter F. Goldschmidt (1974) *As Ye Sow: Three
Studies in the Social Consequences of Agribusiness* to show the influence of the way
labor is organized by the organization of production and the attendant creation
of Mexican communities. However, unlike Goldschmidt, González emphasizes
the overriding importance of cultural activities and of the institutions created
by Mexicans in defining the characteristics of what he terms "village life." This
is exactly my own position, as analyzed in chapter 2, that the Mexican population moves from "victim" to creator and inventor of cultural spaces and places
with many of such inventions continuously influenced by south to north trans-
migration. Robert R. Álvarez (1987) *Familia: Migration and Adaptation in Baja and
Alta California, 1800–1975* is the most descriptive work done on the subject of
south to north migration within the context of the many changes in economy
and polity in the region; and it stands alone in the quality of its anthropology.
    The seminal work in social science is Nick C. Vaca (1970) "The Mexican
American in the Social Sciences: 1912–1970" (Part I: 1912–1935 and Part II:
1936–1970). Jane Hill (1993) "Hasta la Vista Baby" is the most complete study
to date on the social structure determinants of language use in Anglo-Mexican
interaction. Another work along the same lines is my own early "¿Qué Crees?
The Themes and Ramifications of Racism in the Chicano Southwest" (1970).
    Manuel Rojas (1986) *Joaquín Murrieta: "El Patrio"* is the most comprehensive
and accurate historical rendition of the life and death of Joaquín Murrieta. Following the lead provided by James Officer, I am of the opinion that Murrieta
died in Sonora of old age and maintained cross-border household relations in
Baja and Southern California. The head in a jar in Northern California, therefore, is not that of Joaquín Murrieta. Robert J. Rosenbaum (1981) *Mexicano Resis-*

tance in the Southwest: The Sacred Right of Self-Preservation is a well-thought-out and reliable work that provided me with direction and a point of departure for an analysis of the rebellion process in the region. The fundamental work for gaining an insight into the long history of Mexican resistance in Texas is Américo Paredes (1958, 1973) *With His Pistol in His Hand: A Border Ballad and Its Hero.* Another important work is James A. Sandos (1992) *Rebellion in the Borderlands: Anarchism and the Plan of San Diego, 1904–1923.*

Cultural and political resistance through union and communal organization in various areas of the Southwest is investigated by Rodolfo Acuña (1981) *Occupied America, A History of Chicanos;* Juan Gómez-Quiñones (1973) "The First Steps: Chicano Labor Conflict and Organizing 1900–1920," (1973) *Sembradores, Ricardo Flores Magón Y El Partido Liberal Mexicano: A Eulogy and Critique* and (1990) *Chicano Politics: Reality and Promise, 1940–1990;* Vicki L. Ruiz (1987) *Cannery Women, Cannery Lives: Mexican Women, Unionization, and the California Food Processing Industry, 1930–1950;* and Emilio Zamora (1993) *The World of the Mexican Worker in Texas.* For reviews of the functions of mutual aid societies, see Carlos G. Vélez-Ibáñez et al. (1982) "Hispanic American Organizations and Voluntary Associations: A Reference Work of Selected Groups"; José Amaro Hernández (1983) *Mutual Aid for Survival: The Case of the Mexican American;* the Zamora (1990) work cited above; and most specifically my own *Bonds of Mutual Trust: the Cultural Systems of Mexican/Chicano Rotating Credit Associations* (1983) and "Plural Strategies of Survival and Cultural Formation in U.S. Mexican Households in a Region of Dynamic Transformation" (1994).

The section of the text that focuses on household emergence and the inherent cultural systems therein, including statistical information, has been previously published in Carlos G. Vélez-Ibáñez (1993) "Ritual Cycles of Exchange: the Process of Cultural Creation and Management in the U.S. Borderlands" and (1993) "U.S. Mexicans in the Borderlands: Being Poor without the Underclass."

Statistical and demographic information on the various "sadnesses" among Mexican populations, as well as enumerations on gangs, is presented in U.S. Bureau of the Census (1993) *Hispanic Americans Today.* Crucial as well are Jesús M. García (1993) *The Hispanic Population in the United States: March 1992;* Joan W. Moore (1991) *Down to the Barrio: Homeboys and Homegirls in Change;* George J. Warheit et al. (1985) *Psychiatric Symptoms and Dysfunctions among Anglos and Mexican Americans.* Within this same subject area, I offer a special salute to the band of brothers and survivors of E-Company, United States Marine Corps, who fought bravely without training, died many score, and returned, with too many still in the battlefield psychologically and emotionally. They represent so many of all wars.

For critical interpretations of literary works, see Carmen M. del Río (1990) "Chicana Poets: Re-Visions from the Margin"; Héctor Calderón and Ramón

322 « *Bibliographic Note*

Saldívar (1991) *Criticism in the Borderlands: Studies in Chicano Literature, Culture and Ideology;* and Ramón Saldívar (1990) *Chicano Narrative: The Dialects of Difference,* even though I have a distinctly opposite point of view from the authors of the latter two works. Further insights emerge from reading Angie Chabram (1990) "Chicana/o Studies as Oppositional Ethnography"; D. Emily Hicks (1987) "Deterritorialization and Border Writing"; and Yvonne Yarbo-Bejarano (1992) "The Multiple Subject in the Writing of Ana Castillo." Yarbo-Bejarano's discussion of multiple subjectivity as the theoretical source for the discussion of Mexican women's works is invaluable for its fine insights. For Mexican literature of the United States, Justo S. Alarcón (1989) "El Esperpéntico en Miguel Méndez M."; and Juan D. Bruce-Novoa (1976) "La voz del silencio: Miguel Méndez" offer interpretive guidance to Miguel Méndez's work; and for an interpretation of José Antonio Burciaga's work, especially important was my discussion with the author over *cocido* on Sunday morning in Redwood City.

For interpretations of Chicano artwork, the basic studies are Eva Cockcroft (1984) "The Story of Chicano Park"; and Shifra M. Goldman (1990) "How, Why, Where, and When It All Happened: Chicano Murals of California." For a description of the Midwest-Chicago movement, see *The Barrio Murals* (1987). José Antonio Burciaga provided me emotional insight into his murals, which I present in my discussion of his work but which I had not discovered on my own.

Bibliography

Acuña, Rodolfo. 1981. *Occupied America: A History of Chicanos.* 2nd ed. New York: Harper and Row.

Alarcón, Justo S. 1989. "El Esperpéntico en Miguel Méndez M." *The Americas Review* 17, no. 1 (spring): 84–99.

Allen, Peter C. Stanford. 1980. *From the Foothills to the Bay.* Stanford: Stanford Alumni Association & Stanford Historical Society.

Alvarez, Robert R. 1987. *Familia: Migration and Adaptation in Baja and Alta California, 1800–1975.* Berkeley: University of California Press.

Antiguas raíces / Visiones nuevas. Ancient Roots/New Visions. 1968. Tucson: Tucson Museum of Art.

Anzaldúa, Gloria. 1987. *Borderlands: La Frontera.* San Francisco: Aunt Lute Press.

———. 1990. "Internal Affairs o las que niegan a su gente." In *Making Face, Making Soul: Haciendo Caras,* ed. Gloria Anzaldúa. San Francisco: Aunt Lute Press.

———. 1993. "El día de la chicana." In *Infinite Divisions: An Anthology of Chicana Literature,* ed. Tey Diana Rebolledo and Eliana S. Rivero. Tucson: University of Arizona Press.

Aranda, Robert G. 1971. "The Mexican American Syndrome." *American Journal of Public Health* 61 (January): 104–9. Cited in Ronald Angel, "The Health of the Mexican Origin Population." In *The Mexican American Experience,* ed. R. De la Garza et al. (Austin: University of Texas Press, 1985), 415.

Arizona Daily Star, 1992. December 1990–19 February.

Arreola, Daniel D. 1984. "Mexican American Exterior Murals." *The Geographic Review* 74, no. 4 (October): 409–24.

Arthur, Anthony. 1987. *Bushmasters: America's Jungle Warriors of World War II.* New York: St. Martin's Press.

Baca Zinn, Maxine. 1982. "Mexican American Women in the Social Sciences." *Signs, Journal of Women in Culture and Society* 8, no. 2 (winter): 259–72.

Bahr, Donald M. 1971. "Who Were the Hohokam? The Evidence from Pima Papago Myths." *Ethnohistory* 18, no. 3: 245–67.

Barrazas, Maclovio. 1965. Interview by author.

Barrera, Mario. 1979. *Race and Class in the Southwest: A Series of Racial Inequality.* Notre Dame: University of Notre Dame Press.

Barrett, Mark E., George W. Joe, and D. Dwayne Simpson. 1991. "Acculturation Influences on Inhalant Use." *Hispanic Journal of Behavioral Sciences* 13, no. 3 (August): 267–75, 293–94.

The Barrio Murals. 1987. Chicago: The Mexican Fine Arts Center/Museum.

Baugh, Timothy G., and Jonathon E. Ericson. 1992. "Trade and Exchange in a Historical Perspective." In *The American Southwest and Mesoamerica: Systems of Prehistoric Exchange,* ed. Jonathon E. Ericson and Timothy G. Baugh, 3–20. New York: Plenum.

Beals, Ralph L. 1974. Reprint. "Cultural Relations between Northern Mexico and the Southwest United States: Ethnologically and Archaeologically." In *The Mesoamerican Southwest,* ed. Basil C. Hedrick, J. Charles Kelley, and Carroll L. Riley, 51–57. Carbondale: Southern Illinois University Press. Originally appeared in *El norte de México y el sur de Estados Unidos. Tercera reunión de mesa redonda sobre problemas antropológicos de México y Centro América,* 191–99; 245–52. 25 August–2 September, Mexico, 1943.

Bean, Frank, and Marta Tienda. 1987. *The Hispanic Population of the United States.* New York: Russell Sage Foundation.

Becerra, Rosina M. 1982. "The Hispanic Vietnam Veteran: Mental Health Issues and Therapeutic Approaches." In *Mental Health and Hispanic Americans: Clinical Perspectives,* ed. R. M. Becerra, M. Karno, and J. I. Escobar, 169–80. New York: Grune and Stratton.

Brand, Donald. 1939. "Notes on the Geography and Archaeology of Zape, Durango." In *So Live the Words of Men,* ed. Donald Brand and Fred Harvey, 75–106. Albuquerque: University of New Mexico Press.

Browne, J. Ross. 1974. Reprint. *Adventures in the Apache Country.* Tucson: University of Arizona Press, 1869.

Bruce-Novoa, Juan D. 1976. "La voz del silencio: Miguel Méndez." *Diálogos* 12, no. 3 (May–June): 27–30.

Burciaga, José Antonio. 1988. "Last Supper of Chicano Heroes." Reprint, *Los Angeles Times,* 3 May.

———. 1988. "Mythology of Maíz." Reprint and updated, *Los Angeles Times,* 3 May.

———. 1992. Reprint. *Weedee Peepo.* Edinburg: University of Texas–Pan American Press, 1988.

———. 1992. *Drink Cultura: Chicanismo.* Santa Barbara: Capra Press.

Bustamante, Ursula. 1971. Conversation with author. Tucson, Arizona.

Cabrera-Mereb, Claudine. 1992. "The Biocultural Profile of a Population at Risk in the U.S. Mexico Border." Ph.D. diss., Tucson: University of Arizona.

Cabrero, María Teresa. 1989. *Civilización en el Norte de México.* México: Universidad Nacional Autónoma de México.

Calderón, Héctor, and Ramón Saldívar. 1991. *Criticism in the Borderlands: Studies in Chicano Literature, Culture and Ideology.* Durham: Duke University.

California Youth Authority. 1970. *Characteristics of California Youth Authority.* Sacramento: State of California.

———. 1983. *Characteristics of California Youth Authority.* Sacramento: State of California.

———. 1993. *Characteristics of California Youth Authority.* Sacramento: State of California.

Camarillo, Alberto. 1979. *Chicanos in a Changing Society.* Cambridge: Harvard University Press.

Campa, Arthur. 1993. Reprint. *Hispanic Culture in the Southwest.* Norman: University of Oklahoma Press, 1979.

CARA, Chicano Art: Resistance and Affirmation. 1990. Los Angeles: Wight Art Gallery, University of California.

Castañeda, Antonia I. 1992. *Presidarias y Pobladoras: The Journey North and Life in Frontier California.* Renato Rosaldo Lecture Series 1990–1991, vol. 8. N.p., Monograph.

———. 1993. "The Political Economy of Nineteenth Century Stereotypes of Californias." In *Regions of La Raza: Changing Interpretations of Mexican American Regional History and Culture,* ed. Antonio Ríos-Bustamante, 189–211. Encino: Flor y Canto Press.

Castillo, Ana. 1986. *The Mixquiahuala Letters.* Binghamton: Bilingual Press.

Chabram, Angie. 1990. "Chicana/o Studies as Oppositional Ethnography." *Cultural Studies* 4, no. 3 (October): 228–47.

Chávez, Leo. 1988. "Undocumented Mexicans and Central Americans and the Immigration Control and Reform Act of 1986: A Reflection Based on Empirical Data." In *Defense of the Alien,* ed. Lydio F. Tomasi, 137–56. Vol. 10. Staten Island: Center for Migration Studies of New York.

Chávez, Patricio, Madeleine Grynsztejn, and Kathryn Kanjo. 1993. *La Frontera/The Border: Art about the Mexico/United States Border Experience.* San Diego: Centro Cultural de La Raza and Museum of Contemporary Art, San Diego.

Cockcroft, Eva. 1984. "The Story of Chicano Park." *Aztlán: International Center of Chicano Studies Research* 15, no.1 (spring): 79–103.

Cockroft, Eva Sperling, and Holly Barnet-Sánchez, eds. 1990. *Signs from the Heart: California Chicano Murals.* Venice, Calif.: Social and Public Art Resource Center.

Coers, W. C. 1934. "Comparative Achievement of White and Junior High School Pupils." *Peabody Journal of Education* 12:157–62.

Corbin, Alicia. 1937. *Brothers of Light: the Penitentes of the Southwest.* New York: Harcourt, Brace and Co.

Corle, Edwin. 1951. *The Gila: Rivers of the Southwest.* Lincoln: University of Nebraska Press.

Cornelius, Wayne. 1988. "Persistence of Immigrant-Dominated Firms and Industries in the United States: The Case of California." Paper presented at the Conference on Comparative Migration Studies. Paris, France, 20–23 June.

Corrigan, Philip, and Derek Sayer. 1985. *The Great Arch: English State Formation as Cultural Revolution.* Oxford: Basil and Blackwell.

Dean, Jeffrey S., and John C. Ravesloot. 1993. "The Chronology of Cultural Interaction in the Gran Chichimeca." In *Culture and Contact: Charles C. Di Peso's Gran Chichimeca,* ed. Anne I. Woosley and John C. Ravesloot, 83–103. Albuquerque: University of New Mexico Press.

de Jesús, Manuel. 1982–1983. "Zapata's Murals." *La Zapatista.* Reprinted from *La Onda* 1979.

de la Teja, Jesús F., and John Wheat. 1991. "Bexar: Profile of a Tejano Community, 1820–1832." In *Tejano Origins in Eighteenth-Century San Antonio,* ed. Gerald E. Poyo and Gilberto M. Hinojosa, 1–24. Austin: University of Texas Press.

De León, Arnoldo. 1982. *The Tejano Community, 1836–1900.* Albuquerque: University of New Mexico Press.

de Lobbiniere-Harwood, Susanne. 1989. "Interview with Gloria Anzaldúa." *Trivia* (spring): 37–45.

del Río, Carmen M. 1990. "Chicana Poets: Re-Visions from the Margin." *Revista Canadiense de Estudios Hispánicos* 14, no. 2 (spring): 431–45.

Demos, George D. 1962. "Attitudes of Mexican-American and Anglo American Groups Toward Education." *Journal of Social Psychology* (August).

Department of Corrections. 1985. *California Prisoners and Parolees.* Sacramento: State of California.

———. 1993. *California Prisoners and Parolees.* Sacramento: State of California.

Dickerson, R. F. 1919. "Some Suggestive Problems in the Americanization of Mexicans." *Pedagogical Seminary* (September): 288–93.

Diehl, Andrew K., Steven M. Haffner, J. Ava Knapp, Helen P. Hazuda, and Michael P. Stern. 1989. "Dietary Intake and the Prevalence of Gallbladder Disease in Mexican Americans." *Gastroenterology* 97: 1527–33.

Di Peso, Charles. 1974. *Casas Grandes: Medio Period.* Vol. 2. Dragoon, Arizona: The Amerind Foundation.

———. 1983. *Las sociedades no nucleares de Norteamérica: La Gran Chichimeca.* Vol. 7, *Historia general de América: Período indígena.* Caracas: Academia Nacional de la Historia de Venezuela.

Dobyns, Henry F. 1976. *Spanish Colonial Tucson. A Demographic History.* Tucson: University of Arizona Press.

—. 1983. *Their Numbers Become Thinned. Native American Population Dynamics in Eastern North America.* Knoxville: University of Tennessee Press.

—. 1993. "Trails through Casa Grande." *Casa Grande Valley Histories.* Casa Grande Valley Historical Society, 3–26.

Doyel, David E. 1991. "Hohokam Exchange and Interaction." In *Chaco and Hohokam: Prehistoric Regional Systems in the American Southwest,* ed. Patricia L. Crown and W. James Judge, 225–52. Santa Fe: School of American Research Press.

—. 1993. "Interpreting Prehistoric Cultural Diversity in the Arizona Desert." In *Culture and Contact: Charles C. Di Peso's Gran Chichimeca,* ed. Anne I. Woosley and John C. Ravesloot, 39–64. Albuquerque: University of New Mexico Press.

Dunbar Ortiz, Roxanne. 1980. *Roots of Resistance, Land Tenure in New Mexico, 1680–1980.* Los Angeles: Chicano Studies Research Center and the American Indian Studies Center.

Dunitiz, Robin J. 1993. *Street Gallery: Guide to 1000 Los Angeles Murals.* Los Angeles: RJD Enterprises.

Endicott, J., and R. A. Spitzer. 1978. "A Diagnostic Interview: Schedule for Affective Disorder and Schizophrenia." *Archives of General Psychology* 35: 837–44.

Farnham, Thomas Jefferson. 1947. Reprint. Travels in California and Scenes in the Pacific. Oakland, 1844.

Feinman, Gary M. 1991. "Hohokam Archaeology in the Eighties." In *Exploring the Hohokam: Prehistoric Desert Peoples of the American Southwest.* Albuquerque: University of New Mexico.

Ferdon, Edwin N. 1967. "The Hohokam Ball Court: An Alternative View of Its Function." In *The Kiva* 33, no. 1: 1–14.

Fiedel, Stuart J. 1992. *The Prehistory of the Americas.* 2nd ed. Cambridge: Cambridge University Press.

Fish, Paul R. 1989. "The Hohokam: 1,000 Years of Prehistory in the Sonoran Desert." In *Dynamics of Southwest Prehistory,* ed. Linda S. Cordell and George J. Gumerman, 19–63. Washington D.C.: Smithsonian Institution Press.

Foster, Michael S. 1986. "The Mesoamerican Connection: A View from the South." In *Ripples in the Chichimec Sea: New Considerations of Southwestern-Mesoamerican Interactions,* ed. Frances Joan Mathien and Randall H. McGuire, 54–69. Carbondale: Southern Illinois University Press.

Fredrichs, R., C. Aneshenel, and V. Clark. 1982. "Prevalence of Depression in Los Angeles County." *American Journal of Epidemiology* 113: 691–99.

Galarza, Ernesto. 1964. *Merchants of Labor: The Mexican Bracero Story.* Santa Barbara: McNally and Loftin.

————. 1970. *Spiders in the House: Workers in the Fields*. South Bend: University of Notre Dame Press.

García, Jesús M. 1993. *The Hispanic Population in the United States: March 1992*. Current Population Reports, Population Characteristics. Washington, D.C.: U.S. Department of Commerce, July.

García, Mario T. 1981. *Desert Immigrants: The Mexicans of El Paso, 1880–1920*. New Haven: Yale University Press.

————. 1989. *Mexican Americans: Leadership, Ideology, & Identity, 1930–1960*. New Haven: Yale University Press.

Gill, Lois J., and Bernard Spilka. 1962. "Some Nonintellectual Correlates of Academic Achievement among Mexican-American Secondary School Students." *Journal of Educational Psychology* (June): 144–48.

Ginzberg, Eli. 1976. *Labor Market: Segments and Shelters*. Washington, D.C.: Government Printing Office.

Golding, Jacqueline M., and M. Audrey Burnam. 1990. "Immigration, Stress, and Depressive Symptoms in a Mexican-American Community." *Journal of Nervous Disorders* 178, no. 3 (March): 161–71.

Goldman, Shifra M. 1990. "How, Why, Where, and When It All Happened: Chicano Murals of California." In *Signs from the Heart: California Chicano Murals*, ed. Eva Sperling Cockroft and Holly Barnet-Sánchez, 23–54. Venice, Calif.: Social and Public Art Resource Center.

Goldschmidt, Walter F. 1974. *As Ye Sow: Three Studies in the Social Consequences of Agribusiness*. New York: Harcourt, Brace, World.

Gómez-Quiñones, Juan. 1973. "The First Steps: Chicano Labor Conflict and Organizing 1900–1920." *Aztlán: Chicano Journal of the Social Sciences and the Arts* 3, no. 1:13–49.

————. 1973. *Sembradores, Ricardo Flores Magón y el Partido Liberal Mexicano: A Eulogy and Critique*. Monograph no. 5. Los Angeles: Aztlán Publications.

————. 1990. *Chicano Politics: Reality and Promise, 1940–1990*. Albuquerque: University of New Mexico Press.

González, Deena J. 1993. "La Tules of Image and Reality: Euro-American Attitudes and Legend Formation on a Spanish-Mexican Frontier." In *Building with Our Hands: New Directions in Chicana Studies*, ed. Adela de la Torre and Beatriz M. Pesquera, 75–90. Berkeley: University of California Press.

González, Gilbert G. 1994. *Labor and Community: Mexican Citrus Worker Villages in a Southern California County, 1900–1950*. Urbana: University of Illinois Press.

González, Manuel. 1965. Interview by author.

Goody, Jack. 1983. *The Development of the Family and Marriage in Europe*. London: Cambridge University Press.

Grebler, Leo, Joan Moore, and Ralph Guzmán. 1970. *The Mexican American People: The Nation's Second Largest Minority*. New York: Free Press.

Green, Thomas Jefferson. 1845. *Journals of the Expedition against Mier.* New York.

Griswold del Castillo, Richard. 1979. *The Los Angeles Barrio, 1850–1890.* Berkeley: University of California Press.

———. 1984. *La Familia: Chicano Families in the Urban Southwest.* South Bend: Notre Dame Press.

Gullard, Pamela, and Nancy Lund. 1989. *History of Palo Alto, The Early Years.* San Francisco: Scottwall Associates.

Gumerman, George J. 1991. "Understanding the Hohokam." In *Exploring the Hohokam: Prehistoric Desert Peoples of the American Southwest,* ed. George J. Gumerman, 1–27. Albuquerque: University of New Mexico Press.

Gumerman, George J., and Emil W. Haury. 1979. "Prehistory: Hohokam." In *Handbook of North American Indians.* Vol. 9, *Southwest,* ed. Alfonso Ortiz, 75–90. Washington, D.C.: Smithsonian Institution.

Gutiérrez, Ramón A. 1991. *When Jesus Came, the Corn Mother Went Away.* Stanford: Stanford University Press.

Guzmán, Ralph. n.d. "Mexican American Casualties in Vietnam." Unpublished MS. Los Angeles: UCLA Mexican American Studies Project.

Hall, Sharlot. 1946. "Every Day Was Frontier Day in Early Years in Prescott." *Evening Courier,* 29 June, sec. 2, p. 8.

Hargrave, Lyndon L. 1970. *Mexican Macaws: Comparative Osteology and Survey of Remains from the Southwest.* Anthropological Papers of the University of Arizona. Tucson: University of Arizona Press.

Harris, Marvin. 1966. *The Rise of Anthropological Theory.* New York: Thomas & Crowell.

Haury, Emil W. 1957. "A Pre-Spanish Rubber Ball from Arizona." *American Antiquity* 2, no. 4 (1937): 282–88.

———. "An Alluvial Site on the San Carlos Indian Reservation, Arizona." *American Antiquity* 23, no. 1: 2–7.

———. 1976. *The Hohokam: Desert Farmers and Craftsmen.* Tucson: University of Arizona Press.

———. 1986a. "The Greater American Southwest." In *Emil W. Haury's Prehistory of the American Southwest,* ed. J. Jefferson Reid and David E. Doyel, 18–46. Tucson: University of Arizona Press.

———. 1986b. "Thoughts After Sixty Years as a Southwestern Archaeologist." In *Emil W. Haury's Prehistory of the American Southwest,* ed. J. Jefferson Reid and David E. Doyel, 435–63. Tucson: University of Arizona Press.

Hazuda, Helen P., Michael P. Stern, Sharon Parten Gaskill, Steven M. Haffner, and Lytt I. Gardener. 1983. "Ethnic Differences in Health Knowledge and Behaviors Related to the Prevention and Treatment of Coronary Heart Disease." *American Journal of Epidemiology* 117 (June): 717–28. Cited in Ronald Angel, "The Health of the Mexican Origin Population." In *The Mexican Ameri-*

can Experience, ed. R. De la Garza et al., 411–26. Austin: University of Texas Press, 1985.

Heller, Cecilia. 1966. *Mexican American Youth: Forgotten Youth at the Crossroads.* New York: Random House.

Henry, Bonnie. 1992. *Another Tucson.* Tucson: Arizona Daily Star Publications.

Henry, Jules. 1963. *Culture against Man.* New York: Random House.

Hernández, José Amaro. 1983. *Mutual Aid for Survival: The Case of the Mexican American.* Malabar, Florida: Robert E. Krieger.

Herrera-Sobek, María. 1993. *Introduction to Reconstructing a Chicano/a Literary Heritage: Hispanic Colonial Literature of the Southwest.* Tucson: University of Arizona Press.

Heyman, Josiah McC. 1991. *Life and Labor on the Border: Working People of Northeastern Sonora, Mexico, 1886–1986.* Tucson: University of Arizona Press.

Hicks, D. Emily. 1987. "Deterritorialization and Border Writing." In *Literatura de Frontera México/Estados Unidos,* ed. José Manuel Di-Bella, Sergio Gómez Montereo, and Harry Polkinhorn. San Diego: Institute for Regional Studies of the Californias, San Diego State University.

Hill, Jane. 1993. "Hasta la Vista Baby." *Critique of Anthropology* 13, no. 2: 145–76.

Hill, Merton E. 1928. *The Development of an Americanization Program.* Ontario, Calif.: Board of Trustees, Chaffey Union High School and Chaffey Junior College.

Hobsbawn, Eric. 1959. *Social Bandits and Primitive Rebels.* New York: Free Press.

Hoffman, Abraham. 1974. *Unwanted Mexican Americans in the Great Depression: Repatriation Pressures, 1929–1939.* Tucson: University of Arizona Press.

Hogue, W. Lawrence. 1992. "An Unresolved Modern Experience: Richard Rodríguez's Hunger of Memory." *The Americas Review* 20, no. 1: 52–64.

Houghton, Neal D. 1969. "What Price Development for Mass-Poverty Areas?" *Western Political Quarterly* 22: 774–89.

Islas, Arturo. 1993. Introduction to *Drink Cultura: Chicanismo,* by José Antonio Burciaga. Santa Barbara: Capra Press.

Ives, Ronald L. 1984. *José Velásquez: Saga of a Borderlands Soldier.* Tucson: Southwestern Mission Research Center.

James, Franklin J. 1988. *Persistent Urban Poverty and the Underclass: A Perspective Based on the Hispanic Experience.* Paper presented at the Conference on Persistent Poverty, Trinity University, Tomás Rivera Center, San Antonio, 8 April.

Jiménez Moreno, Wigberto. 1966. "Mesoamerica before the Toltecs." In *Ancient Oaxaca,* ed. John Paddock, 1–82. Stanford: Stanford University Press.

Johansen, Bruce, and Roberto Maestas. 1983. *El Pueblo: The Gallegos Family's American Journey, 1503–1980.* New York: Monthly Review Press.

Johns, Elizabeth. 1975. *Storms Brewed in Other Men's Worlds.* College Station: Texas A&M Press.

————. 1991a. "Independent Indians and the San Antonio Community." In *Tejano Origins in Eighteenth-Century San Antonio,* ed. Gerald E. Poyo and Gilberto M. Hinojosa, 123–35. Austin: University of Texas Press.

————. 1991b. "Settlement and Development: Claiming the West." In *The West as America: Reinterpreting Images of the Frontier,* ed. William H. Truettner, 191–235. Washington, D.C.: Smithsonian Institution Press.

Jorgensen, Joseph G. 1980. *Western Indians: Comparative Environments, Languages, and Cultures of 172 Western American Indian Tribes.* San Francisco: W. H. Freeman.

Keefe, Susan E., and Amado Padilla. 1987. *Chicano Ethnicity.* Albuquerque: University of New Mexico Press.

Keefe, Susan E., Amado M. Padilla, and Manuel L. Carlos. 1978. *Emotional Support Systems in Two Cultures: a Comparison of Mexican Americans and Anglo Americans.* Occasional Paper, no 7. Los Angeles: Spanish Speaking Mental Health Research Center, University of California.

————. 1979. "Mexican American Extended Family as an Emotional Support System." *Human Organization* 38: 144–52.

Kelley, Charles J., and Ellen Abbott Kelley. 1975. "An Alternative Hypothesis for the Explanation of Anasazi Culture History." In *Collected Papers in Honor of Florence Hawley Ellis,* ed. Theodore R. Frisbie, 178–233. Papers of the Archaeological Society of New Mexico No.2.

Kingsolver, Barbara. 1989. *Holding the Line: Women in the Great Arizona Strike of 1983.* Ithaca: Cornell University Press.

Knight, George P., Martha E. Bernal, Camille A. Garza, and Marya K. Cota. 1993. "Family Socialization and the Ethnic Identity of Mexican-American Children."*Journal of Cross-Cultural Psychology* 24, no. 1 (March): 99–114.

Lafaye, Jacques. 1976. *Quetzalcoatl and Guadalupe: The Formation of Mexican National Consciousness, 1531–1813.* Chicago: University of Chicago Press.

LeBlanc, Steven A. 1989. "Cultural Dynamics in the Southern Mogollon Area." In *Dynamics of Southwest Prehistory,* ed. Linda S. Cordell and George J. Gumerman, 179–207. Washington, D.C.: Smithsonian Institution Press.

Leach, Edmund. 1979. *Political Systems of Highland Burma.* 2nd ed. Austin: Beacon Press.

Litwak, E. 1960. "Geographic Mobility and Extended Family Cohesion." *American Sociological Review* 25: 9–21.

Lomelí, Francisco. 1993. "Poetics of Reconstructing and/or Appropriating a Literary Past: The Regional Case Model." In *Recovering the U.S. Hispanic Literary Heritage,* ed. María Herrera-Sobek, 221–39. Houston: Arte Público Press.

Lomnitz, Larissa D. n.d. "Horizontal and Vertical Relations and the Social Structure of Urban Mexico." Typescript.

Long, Jeffrey C., et al. 1991. "Genetic Variation in Arizona Mexican Americans:

Estimation and Interpretation of Admixture Proportions." *American Journal of Physical Anthropology* 84: 142–57.

Manuel, Herschel T. 1965. *Spanish-Speaking Children of the Southwest.* Austin: University of Texas Press.

Markides, Kyriakos S., and Jeannine Coreil. 1986. "The Health of Hispanics in the Southwestern United States: an Epidemiologic Paradox." *Public Health Reports* 101, no. 3 (May–June): 253–65.

Martin, Jeanne, and Lucina Suárez. 1987. "Cancer Mortality among Mexican Americans and Other Whites in Texas, 1969–1980." *American Journal of Public Health* 77, no. 7 (July): 851–53.

Mathien, Frances Joan. 1986. "External Contact and the Chaco Anasazi." In *Ripples in the Chichimec Sea: New Considerations of Southwestern-Mesoamerican Interactions,* ed. Frances Joan Mathien and Randall H. McGuire, 220–42. Carbondale: Southern Illinois University Press.

McBride, Anthony A., George W. Joe, and D. Dwayne Simpson. 1991. "Prediction of Long-Term Alcohol Use, Drug Use, and Criminality among Inhalant Users." Special Issue: "Inhalant Use by Mexican American Youth: Findings from a Longitudinal study." *Hispanic Journal of Behavioral Sciences* 13, no. 3 (August): 315–23.

McGuire, Randall H. 1986. "Economies and Modes of Production in the Prehistoric Southwestern Periphery." In *Ripples in the Chichimec Sea: New Considerations of Southwestern-Mesoamerican Interactions,* ed. Frances Joan Mathien and Randall H. McGuire, 243–69. Carbondale: Southern Illinois University Press.

———. 1993. "The Structure and Organization of Hohokam Exchange." In *The American Southwest and Mesoamerica: Systems of Prehistoric Exchange,* ed. Jonathan E. Ericson and Timothy G. Baugh, 95–119. New York: Plenum.

McWilliams, Carey. 1990. Reprint. *North from Mexico: The Spanish-Speaking People of the United States.* Original edition, New York: Praeger, 1948.

Méndez, Miguel. 1992. Reprint. *Pilgrims in Aztlán.* Tempe, Arizona: Bilingual Press. Original edition, Tucson: Editorial Peregrinos, 1974.

Meriam, J. C. 1933. "Activity Curriculum in a School of Mexican Children." *Journal of Experimental Education* (June): 304–8.

Mesa-Bains, Amalia. 1991. "El Mundo Femenino: Chicana Artists of the Movement—A Commentary on Development and Production." *CARA, Chicano Art: Resistance and Affirmation.* 131–40. Los Angeles: Wight Art Gallery, University of California.

Mickey, M.R. et al. 1983. "Paternity Probability Calculations for Mixed Races." In *Inclusion Probabilities in Parentage Testing,* ed. R. H. Walker, 325–47. Arlington: American Association of Blood Banks.

Mirandé, A., and Evangelina Enríquez. 1986. *La Chicana.* Chicago: University of Chicago Press.

Mitchell, Braxton D., Michael P. Stern, Steven M. Haffner, Helen P. Hazuda, and Judith K. Patterson. 1990. "Risk Factors for Cardiovascular Mortality in Mexican Americans and Non-Hispanic Whites." *American Journal of Epidemiology* 131, no.3: 423–33.

Mitchell, J. Clyde. 1969. *Social Networks in Urban Situations.* Manchester: Manchester University Press for the Institute for Social Research, University of Zambia.

Moll, Luis C., Carlos G. Vélez-Ibáñez, and James B. Greenberg. 1988. "Community Knowledge and Classroom Practice: Combining Resources for Literacy Instruction." *Innovative Approaches Research Project Grant, Development Associates.* N.p.

———. 1990. "Community Knowledge and Classroom Practice: Combining Resources for Literacy Instruction: a Technical Report from the Innovative Approaches Research Project." U.S. Department of Education.

Monroy, Douglas. 1990. *Thrown among Strangers: The Making of Mexican Culture in Frontier California.* Berkeley: University of California Press.

Montejano, David. n.d. "Anglos and Mexicans in the 21st Century: Speculations and Considerations." Typescript.

———. n.d. "Anglos and Mexicans in the 21st Century: Speculations and Considerations." Typescript. Synthesized from Tom W. Smith. *Ethnic Images.* General Social Survey Topical Report. No. 19, December National Opinion Research Center, University of Chicago, 1990.

Moore, Joan W. 1978. *Homeboys: Gangs, Drugs, and Prison in the Barrios of Los Angeles.* Philadelphia: Temple University Press.

———. 1991. *Down to the Barrio: Homeboys and Homegirls in Change.* Philadelphia: Temple University Press.

Morgan, Patricia M. 1990. "The Making of a Public Problem." In *Mexican Labor in California and the Marijuana Law of 1937, Drugs in Hispanic Communities,* 233–52. New Brunswick: Rutgers University Press.

Morris, Desmond. 1968. *The Naked Ape.* New York: Knopf.

Murals: Guide to Murals in Tucson. 1993. Tucson: Tucson/Pima Arts Council.

Murguía, Víctor. 1986. *Capital Flight and Economic Crisis: Mexican Post-Devaluation Exiles in a California Community.* San Diego: Center for U.S.-Mexican Studies, University of California.

Nash, June. 1979. *We Eat the Mines and the Mines Eat Us.* New York: Columbia University Press.

Navarro, Armando. 1995. *Mexican American Youth Organization: Avant-Garde of the Chicano Movement in Texas.* Austin: University of Texas Press.

Neitzel, Jill. 1989. "Regional Exchange Networks in the American Southwest: A Comparative Analysis of Long-Distance Trade." In *Sociopolitical Structure of Prehistoric Southwestern Societies,* ed. Steadman Upham, Kent G. Lightfoot, and Roberta A. Jewett, 149–89. Boulder: Westview Press.

Officer, James E. 1987. *Hispanic Arizona, 1536–1856.* Tucson: University of Arizona Press.

———. n.d. Unpublished Notes. James Officer Library, Bureau of Applied Research in Anthropology. Section 48. University of Arizona.

Olson, Ronald. 1933. "Clan and Moiety in Native America." University of California Publications in American Archaeology and Ethnology. Berkeley. Quoted in David R. Wilcox, "The Mesoamerican Ballgame in the American Southwest." In *The Mesoamerican Ballgame,* ed. Vernon L. Scarborough and David R. Wilcox (Tucson: University of Arizona Press, 1991), 101.

Organista, Ricardo. 1983. *The Chicano Mural: Its Analysis and Use for Increasing Cultural Awareness among Educators.* Ann Arbor: University Microfilms International.

Paredes, Américo. 1973. Reprint. *With His Pistol in His Hand: A Border Ballad and Its Hero.* Austin: University of Texas Press, 1958.

Park, Joseph F. 1961. "The History of Mexican Labor in Arizona during the Territorial Period." Master's thesis. Tucson, Arizona: Department of History, University of Arizona. Quoting the *Bisbee Daily Review.* 2, 3, 5 June 1903.

Peterson, Fredrick A. 1990. *Ancient Mexico: An introduction to the Pre-Hispanic Cultures.* New York: Putnam.

Pike, Fredrick B. 1992. *The United States and Latin America: Myths and Stereotypes of Civilization and Nature.* Austin: University of Texas Press.

Pitt, Leonard. 1971. *The Decline of the Californios: A Social History of the Spanish Speaking Californians, 1846–1890.* Berkeley: University of California Press.

Poepone, Paul, and Roswell H. Johnson. 1933. *Applied Eugenics.* New York: Macmillan.

Poyo, Gerald E. 1991. "Immigrants and Integration in Late Eighteenth-Century Bexar." In *Tejano Origins in Eighteenth-Century San Antonio,* ed. Gerald E. Poyo and Gilberto M. Hinojosa, 85–103. Austin: University of Texas Press.

Pumpely, Raphael. 1871. *Across America and Asia.* 5th ed., rev. New York: Leypodt and Holt.

Quesada, Gustavo M., and Peter L. Heller. 1977. "Sociocultural Barriers to Medical Care among Mexican Americans in Texas: A Summary Report of Research Conducted by the Southwest Medical Sociology Ad Hoc Committee." *Medical Care* 15 (May): 93–101. Cited in Ronald Angel, "The Health of the Mexican Origin Population." In *The Mexican American Experience,* ed. R. De la Garza et. al., 411–26 (Austin: University of Texas Press, 1985), 415.

Quijada Hernández, Armando, and Juan Antonio Ruibal Corella. 1985. *Período del México independiente: 1831–1883.* Vol. 3 of *Historia general de Sonora.* Hermosillo: Gobierno del Estado de Sonora.

Radloff, L. 1977. "The CES-D Scale: A Self-Report Depression Scale for Research in the General Population." *Applied Psychological Measures* 1: 385–401.

Ramírez, Oscar. 1994. *Border People: Life and Society in the U.S.-Mexico Borderlands.* Tucson: University of Arizona Press.

Reff, Daniel T. 1991. *Disease, Depopulation, and Culture Change in Northwestern New Spain, 1518–1764.* Salt Lake City: University of Utah Press.

Reyes, Pedro, and Richard R. Valencia. 1993. "Educational Policy and the Growing Latino Student Population: Problems and Prospects." *Hispanic Journal of Behavioral Sciences* 15, no. 2 (May): 258–83.

Reyman, Jonathan Eric. 1971. "Mexican Influence on Southwestern Ceremonialism." Ph.D. diss., Southern Illinois University.

Riding, Alan. 1989. *Distant Neighbors: A Portrait of the Mexicans.* New York: Random House.

Riley, Carroll L. 1982. *The Frontier People: The Greater Southwest in the Protohistorical Period.* Carbondale: Southern Illinois Press.

Rodríguez, Luis J. 1993. *Always Running, La Vida Loca: Gang Days in L.A.* New York: Touchstone.

Rodríguez, Richard. 1982. *Hunger of Memory.* New York: David R. Godine.

———. 1992. *Days of Obligation: An Argument with my Mexican Father.* New York: Penguin Books.

Rojas, Manuel. 1986. *Joaquín Murrieta: "El Patrio."* Mexicali, B.C.: Estado de Baja California.

Romo, Ricardo. 1983. *East Los Angeles: History of a Barrio.* Austin: University of Texas Press.

Rosaldo, Renato. 1989. *Culture and Truth: The Remaking of Social Analysis.* Boston: Beacon Press.

Rosenbaum, Robert J. 1981. *Mexicano Resistance in the Southwest: The Sacred Right of Self-Preservation.* Austin. University of Texas Press.

Rowe, Alan. 1991. "Note on Education and Self-Worth among Anglo-American, Black American, and Mexican American Men in San Antonio." *Perceptual and Motor Skills* 73, no. 2 (October): 433–34.

Ruiz, Vicki L. 1987. *Cannery Women, Cannery Lives: Mexican Women, Unionization, and the California Food Processing Industry, 1930–1950.* Albuquerque: University of New Mexico Press.

Saldívar, Ramón. 1990. *Chicano Narrative: The Dialects of Difference.* Madison: University of Wisconsin Press.

San Miguel, Guadalupe. 1987. *"Let All of Them Take Heed": Mexican Americans and the Campaign for Educational Equality in Texas, 1910–1981.* Austin: University of Texas Press.

Sánchez, George. 1984. *"Go after the Women": Americanization of the Mexican Immigrant Woman, 1915–1929.* Working Paper, no. 6. Stanford Center for Chicano Research, Stanford, California, June.

Sánchez, George I. 1967. *Forgotten People: A Study of New Mexicans.* Albuquerque: University of New Mexico Press.

Sánchez-Tranquilino, Marcos. 1991. "Mi casa no es su casa: Chicano Murals and Barrio Calligraphy as Systems of Signification at Estrada Courts: 1972–1978." Master's thesis, Los Angeles: University of California.

Sandos, James A. 1992. *Rebellion in the Borderlands: Anarchism and the Plan of San Diego, 1904–1923.* Norman: University of Oklahoma Press.

Santos, Richard. 1992. "US and Foreign Born Mexican American Youth: A Socioeconomic Comparison." *International Journal of Adolescence and Youth* 3, no. 3–4: 319–31.

Schaefer, Jack. 1973. *Heroes without Glory: Some Good Men of the Old West.* Boston: Houghton-Mifflin, 1965. Reprint of Pedro Castillo and Albert Camarillo. *Furia y muerte: Los bandidos chicanos.* Monograph No. 4, Los Angeles: Aztlán Publications, Chicano Studies Center, University of California, Los Angeles.

Schroeder, Harold E. 1979. "Shifting for Survival in the Spanish Southwest." In *New Spain's Far Northern Frontier,* ed. David J. Weber, 247–55. Albuquerque: University of New Mexico Press. First published in *New Mexico Historical Review* 42, no. 4 (October 1968): 291–310.

Segade, Gustav V. 1973 "Toward a Dialectic of Chicano Literature." *Mester* 4, no.1 (November): 4–5.

Segura, Denise A. 1989. "The Interplay of Familism and Patriarchy on Employment among Chicana and Mexican Women." Renato Rosaldo Lecture Series, 1987–1989. Vol. 5. Monograph.

Sena-Rivera, J. 1980. "La familia hispana as a Natural Support System: Strategies for Prevention." In *Hispanic Natural Support Systems,* ed. R. Valle and W. Vega, 75–81. Sacramento: California Department of Mental Health, Office of Prevention.

Sheridan, Thomas E. 1986. *Los Tucsonenses: The Mexican Community in Tucson, 1854–1941.* Tucson: University of Arizona Press.

Simic, Andrei, and Barbara Myerhoff. 1978. "Conclusions." In *Life's Career— Aging: Cultural Variations in Growing Old,* ed. Barbara G. Myerhoff and Andrei Simic, 231–49. Beverly Hills: Sage Press.

Simmons, Marc. 1964. "Tlascalans in the Spanish Borderlands." *New Mexico Historical Review* 39: 101–10.

———. 1979. "History of Pueblo-Spanish Relations to 1821." In *Handbook of North American Indians: Southwest,* ed. Alfonso Ortiz, Washington, D.C.: Smithsonian Institution.

Smith, Cornelius. n.d. *Tanque Verde: The Story of a Frontier Ranch.* Privately Published. Quoted in Thomas E. Sheridan, *Los Tucsonenses: The Mexican Community in Tucson, 1854–1941.* (Tucson: University of Arizona Press, 1986.)

Smith, Stephanie S., George W. Joe, and D. Dwayne Simpson. 1991. "Parental Influences on Inhalant Use by Children. Special Issue: Inhalant Use by Mexican American Youth: Findings from a Longitudinal study." *Hispanic Journal of Behavioral Sciences* 13, no. 3 (August): 267–75.

Smithwick, Noah. *The Evolution of a State: or, Recollections of Old Texas Days.* 1st ed., 1900; Original edition, Austin: 1935, p. 45. Quoted in David J. Weber, ed. *New Spain's Far Northern Frontier: Essays on Spain in the American West, 1540–1821* (Albuquerque: University of New Mexico Press, 1979), 296.

Sonnichsen, C. I. 1974. *Colonel Green and the Copper Skyrocket.* Tucson: University of Arizona Press.

Stanley, Grace C. 1920. "Special Schools for Mexicans." *Survey* 44 (15 September): 714–20.

Stark, Miriam. 1984. "La Chicana: Changing Roles in a Changing Society." Unpublished MS. Honors Thesis, Ann Arbor: University of Michigan.

Stern, M. P., et al. 1986. "Association between NIDDM, RH Blood Groups, and Haploglobin Phenotype: Results from the San Antonio Heart Study." *Diabetes* 35: 387–91.

Street Gang Guide. 1981. Tucson: Gang Investigators League of Arizona.

Suárez, Lucina and Jeanne Martin. 1987. "Primary Liver Cancer Mortality and Incidence in Texas Mexican Americans, 1969–80." *American Journal of Public Health* 77, no. 5: 631–33.

Swadesh, Frances Leon. 1977. *Los primeros pobladores: Hispanic Americans of the Ute Frontier.* Notre Dame: University of Notre Dame Press.

Swartz, Marc J. 1972. "The Perceptual Approach in the Study of Local Level Politics." La Jolla: University of California, San Diego. Mimeographed.

Tapia, Javier. 1989. "The Recreation of School at Home through Play." Typescript, Tucson: Bureau of Applied Research in Anthropology.

Tenenbaum, Shelly. 1993. *A Credit to their Community: Jewish Loan Societies in the United States, 1880–1945.* Detroit: Wayne State University.

Testa, Mark. 1988. "The Re-creation of School at Home through Play." Paper prepared for the Population Association of American Session on Welfare Policies, April.

Trujillo, Charley. 1990. *Soldados: Chicanos in Viet Nam.* San Jose: Chusma Publications.

Tucson Daily Citizen, 1987–1994. 4 April–1 January.

U.S. Bureau of the Census. 1989. *The Hispanic Population in the United States, March 1989.* Current Population Reports, Population Characteristics. Washington, D.C.: Government Printing Office.

———. 1993a. *Hispanic Americans Today.* Current Population Reports, 23–183. Washington, D.C.: Government Printing Office.

———. 1993b. *Persons of Hispanic Origin in the United States: August 1993.* Current Population Reports, 1990 CP-3-3. Washington, D.C.: Government Printing Office.

U.S. Commission on Civil Rights. 1970. *Mexican Americans and the Administration of Justice in the Southwest.* Washington, D.C.: U.S. Government Printing Office.

U. S. Department of Defense. n.d. *Hispanics in America's Defense.* 71–90. Washington, D.C.

U.S. Department of Justice. 1954. *Annual Report of the Immigration and Naturalization Service.*

Vaca, Nick C. 1970. "The Mexican-American in the Social Sciences: 1912–1970, Part I: 1912–1935." *El Grito: A Journal of Mexican-American Thought* 3, no. 3 (spring): 3–24.

———. 1970. "The Mexican-American in the Social Sciences: 1912–1970, Part II: 1936–1970." *El Grito: A Journal of Mexican-American Thought* 4, no.1 (fall): 17–51.

Van Velsen, Johansen. 1967. "The Extended Case Method and Situational Analysis." In *The Craft of Social Anthropology,* ed. A. L. Epstein. London: Tavistock Publication.

Vega, William A., George J. Warheit, and Kenneth Meindardt. 1984. "Marital Disruption and the Prevalence of Depressive Symptomatology among Anglos and Mexican Americans." *Journal of Marriage and the Family* (November): 817–24.

Vega, William A., James F. Sallis, Thomas L. Patterson, Joan W. Rupp, Julie A. Morris, and Philip R. Nader. 1988. "Predictors of Dietary Change in Mexican American Families Participating in a Health Behavior Change Program." *American Journal of Preventive Medicine* 4, no. 4: 194–99.

Vélez, María T. 1983. "The Social Context of Mothering: A Comparison of Mexican American and Anglo Mother-Infant Interaction Patterns." Ph.D. diss., Wright Institute, Los Angeles.

Vélez-Ibáñez, Carlos G. 1970. "¿Qué crees? The Themes and Ramifications of Racism in the Chicano Southwest." Typescript, 1 May.

———. 1979. "Ourselves through the Eyes of an Anthropologist." In *Chicanos as We See Ourselves,* ed. Arnulfo Trejo, 37–48. Tucson: University of Arizona.

———. 1980. "Los movimientos chicanos: problemas y perspectivas." In *Las relaciones México y Estados Unidos,* ed. David Barkin et al., 217–34. México D.F.: Nueva Editorial Imagen.

———. 1983. *Bonds of Mutual Trust: the Cultural Systems of Mexican / Chicano Rotating Credit Associations.* New Brunswick: Rutgers University Press.

———. 1988a. "Networks of Exchange among Mexicans in the U.S. and Mexico: Local Level Mediating and International Transformations." *Urban Anthropology* 17, no. 1: 27–51.

———. 1988b. "Forms and Functions among Mexicans in the Southwest: Implications for Classroom Use." Paper Presented to Invited Session of the American Anthropological Association. N.p., 20 November.

————. 1990. "Los Chavalones of E Company: Extraordinary Men in Extraordinary Events." Address to the 40th Reunion of E Company. Tucson, Arizona, 28 July.

————. 1993a. "Ritual Cycles of Exchange: The Process of Cultural Creation and Management in the U.S. Borderlands." In *Celebrations of Identity, Multiple Voices in American Ritual Performance,* ed. Pamela R. Frese. Westport: Bergin & Garvey.

————. 1993b. "U.S. Mexicans in the Borderlands: Being Poor without the Underclass." In *The Barrios: Latinos and the Underclass Debate,* ed. Joan Moore and Raquel Pinderhughes, 195–220. New York: Russell Sage Foundation.

————. 1994. "Plural Strategies of Survival and Cultural Formation in U.S. Mexican Households in a Region of Dynamic Transformation." In *Diagnosing America: Anthropology and Public Engagement,* ed. Shepherd Foreman. Ann Arbor: University of Michigan Press.

————. 1995. "The Challenge of Funds of Knowledge in Urban Arenas: Another Way of Understanding the Learning Resources of Poor Mexicano Households in the U.S. Southwest and Their Implications for National Contexts." In *The Anthropology of Lower Income Urban Enclaves: The Case of East Harlem,* ed. Judith Freidenberg, 253–80. Vol. 749. New York: Annals of New York Academy of Sciences.

Vélez-Ibáñez, Carlos G., with Bradford Bagasao, Adelaida del Castillo, Rosa Colorado, and Carmen Dávila. 1982. "Hispanic American Organizations and Voluntary Associations: A Reference Work of Selected Groups, A Report." Typescript, 20 June, 181–186.

Vélez-Ibáñez, Carlos G., Gerardo Bernache, and Ana O'Leary. 1992. "Confidential Report of the Southwest Utility Corporation." Typescript. Bureau of Applied Research in Anthropology, University of Arizona.

Vélez-Ibáñez, Carlos G., and James B. Greenberg. 1986. "Multidimensional Functions of Non-Market Forms of Exchange among Mexicans/Chicanos in Tucson, Arizona." NSF Project, BNS-8418906.

————. 1992. "Formation and Transformation of Funds of Knowledge Among U.S.-Mexican Households." *Anthropology and Education Quarterly* 23, no. 4: 313–35.

Vélez-Ibáñez, Carlos G., James B. Greenberg, and Byron Johnstone. 1984. "The Ethnic, Economic, and Educational Structure of Tucson, Arizona: The Limits of Possibility for Mexican Americans in 1982." In *Proceedings of the 1984 Meeting of the Rocky Mountain Council on Latin American Studies.* Las Cruces: New Mexico State University, 154–64.

Vernon, S., and R. Roberts. 1982. "Prevalence of Treated and Untreated Psychiatric Disorders in Three Ethnic Groups." *Social Science Medicine,* 1575–82.

Vidaurrieta Tjarks, Alicia. 1979. Reprint. "Comparative Demographic Analysis of Texas, 1777–1793." In *New Spain's Far Northern Frontier: Essays on Spain in* the *American West, 1540–1821*, ed. David J. Weber, 137–69. Albuquerque: University of New Mexico Press. Appeared originally in *Southwestern Historical Quarterly* 77 (1974): 291–338.

Vigil, James Diego. 1988. "Street Socialization, Locura Behavior, and Violence among Chicano Gang Members." In *Violence and Homicide in Hispanic Communities*, ed. J. Kraus et al., 231–41. Washington D.C.: Office of Minority Health, National Institute of Mental Health.

Warheit, George J., William Vega, Joanne B. Auth, and Kenneth Meinhardtet. 1985. "Psychiatric Symptoms and Dysfunctions among Anglos and Mexican Americans." *Research in Community and Mental Health*. Vol. 5: 3–32.

Weber, David J. 1968. *The Taos Trappers: The Fur Trade in the Far Southwest, 1540–1846*. Norman: University of Oklahoma Press.

———. 1988. *Myth and the History of the Hispanic Southwest*. Albuquerque: University of New Mexico Press.

———. 1992. *The Spanish Frontier in North America*. New Haven: Yale University Press.

Weber, Devora Anne. 1973. "The Organizing of Mexicano Agricultural Workers: Imperial Valley and Los Angeles, 1928–34, An Oral History Approach." *Aztlán: Chicano Journal of the Social Sciences and the Arts* 3, no. 2: 307–47.

———. 1994. *Dark Sweat, White Gold: California Farm Workers, Cotton, and the New Deal*. Berkeley: University of California Press.

Weigan, Phil C., Garman Harbottle, and Edward V. Sayre. 1977. "Turquoise Sources and Source Analysis: Mesoamerican and the Southwestern U.S.A." In *Exchange Systems in Prehistory*, ed. Timothy K. Earle and Jonathon E. Ericson, 1–34. New York: Academic Press.

Welch, Susan, John Gruhl, and Cassia Spohn. 1984. "Dismissal, Conviction, and Incarceration of Hispanic Defendants: A Comparison with Anglos and Blacks." *Social Science Quarterly* 65, no. 2 (June): 257–64.

Wicke, Charles R. 1965. "Pyramids and Temple Mounds: Mesoamerican Ceremonial Architecture in Eastern North America." *American Antiquity* 30, no. 4: 409–21.

Wilcox, David R. 1986. "The Tepiman Connection: A Model of Mesoamerican-Southwestern Interaction." In *Ripples in the Chichimec Sea: New Considerations of Southwestern-Mesoamerican Interactions*, ed. Frances Joan Mathien and Randall H. McGuire, 134–54. Carbondale: Southern Illinois University Press.

———. 1991a. "Hohokam Social Complexity." In *Chaco and Hohokam: Prehistoric Regional Systems in the American Southwest*, ed. Patricia L. Crown and W. James Judge, 253–75. Santa Fe: School of American Research Press.

———. 1991b. "The Mesoamerican Ballgame in the American Southwest." In *The Mesoamerican Ballgame*, ed. Vernon L. Scarborough and David R. Wilcox, 101–25. Tucson: University of Arizona Press.

Wilbur-Cruce, Eva Antonia. 1987. *A Beautiful, Cruel Country.* Tucson: University of Arizona Press.

Wilkerson, S. Jeffrey K. 1991. "And Then They Were Sacrificed: The Ritual Ballgame of Northeastern Mesoamerica through Time and Space." In *The Mesoamerican Ballgame,* ed. Vernon L. Scarborough and David R. Wilcox, 45–71. Tucson: University of Arizona Press.

Williams, Brett. 1984. "Why Migrant Women Feed their Husbands Tamales: Foodways as a Basis for a Revisionist View of Tejano Family Life." In *Ethnic and Regional Foodways in the United States: The Performance of Ethnic Identity,* ed. L. K. Brown and K. Mussell, 113–26. Knoxville: University of Tennessee.

Williams, Raymond. 1977. *Marxism and Literature.* Oxford: Oxford University Press.

Wolf, Eric R. 1988. "Afterword." *Urban Anthropology* 17, no 1: 105–9.

Wollenberg, Charles. 1973. "Working on El Traque: The Pacific Electric Strike of 1903." *Pacific Historical Review* 42 (August): 358–69.

Yarbo-Bejarano, Yvonne. 1992. "The Multiple Subject in the Writing of Ana Castillo." *The Americas Review* 20, no. 1: 65–72.

Zamora, Emilio. 1993. *The World of the Mexican Worker in Texas.* College Station: Texas A&M University Press.

Zatz, Marjorie S. 1985. "Pleas, Priors, and Prison: Racial/Ethnic Differences in Sentencing." *Social Science Research* 14: 169–183.

Zavella, Patricia. 1987. *Women's Work and Chicano Families: Cannery Workers of the Santa Clara Valley.* Ithaca: Cornell University Press.

Zink, Sally. 1993. "Introduction." *Casa Grande Valley Histories.* Casa Grande, Ariz.: Casa Grande Historical Society.

Index

inequality: and literature, 214, 311n.6
intermarriage: and blurred culture lines,
52; and border balanced households,
143; and clustered households, 149,
155–56; and cultural subordination, 58,
59–60, 61–62; of elites, 58, 59–60,
61–62, 67–68, 300n.22; Irish/Mexican,
316n.17; and land grant control, 247,
314–15n.8; and population growth, 38;
prevalence of, 67–68; racial construction and, 268; waning of, 68. *See also*
marriage
Introduction of Maize (Burciaga), 249,
250–51
Ipais, 54
IRCA, 83
Irish Catholicism and culture, 230–31,
252, 315–16n.17
irrigation, 39, 41, 47

Japanese Mexican Labor Association
(JMLA), 110–11
Japanese population, 110, 113
Jesuit missionaries, 41, 285n.117
Jewish population, 124, 268
Jim Crow laws, 70
JMLA. *See* Japanese Mexican Labor Association
juridical system: benevolent associations'
improvement of, 126; ethnic bias and,
192–96; improvements through,
128–29; racism and commodity identity
in, 78–79
juries, 129

Katsina murals, 314n.3
Kennedy, Jacqueline, 252
Kennedy, John F.: persona of, 252–53;
political campaigns, 127, 129
Kino, Eusebio Francisco, 41
kinship: and cross-border households.
See cross-border clustered households;
and cultural subordination, 58,
59–60, 61–62; immigration restrictions and, 82–83; and south to north

movement, 63, 67, 69, 70, 174–75; and
union organizing, 110. *See also* households; intermarriage; social density
Korean War, 129, 201, 203–04

labor: and Chicano movement, 128; dual
wage/labor structure, 65–66, 79–81, 82,
108, 115, 117–18, 119–20; of household,
and patriarchy, 139, 148; immigration
policy and. *See* immigration policies;
slavery, 21, 37, 38, 282n.71. *See also* employment
labor unions: agricultural, 110–14, 130;
Anglo-only, 79, 81–82, 115, 117, 119,
120; and commodity identity, 82; cultural
basis of development, 109–10; dual
wage/labor structures supported by,
79, 80, 117; households and, 137, 296–
97n.3; ideologies of, 111–12, 130; mining, 114–18; as platform for change, 93;
railroads, 119–21; union busting, 112,
113, 115, 116–17, 120; women and, 109–
10, 112–13, 120–21. *See also specific unions*
labradores, 52
land, U.S. strategy for acquiring, 62
land grants: Apache attacks and abandonment of, 46–47; and Californios, 54, 56;
intermarriage and, 62, 247, 314–15n.8;
loss of, 57, 62, 64, 247; squatters and,
247; as symbol, 57
language: Americanization and, 66,
82–83, 85, 227; bilingualism. *See* bilingualism; cultural designation with,
309n.76; and Easter celebration, 176;
employment and, 81; and extended
familism, 144–45, 155; Jackie Kennedy's
use of, 252; literacy, 85, 289–90n.81; and
mental health, 197; parody of, 85–86;
racism affecting, 91–92
Last Supper of Chicano Heroes (Burciaga),
249
Latino, as term, 86
laundries, 80, 121
la vida loca, 191–92
Lawrence, Lester, 16, 275

Index » 353

associations, 125; and Catholic Church, 155, 304n.33; and population growth, 70

Mexicans: and Easter, 175, 176; as pejorative term, 71–77, 86, 91, 268; pre-Mexican Independence. See Hispanos/Mexicanos; racism and. See racism; of U.S., post-Mexican war. See Mexicans, U.S.; violence against. See violence. See also south to north movement

Mexicans, U.S.: denial of heritage by. See self-denial; Spanish descent, claiming of; discrimination against. See discrimination; distinguished from Mexicans, 82, 266; "Hispanic" as referent for, 86; identity of. See identity; inclusiveness of, 270; non-U.S.-born, poverty and education of, 187–88; origins of, 63–64, 132; population statistics of, 182–85; referent terms for, 86–87, 219; struggles of. See political struggles; resistance; underclass and, 298–99; well-being and sadness of. See distribution of sadness

Mexican war of 1846: and cultural subordination of Hispanos/Mexicanos, 58, 61–62, 267–68; process leading to, 57–62; San Patricio Brigade and, 252, 315–16n.17

Mexico: citizenship policy of, 58–59; flight of capital from, 300n.22; people of. See Mexicans; trade policy of, 58. See also Mesoamerican populations

middle class: and barrioization, 65; benevolent associations and, 68–69, 125; class stratification and, 66–67; clustered households of, case study, 154–57; household struggles of, 138; literature and, 227–32; percentage of households as, 141, 299–300n.21. See also class

migration: and bumping, 6; and cultural integration, 8–9; ethnobiography of, 13–19; a historical view of, 229, 232; immigration distinguished from, 8, 229; industrialization and, 186, 196, 200; mining and. See mining; population growth and, 38–39, 108–09; recent, and poverty, 188; scale of, 108–09; union ac-

tivities and, 115. See also south to north movement

military: and Logan Heights, 209, 310n.2; occupational injury and, 161–62; support of, 150, 158–59, 160, 161–62. See also war

"million dollar wound," 200–201

Milton, 208

Mine, Mill, and Smelter Workers, 117, 121

mining: alcohol and, 153; and Apache raiding, 76; and commodity identity, 78–79; dual wage/labor structure, 79, 108, 115, 117–18; early trade and, 33–34; expertise in, 94, 96, 108; Foreign Miners Tax, 78, 97, 291–92n.19; and Hispanos/Mexicanos settlement, 44, 76; labor unions and activities, 95, 114–18; language restrictions and, 81; migration and, 78; peonage system of, 108, 117; pre-Hispanic, 33, 281n.60; violence against Mexicans in, 94–100, 100, 102; women and, 118, 121

missionaries: as first line of defense, 47; and Hispanos/Mexicanos settlement, 37, 38, 41, 285n.117; secularization of, 54, 56, 247; in Texas, 48

Missouri-Santa Fe trail, 60

Mixquiahuala Letters, The (Castillo), 216, 233–37

Mogollon: culture of, 20; fall of, 34; interactive culture of, 31; Mesoamerican influence on, 20, 22, 24, 30, 31

mojados (wetbacks), 82, 289n.73

moradas, 124

More Chicano Heroes and Heroines (Burciaga), 249, 253–54

Moreno, José, 64

Morris, W. T. "Brack," 105

movement, south to north. See migration; south to north movement

movimiento. See Chicano cultural convulsive transition movement

Movimiento Estudiantil Chicano de Aztlán (MECHA), 130, 210

murals and mural movement: of Burciaga. See Burciaga, José Antonio; as com-

About the Author

CARLOS G. VÉLEZ-IBÁÑEZ is Dean of the College of Humanities, Arts, and Social Sciences and Professor of Anthropology at the University of California in Riverside. He was formerly Director of the Bureau of Applied Research in Anthropology at the University of Arizona.

He received a doctorate in anthropology from the University of California at San Diego and a master's degree in English from the University of Arizona. His awards include Fellow at the Center for Advanced Study in the Behavioral Sciences at Stanford University, 1993; Smithsonian Institution Visiting Associates Program, 1986; and Fellow, Rockefeller Foundation, 1981–82.

Vélez-Ibáñez is the author of *Bonds of Mutual Trust: The Cultural Systems of Rotating Credit Associations Among Urban Mexicans and Chicanos* and *Rituals of Marginality: Politics, Process, and Culture Change in Central Urban Mexico.* Both books have been published in Spanish as well as in English. His research specialties include peoples of North America, especially ethnic and minority groups in the United States and Mexico as well as peoples of the Hispanic Caribbean, and he has numerous publications in these areas.

4/02   Ø   12/01
3/03   4   1/03
6/05   4   1/03